A Century of Sports
Missouri Valley Conference
1907-2007

by Steve Richardson

St. Louis, Missouri

MathisJones Communications, LLC

ISBN 1-933370-09-2

Library of Congress Control Number: 2006930358

*The Missouri Valley Conference wishes to express
its appreciation for the sponsorship support
provided by State Farm Insurance.*

Contributing Writers
Dave Dorr
Matthew Heidenry

Additional Photography and Cover Photo Illustration
William Mathis

Design, Layout and Photo Restoration:
Ellie Jones • William Mathis
Design Copyright © 2006 MathisJones Communications, LLC

MathisJones Communications, LLC
1 Putt Lane
Eureka, Missouri 63025
Info@MathisJones.com

Table of Contents

Creighton celebrates 2000 MVC Tournament championship

Foreword

As we stand at the end of our first century, we have learned that the Missouri Valley Conference's history is very much like a maze. The Valley's story includes many familiar faces and places, but it also contains endless twists and turns, dead ends and new passages. The people, schools and rivalries most often identified with the Valley–Larry Bird and Oscar Robertson, Bradley and Wichita State, Robertson Field House and Drake Stadium–share their histories with elements as unlikely as Olympic gold medalists from Grinnell and Nebraska's legendary football program.

This book project revived the legends and lore associated with the MVC and, during its undertaking, countless new stories surfaced. As we look back, we have discovered that beneath the triumphs and the trials that have taken place in the competitive arena lies a college athletic conference that has survived and endured through adaptability and perseverance.

I am indebted to the MVC staff, to those individuals present and past who have blazed a trail of excellence through the years. The Valley has returned to national prominence on many fronts, thanks in no small part to the good work of my longest-tenured associates–Joe Mitch, Patty Viverito, Jack Watkins and Mike Kern–who are pictured on page 22 along with the full MVC staff.

The contribution of business and civic leaders like John Q. Hammons of Springfield, MO, symbolize the commitment to Atheletics that is taking place on MVC campuses.

My thanks are also extended, on behalf of the Conference, to the trio that has simply made this book happen and who have made their way through the labyrinth unscathed: Steve Richardson, William Mathis and Ellie Jones, all of whom dug deeper into the Conference's history than what seemed possible.

Steve's storytelling makes the Valley's history very readable and his interviews and research give an excellent perspective on the past century. William and Ellie, in addition to providing the design of the book, combined endless hours of photo research in the archives of nearly every school that has been a member of the league. Their tireless work resulted in the unearthing of countless rich stories that have long been buried or forgotten, and the discovery of literally hundreds of amazing photos and other documents, which are preserved herein for the generations to come.

Thanks, as well, to Dave Dorr and Matthew Heidenry for additional writing and to Josh Stevens for making the book much more visible to the public, and to the many other individuals–administrators, coaches, student-athletes–who helped to build and nurture the MVC through the past 100 years.

As we celebrate the uniqueness and the importance of the Missouri Valley's rich and storied past, we also share an unbridled excitement over prospects for its future.

In March of 2006, the Valley captivated the interest of college basketball fans throughout the nation by placing four men's teams in the NCAA Tournament, with two storied programs–Bradley and Wichita State–advancing to the Sweet 16. It was clear that the MVC was truly back among the nation's elite conferences in men's basketball, and it has been no secret that the league has been excellent in many other programs as well.

The strength of the Valley has been in its campus leadership–our presidents, our athletics administrators and our coaches. There has been a boom in athletics facilities construction and in the expansion of our great universities in recent years. There is no better indication of this than at Missouri State University, where John Q. Hammons, Springfield, Missouri business leader and philanthropist, recently provided the lead gift to construct a $65 million, 11,000-seat on-campus basketball arena. Indeed, virtually all of the current ten Valley member schools have made significant investment in, and commitment to, their athletics programs and to the conference. We believe that our future appears as bright as our past.

Finally, as we pause to look ahead to our second century, we have realized that there is no better corporate friend in college athletics than State Farm Insurance, a company based in the heart of the MVC in Bloomington, Illinois. All of us in the Valley wish to express our gratitude for the support State Farm has provided our championship sports through the years.

We toast our good friends at State Farm, and our past and future successes. Here's to the next century!

J. Douglas Elgin

J. Douglas Elgin, MVC Commissioner

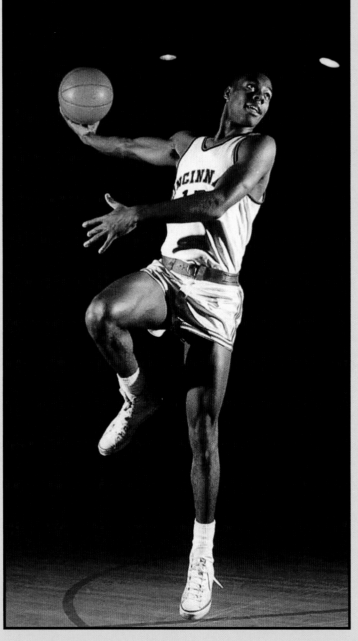

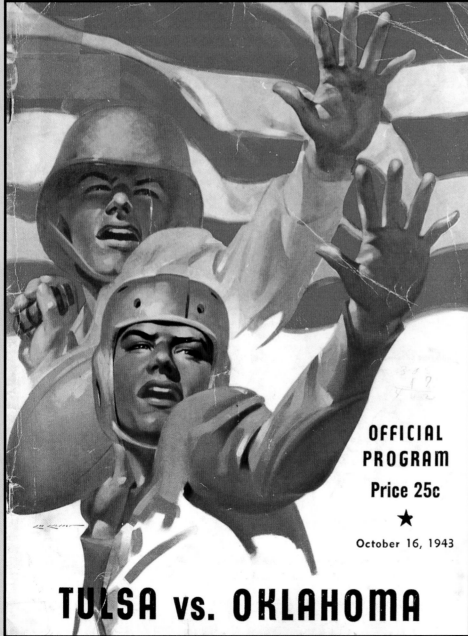

OFFICIAL
PROGRAM

Price 25c

★

October 16, 1943

TULSA vs. OKLAHOMA

F. W. TUTTLE
INSTRUCTOR IN PHYSICAL TRAINING

MARY IDA MANN
INSTRUCTOR WOMEN'S GYMNASIUM

JOHN F. McCLEAN
COACH OF TEAMS

ROBERT B. CALDWELL
INSTRUCTOR IN PHYSICAL TRAINING

UNIVERSITY OF MISSOURI
DEPARTMENT OF PHYSICAL TRAINING
AND ATHLETICS

CLARK W. HETHERINGTON
DIRECTOR

COLUMBIA December 19, 1905.

Chancellor Frank Strong ,

    University of Kansas,

        Lawrence, Kas.

Dear Sir: - -

    The time seems ripe for some deeper understanding and, perhaps, organization between the Universities of the Southwest concerning intercollegiate athletics.   Hence, I am writing to ask if you would be willing to send a faculty representative acquainted with the conditions in you institution to Columbia in February to take part in a conference help under the auspices of Missouri University, in which there shall be a thorough discussion of previously submitted problems and remedies and the possibilities for the formation of an intercollegiate conference and association that will make the athletic relations of the colleges of the Southwest, along all lines, better and stronger.   February is suggested as we expect to have a formal opening of our new gynasium at that time.

    A similar letter has been sent to Washington University, Nebraska, Oklahoma, Kentucky, Arkansas and Texas.   Would you suggest other institutions?

        Very Truly yours,

        Clark W. Hetherington

Dict.

Clark Wilson Hetherington
&
the Founding of the Missouri Valley Conference

The first meeting to develop the Missouri Valley Conference occurred at the Midland Hotel in Kansas City on Jan. 12, 1907. The attending schools were Washington University in St. Louis, Kansas University, University of Iowa, University of Missouri, and University of Nebraska. Representatives from the schools were highly regarded professors from the health and athletics fields, including Dr. James Naismith of Kansas, the inventor of basketball. The chairman of the meeting, however, was Clark Wilson Hetherington from the University of Missouri, who was the catalyst for the meeting as well. He began campaigning for a conference four years prior to its founding. Although the MVC is the result of a committee, Hetherington is arguably the one individual who is most responsible for its formation.

Clark Hetherington is an often-overlooked figure in the world of college athletics who, as one of the most influential people in pre–World War I athletics, pioneered the development of college sports in the United States. His theories of athletics are profound and insightful, focusing on developmental and educational aspects of athletics. He foresaw many issues in college sports that still persist, including the importance of differentiating between the amateur and the professional. He also believed that inter-school competition was an educational responsibility of each college. This belief drove Hetherington to be influential in the formation of not only the Missouri Valley Conference but also the National Collegiate Athletic Association.

Hetherington was born in Minnesota in 1870 and moved with his family to California at age four. After being refused admission to the University of California, Clark was accepted into Stanford University in 1891, graduating four years later with a degree in Health. His postgraduate work was in Physical Training at Stanford and Whittier State School, and in Psychology at Clark University.

In 1900, Hetherington became a professor of Physical Education and the director of Gymnasia and Athletics at the University of Missouri, a position that he held for 10 years. Although his career continued to high acclaim—both in New York and in California—his Missouri years had a great impact in amateur athletics. While at Missouri, Hetherington helped legitimize physical education as a discipline, and he supported women's activities. He also was involved with the 1904 Olympic Games, which were held in St. Louis in conjunction with the Louisiana Purchase Exposition.

The American Academy of Kinesiology and Physical Education honors Hetherington by offering the annual C. W. Hetherington Award. The award recognizes significant contributions to the study of physical education and kinesiology.

Matthew Heidenry

James Naismith had 14 days to create an indoor game that would provide an "athletic distraction" for a rowdy class through the brutal New England winter. Naismith' invention didn't come easily. Getting close to the deadline, he struggled to keep the class's faith. His first attempt was to bring outdoor games indoors, i.e., soccer and lacrosse. These games proved too physical and cumbersome. At his wits' end, Naismith recalled a childhood game that required players to use finesse and accuracy to become successful. After brainstorming this new idea Naismith developed basketball's original 13 rules and, consequently, the game of basketball.

The Midland Hotel

Kansas City, Missouri

Site of the First Meeting of the Founding Fathers
of the Missouri Valley Conference
January 12, 1907

C. W. Hetherington
University of Missouri

James Naismith
University of Kansas

TIME LINE
1907-2006

W. C. Lansdon
University of Kansas

Captain James Werkizer
University of Nebraska

A. N. Walker
University of Kansas

Dr. W. J. Monilaw
University of Missouri

FOUNDING
FATHERS

Mark Catlin
Iowa University

Professor Calvin Woodward
Washington University

Jan. 12", 1907
A letter from the Univ. of Missouri being read as to the formation of a proposed "Missouri Valley Conference"; it was moved and carried.

MVC First Track Meet

190

FEBRUARY 16, 1908 IOWA & NEBRASKA SHARE FIRST MVC FOOTBALL TITLE.

THE ORIGINAL SEVEN

 WASHINGTON U

 NEBRASKA

 KANSAS

 MISSOURI

 DRAKE

 IOWA

 AMES TEACHERS COLLEGE

CLARENCE E. McCLUNG
FIRST MVIAA SECRETARY

APRIL 1
MISSOURI VALLEY INTERCOLLEGIATE ATHLETIC ASSOCIATION ADOPTED AS OFFICIAL NAME.

MAY 1907
FIRST MVC MEN'S TRACK OUTDOOR CHAMPIONSHIP (IOWA STATE WINS MEET HELD AT KANSAS CITY).

NOVEMBER 10, 1907
MISSOURI VALLEY BASKETBALL LEAGUE FORMED WITH KANSAS, MISSOURI, & WASHINGTON UNIVERSITY (ST. LOUIS) IN THE SOUTHERN DIVISION & NEBRASKA, AMES (IOWA STATE), & DRAKE IN THE NORTHERN DIVISION. A CHAMPIONSHIP SERIES BETWEEN THE DIVISIONS WAS HELD. KANSAS DEFEATED IOWA STATE FOR THE TITLE.

NEBRASKA FOOTBALL EARLY 1900S.

IOWA FOOTBALL COACH MARK S. CATLIN WINS OLYMPIC HURDLES & TAKES 2ND IN DISCUS IN 1904 ST. LOUIS OLYMPICS CATLIN REPRESENTS IOWA AT FIRST MVC MEETING.

THE LEGENDARY PHOG ALLEN.

CAL McCRACKEN, JOHN OUTLAND (OUTLAND TROPHY NAMED AFTER HIM), & BERT KENNEDY, PLAYERS IN THE 1890S. OUTLAND WAS WINNINGEST COACH WITH 53 WINS FROM 1904-1910 AT IOWA STATE.

BURCH THE BEAR WAS IOWA'S MASCOT.

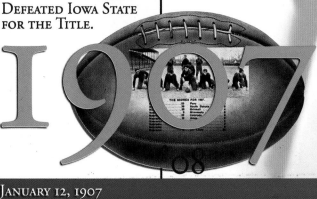

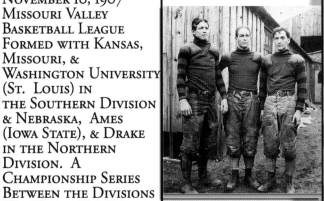

1907

'08

BLACK THE TIGERS EY
TWIST THE TIGERS TAI

Mo. 11 – Drake 8 Des Moines. Iowa Nov. 7, 08.

They twisted our tail in first half, but we ble Their eye in the second half.

Missouri 3 Kansas 0 "Mo" kicks goal

'09

'10

'11

JANUARY 12, 1907
FIRST MEETING OF UNIVERSITY REPRESENTATIVES IN KANSAS CITY TO FORM THE MVC.

1907-1927
NEBRASKA WINS 12 FOOTBALL CHAMPIONSHIPS.

MAY 26, 1911
UNIVERSITY OF IOWA WITHDRAWS FROM MISSOURI VALLEY CONFERENCE.

AMES FOOTBALL GAME 1912

DEC. 26, 1912 KANSAS STATE ADMITTED.

1914 IOWA STATE COMPLETES THE WEST STADIUM AT WEST FIELD. A RECORD CROWD OF 8,000 WATCHED THE HOMECOMING GAME CHAMPIONSHIP.

AMES. 1913.

1913 IOWA STATE FOOTBALL TEAM.

FOURTH ANNUAL.
DRAKE RELAY CARNIVAL
DRAKE STADIUM
APRIL 19, 1913
DES MOINES - IOWA
OFFICIAL PROGRAM
PRICE TEN CENTS

DRAKESTAD WINS 2 MILE STATE MEET 1914

He had a big lead

1912 MISSOURI BASEBALL TEAM.

EARLY KANSAS FOOTBALL GAME.

MVC YELL LEADERS, EARLY 1900S.

'12 FIRST MVC MEN'S TENNIS CHAMPIONSHIP TAKES PLACE IN COLUMBIA, MISSOURI, WITH WASHINGTON U TAKING THE TITLE.

Coach Stiehm

Missouri Valley Track Records

Event	Contestant	School	Date	Record
100 yd. dash	Wilson	Coe	May 28, '10	:10
	Haddock	Kansas	June 5, '09	:10
One mile run	Farquhar	Ames	May 25, '12	4:22 2-5
120 yd. hurdles	Nicholson	Missouri	May 25, '12	:15 2-5
440 yd. dash	Reed	Nebraska	May 27, '11	:50
220 yd. hurdles	Kirksey	Missouri	May 27, '11	:25
1-2 mile run	Bermond	Missouri	May 25, '12	1:57
220 yd. dash	Wilson	Coe	May 27, '11	:22
1 mile relay		Nebraska	May 25, '12	3:27 3-5
2 mile run	Durey	Des Moin's	May 27, '11	9:46
1-2 mile relay		Nebraska	May 25, '12	1:32 1-5
Pole vault	Lambert	Wash'ng't'n	May 27, '11	11.8 7-8
Discus throw	Thatcher	Missouri	May 25, '12	126.5 3-4
High jump	Nicholson	Missouri	May 25, '12	5.11 3-4
Shot put	Howe	Wash'ng't'n	May 28, '10	42.6 1-2
Broad jump	Wilson	Kansas	May 28, '10	22.10 1-2
Hammer throw	Lambert	Ames	June 5, '09	144.5

COACH PHOG ALLEN & HIS KANSAS BASKETBALL TEAM.

W. MILLER. COACH ALLEN. CAPT. M'CUNE. BERGEN. M. MILLER. WOODWARD. PEARD. WOHLER.

MISSOURI

WASHINGTON U

IA STATE COLLEGE TRACK TEAM 1914

Merriam's fast runners

WHERE THE PRESS REPORTS CAME FROM

1912

'13

'14

'15

'16

'12-13 NEBRASKA COACH "JUMBO" STIEHM WINS FOOTBALL & BASKETBALL TITLES IN THE SAME YEAR.

1914 AN IOWA FOOTBALL RESERVED SEAT SEASON TICKET COST $2.00 FOR FOUR HOME GAMES.

1915 NEBRASKA FOOTBALL GOES 8-0 OVERALL AND OUTSCORES ITS OPPONENTS, 282-39.

1911-1916 NEBRASKA GOES 49-5 IN MEN'S BASKETBALL LEAGUE PLAY.

DEC. 13, 1918 GRINNELL (IOWA) ADMITTED.

DEC. 5, 1919 OKLAHOMA ADMITTED.

GRINNELL'S BEN DOUGLAS EARNS NINE LETTERS IN FOOTBALL, BASKETBALL, & TRACK.

GRINNELL'S WENDELL "SONNY" DAVIS CAPTAINS FOOTBALL & BASKETBALL, EARNING THREE LETTERS IN EACH. DAVIS ALSO EXCELS ON THE TRACK & DECATHLON. IN FOOTBALL, HE WAS ALL-VALLEY.

AMERICAN OLYMPIC TEAM 1920

VIIe OLYMPIAD Antwerp, Belgium April-September 1920

1920 IOWA STATE'S ALL-AMERICAN POLLY WALLACE.

1920-21 NEBRASKA READMITTE[D]

KANSAS' EVERETT BRADLEY WINS SILVER MEDAL IN PENTATHLON IN OLYMPIC GAMES AT ANTWERP.

bradley american olympic team anvers

everett bradley

252/20 Lawrence KS 14 WU

congratulations-university proud your-victory

Lindley chancellor Allen director

IOWA STATE CROSS COUNTRY MEET

MEN'S GYMNASIUM, GRINNELL.

VIIe OLYMPIA[D] ANVERS (BELGIQ[UE]) AOÛT-SEPTEMBRE-1920

KANSAS JAYHAWK ATHLETIC DIRECTOR JAMES NAISMITH "THE FATHER OF BASKETBALL."

1917

'18

'19

'20

'21

1918-1919 NEBRASKA SUSPENDED.

1919 ARTHUR EILERS BECOMES MVC SECRETARY.

1917-1922 MISSOURI GOES 75-7 IN MEN'S BASKETBALL.

1921 LEONARD PAULU WINS FIRST OF THREE NCAA CHAMPIONSHIPS IN TRACK.

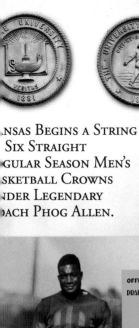

Drake University 1881 Veritas
The University of Oklahoma 1892
Collegium Iowense Grinnell
Iowa State College of Agriculture and Mechanic Arts
Science with Practice
Universitatis Missouriensis
Sigillum Universitatis Kansiensis
Washington University Saint Louis 1853
Per Veritatem Vis

ansas Begins a String
Six Straight
gular Season Men's
sketball Crowns
nder Legendary
oach Phog Allen.

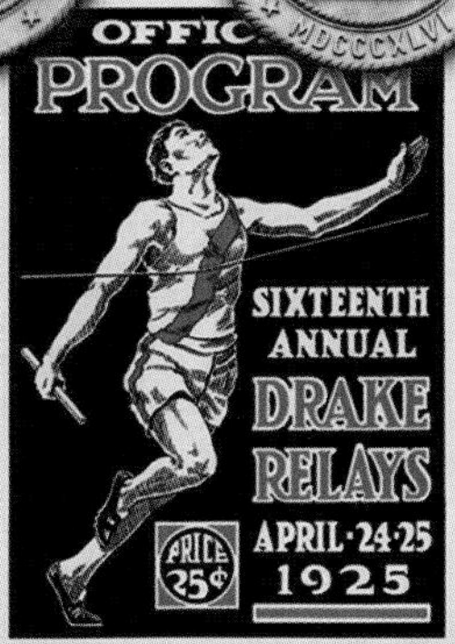

Offici
Program
Sixteenth
Annual
Drake
Relays
April · 24 · 25
1925
Price 25¢

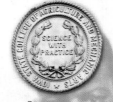

Seals Located on Nebraska's Football Stadium Depicting the MVC Football League Schools in the 1920s. These Seals Are Still on the Facility Today.

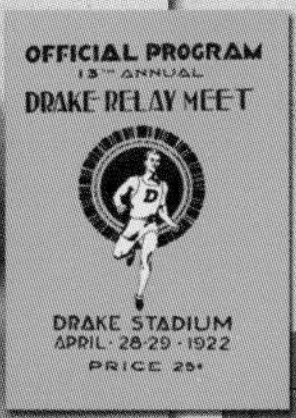

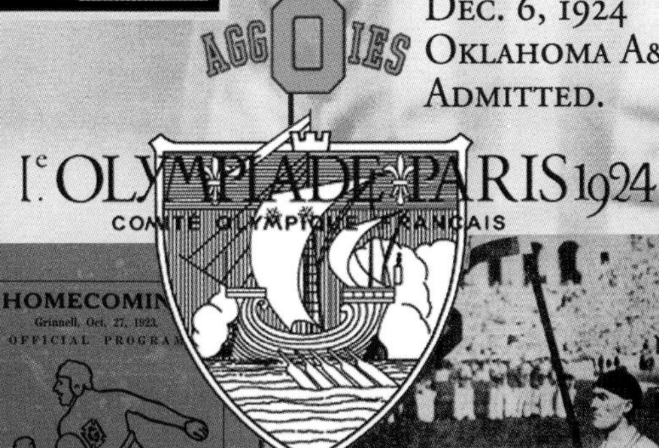

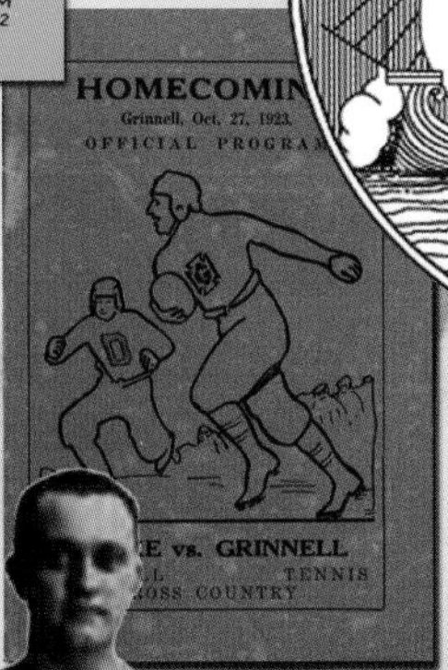

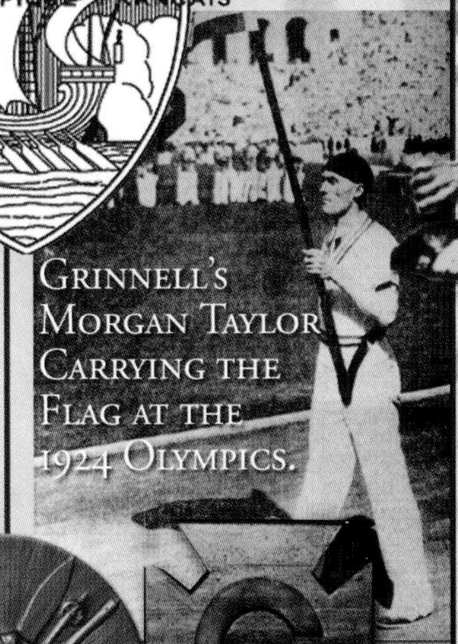

Oklahoma A&M Declared MVC Football Champions

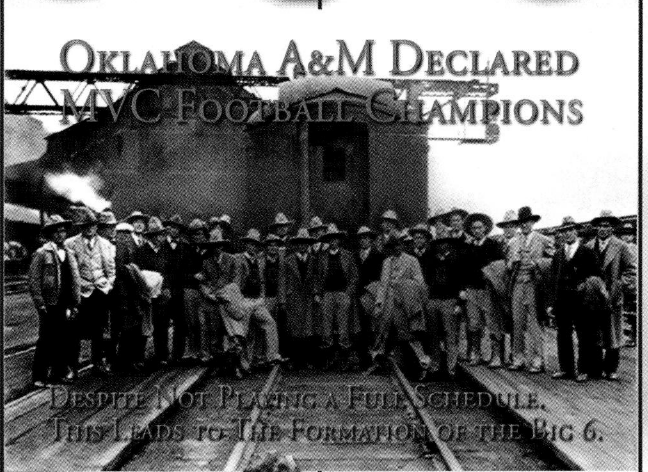

Despite Not Playing a Full Schedule. This Leads to The Formation of the Big 6.

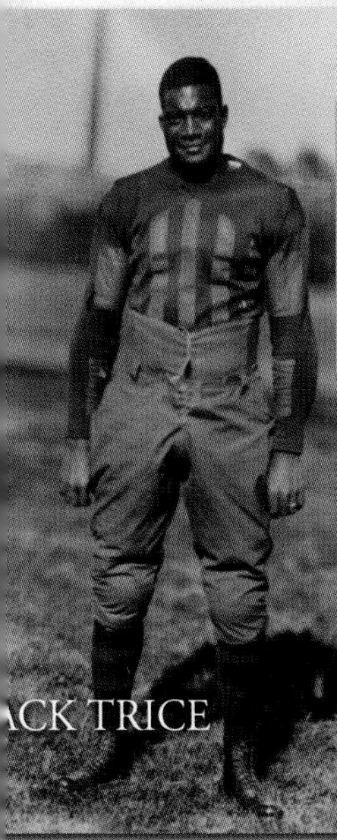

Ack Trice

Official Program
13th Annual
Drake Relay Meet
Drake Stadium
April · 28 · 29 · 1922
Price 25¢

Dec. 6, 1924
Oklahoma A&M Admitted.

Aggies
I^e Olympiade Paris 1924
Comité Olympique Français

Homecomin
Grinnell, Oct. 27, 1923.
Official Progra
e vs. Grinnell
Tennis
oss Country

Grinnell's Morgan Taylor Carrying the Flag at the 1924 Olympics.

1924
Grinnell's Morgan Taylor Sets World Record in 400 Meter Hurdles.

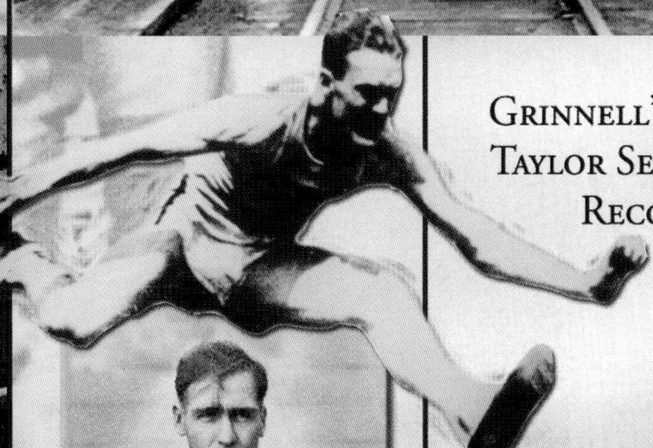

wa State's Jack Trice:
y thoughts Just
fore the First
al College Game
My Life: The Honor
My Race, Family,
Self Is at Stake.
eryone Is Expecting
to Do Big Things.
Vill." During the
rst Half of the Game
e Next Day, Trice
ffered a Broken
llarbone, Continued
Play, but Was Thrown
His Back & Trampled
Three Minnesota
ayers. He Died
ree Days Later.

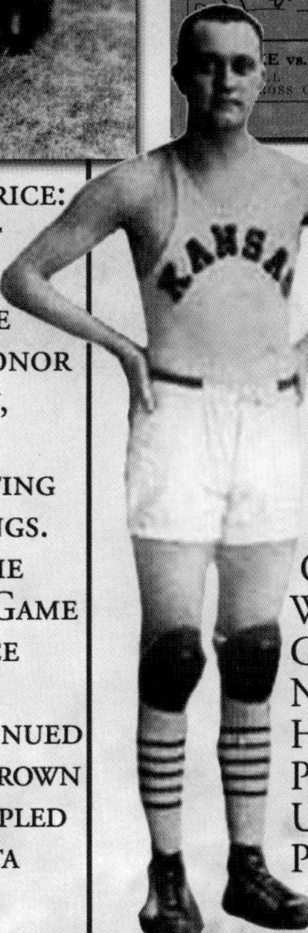

Kansas

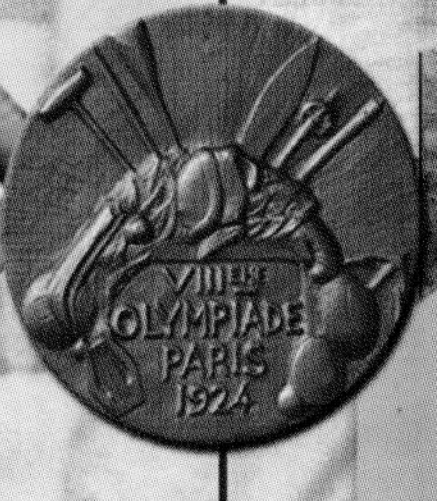

VIIIe Olympiade Paris 1924

Adolph Rupp, One of the Winningest Coaches in NCAA History, Played Under Phog Allen at Kansas.

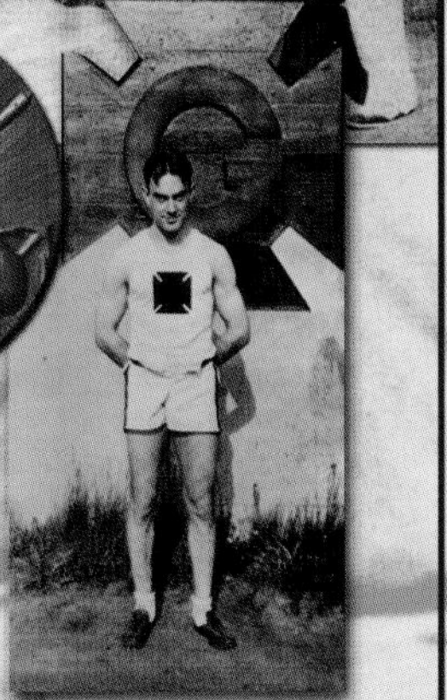

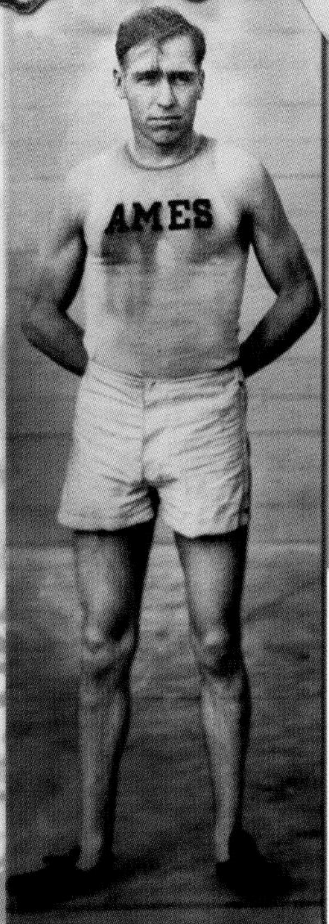

Ames

Lloyd Rathbun Is Iowa State's First National Champion. Rathbun Captures MVC Titles in the Two-Mile Run From 1920 to 1922, & the Cross Country Crown in 1920 & 1921.

Paris _ 1924
VIIIe Olympiade
Jeux Olympiques

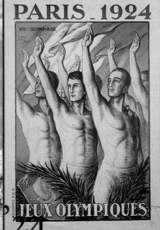

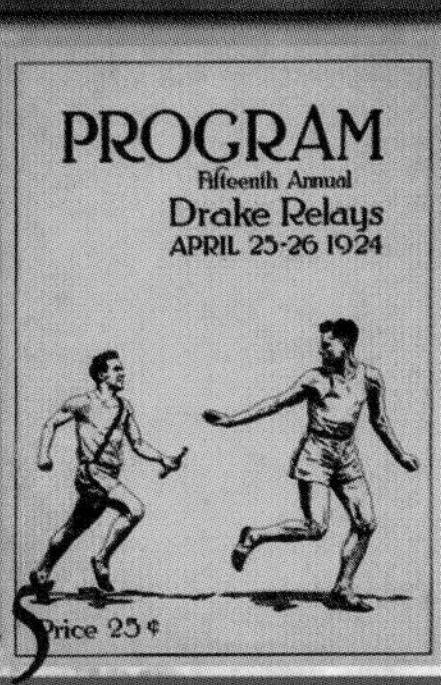

Program
Fifteenth Annual
Drake Relays
April 25-26 1924
Price 25¢

The Missouri Alumnus
Volume XIII December 1924 Number 4
Jackson's Touchdown
How Missouri Won the Valley Championship

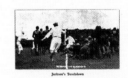

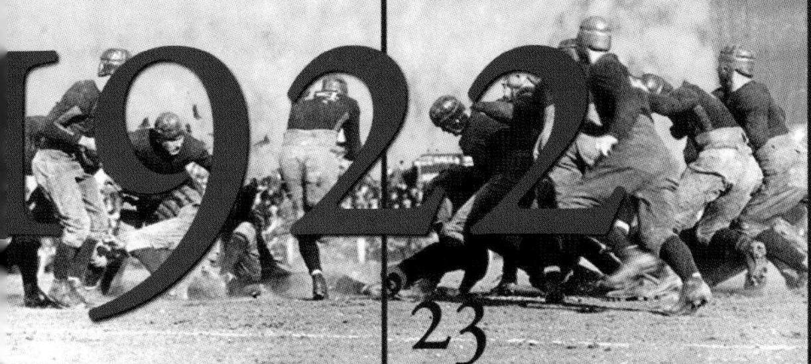

1922 '23 '24 '25 '26

nsas Wins a Record
Straight League
mes In Men's
sketball.

1922-23
Kansas Wins Back-to-Back National Championships in Men's Basketball.

December 1925
Arthur E. Eilers Is Appointed Permanent Secretary of the Missouri Valley Conference.

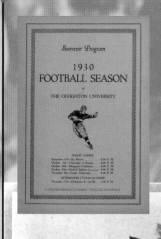

Souvenir Program
1930
FOOTBALL SEASON
at
THE CREIGHTON UNIVERSITY

1928
CREIGHTON
ADMITTED.

BILLY APPEARED
AS REALISTIC
BLUEJAY IN 1927.

Oklahoma A.-M. 13
Creighton 6

GOAL

Brock

1927
MISSOURI CONVERTS A
FIELD GOAL DURING
1927 CHAMPIONSHIP
SEASON.

1928
GRINNELL'S
MORGAN TAYLOR
WINS OLYMPIC
SILVER MEDAL
IN 400 METER
HURDLES.

GRINNELL'S HARRIS
COGGESHALL
REACHES THE FINALS
OF THE EASTERN
INTERCOLLEGIATE
CHAMPIONSHIPS,
PLAYS ON THE
BASKETBALL TEAM,
AND IS ELECTED
TO THE IOWA SPORTS
HALL OF FAME IN 1959.
COGGESHALL IS
CONSIDERED THE BEST
TENNIS PLAYER IN
IOWA'S HISTORY.

Dave Miller
OKLAHOMA
AGGIES
Season
1930
Programme

Oklahoma A. and M. vs. Washington University
October 24   Price 10

Drake Relays
Drake Stadium
April 27, 28, 1928

GOOD ONLY
SATURDAY
APRIL
28

Admission $2.50

Director

OKLAHOMA A&M'S
RANSOM "PAT" BOWMA
"A PLOUGHING, PUSHI
PLUNGING MACHINE,"
LEADS AGGIES TO A
VALLEY CHAMPIONSHI

NOTRE DAME

SOLDIER FIELD

Saturday,
Nov. 9, 1929   DRAKE   Official
25 Cents

OKLAHOMA A&M TR

1927

'28

'29

'30

'31

MISSOURI, IOWA STATE,
OKLAHOMA, KANSAS,
KANSAS STATE, &
NEBRASKA WITHDRAW
TO FORM BIG SIX.

1931
DRAKE UNIVERSITY
CELEBRATES ITS 50TH
ANNIVERSARY.

JOHN BROOKS OF CHICAGO JUMPS TO VICTORY IN THE LONG JUMP WITH A NEW DRAKE RELAYS RECORD F 24'8 3/4".

1932 BUTLER ADMITTED.

A World's Record Hurdler

MORGAN TAYLOR

1936-40 OKLAHOMA A&M'S HENRY IBA WINS OR SHARES FIVE CONSECUTIVE MVC BASKETBALL CHAMPIONSHIPS.

CREIGHTON VS. GRINNELL COLLEGE

October 10, 1936

1934 TULSA & WASHBURN (KANSAS) ADMITTED.

1935 DRAKE'S LINN PHILSON WINS NCAA HIGH JUMP TITLE, THE BULLDOGS' FIRST NCAA OUTDOOR MEN'S TRACK INDIVIDUAL TITLE.

RONALD REAGAN AT THE DRAKE RELAYS.

TULSA WINS 12 FOOTBALL CHAMPIONSHIPS BETWEEN 1935 AND 1951.

JACK TORRANCE OF LOUISIANA STATE BREAKS THE WORLD RECORD IN SHOT PUT. THE DISTANCE OF 55'1/2" ALSO SET A DRAKE RELAYS, A COLLEGIATE & AN AMERICAN RECORD.

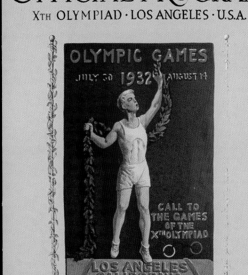

OFFICIAL PROGRAM
XTH OLYMPIAD · LOS ANGELES · U.S.A.

OLYMPIC GAMES
JULY 30 1932 AUGUST 14

CALL TO THE GAMES OF THE XTH OLYMPIAD

LOS ANGELES CALIFORNIA

1932

OL MPIC P RK 10

SAT RDAY AUG ST 6, 1932

GRINNELL'S MORGAN TAYLOR EXCELS AT THE 1932 OLYMPIC GAMES IN LOS ANGELES.

HELMS ATHLETIC FOUNDATION
FOUNDED 1936

MORGAN TAYLOR'S HELMS HALL OF FAME AWARD.

DRAKE RELAYS QUEEN MARTHA STULL (CENTER).

'33

'34

'35

'36

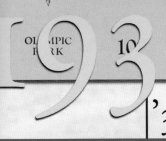

34 OACH HENRY IBA'S RST YEAR AT OKLAHOMA &M.

1934 BUTLER WITHDRAWS.

1936 OKLAHOMA A&M WINS FIRST OF 5-STRAIGHT MEN'S BASKETBALL TITLES.

JANUARY 11, 1936 OKLAHOMA A&M WINS FIRST OF 41-STRAIGHT LEAGUE HOME GAMES IN MEN'S BASKETBALL.

OKLAHOMA A.&M. FOOTBALL STAFF

COACHING STAFF, L TO R: RALPH HIGGINS JOHN B. MCDANIEL TED COX ELWAN DEES AL PADDOCK.

OKLAHOMA A&M'S COACH RALPH HIGGINS WINS 17 STRAIGHT TEAM CHAMPIONSHIPS IN TRACK & FIELD FROM 1938 TO 1957.

LONG ISLAND U. . . . . ROANOKE . . . NEW MEXICO AGGIES BRADLEY TECH. . . . ST. JOHN'S U. . . . LOYOLA U.

NATIONAL CHAMPIONSHIP TROPHY

NATIONAL INVITATION TOURNAMENT
MARCH 22nd 1939   SOUVENIR PROGRAM 15c

CREIGHTON'S EDDIE HICKEY WINS THREE STRAIGHT MVC BASKETBALL TITLES FROM 1941 TO 1943.

1941 CREIGHTON MAKES MVC'S FIRST MEN'S BASKETBALL APPEARANCE IN NCAA TOURNAMENT.

DRAKE RELAYS $2.20
EXCHANGE TICKET
This ticket has a value of TWO DOLLARS and TWENTY CENTS on the purchase price of any ticket or tickets at the Drake Relays either Friday or Saturday. Federal Revenue Tax included.
FRIDAY, APRIL 28 1939 SATURDAY, APRIL 29

CENTRAL vs TULSA

1937 SLU FOOTBALL VS. WASHINGTON U.

1937 SAINT LOUIS ADMITTED.

1936 OLYMPIC WRESTLING TEAM IS HONORED DURING A CEREMONY AT THE AGGIE–OU GAME. ON THE PLATFORM ARE ROY DUNN, ROSS FLOOD, FRANK LEWIS, HARLEY STRONG, & FRED PARKEY. JOE COOK, MAYOR OF CUSHING, OKLA.,(L), CONGRATULATES A&M COACH ED GALLAGHER.

GRINNELL SWIMMING TROPHY

OKLAHOMA A&M'S TRAVELING SQUAD VISITS ACTING GOVERNOR JAMES E. BARRY BEFORE LEAVING FOR THE NIT.

1941 JOHNNY "SLINGSHOT" KNOLLA WAS CREIGHTON'S ALL-MVC, UPI & AP ALL-AMERICAN.

TULSA VS. OKLAHOMA A. & M. COWBOYS STILLWATER, OKLAHOMA
HOMECOMING OCTOBER 22, 1938

1937

'38

'39

'40

'41

OKLAHOMA A&M'S MOST FAMOUS OF ALL WRESTLING COACHES, EDWARD CLARK GALLAGHER, IS NICKNAMED "KNUTE ROCKNE OF THE MAT."

1937 THE STITCHES ARE REMOVED IN THE NEW DESIGN OF THE BASKETBALL.

1939 GRINNELL COLLEGE (IOWA) WITHDRAWS.

1941 WASHBURN (KANSAS) WITHDRAWS.

42
**ULSA IS UNBEATEN
ND UNTIED DURING
EGULAR SEASON, BUT
OSES 14-7 TO TENNESSEE
N SUGAR BOWL.**

TULSA'S HURRICANE.

1945
DRAKE'S FRED FEILER
WINS BACK-TO-BACK
MEN'S CROSS COUNTRY
TITLES IN 1944 AND
1945, AND DRAKE TAKES
NCAA TEAM TITLES
IN THE SPORT IN 1944,
1945, & 1946.

MARCH 23-24, 1945
OKLAHOMA A&M PLAYS
IN THE NCAA WESTERN
CHAMPIONSHIP FINALS.

N·C·A·A
Western Championship Finals

MUNICIPAL AUDITORIUM
KANSAS CITY, MISSOURI
MARCH 23-24, 1945

OFFICIAL
25¢
PROGRAM

RELAYS QUEEN JOYCE
BEELER, 1946.

1946
OKLAHOMA A&M'S
BOB KURLAND SCORES 58
POINTS—AN MVC
RECORD FOR 14 YEARS
UNTIL OSCAR ROBERTSON
SCORES 62 AGAINST
NORTH TEXAS IN 1960.

OKLA. GOV. BOB KERR, PRES. AND
ENNETT (R) SURROUND I.A. GOV

DRAKE
13
OKLA.ST.
9

1944
MVC VOTES
OKLAHOMA
A&M MVC
CHAMPS
BECAUSE
TEAMS DURING
WORLD WAR II
DID NOT PLAY LEAGUE
SCHEDULE.

1945
WICHITA (NOW
WICHITA STATE)
ADMITTED.

JANUARY 1, 1945
TULSA BEATS GEORGIA
TECH 26-12 TO BECOME
ORANGE BOWL CHAMPS.

america's best

NATIONAL COLLEGIATE ATHLETIC ASSOCIATION
BASKETBALL TOURNAMENT · EAST-WEST FINALS
MADISON SQUARE GARDEN   MARCH 27, 1943   SOUVENIR PROGRAM 15c

42
**ULSA'S
LENN
OBBS
ADS
ATION**

**NTING
TH 48.3
ERAGE.**

SUGAR BOWL
CLASSIC
1943

45

S.
ESSEE

SOUVENIR

11TH ANNUAL
ORANGE BOWL CLASS
JAN. 1-1945   MIAMI, FLA.

WARTIME FOOTBALL AT
OKLAHOMA A. and M.

OKLAHOMA A&M
football
1945

GEORGIA TECH
VS
TULSA

1946
BOB KURLAND'S 25
FIELD GOALS AGAINST
SLU STILL STAND AS
MVC RECORD.

AGGIES
85
AGGIES
90
AGGIES
77

ANNUAL DRAKE RELAYS
FRIDAY
SATURDAY
APRIL 24-25
1942
KE STADIUM · DES MO

MID-1940S
HENRY IBA CREDITS
BOB KURLAND WITH
FIRST DUNK IN GAME
AGAINST TEMPLE.

1944-45
OKLAHOMA A&M
IS ONLY SCHOOL IN
MVC TO PLAY A
FULL BASKETBALL
SCHEDULE DURING
WORLD WAR II.

1945 & 1946
OKLAHOMA
A&M NCAA
BASKETBALL
CHAMPS.

1946
ALL FIVE FIRST-TEAM
MVC PLAYERS WERE
FROM OKLAHOMA
A&M: KURLAND,
AUBREY, PARKS, KERN,
& WILLIAMS.

1942

WARTIME FOOTBALL AT

'43

'44

'45

'46

1-43
EIGHTON WINS
REE STRAIGHT
EN'S BASKETBALL
TLES.

1943
ONLY TULSA,
OKLAHOMA A&M, &
DRAKE FIELD FOOTBALL
TEAMS.

1945
OKLAHOMA A&M'S BOB
FENIMORE IS THIRD IN
HEISMAN TROPHY
BALLOTING.

100 YEARS OF ATHLETICS EXCELLENCE

1948

SLU Basketball Team.

DETROIT
1947
Detroit Admitted. Washington U. (St. Louis) & Creighton Withdraw.

Early Color Image (1946) from the Drake Relays.

"Easy" Ed Macauley.

1948
Bradley Legendary Coach A. J. Robertson Dies (Coached Football, Basketball, & Baseball & Also Served as A.D.).

Johnny Bright

CONTESTANT
DRAKE
WARE!
NON TRANSFERABLE
1948

ADMISSION
RELAYS
FRIDAY
APRIL 23, 1948

1950
Legendary Head Coach Leads Bradley to First Appearance in the NCAA Baseball College World Series.

BU
1948
Bradley Admitted.

UH
1950
Houston Admitted.

October 20, 1951
Don Ultang & John Robinson Win Pulitzer Prize for Drake's Bright Incident Photos.

UNIVERSITY OF WICHITA
vs.
BRADLEY UNIVERSITY
of Peoria, Illinois
SHOCKER
OFFICIAL FOOTBALL MAGAZINE
VETERANS FIELD
OCTOBER 4
Golden Anniversary

1951
Drake's Johnny Bright Accounts for 6,000 Total Yards in His Career.

NCAA WESTERN FINALS

11TH ANNUAL
NCAA
NATIONAL COLLEGIATE BASKETBALL TOURNAMENT
35¢
EAST-WEST FINALS
KENTUCKY vs. OKLAHOMA A&M
OREGON STATE vs. ILLINOIS
March 26, 1949

1950
Bradley Finishes #1 In Final Team AP Basketball Poll.

BRADLEY vs. DRAKE
OFFICIAL PROGRAM
25¢
50

25¢ SOUVENIR PROGRAM

Tulsa's Jim Finks Is the Nation's Second Leading Passer with 1,363 Yards & 7 Touchdowns. NFL Hall of Fame 1995.

QUARTERBACK CLUB
PEORIA, ILLINOIS
1948 SCHEDULE
No. 360
1948

DELTA BOWL
WILLIAM & MARY
vs.
OKLAHOMA A&M
CRUMP STADIUM
JANUARY 1, 1

THIS FIELD HOUSE DEDICATED TO THE MEMORY OF
ALFRED JAMES ROBERTSON

1947
1948
THIS FIELD HOUSE

'47
'48
'49
'50
'51

1947
SLU Billikens Win Their First MVC Title.

1948
Ed Macauley of SLU Earns First of Back-to-Back National Player of the Year Honors.

1949
Oklahoma A&M Wins Six of the Valley's Seven Team Championships.

1950
Bradley Plays in Finals of NIT and NCAA Tournament.

1951
Drake's Johnny Bright Is Fifth in Heisman Trophy Balloting.

100 Years Of Athletics Excellence

1952
Tulsa's Howard Waugh Leads Nation in Rushing With 1372/8.4 Yards a Carry.

1954-55
Tulsa's Clarence Iba is Voted MVC Basketball Coach of the Year.

1954-55
Bob Patterson Is Tulsa's First All-American, Leads the MVC in Scoring and Wins His First MVP Title.

The 1954 NCAA Tournament Championship Game Matching Bradley Against LaSalle Was the First Ever Championship Contest Televised to a National Audience.

Bobby Joe Mason.

1956
Cincinnati Admitted.

1956
North Texas State Admitted.

MEAN GREEN

51-52
Marvin Matuszak Is the First Tulsa Gridder to be Honored by the Associated Press as an All-American Two Years in a Row.

1953
Oklahoma A&M Coach Ralph Higgins with Aggie Runners.

Parry O'Brien Held the World Record in the Shot Put from 1953 until 1959. At the Drake Relays in 1954, He Increased His World Record to 59' 9 3/4".

1955
Bradley Team.

1956
Houston Wins First of Five Straight NCAA Men's Golf Championships.

1956 Drake Readmitted.

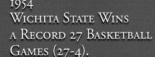

1952
'53
'54
'55
'56

1952
Tulsa's Howard Waugh Rushes for 250 Yards. The Record Stands for 30 Years.

1954
Wichita State Wins a Record 27 Basketball Games (27-4).

1955
Okla. A&M's J. W. Mashburn Wins First of Two-Straight NCAA Outdoor Track Titles.

1956
Kansas Coach Phog Allen Retired with a 48-Year Record of 746–264.

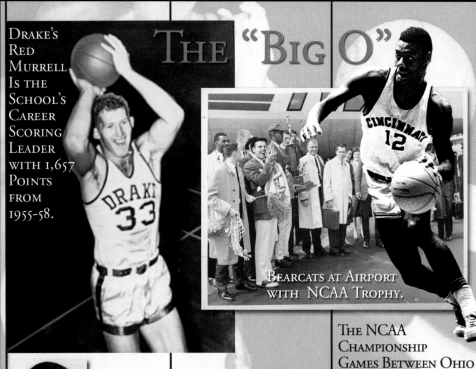

DRAKE'S RED MURRELL IS THE SCHOOL'S CAREER SCORING LEADER WITH 1,657 POINTS FROM 1955-58.

THE "BIG O"

BEARCATS AT AIRPORT WITH NCAA TROPHY.

CINCINNATI'S BOB WIESENHAHN (WICHITA STATE VS. CINCINNATI).

1961-62 CINCINNATI WINS BACK-TO-BACK NCAA MEN'S BASKETBALL TITLES DURING A STREAK OF SIX STRAIGHT MVC REGULAR-SEASON CROWNS.

CINCINNATI BASKETBALL COACH ED JUCKER.

1957 NORVALL NEVE APPOINTED COMMISSIONER.

1957 OKLAHOMA A&M WITHDRAWS.

CINCINNATI'S JACK LEE, "THE GENERAL," FINISHES HIS COLLEGE CAREER WITH A 55 PASS COMPLETION PERCENTAGE—THE BEST IN SCHOOL HISTORY. LEE WAS NAMED ALL-MVC IN 1958 & 1959.

1958 TO 1960 CINCINNATI BEARCATS COMPILE 39-3 MVC RECORD AND WIN THREE LEAGUE CHAMPIONSHIPS.

1957-58 TO 1959-60 CINCINNATI'S OSCAR ROBERTSON LEADS DIVISION I IN SCORING THREE STRAIGHT SEASONS WITH AVERAGES OF 35.1, 32.6 & 33.7 POINTS.

THE NCAA CHAMPIONSHIP GAMES BETWEEN OHIO STATE & CINCINNATI IN 1961 & 1962 MARKED THE ONLY TIMES DURING THE 20TH CENTURY THAT TWO TEAMS FROM THE SAME STATE MET IN THE NCAA FINALS.

JANUARY 16, 1960 BRADLEY DEFEATS CINCINNATI 91-90. GAME VOTED BY BRADLEY FANS AS GREATEST BASKETBALL GAME IN SCHOOL'S HISTORY.

1960 THE "BIG O" SETS MISSOURI VALLEY CONFERENCE SINGLE GAME SCORING RECORD AGAINST NORTH TEXAS WITH 62 POINTS.

DRAKE 20 IOWA ST. 0

1959 DRAKE RELAYS
APRIL 24-25
DRAKE STADIUM
DES MOINES, IOWA
RESERVED SEAT $3.00
RESERVED $3.00
GATES OPEN AT 12:30 P.M.
EVENTS START AT 1:15 P.M.

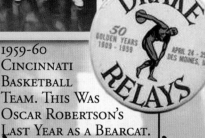

1959-60 CINCINNATI BASKETBALL TEAM. THIS WAS OSCAR ROBERTSON'S LAST YEAR AS A BEARCAT.

1960 HOUSTON WITHDRAWS.

A MAJORETTE PERFORMING IN FRONT OF THE POLE VAULT COMPETITION AT THE DRAKE RELAYS.

DRAKE RELAYS
50 GOLDEN YEARS 1909-1959
APRIL 24-25 DES MOINES, IA.

1957

'58

'59

'60

'61

1957 BRADLEY WINS NIT.

1957 CINCINNATI WINS FIRST OF NINE CONSECUTIVE MVC MEN'S SWIMMING TITLES.

1959 HOUSTON'S DICK CRAWFORD WINS BACK-TO-BACK MEDALIST HONORS AT NCAA GOLF CHAMPIONSHIP.

1960 BRADLEY WINS NIT.

TULSA FOOTBALL

1966

1963-64
LOUISVILLE BREAKS COLOR BARRIER WITH WADE HOUSTON, SAM SMITH, & EDDIE WHITEHEAD.

3-64
ILSA'S JERRY RHOME ROWS FOR 4,779 RDS AND 42 UCHDOWNS.

2-63
CHITA BEATS OHIO ATE 71-54 IN FRONT OF RGEST CROWD (11,375) HISTORY OF UNDHOUSE.

COACH JUCKER WITH CINCINNATI'S ALL-AMERICANS.

ARCH 17, 1962
CAA MIDWEST GIONAL IN MANHATTAN, NSAS.

1963
LOUISVILLE SIGNS MOST IMPORTANT RECRUIT IN SCHOOL'S HISTORY—WES UNSELD.

1965
BILLY GUY ANDERSON LEADS TULSA TEAM TO BLUEBONNET BOWL, WHERE THE HURRICANE LOSES TO TENNESSEE 27-6.

WES UNSELD

DECEMBER 1964
WICHITA IS RANKED #1 FOR ONE WEEK IN BASKETBALL.

1964
LOUISVILLE ADMITTED.

1964-65
TULSA'S JERRY RHOME & HOWARD TWILLEY FINISH RUNNERS-UP IN THE HEISMAN TROPHY BALLOTING IN CONSECUTIVE YEARS.

CINCINNATI COACH ED JUCKER WITH RON BONHAM (LEFT) AND GEORGE WILSON (RIGHT).

1965
TULSA'S BILLY GUY ANDERSON THROWS FOR A THEN-NCAA RECORD 502 YARDS AGAINST COLORADO STATE.

1965
TULSA'S HOWARD TWILLEY SETS NCAA RECORD FOR CAREER PASS RECEPTIONS WITH 261.

DECEMBER 30, 1966
BRADLEY WINS SUGAR BOWL BASKETBALL TOURNAMENT AGAINST UTAH 64-62.

1966
MEMPHIS STATE ADMITTED.

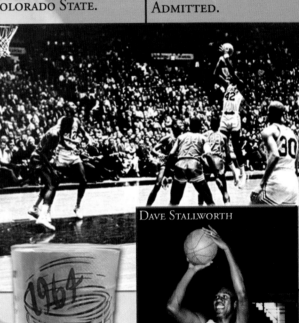

DAVE STALLWORTH

1965-66
DRAKE FRESHMEN McCARTER, PULLIAM, & WRIGHT OUTPLAY VARSITY TEAM IN PRACTICE, AND AFTERWARDS ARE NOT ALLOWED TO PLAY TOGETHER AGAINST THE VARSITY TEAM.

JERRY RHOME'S HELMET.

1962

DRAKE RELAYS
Drake Stadium
April 27-28, 1962

'63

'64

'65

'66

9-63
NCINNATI REACHES FIVE RAIGHT FINAL FOURS, NNING TITLES IN 1961 & '62.

1963
CINCINNATI'S ED JUCKER IS NATIONAL COACH OF THE YEAR IN MEN'S BASKETBALL.

1964
TULSA'S JERRY RHOME IS SECOND IN HEISMAN TROPHY BALLOTING.

1965
TULSA'S HOWARD TWILLEY IS SECOND IN HEISMAN TROPHY BALLOTING.

PAUL MORRISON • DRAKE

1967
LOUISVILLE CARDINALS
WIN FIRST OF SEVEN MVC
TITLES IN BASKETBALL.

1967-68
LOUISVILLE'S WES UNSELD
SETS SCHOOL SINGLE-
GAME SCORING RECORD
WITH 45 POINTS
AGAINST GEORGETOWN.

BOBBY "BINGO" SMITH

1968
BRADLEY WINS
TENNIS
CHAMPIONSHIP.

1968-69 DRAKE TEAM
WINS CONSOLATION
GAME IN FINAL FOUR
SEMIFINALS (THE NCAA
DISCONTINUED THE
CONSOLATION GAME
FOLLOWING THE
1981 FINAL FOUR).

1968 TO 1970
DRAKE'S MAURY JOHN
IS ONLY COACH IN
MVC HISTORY TO
BE NAMED COACH OF
THE YEAR FOR THREE
CONSECUTIVE YEARS.

1968-69
TULSA'S BOBBY "BINGO"
SMITH LEADS MVC IN
SCORING AND NAMED
LEAGUE MVP.

1970 TO 1972
TULSA'S DREW PEARSON
CATCHES 55 PASSES FOR
1,119 YARDS.

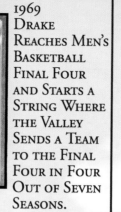

BE IT RESOLVED: THE DES MOINES BRANCH
OF THE NAACP RECOGNIZES AND HONORS

DRAKE'S GREATEST TEAM:
BLACK & WHITE TOGETHER

BRAVO! TO THE 1968-69 DRAKE MEN'S BASKETBALL
TEAM, WHOSE EXCEPTIONAL TEAMWORK AND PLAY
NOT ONLY RESULTED IN OUTSTANDING SUCCESS ON
THE HARDWOOD, BUT WHOSE INTERRACIAL CAMARADERIE
TAUGHT AN ENTIRE COMMUNITY EXTRAORDINARY
LESSONS ON RACIAL DIVERSITY AND LIFE.

BRAVO! TO COACH MAURY JOHN, JEAN JOHN,
ASSISTANT COACHES GUS GUYDON AND DAN CALLAHAN
AND DRAKE UNIVERSITY, FOR CREATING A WELCOMING
ENVIRONMENT FOR THE AFRICAN-AMERICAN MEMBERS
OF THE TEAM AT A TIME WHEN OUR NATION WAS
STRUGGLING TO COME TO GRIPS WITH ITS UNFORTUNATE
RACIAL LEGACY, AND FOR BUILDING A TEAM CHEMISTRY
THAT WAS TRULY BLACK-AND-WHITE TOGETHER.

RESOLUTION PASSED UNANIMOUSLY, DECEMBER 18, 2003

PRESENTED JANUARY 2004
BY THE DES MOINES BRANCH NAACP
LINDA CARTER, PRESIDENT

1969
DEWITT T. WEAVER
APPOINTED
COMMISSIONER.

1969 CINCINNATI
WITHDRAWS.

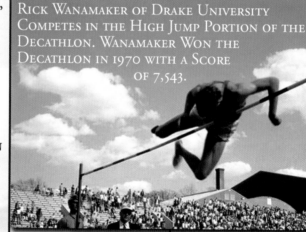

RICK WANAMAKER OF DRAKE UNIVERSITY
COMPETES IN THE HIGH JUMP PORTION OF THE
DECATHLON. WANAMAKER WON THE
DECATHLON IN 1970 WITH A SCORE
OF 7,543.

1969
DRAKE'S MAURY JOHN
USES "BELLY BUTTON
DEFENSE," A PHRASE
COINED BY
RESTAURATEUR
BABE BISIGNANO.

1969
DRAKE
REACHES MEN'S
BASKETBALL
FINAL FOUR
AND STARTS A
STRING WHERE
THE VALLEY
SENDS A TEAM
TO THE FINAL
FOUR IN FOUR
OUT OF SEVEN
SEASONS.

OCTOBER 2, 1970
WICHITA STATE
FOOTBALL TEAM
PLANE CRASHES
IN COLORADO.

1968 AL WILLIAMS
ATTENDS DRAKE &
HELPS BULLDOGS
REACH 1969 NCAA
BASKETBALL FINAL FOUR.

1970
DRAKE'S RICK
WANAMAKER WINS
NCAA DECATHLON,
AND, A YEAR LATER,
WINS THE DECATHLON
IN THE PAN AM GAMES.

1970
MVC COMMISSIONER
DEWITT WEAVER MOV
MVC OFFICE FROM
KANSAS CITY TO DALL

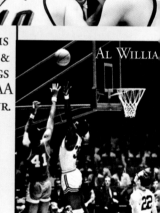

LOUISVILLE'S DEN
CRUM TAKES T
CARDINALS TO T
FINAL FO

DRAKE'S MAURY JO

AL WILLIA

1970
WEST TEXAS
STATE
&
NEW MEXICO
STATE
ADMITTED.

1967

DREW PEARSON   '68   '69   '70   '71

1968
DRAKE WINS FIRST OF
EIGHT STRAIGHT MVC
INDOOR TRACK TITLES.

1969
TULSA WINS FIRST OF
SEVEN CONSECUTIVE
MVC BASEBALL TITLES.

1970
PRESIDENT NIXON
CONTRIBUTES $500 TO A
FUND FOR SURVIVORS OF THE
WICHITA STATE PLANE CRASH.

1971
RB HOWARD STEVENS OF
LOUISVILLE WINS FIRST C
TWO STRAIGHT MVC FOO
BALL OFFENSIVE MVPS.

'73
Tulsa's Ray Rhodes [h]as 19 Kickoff Returns [fo]r 501 Yards, a School [R]ecord that Stood for [?] Years.

1973
Sub Four-Minute Miler, Jim Ryun, Runs the Mile at the Drake Relays.

1973
Memphis State Loses to UCLA in NCAA Final Four Title Game in St. Louis.

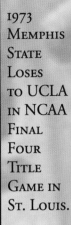

6th drake relays
April 23-24, 1976 • Drake Stadium • Des Moines, Iowa

$1.00

1975
Louisville Cardinals Win 7th and Final MVC Basketball Title.

1974-75
Steve Largent Leads the Nation in Touchdown Receptions.

'72
[De]Witt Weaver [Re]signs as [Co]mmissioner.

1973
Memphis State Withdraws.

'72
[M]ickey Holmes [A]ppointed [Co]mmissioner.

'72
[Lo]uisville Reaches [th]e Final Four.

Then California Governor Ronald Reagan and Iowa Governor Robert D. Ray Pose with the 1974 Drake Relays Queen Gloria Watson.

1972-73
Memphis State's Larry Kenon's 501 Rebounds and 273 Field Goals Remain Memphis' Single-Season Records.

SALUKIS

1974
Southern Illinois Admitted.

1974
Saint Louis & North Texas State Withdraw.

1975
Univ. of Louisville Withdraws from MVC.

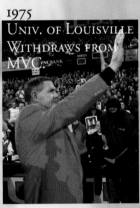

1975
Southern Illinois Begins a Stretch of Ten Straight Outdoor Men's Track Crowns.

1976
Indiana State Admitted.

ISU

1975-76
SIU's Mike Glenn Is MVC Player of the Year and Goes on to a 10-Year Career in the NBA.

1976
Creighton Re-admitted.

Tulsa Alumni Ray Rhodes & Steve Largent Meet at Tulsa HOF Dinner.

1972

'73

'74

'75

'76

1973
First NCAA Title Game Broadcast on Monday Night Television, UCLA & Memphis.

1974-75
Tulsa Is a Perfect 10-0 in Conference Play, Winning Back-to-Back MVC Football Titles.

1975
Louisville Reaches NCAA Final Four.

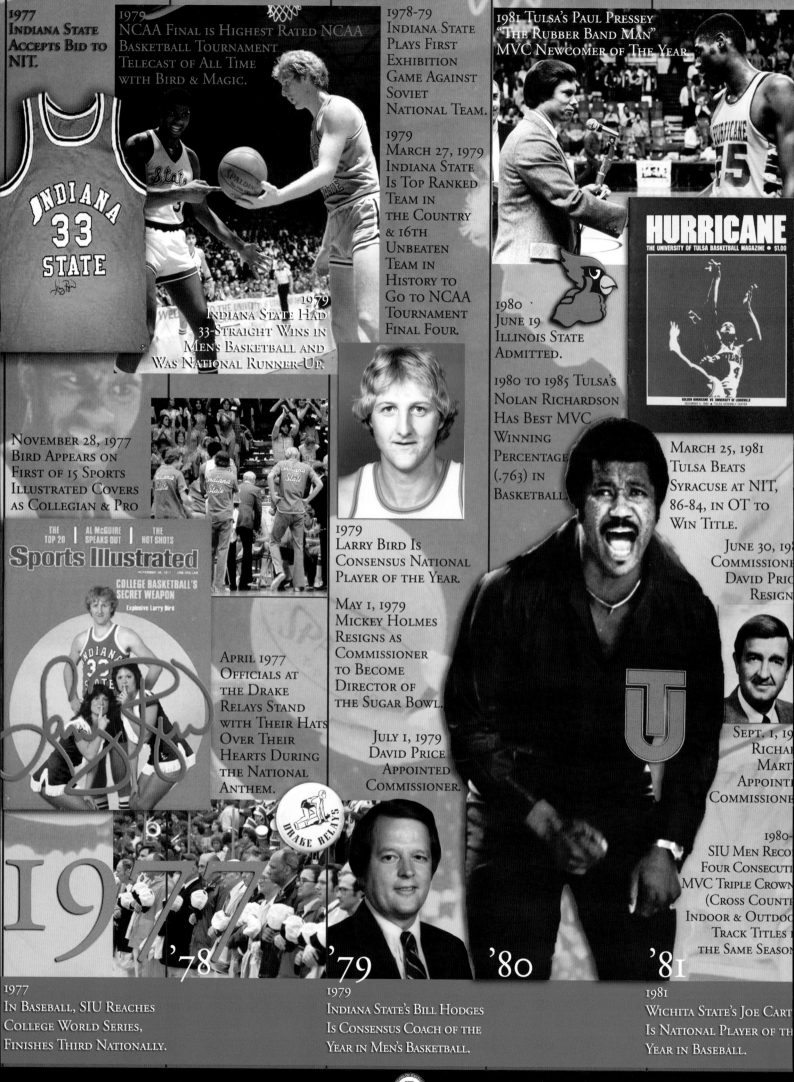

1977
INDIANA STATE ACCEPTS BID TO NIT.

1979
NCAA FINAL IS HIGHEST RATED NCAA BASKETBALL TOURNAMENT TELECAST OF ALL TIME WITH BIRD & MAGIC.

1978-79
INDIANA STATE PLAYS FIRST EXHIBITION GAME AGAINST SOVIET NATIONAL TEAM.

1979
MARCH 27, 1979 INDIANA STATE IS TOP RANKED TEAM IN THE COUNTRY & 16TH UNBEATEN TEAM IN HISTORY TO GO TO NCAA TOURNAMENT FINAL FOUR.

1981 Tulsa's Paul Pressey "The Rubber Band Man" MVC Newcomer of The Year.

INDIANA 33 STATE

HURRICANE
THE UNIVERSITY OF TULSA BASKETBALL MAGAZINE • $1.00

GOLDEN HURRICANE VS UNIVERSITY OF LOUISVILLE
DECEMBER 4, 1980 • TULSA ASSEMBLY CENTER

1979
INDIANA STATE HAD 33-STRAIGHT WINS IN MEN'S BASKETBALL AND WAS NATIONAL RUNNER-UP.

1980
JUNE 19 ILLINOIS STATE ADMITTED.

1980 TO 1985 TULSA'S NOLAN RICHARDSON HAS BEST MVC WINNING PERCENTAGE (.763) IN BASKETBALL.

NOVEMBER 28, 1977 BIRD APPEARS ON FIRST OF 15 SPORTS ILLUSTRATED COVERS AS COLLEGIAN & PRO

MARCH 25, 1981 TULSA BEATS SYRACUSE AT NIT, 86-84, IN OT TO WIN TITLE.

JUNE 30, 19 COMMISSIONE DAVID PRIC RESIGN

THE TOP 20 | AL McGUIRE SPEAKS OUT | THE HOT SHOTS
Sports Illustrated
NOVEMBER 28, 1977 ONE DOLLAR
COLLEGE BASKETBALL'S SECRET WEAPON
Explosive Larry Bird
INDIANA STATE 33

1979
LARRY BIRD IS CONSENSUS NATIONAL PLAYER OF THE YEAR.

MAY 1, 1979 MICKEY HOLMES RESIGNS AS COMMISSIONER TO BECOME DIRECTOR OF THE SUGAR BOWL.

APRIL 1977 OFFICIALS AT THE DRAKE RELAYS STAND WITH THEIR HATS OVER THEIR HEARTS DURING THE NATIONAL ANTHEM.

JULY 1, 1979 DAVID PRICE APPOINTED COMMISSIONER.

SEPT. 1, 19 RICHA MART APPOINT COMMISSIONE

DRAKE RELAYS

1980- SIU MEN RECO FOUR CONSECUTI MVC TRIPLE CROWN (CROSS COUNTR INDOOR & OUTDOO TRACK TITLES THE SAME SEASON

19**77**

'**78**

'**79**

'**80**

'**81**

1977
IN BASEBALL, SIU REACHES COLLEGE WORLD SERIES, FINISHES THIRD NATIONALLY.

1979
INDIANA STATE'S BILL HODGES IS CONSENSUS COACH OF THE YEAR IN MEN'S BASKETBALL.

1981
WICHITA STATE'S JOE CART IS NATIONAL PLAYER OF TH YEAR IN BASEBALL.

1907 2007
100 YEARS OF ATHLETICS EXCELLENCE

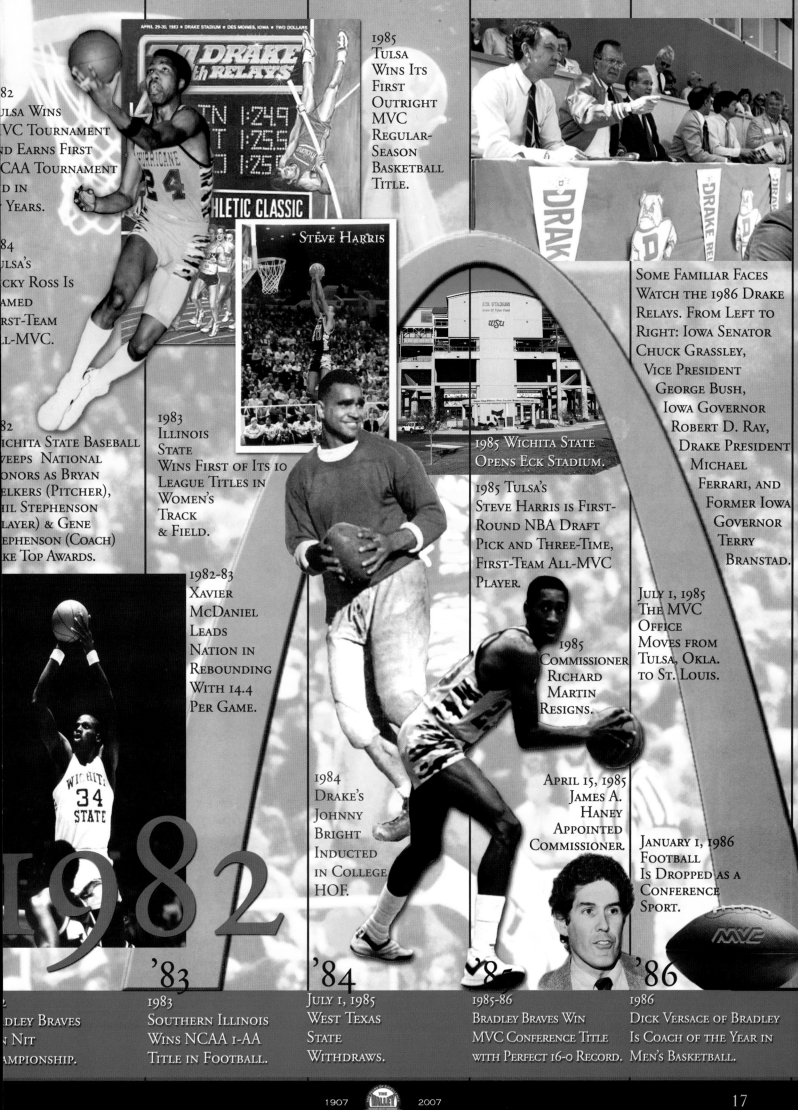

1982 TULSA WINS MVC TOURNAMENT AND EARNS FIRST NCAA TOURNAMENT ... IN ... YEARS.

1984 TULSA'S RICKY ROSS IS NAMED FIRST-TEAM ALL-MVC.

1982 WICHITA STATE BASEBALL SWEEPS NATIONAL HONORS AS BRYAN OELKERS (PITCHER), PHIL STEPHENSON (PLAYER) & GENE STEPHENSON (COACH) TAKE TOP AWARDS.

STEVE HARRIS

1983 ILLINOIS STATE WINS FIRST OF ITS 10 LEAGUE TITLES IN WOMEN'S TRACK & FIELD.

1982-83 XAVIER McDANIEL LEADS NATION IN REBOUNDING WITH 14.4 PER GAME.

1985 WICHITA STATE OPENS ECK STADIUM.

1985 TULSA WINS ITS FIRST OUTRIGHT MVC REGULAR-SEASON BASKETBALL TITLE.

1985 TULSA'S STEVE HARRIS IS FIRST-ROUND NBA DRAFT PICK AND THREE-TIME, FIRST-TEAM ALL-MVC PLAYER.

1985 COMMISSIONER RICHARD MARTIN RESIGNS.

SOME FAMILIAR FACES WATCH THE 1986 DRAKE RELAYS. FROM LEFT TO RIGHT: IOWA SENATOR CHUCK GRASSLEY, VICE PRESIDENT GEORGE BUSH, IOWA GOVERNOR ROBERT D. RAY, DRAKE PRESIDENT MICHAEL FERRARI, AND FORMER IOWA GOVERNOR TERRY BRANSTAD.

JULY 1, 1985 THE MVC OFFICE MOVES FROM TULSA, OKLA. TO ST. LOUIS.

APRIL 15, 1985 JAMES A. HANEY APPOINTED COMMISSIONER.

1984 DRAKE'S JOHNNY BRIGHT INDUCTED IN COLLEGE HOF.

JANUARY 1, 1986 FOOTBALL IS DROPPED AS A CONFERENCE SPORT.

1982

'83

'84

'85

'86

BRADLEY BRAVES ... NIT ...AMPIONSHIP.

1983 SOUTHERN ILLINOIS WINS NCAA 1-AA TITLE IN FOOTBALL.

JULY 1, 1985 WEST TEXAS STATE WITHDRAWS.

1985-86 BRADLEY BRAVES WIN MVC CONFERENCE TITLE WITH PERFECT 16-0 RECORD.

1986 DICK VERSACE OF BRADLEY IS COACH OF THE YEAR IN MEN'S BASKETBALL.

1989 TO 1992 SIU BASKETBALL TEAM MAKES FOUR STRAIGHT NITS.

1990 TO 1995 SIU COACH RICH HERRIN'S SALUKIS WERE DOMINANT, WINNING TWO REGULAR SEASON TITLES & THREE CONSECUTIVE VALLEY TOURNAMENT CHAMPIONSHIPS (1993-1995).

WICHITA STATE BASEBALL COACH, GENE STEPHENSON

TWO LEAGUE TEAM CREIGHTON & WICHI STATE, REACH COLLEG WORLD SERI IN BASEBA

1988 JAMES A. HANEY RESIGNS AS COMMISSIONER.

Missouri Valley Legend

HERSEY HAWKINS
1984 · BRADLEY · 198

ILLINOIS STATE'S REDBIRD ARENA UNDER CONSTRUCTION.

1988 DIET PEPSI BECOMES LEAGUE'S FIRST MAJOR CORPORATE SPONSOR.

DIET PEPSI

1988 BRADLEY'S HERSEY HAWKINS IS NATIONAL PLAYER OF THE YEAR.

MAY 17, 1988 DOUG ELGIN APPOINTED COMMISSIONER.

DECEMBER 22, 1988 BRADLEY'S HERSEY HAWKINS SETS ALL-TIME MVC SINGLE-GAME SCORING RECORD WITH 63

1991-92 DARREN PLAB OF SIU WINS BACK-TO-BACK NCAA OUTDOOR HIGH JUMP TITLES.

1990 SOUTHWEST MISSOURI STATE ADMITTED.

NORTHERN I·O·W·A

1991 NORTHERN IOWA ADMITTED.

1987

'88

'89

90

1988 BRADLEY'S HAWKINS IS VOTED MVC'S FINAL 1ST TEAM ALL-AMERICAN OF 20TH CENTURY.

1989 WICHITA SHOCKERS WIN NCAA BASEBALL CHAMPIONSHIP.

1991 MVC HOSTS FIRST MEN'S BASKETBALL TOURNAMENT IN ST. LO AT KIEL AUDITORIUM.

1907 2007

100 YEARS OF ATHLETICS EXCELLENCE

1991
CREIGHTON MEN'S SOCCER BEGINS A STRING OF 15 CONSECUTIVE APPEARANCES IN THE NCAA MEN'S SOCCER TOURNAMENT.

1993
WICHITA STATE'S DARREN DREIFORT IS NAMED NATIONAL COLLEGIATE BASEBALL PLAYER OF THE YEAR WHILE LEADING SHOCKERS TO NATIONAL CHAMPIONSHIP GAME.

1996
EINARS TUPURITIS OF WICHITA STATE SWEEPS INDOOR AND OUTDOOR 800M NCAA TITLES.

1995
SIU'S CHRIS CARR IS MVC'S LEADING SCORER AND LEAGUE MVP.

1996
CREIGHTON'S JOHNNY TORRES RECEIVES FIRST OF TWO CONSECUTIVE NATIONAL COLLEGIATE SOCCER PLAYER OF THE YEAR LAURELS.

...ARCH 1993 ...VC HOSTS ...E FIRST ...SEVEN ...CAA ...SKETBALL ...ENTS ...ST. LOUIS IN ...3-YEAR ...RIOD.

HAVE A BALL!

THE VALLEY

...2 ...SSOURI STATE ...VANCES TO ...MEN'S FINAL FOUR ...BASKETBALL.

MISSOURI VALLEY CHAMPS

1994
TULSA'S GARY COLLIER IS MVC PLAYER OF THE YEAR.

1994
INDIANA STATE'S HOLLI HYCHE CAPTURES HER 7TH NCAA SPRINT TITLE IN TWO-YEAR SPAN.

STATE FARM INSURANCE

Auto Life Fire

1996
STATE FARM INSURANCE BECOMES MAJOR MVC CORPORATE PARTNER.

1996
THE VALLEY SENDS BOTH TULSA AND BRADLEY TO THE NCAA TOURNAMENT.

N·C·A·A

WOMEN'S FINAL FOUR ...OS ANGELES ·9·9·2

1993 TO 1995
SIU WINS AN UNPRECEDENTED THREE-STRAIGHT MVC TOURNAMENT CHAMPIONSHIPS.

1994
TULSA'S SHEA SEALS IS MVC FRESHMAN OF THE YEAR AND LOU DAWKINS IS MVC DEFENSIVE PLAYER OF THE YEAR.

1996
CREIGHTON BECOMES THE FIRST OF FOUR MVC TEAMS TO REACH THE COLLEGE CUP IN MEN'S SOCCER, WHICH INCLUDES A BLUEJAY NATIONAL CHAMPIONSHIP GAME APPEARANCE IN 2000.

SATURDAY APRIL 27, 1996
9-10 J 3 19
...ate Sec. Row Seat
...AKE RELAYS

DRAKE 2305

Tulsa

NOV. 4, 1993
EVANSVILLE ADMITTED TO MVC, EXPANDING MEMBERSHIP TO 11, THE LARGEST NUMBER OF SCHOOLS AT ONE TIME IN VALLEY HISTORY.

1992

1993
MISSOURI STATE'S WOMEN'S BASKETBALL TEAM REACHES THE SWEET 16.

1994-95
TUBBY SMITH COACHES FINAL SEASON AT TULSA WITH A 24-8 RECORD AND A TRIP TO THE SWEET 16.

1995
SIU'S PAUL LUSK COLLECTS THREE MVC TOURNAMENT CHAMPIONSHIP RINGS.

'93

'94

'95

'96

1996
TULSA WITHDRAWS.

...C TOURNAMENT ...VES FROM THE OLD ...L TO THE ST. LOUIS ...NA.

1992
MEN'S & WOMEN'S SPORTS PROGRAMS MERGE UNDER MVC BANNER.

1994-95
TULSA ADVANCES TO BACK-TO-BACK SWEET 16'S IN NCAA TOURNAMENT.

1995
MVC TOURNAMENT MOVES FROM THE ARENA TO SAVVIS CENTER.

Henry Iba

Hersey Hawkins

Larry Bird

Oscar Robertson

Ed Macauley

Dave Stallworth

Wes Unseld

1997
August 26
Charter Class of
MVC Athletics
Hall of Fame
Announced.
Inductees Include
Larry Bird,
Hersey Hawkins,
Ed Macauley, Oscar
Robertson, Dave
Stallworth, Wes
Unseld, &
Henry Iba.

1999 Three Teams
Reach NCAAs in Men's
Basketball, Beginning
a String of Eight
Straight Years with
Two or
More Bids.

1998-02
Northern Iowa Goes
88-2 in Conference
Volleyball & Wins
Five Straight MVC
Regular-Season Titles.
UNI Reaches Sweet 16
Three Times & Has
Two National Coach
of the Year
Honors (Iradge
Ahrabi-Fard &
Bobbi Peterson).

2001
Jackie Stiles
Breaks NCAA
Division I
Women's
Scoring Record
& Receives the
Wade Trophy
& the Honda-
Broderick Cup
& Leaps Bears
to 2001 NCAA
Final Four.

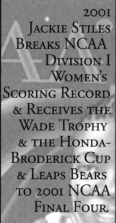

2001 NCAA. DIVISION I WOMEN'S BASKETBALL CHAMPIONS
Savvis Center · St. Louis, Missouri · March 30 & April 1

The Missouri Valley
Conference Hosts
the 2001 Women's
Final Four at Savvis
Center. The Sold-O[ut]
Event Represents
the First NCAA
Division 1 Women's
Tournament
Ever Hosted in the
City of St. Louis.

1997
Kevin Little, 1997
World Indoor 200
Meter Champion &
Drake Graduate,
Prepares to
Run in the Men's
Special Invitational
400-Meter Dash at the
Drake Relays.

2000
SIU's Connie Price-
Smith Competes in
Fourth Straight
Olympics,
Representing
the USA in
the Shot
Put.

1999
to
2003
Kent
Williams
Is Only
Player in
SIU History
to Lead Saulkis
in Scoring Four
Straight Seasons.

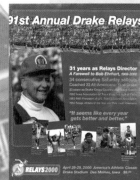
JACKIE STILES DAY
FRIDAY, APRIL 13, 2001

Hometown 'star' gets hero's welcom[e]

91st Annual Drake Relays

31 years as Relays Director
A Farewell to Bob Ehrhart, 1969-2000
34 consecutive Saturday sellouts
Coached 25 All-Americans; 16 at Drake

"It seems like every year
gets better and better."

RELAYS 2000
April 28-29, 2000 America's Athletic Classic
Drake Stadium, Des Moines, Iowa

SATURDAY, APRIL 14, 2001
CLAFLIN, KANSAS
SCHEDULE

THE STILES FILE
To be continued ...

1907   2007
1997   '98   '99   '00   01

1997-98
Illinois State Wins
Back-to-Back Regular
Season & Tournament
Titles in Men's Basketball.

1998
Missouri State is the
First League School to
Win Three Straight Soft-
Ball Tournament Titles.

1999
Missouri State
Advances to Sweet 16
in Men's Basketball.

2000
In Men's Soccer,
Creighton & SMU Both
Represent the MVC
in the College Cup.

2001
SMU's Luchi Gonzalez
Is National Player of t[he]
Year in Men's Soccer.

2002
Illinois State's Christian Goy Wins NCAA [Ind]oor Title [in] the Mile.

2003
Missouri State Advances to College World Series.

2003
MVC Takes Part in ESPN Bracket Busters Series for the First Time, Going 4-0 in the Initial Event.

SIU's Darren Brooks

2004
State Farm Agrees to Title Sponsorship of 17 Valley Sports.

2004
Creighton Women's Basketball Wins the WNIT Title, the First League Team to Do So.

2005
April 2-4 - The MVC Hosts the 2005 NCAA Men's Final Four at the Edward Jones Dome, Culminating an 8-Year Stretch of Six NCAA Tournament Hosting Opportunities.

2005
Missouri State Women's Basketball wins the WNIT Crown

2006
In Men's Basketball, League Sends Four Teams to NCAA Tournament for First Time & Two Teams to the NIT, Posting Seven Postseason Victories & Advancing Two Men's Basketball Teams to the Sweet 16 in the Same Season (Bradley & Wichita).

2006
Former Drake Alumnus Zach Johnson Becomes First MVC Golfer to Qualify for a U.S. Ryder Cup Team.

[20]0[2]
[th]e MVC has Five [Sw]eet 16 Teams [SI]U-Men's Basketball; [D]rake-Women's [Ba]sketball, SMU & [Cr]eighton-Men's [So]ccer; UNI-Volleyball) [in] the Same Year [Pic]tured [is] SIU's [Jer]maine [De]arman

STATE FARM
Auto Life Fire
INSURANCE

1999-2006 Creighton's Dana Altman's Eight Straight 20-Victory Seasons is the Most in MVC History.

NCAA FINAL FOUR 2005 ST. LOUIS

Sweet Surprises
Marcellus Sommerville Leads Bradley into The Sixteen as Upsets Rattle the Brackets
BY GRANT WAHL

2006 MVC Tournament Final Moves from Monday Night to Sunday Afternoon & from ESPN to CBS.

2006
MVC Tournament Scores Record Crowd of 63,739 Attendance.

St. Louis' Scottrade Center.

2006
SAVVIS Center Is Renamed the Scottrade Center.

Sweet Surprises

2005
Amy Harre SIU Softball

2002   '03   '04   '05   '06

[20]02
[In]diana State Hosts [the] First of Four [N]CAA Cross Country [Ch]ampionships.

2003
Missouri State Advances to Baseball College World Series.

2004
Valley Plays Host to NCAA Men's Basketball Regional at the Dome.

2005
MVC Mens Basketball Sends 3 Teams to NCAA Tournament for Third Time in League History.

2005-2006
MVC Softball Sends Record Three Teams to NCAA Tournament in Back-to-Back Years.

The present Missouri Valley Conference staff, left to right: First row: Mary Mulvenna, Director of Compliance/Community Relations; Patty Viverito, Senior Associate Commissioner; Carla Fight, Assistant to the Commissioner; Erica Stelling, Director of Communications. Second row: Mike Kern, Associate Commissioner for Communications; SuMeyko Jones, Receptionist; Dave Biancamano, Director of Operations; Matt Marchal, Assistant Commissioner for Corporate Relations; Maxine Day, Executive Assistant. Third row: Jack Watkins, Associate Commissioner for Marketing/Television; Rich Steed, Chief Financial Officer, Doug Elgin, Commissioner, Joe Mitch, Associate Commissioner

Mark Turgeon, Wichita State

Barry Hinson, Missouri State

For the first time in its storied history, the Missouri Valley Conference placed four teams in the NCAA Men's Tournament in 2006. The Valley also advanced two teams—Bradley and Wichita State—to the Sweet 16 for the first time in the same year. And the MVC— with 38 starters returning for the 2006–07 season—certainly may not be finished with its NCAA Tournament runs. The MVC's 2006 regular-season champion Wichita State returns four starters, and 2006 league tournament champion SIU returns all of its front-line players.

Hence the new moniker for the league: "Big Valley." "We are not mid-major," said Missouri State Coach Barry Hinson. "We are high major in basketball. There are 31 conferences, and we were sixth (in the RPI in 2005–06). I am not that good in math, but we are a high major."

The momentum should continue beyond 2005–06 for many reasons:

- New basketball facilities will appear at UNI in 2006 and at Missouri State in 2008. Wichita State's arena has been face-lifted. Southern Illinois' is scheduled to be renovated.
- Creighton's spectacular new 15,700-seat Qwest Center OMAHA drew 226,295 spectators in 2005–06, the first time an MVC school has surpassed 200,000 for home attendance in a single season.
- For the first time, CBS aired the 2006 MVC Tournament final and will again in 2007.
- League officiating has been upgraded. A more financially lucrative pay scale allows the MVC to compete with other major conferences for the best officials.
- After a banner year, the MVC lost only one of its men's head coaches—UNI's Greg McDermott—to Iowa State during the offseason.

The MVC's "Drive for Five" NCAA Tournament teams hit high gear during the MVC postseason tournament in St. Louis. Southern Illinois beat surging Bradley for the Salukis' first tournament title since 1995 and became the league's automatic qualifier to go along with three NCAA at-large teams for the first time (UNI, Bradley, and Wichita State).

"We had six teams that were really good enough to get in this tournament," said Wichita State Coach Mark Turgeon. Hinson's Bears and

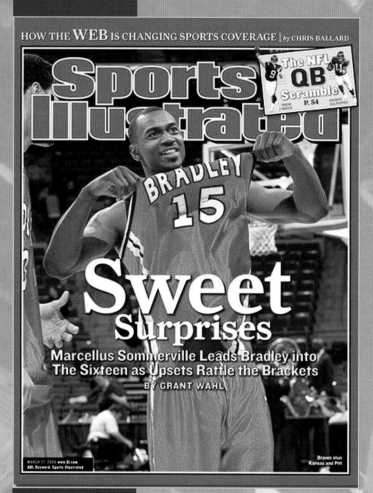

Creighton, both Top 40 RPI teams, could have made the field at-large but had to settle for National Invitation Tournament berths.

Southern Illinois and UNI lost in the NCAA first round to two Big East teams (West Virginia and Georgetown), but Bradley and Wichita State carried the MVC torch, beating two teams from the Big East and one each from the Big 12 and SEC. The Braves toppled Kansas and Pittsburgh at Auburn Hills and the Shockers ousted Seton Hall and Tennessee in Greensboro. Doug Elgin said league teams have recently built up strong RPIs to get in the field at-large, and once in the NCAA field they are formidable. "Our athletics directors and coaches understand the importance of playing tough nonconference schedules," said commissioner Doug Elgin, a former member of the NCAA Division I Men's Basketball Committee. "Coaches in the Valley have clearly raised the bar for our league, and what our teams have accomplished has many other conferences trying to emulate what we've done."

"Our league goes and plays on the road," SIU Coach Chris Lowery said. "We are willing to go and play other people. Other people stay at home the whole month of December and rack up wins. I think that is why our league is successful."

Certainly college basketball's rules have changed as well, allowing the MVC to make inroads on other power conferences. "There's obviously tremendous parity," said Bradley Coach Jim Les. "Just because we maybe don't get as much exposure doesn't mean we are any less of a basketball team or a basketball conference. The MVC is a major basketball conference. You can look back when scholarships got trimmed from 15 to 13, I think that also created a lot of parity across the country in terms of maybe those guys who would have gone to bigger schools now were more receptive to coming to a smaller university. I also think (AAU basketball tournaments have helped) our ability to see young men, recruit, and expand our recruiting base. We didn't necessarily have the resources that the big schools have to fly to all those high schools. Now we can go to a tournament and see 400–500 of those kids. It has leveled the playing field."

Both Bradley and Wichita State, long-time MVC members, broke NCAA Tournament droughts. Elgin said it is important that such traditional MVC powers become strong again for the league to move forward. Bradley won 11 of its last 14 games to make its first NCAA Tournament since 1996. As a No. 13 seed, the Braves stunned fourth-seeded Kansas in the first round, and then upset fifth-seeded Pittsburgh in the second round before falling in the Sweet 16 to Memphis, the region's top seed.

Bradley had not won an NCAA Tournament game since the days of Hersey Hawkins in 1986. "We knew we were a good team all year," said Bradley's 7-foot, 260-pound sophomore Patrick O'Bryant. "We knew we could compete with anybody."

O'Bryant—one of those "AAU finds" perhaps—averaged 13.4 points and 8.3 rebounds and led the MVC in blocks with 2.9 a game. Those were good enough averages for him to opt out of school two years early and declare for the 2006 NBA Draft. Otherwise, the MVC would have had 39 returning starters for 2006–07.

Meanwhile, seventh-seeded Wichita State, in its first NCAA Tournament since 1988, wiped out No. 10 seed Seton Hall and No. 2 seed Tennessee in the first two rounds before losing to George Mason in the regional semifinals. The Shockers' overall inside-outside balance with MVC regular-season MVP senior center Paul Miller and its three-point shooting were key ingredients. But so was attitude going into March.

Wichita State had not won an NCAA Tournament game since 1981 when it won three before losing to LSU in a regional final, and it had almost been as long since the Shockers had finished atop the MVC regular-season standings. "We had carried a 23-year weight around with us," Turgeon said of WSU's MVC regular-season title drought. "You can tell our kids were under a tremendous amount of pressure to get this done. I feel like the world is off our shoulders."

Then it became a matter of MVC pride. "All season long people have been talking about the Missouri Valley and how everybody else should be getting more picks in the tournament," Wichita State guard Ryan Martin said. "Now, we're just trying to prove everybody wrong."

After his Salukis won the 2006 State Farm MVC Tournament title, Lowery cautioned other coaches and the league hierarchy in general about ending the season without an exclamation point in the NCAA Tournament. "Obviously, validation will come for the Missouri Valley only if our teams can win games in the NCAA Tournament, or better yet, make it to the Sweet 16," Lowery said. "If we are truly the sixth-ranked RPI league, we need to prove that to the rest of the country.

Mission accomplished!

Melanie Boeglin, Indiana State, and Patty Viverito, MVC

Paul Miller, Wichita State

Tulsa Coach Henry Frnka

MVC FOOTBALL

A ROLLER-COASTER RIDE WITH MEMBERSHIP, RESULTS

The popularity of college football increased in the Midwest at the beginning of the 20th century, and seven years into the new century the oldest NCAA Division I conference west of the Mississippi—the Missouri Valley—took off with a 78-year run of college football competition.

Starting in 1907 with five charter members, the MVC conducted football competition through the 1985 season. Over the course of the nearly eight decades, 29 schools from Michigan to New Mexico competed for the MVC football title.

Iowa was one of the charter football-playing members of the MVC, along with Nebraska, Kansas, Missouri, and Washington University in St. Louis. The Hawkeyes, however, never competed in basketball and only four seasons in MVC football before becoming full-fledged members of the Western Conference (Big Ten Conference) in 1911.

A year after the initial football competition, Drake and Iowa State joined the MVC. Kansas State was added in 1913, restoring the league to seven football-playing members through 1917, the year before league competition was interrupted one season because of World War I.

NEBRASKA DOMINATED EARLY MVC PLAY

Nebraska was the early MVC power, winning or tying nine of the first 11 titles. Included in that era was a 34-game unbeaten string (longest in school history) and Cornhusker claims of mythical national championships in 1914 and 1915 under Coach Jumbo Stiehm, who won the Missouri Valley Conference title in each of his five seasons. His 1915 football team beat Notre Dame, 20–19, handing the Irish their only loss of the season. Stiehm also doubled as the school's basketball coach.

The Cornhuskers were suspended from league play in 1919 and 1920 after they scheduled a game against Oklahoma in Omaha in 1919 at a time when the league mandated league schools play games at campus sites. Hoping for a big payday, while enticing Creighton and Marquette to play a second game as a "doubleheader," the Cornhuskers only broke even in the endeavor.

Nebraska played as an independent during those two seasons, but after resuming MVC competition in 1921, the Cornhuskers won three MVC titles in succession.

Nebraska played an 11-game series with powerhouse Notre Dame through 1925. It proved to be highly competitive and drew attention to the MVC. Nebraska moved into the bigtime of college football in 1923 with the opening of Memorial Stadium and drew 30,000 fans for a game against the Fighting Irish that season.

Nebraska produced two later-to-be-recognized consensus NCAA All-Americas during that era, end Guy Chamberlin in 1915 and tackle Ed Weir in 1924 and 1925. They were the MVC's only NCAA consensus All-Americas until Oklahoma A&M's running back Bob Fenimore in 1945. "Guy was an end and blocked and played defense, but I don't think they threw to him much because he doesn't rank up there in our receiving statistics," said long-time Nebraska Sports Information Director and newsman Don Bryant with a chuckle. "Ed Weir had the reputation of being the first of the red-dogging linemen. He was a hurdler in high school and college. He was our first two-time All-America and later our track coach. He was a tremendous rusher."

By the 1928 season, Nebraska had left the MVC, along with Missouri, Kansas, Kansas State, Iowa State, and Oklahoma (which had joined the MVC in 1920). Those schools left to form the Big Six, a forerunner of the future Big Eight Conference. Only Oklahoma A&M remained, but it eventually joined the others about 30 years later.

One of the major reasons for the MVC's lack of notoriety in football was the fact that the large state universities— Iowa, Nebraska, Kansas, and Missouri—which helped found the league, were all gone from the MVC barely two decades later.

Such conference membership gyrations were commonplace in the MVC, giving rise to the phrase over the years, "Football in the Valley has survived war and the pestilence of changing Valley membership."

The MVC, which had been a 10-team league in 1927, was reduced to a five-team football league in 1928, the fewest number of teams it had had since its inaugural year. Creighton joined in 1928 to give the league members with a definite private flavor: Drake, Grinnell, Washington University, with Oklahoma A&M as the only public school.

Creighton's famous basketball coach Eddie Hickey, who later went to Saint Louis University and Marquette in the same capacity, actually coached a season of football in 1934 (2–7 overall record). Hickey, who played football at Creighton, became the Bluejays basketball coach in 1935.

Butler (1933 and 1934) and Washburn (1935–1940) came and went as members. Saint Louis joined in 1937 and stayed through the 1949 season as a football-playing member, but the major development was the addition of Tulsa in 1935.

Ed Weir, Nebraska

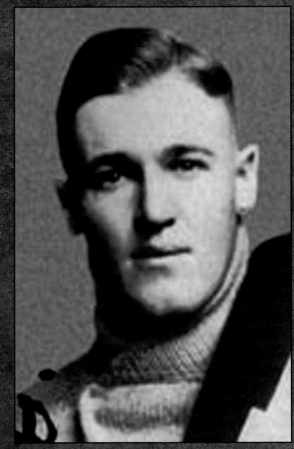

Guy Chamberlin, Nebraska

Some Creighton Bluejays found motivation any way they could

Saint Louis and Tulsa battle in the snow

TULSA A FORCE
IN CHANGING LEAGUE

Tulsa was the dominant MVC team for the next half-century, winning or tying for 25 conference crowns (19 outright, six co-titles). The Golden Hurricane won or tied for 10 of the first 13 MVC races in which they competed. During that period, Tulsa compiled a 36–4–1 record against MVC teams and outscored them, 1,043–273.

In the early and mid-1940s, many of the top programs, outside of Army and Navy, were struggling to field teams because of World War II. Creighton and Washington University played their last MVC football seasons in 1942. Twenty-eight of Creighton's 35 players on the 1942 team were called to serve their country, making it impossible for the Omaha-based Jesuit school to field a team. Saint Louis University, another pri-

WARTIME FOOTBALL AT
OKLAHOMA A. and M.
The 1944 Dope Book and Souvenir Brochure of the Cowboys

vate Jesuit school, cancelled football during the 1943 and 1944 seasons because of manpower shortages.

Tulsa and Oklahoma A&M carried the league during 1943 and 1944 when only they and Drake fielded football teams. "So great were the Aggie and Hurricane records that the winner of the Aggie–Tulsa game each year was voted the champion," said a story in the MVC Diamond Anniversary football media guide. "Thus, while football was curbed shortly in the Valley by World War II, it never knew greater national prominence in its long history than during those turbulent seasons."

In 1944, Oklahoma A&M defeated Tulsa, 46–40, to win the MVC title and followed that up with a 34–0 shutout of Texas Christian University in the Cotton Bowl. The following season, the Aggies beat Tulsa, 12–6, for the MVC title again, and then engineered a 33–13 victory over St. Mary's in the 1946 Orange Bowl.

Tulsa, however, was the first school in NCAA history to appear in five straight New Year's Day games: 1942 Sun Bowl, 1943 and 1944 Sugar Bowls, 1945 Orange Bowl, and 1946 Oil Bowl. During that five-year period, Tulsa Coach Henry Frnka compiled a dazzling 40–9–1 record.

Drake's 1945 team went to the Raisin Bowl, giving the MVC three bowl teams for the only time in its football history.

One of the stars of those Tulsa teams in the 1940s, Glenn Dobbs, returned to coach Tulsa in 1961 and made the Golden Hurricane the top passing team in college football. The 5-8, 128-pound Dobbs led Tulsa to a 25–6 record and three straight Missouri Valley titles from 1940 to 1942 as a starting back who threw the ball and also kicked and punted. Tulsa led the nation in passing his senior year, when the team finished the regular season 10–0 before losing to Tennessee in the Sugar Bowl.

Dobbs wound up ninth in the Heisman Trophy balloting that year and was a first-round draft choice by the NFL's Chicago Cardinals in the spring of 1943, but he never signed with an NFL team. He played in the All-America Football Conference and passed for more than 400 yards in one game in 1948. Dobbs developed even more of a penchant for passing by playing in the wide-open Canadian Football League. "He loved the game and wanted to throw every down," said F. A. Dry, who was an assistant coach under Dobbs at Tulsa in the 1960s. "We had to wrestle with him to run it."

Glenn Dobbs, Tulsa

Tulsa coach Henry Frnka

Tulsa U. Sugar Bowl Team, 1942

Undefeated - Untied

MORE CHANGES HIT THE MVC

The MVC had to undergo more membership turnover and then turmoil involving Drake, Bradley, and Oklahoma A&M.

After World War II, Creighton dropped football altogether, and Saint Louis University re-instituted its football program for five years but, because of the rising costs, discontinued it for good following the 1949 season.

The MVC, which had picked up Wichita in 1945, added both Detroit and Bradley in 1949 and Houston in 1951 for a seven-team league to go along with the "War-Time Three" of Drake, Oklahoma A&M, and Tulsa.

The Johnny Bright–Oklahoma A&M incident—in which Drake's star running back was intentionally slugged in a game, but had no repercussions—so enraged Drake that the Bulldog officials decided to leave the MVC before the 1952 season began. Bradley, in sympathy with Drake, also bolted. Although both Drake and Bradley were readmitted in 1955 for basketball, the Braves never played football in the league again and eventually dropped the sport altogether in 1970 for financial reasons. Drake didn't play football in the MVC again until the 1971 season. "The Valley, to my mind, didn't take any action (over the Bright incident)," said Paul Morrison, long-time Drake historian and the school's former SID. "The Drake fans went on for awhile with no action. Finally, our athletic council felt it was such a severe thing we felt we had to do something to satisfy our fans, so we dropped out of the Valley."

In 1957, Oklahoma A&M (Oklahoma State) left the MVC and eventually joined six former MVC schools, plus Colorado, to form the Big Eight in 1960.

In 1942, Coach Frnka produced the nation's only unbeaten and untied teams.

Top Row, Left to Right: Cramer, Spangler, Ramage, Judd, Berry, Patillo, Furney, Annex, Pitcock, Bland, Schad, and Simmons, student manager.
Third Row: Herriman, Winfrey, Daniels, Goerner, Sharp, Burris, Hightower, Parton, Green, Ewbanks, Goodnight.
Second Row: Coach Middigan, Jones, Burgeis, Taylor, Hendrix, Judd, Dobbs, B. Dobbs, LeForce, Hail, Lancaster.
Front Row: Coach Henry Frnka, Erickson, Hendrick, Cooper, D'Arcy, Greene, McGinley, Dost, Purdin, Spilman, Keithley, and Coach Brothers.

Glenn Dobbs

Oklahoma A&M's departure caused the MVC fathers to once again scramble for members. "Mr. Iba always wanted to get into the Big Six," said former Oklahoma A&M basketball center Bob Kurland. "The Missouri Valley was looked upon as a secondary league to the Big Six. He was tickled to death. It made his job as an AD a better situation. The business aspect of being at a larger-school conference was an advantage to him." To help ease the loss of Oklahoma A&M and also Detroit after the 1956 season, North Texas and Cincinnati came into the MVC in 1957. With Houston, Tulsa, and North Texas in the league, the MVC was taking on a southwestern flavor.

North Texas became an immediate factor in the MVC race when running back Abner Haynes, the first African American to play major-college football in the Southwest, starred for the Eagles. Later a star with the Dallas Texans and the Kansas City Chiefs in the American Football League, Haynes, a Denton, Tex., native, would lead his hometown school in rushing three straight seasons and to two MVC titles in 1958 and 1959. "He wasn't a big person," said Fred McCain, an assistant coach for that North Texas team and later the school's athletic director. "He had good speed and strength. He just had all the assets for a good running back."

McCain admits that had Haynes come along a decade later, he might have enrolled at SMU or another Southwest Conference school. Jerry LeVias broke the color barrier in that league under SMU Coach Hayden Fry in 1966.

Haynes and his African American teammate, Leon King, had to live "cross-town" from the school. But McCain said they competed for North Texas without incident, and it started a stream of top African American athletes going to North Texas, which won five conference titles and placed

second six times during 18 years of Missouri Valley competition. "A lot of schools were not picking black athletes," McCain said. "We had an early beginning. We were fortunate in getting a great number of them."

From 1957 through 1974, North Texas' final season in the MVC, the Mean Green had 43 players selected in the NFL Draft. That included first-round picks in three consecutive drafts, defensive tackle Mean Joe Greene (1969, Pittsburgh Steelers), defensive end Cedric Hardman (1970, San Francisco 49ers), and defensive back Leonard Dunlap (1971, Baltimore Colts).

Henry Iba (third from right) sits in with Big Eight officials

Abner Haynes, North Texas

Mean Joe Greene, North Texas

After North Texas won back-to-back titles to close out the 1950s (tying Houston in 1959), Houston left to become an independent in 1960 and eventually wound up in the Southwest Conference. "Houston pulled out for financial reasons," said Johnny Overby, who was an MVC basketball official. "The travel was tough for them to get from Houston, Tex., to Peoria, Ill., for basketball. And the Valley was awfully strong in basketball and average in football. (Later) when they built the Astrodome, Houston thought they would go strong both ways and they did."

The four remaining schools—Wichita State, Tulsa, Cincinnati, and North Texas—stuck together in the MVC during the 1960s. Louisville joined the MVC in 1963 with Memphis State coming in 1968.

Wichita State won back-to-back MVC titles in 1960 and 1961, and WSU made it three in four seasons by tying Cincinnati for the title in 1963, when Bill Parcells starred for the Wheat Shockers at defensive tackle. Parcells, a three-year WSU letterman and later an assistant coach for the Shockers, went on to a Super Bowl–winning coaching career in the NFL with the New York Giants (1986 and 1990) and also with three other NFL teams, the New England Patriots, New York

Hayden Fry

Jets, and Dallas Cowboys. But the 1963 crown was the last Missouri Valley football title in Wichita State history—23 years before the school dropped football following the 1986 season.

PASSING FRENZY AT TULSA
Dobbs had returned to Tulsa to coach the Golden Hurricane in 1961, and from 1962 to 1966, Tulsa led the nation in passing yards per game each season. Dobbs came in and filled Skelly Stadium with an offense that had fans wondering if the passing would ever stop.

In 1964, Tulsa quarterback Jerry Rhome led the country in total offense and passing yards. The following season, Tulsa quarterback Bobby Anderson did the same. In both those seasons, Howard Twilley, a consensus NCAA All-American, led the country in receiving yards.

"We would wear the defense down," Dry said. "They would have to rush the passer, and they were used to playing against the running game. The defensive line would tire. We would not get that much of a pass rush during the latter part of the game. They aren't geared like they are now. We were facing three-deep zones. Everything worked to our advantage."

Tulsa parlayed the potent passing attack into two Bluebonnet Bowl berths in Houston (1964, 1965), two MVC titles (1962, 1965), and two Top 20 rankings at the end of those bowl seasons. The MVC really never captured that magic again, but it consistently was producing top players in the 1960s and into the 1970s.

TEXAS INFLUENCE
The best MVC player of the late 1960s was Mean Joe Greene, a defensive tackle whose picture still hangs on the side of the stadium at Fouts Field in Denton. The 10-time All-Pro selection for the Pittsburgh Steelers led the Mean Green to back-to-back MVC titles in 1966 and 1967 and a second-place finish behind Memphis State in 1968, when the team finished 8–2 overall. Greene was a three-time All-MVC selection from 1966 to 1968. "I recruited Mean Joe Greene, from Temple (Texas)," McCain said. "The first time you saw him, you thought he would be good. He was big and very handsome, very physical, very athletic, a good student. He had a ton of assets and he could use them all. He wouldn't have played in the pros that long if he wasn't a very, very good individual."

TEXAS INFLUENCE OF A DIFFERENT KIND
Before the 1969 football season, DeWitt Weaver was appointed MVC commissioner. He replaced Norvall Neve, who left for a job with the Atlantic Coast Conference. Weaver immediately was faced with membership issues. Cincinnati withdrew from the conference following the 1969 season, leaving the MVC with just five football teams again.

The league was further weakened during the 1970 football season when the tragic crash occurred with one of the planes carrying the

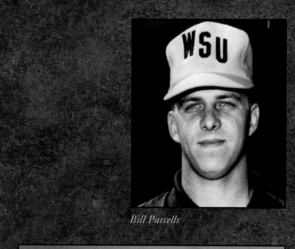

Bill Parcells

Howard Twilley

Jerry Rhome

Wichita State football team to a game at Utah State. The Wichita Shockers, however, showing great courage, finished the season with a 0–9 record.

Weaver had designs on making the MVC a football league. He had a football background—playing guard at Tennessee in the 1930s and later becoming the head football coach at Texas Tech for 10 seasons. Before becoming MVC commissioner, Weaver had worked most recently as executive director for SMU's Mustang Club in Dallas.

In 1970, Weaver moved the MVC headquarters from Kansas City to Dallas. The move to Texas, a big professional, college, and high school football state, was symbolic to many in the MVC. "He wanted to move into football," Overby said. "I told him he was kicking a good thing in the mouth. The basketball was solid. . . . West Texas State and New Mexico State wanted in, and we were going strong into football. But we had had Drake just go to the Final Four in 1969, and if a couple of calls had gone against Lew Alcindor (of UCLA), they would have been in the title game against Purdue. We had a clinic in Wichita. I said, 'DeWitt, don't talk about football.'"

By the 1971 season, West Texas State was in the MVC, and by 1972, New Mexico State was in the league as well. The eight-team football MVC stretched from Louisville, Ky., in the East to Las Cruces, N.M., in the West.

In 1972, North Texas was the only MVC team to play every other member. And schools had scheduling differences, worries over the expensive travel, and differences in basketball philosophies. And eventually some left, forcing more changes. "When I became Mid-American Conference commissioner in 1971, we had only six schools," said Fred Jacoby. "We had a meeting with Cincinnati (then an independent) and they said, 'Give us two weeks.' And they said if we come, the two of us (Louisville) will come together. That's when we expanded and took Central Michigan, Eastern Michigan, Ball State, and Northern Illinois."

Weaver retired as MVC commissioner in 1972 and was replaced by Mickey Holmes, who had worked at the Big Eight Conference. Before Holmes got the job,

DeWitt Weaver

the league had decided to move its office from Dallas to Tulsa. Holmes said he spent exactly one day in Dallas in an office filled with boxes readied for the moving van. Getting out of Texas eventually signaled another shift in the league membership.

SCHEDULING CAUSES PROBLEMS

"The thing that was the bone of contention was the football championship," Holmes said. "There was an extreme desire on the part of the majority to establish round-robin play in football and therefore have a true champion. And there was interest on the part of a minority to have extreme flexibility in football scheduling."

Memphis State didn't want to be bound playing seven or eight conference football games, rather being able to schedule games with Ole Miss, Southern Mississippi, Florida State, South Carolina, and Tennessee. So Memphis State left to become a football independent following the 1972 season.

In a period of four years, from 1973 to 1976, there was a flurry of activity with MVC membership, mostly caused by this football scheduling controversy. After the 1974 season, North Texas left and became an independent under Coach Hayden Fry. The Mean Green had aspirations of eventually joining the Southwest Conference. "We, in the MVC, were stretched all over the nation," said Fry, whose Mean Green won the MVC title in 1973 in one of his two seasons in the league. "People here were not interested in watching these teams (in the MVC). . . . I got games against Texas, Tennessee, Oklahoma State, and Houston. I wanted to beef up the schedule and make it more interesting for the fans and make more money. . . . I had some good players at North Texas and there was no reason we couldn't have a good team. Had I stayed at North Texas (he left for Iowa following the 1978 season) we would have gotten into the SWC."

Louisville also dropped out before the 1975 football season. Colorful Lee Corso had a brief stint in the league, leading the Louisville Cardinals to MVC titles in 1970 and 1972 and a berth in the Pasadena Bowl in 1970. But basketball entered into Louisville's decision. "It was a better fit for us," former Louisville basketball Coach Denny Crum said of leaving the MVC. "I loved playing in the Valley. I had great relationships with all the coaches and the competition was always tough. But

a lot of those places were tough to get to. The Metro Conference, with headquarters located initially in St. Louis, became the alternative for Louisville, Cincinnati, and Memphis State. They found a basketball conference without any requirements in football scheduling.

Saint Louis University had left the MVC following the 1973–74 season, ending a 36-year relationship to join the Metro Conference, which began competition as a basketball league in 1976–77. "With four MVC schools coming into the league, the Metro Conference had instant credibility," said Joe Mitch, who was an assistant commissioner at the Metro for eight years before joining the MVC as an associate commissioner.

The MVC brought in Southern Illinois and Indiana State to bolster the football playing side, and old MVC member Creighton replaced Saint Louis in basketball. Tulsa remained in the Missouri Valley and won three straight league football championships from 1974 to 1976, while North Texas State and Louisville were leaving and Indiana State and SIU were assimilating into the Missouri Valley Conference.

During that era, receivers Drew Pearson, later of "Hail Mary" Dallas Cowboys fame, and Steve Largent, who became an NFL Hall of Famer for the Seattle Seahawks, were stars for the Golden Hurricane.

DRAKE
WICHITA

VETERANS FIELD
8 p.m.
Saturday
September 30, 1967

END OF THE LINE!

Two fantastic goal-line stands highlighted Wichita State's opening 3-3 deadlock with Utah State. This action came on the Aggies' first series of downs which resulted in being stopped by Shocker defenders on the one-yard line. WSU stopped another Aggie drive at the one late in the fourth quarter to salvage the tie. (Photo courtesy of Harry G. Schraeder.)

WSU, DRAKE
EYE FIRST
GRID WIN!
See Page 19...

25¢ OFFICIAL PROGRAM

1907   2007

Steve Largent

By this time, Dry was Tulsa's head football coach and athletic director. He had been drafted into the coaching post in the middle of the 1972 season. Tulsa very well could have jumped to independent football status. "Mickey was trying to stabilize them (league members)," Dry said. "And the feeling was within our athletic council, Tulsa had decided to be stable and stay and see what Mickey was able to do. We were still able to schedule (outside the league) . . . Memphis State. . . . We had been able to play Tennessee. We signed a long-time contract, something like 10 years, to play Arkansas . . . and the Oklahoma State series was renewed."

Tulsa, in fact, remained in the league for the rest of its football years, all the way through 1985.

MAKING HISTORY AT WICHITA STATE

Wichita State made history in 1978 when flamboyant athletic director Ted Bredehoft hired Willie Jeffries as the Shockers' head coach. Jeffries was the first African American head football coach at a predominantly white major college institution. "Jeffries looked like the best person for the job," said long-time Wichita State faculty representative Martin Perline. "I don't think the race issue entered too many people's minds. I don't think that was an issue. I really don't. I didn't see any backlash. I think many people lauded us for going out and getting the best person."

Jeffries had been a successful coach at South Carolina State and was given the task of trying to make Wichita State a winner. The Shockers had posted just one winning season since 1963, a 6–5 mark in 1972, two seasons after the plane crash.

Jeffries knew he wouldn't have been at Wichita State if the program hadn't been down. Still, he was a little taken back that he got the call. "I was surprised," Jeffries said at the time he got the job. "It hit me in a way. No, it wasn't a Joe Louis punch. I knew they had thought of hiring a black coach. And

Drew Pearson and Howard Twilley

because they had talked to Rudy Hubbard (who had coached at Florida A&M) before, that made me feel good about them."

Jeffries wound up being Wichita State's next-to-last football coach because he couldn't sustain success. And he helped put the school on an NCAA football probation, which, along with a basketball infractions case, eventually resulted in Bredehoft's pressured resignation.

In five seasons, Jeffries had one winning record (8–3 in 1982). During the 1982 season, Wichita State quarterback Prince McJunkins became the first quarterback in NCAA Division I-A history to pass for more than 4,000 yards and run for more than 2,000 in a career. McJunkins engineered a 13–10 upset of Kansas in Lawrence. The scene at the end of that game will be forever etched in Wichita State football lore. The diminutive Bredehoft jumped into the arms of Jeffries as he left the field in a victory celebration on the Jayhawks' home field.

After the 1986 season, Wichita State's financially strapped football program folded. Studies showed the athletic department needed a substantial infusion of capital—$3.6 million—to retire debt and put it on solid footing if football was to continue.

Willie Jeffries

Ted Bredehoft

Martin Perline points to a 36–35 loss to Morehead State during that 3–8 season as the death blow. Wichita State led 35–3 at halftime, only to be outscored 33–0 in the second half. At that point, it was the biggest comeback in NCAA history. "You keep losing, losing, which is depressing," Perline said. "Plus, you are losing all this money. And I guess the killer was the loss to Morehead State. That was the straw that did it. If we had won that game, would we be playing football today? No. It would have just taken a little longer. Within a year we were out of college football."

DRAKE, TULSA SHINE; SIU WINS I-AA TITLE
Back on the field, Tulsa, under Head Coach John Cooper, dominated the final years of the MVC football competition. The Tulsa job served as a springboard for Cooper to move on to Arizona State and later Ohio State.

After a disappointing 3–8 mark in 1977, Cooper then rattled off seven straight winning seasons at Tulsa and won or tied for five MVC titles. Cooper left for Arizona State following the 1984 season.

"We coached them hard," said Cooper. "We ran the option, the split-back veer and we ran it for eight years. We did not make many mistakes and we had a good kicking game and we didn't turn it over. Those were the same principles I had at ASU and Ohio State. . . . I made people at Ohio State mad when I said some of the players I had at Tulsa could play anywhere."

During Cooper's tenure, Tulsa had the league's toughest non-conference schedule, playing ranked teams such as Arkansas, Oklahoma, Oklahoma State, Florida State, and BYU—usually on the road.

The Golden Hurricane picked up a big payday for what Cooper said was a "shoe-string budget." It was still more than enough to finance an MVC champion most seasons.

"We beat Florida, Virginia, Louisville, Kansas, Air Force, and Texas Tech," Cooper said of several other opponents from larger conferences. "Those were some good times. There were times, we get up on Saturday morning, fed our team a breakfast, got on a plane and then checked into a Holiday Inn (and played the game). I remember we went to Texas Tech and hung one on them, 59–20, gave our kids a box of Kentucky Fried Chicken, got on the plane, and went home."

The 1980 season, which was the MVC's 73rd year of competition, was a banner year. MVC schools completed a 19–18 record against outside competition, the league's first winning non-conference record since 1967. The record included a 3–0 mark against the Big Eight Conference:

Drake 41, Colorado 22; West Texas 20, Oklahoma State 19; Tulsa 3, Kansas State 0.

Drake, which had re-entered the MVC as a football-playing member in 1971, had one last fling with big-time football success under Coach Chuck Shelton. The Bulldogs posted 8–3 and 10–1 records in 1980 and 1981, respectively, and beat Colorado in 1979 and 1980 in Boulder.

Shelton ran the "West Coast Offense" and the Bulldogs led the nation (Division I-AA) in total offense once during his tenure. But the reward for tying Tulsa for the MVC title in 1981 was staying home. "In those days, bowl game (invitations) were based on attendance," Shelton said. "I wouldn't have invited us either. You have to have large followings to make it go."

By the next season, the NCAA passed increased attendance rules and several Valley schools, including Drake, were relegated to Division I-AA status. Drake dropped Division I-A football after the 1985 season when the MVC ceased to play for a football title. They

Chuck Shelton

Ray Dempsey

played an exhibition schedule in 1986, then moved to Division III non-scholarship football in 1987. "I thought it was damaging," said Shelton. "We were able to recruit when we were in Division I-A and were able to play and schedule and entertain. I fought becoming a Division I-AA team."

Tulsa, meanwhile, remained in Division I-A and won the last 23 games it played against MVC competition from 1981 to 1985. And the Golden Hurricane won five of the last six conference titles outright and shared the other one.

Besides Tulsa's domination, it was increasingly difficult to satisfy members, which had become more diverse. "At that time, it was a mixture of I-A and I-AAs and non-football playing schools," said Jeff Hurd, the MVC's publicist from 1978 to 1985. "Football was always an issue in a league where programs were at different levels and with different commitments. It was somewhat of a divisive force in the conference. We were in the early stages of re-classification. The league tried to hold together as a football conference, but it was obvious it was not going to work."

Southern Illinois took advantage of the re-classification in 1983. The Salukis, under Coach Ray Dempsey, finished second to Tulsa (5–0) in the MVC standings with a 4–1 record (never playing the Golden Hurricane during the regular season). But SIU, which lost only to Wichita State, was competing as a I-AA member and qualified for the NCAA Division I-AA playoffs.

During the playoffs, the Salukis gave up a total of 21 points in three games and just an average of 125 yards per contest. After a first-round bye, SIU beat fellow MVC member Indiana State, 23–7, in the quarterfinals. The Salukis followed that up with a 23–7 victory over Nevada–Reno in the semifinals and hammered Western Carolina, 43–7, in the final to cap a 13–1 season and win the I-AA title. Dempsey left following that season to become coach of Memphis State. SIU's title did little to stave off the death knell of the MVC.

In order to remain in Division I-A, Tulsa and Wichita State had continued playing big-time opponents outside the league to meet attendance requirements. In some cases,

Dempsey returns triumphant with the I-AA title

those contests were designated as conference games. Wichita State was unclassified for a time as it struggled to meet I-A attendance requirements. "MVC teams had compromised," said Holmes, who resigned as commissioner in 1979 and became executive director of the Sugar Bowl. "They would play designated non-conference games to count in the conference standings, which some of them thought was a real disadvantage to them. Inevitably they would pick the strongest non-conference opponent for a Wichita State or Tulsa and designate that as a conference game."

During those turbulent football times from 1972 to 1985, the MVC had four commissioners, Holmes, David Price, Richard Martin, and finally Jim Haney.

On Jan. 1, 1986, the MVC dropped football as a league sport. Tulsa and Wichita State became independents, before Wichita State dropped the sport altogether following the 1986 season. Drake allowed its scholarship athletes to go elsewhere by dropping the sport in 1986 for one year. West Texas State became a Division II program. SIU and Illinois State had held dual football memberships in the Gateway Conference and the MVC in 1985, so they played a full Gateway schedule in 1985. In 1986, Indiana State joined them. Commissioner Haney oversaw the final season of MVC football in 1985 when

Tulsa was crowned champion. Even the MVC and Tulsa couldn't agree on whether the Golden Hurricane's final conference record was 3–0 or 5–0 because two of the "designated league games" were against non-conference teams Houston and East Carolina.

The MVC offices moved from Tulsa to St. Louis prior to the 1985 football season, which was another signal that the focus was shifting from football to basketball. The last Texas team in the league, West Texas State, withdrew from the league altogether in the summer of 1986.

"I loved the school and it was a great conference and they had a bunch of coaches who had a lot of success," said Shelton, who left Drake to coach at Utah State after the 1985 season. "I would have stayed forever. I enjoyed the competition. . . . I had some of the more enjoyable times in my career."

After nearly 80 years of competition, it was time to shut the door on MVC football.

Phog Allen

MVC BASKETBALL

F rom the very beginning, the Missouri Valley Conference fathers were influenced by a basketball icon. At the initial meeting to form the conference on Jan. 12, 1907, at the old Midland Hotel in Kansas City, the inventor of basketball was in attendance.

The University of Kansas' Dr. James Naismith was one of three representatives from the school at the meeting. He had great input as the league moved forward with a basketball competition in 1907–08 consisting of three-team North and South Divisions.

Kansas, with Coach Forrest C. "Phog" Allen, dominated the early MVC races, winning or sharing seven of the first eight titles. The Jayhawks, who claimed two Helms Foundation national championships in 1922 and 1923 as MVC members, also captured six of the last seven MVC titles they competed for under the legendary Allen before departing the MVC in 1928.

Kansas left the MVC with five other state universities—Missouri, Nebraska, Iowa State, Oklahoma, and Kansas State—to form the Big Six after the 1927–28 season. Later to become known as the Big Eight Conference with the additions of Colorado and Oklahoma State, it was a league where football at most schools was the major staple most of the 20th century.

The defection of those schools signaled a century of MVC membership diversity and fluidity. Basketball would always be the focal point for a group of schools that often had little else in common. Football would always be a source of scheduling controversy and often be a reason for MVC schools to look for greater financial rewards in other more powerful football leagues.

"In the Missouri Valley, you had land-grant colleges, Catholic, and non-denominational private schools, and the philosophies of the members didn't always jell," said Dick Martin, MVC commissioner from 1981 to 1985. "The Big Eight had land-grant colleges with similar philosophies. The Valley was a mixture of land-grant, private, and parochial that sometimes you couldn't equate with economics, football issues, and small markets."

The mixture of schools, however, was the MVC's charm over the years. Memphis, Tulsa, Louisville, Saint Louis, Detroit, Butler, Houston, and Cincinnati gave the MVC a diverse middle-size city, big-city look. Oklahoma A&M, North Texas, West Texas State, and

"In the Missouri Valley, you had land-grant colleges, Catholic, and non-denominational private schools, and the philosophies of the members didn't always jell."

Ed Macauley, Saint Louis U

Phog Allen instructing Jayhawk basketball players

New Mexico State added a southwestern flavor. Communities in the Midwest such as Peoria, Ill., Omaha, Neb., Des Moines, Ia., and Wichita, Kan., provided the midwestern core of schools that would endure.

The MVC was like a giant amoeba. It stretched at one point from Detroit to Oklahoma and another time from Kentucky to New Mexico. All in one weekend a team could be playing at Louisville's Freedom Hall, and only hours later be in the desert in Las Cruces; or listening to Motown in the morning, and Country Western in the evening. "You'd start in the Eastern time zone," said MVC official and later supervisor of officials, Johnny Overby, who once had to change into his officials' stripes in a police car because his plane was late arriving. "Then, you would go to West Texas and go through two time zones."

Valley teams played all over the country during the non-conference portions of their schedules during an era when anybody would play anybody who would travel the distance. "They would play teams all the way to the West Coast," said Bradley's Roger Phegley. "The Eastern schools would play further out East. The MVC had a recognized non-conference schedule across the country."

MAKING A NAME FOR THE OLD MVC

Starting in the 1940s, when college basketball became a national sport with the advent of big-time intersectional games at Madison Square Garden and the popularity of the NCAA Basketball Tournament increased, the MVC really took off.

Oklahoma A&M, under Henry Iba, won back-to-back NCAA titles in 1945 and 1946 with towering Bob Kurland, who became the first player to win the NCAA Tournament's Most Outstanding Player in back-to-back years. Iba was not only a great innovator on the floor, but also in the administration of the game. He took his team on regular-season trips to the East Coast and Madison Square Garden, where they were showcased for all the Eastern writers to see what they were missing back in the middle part of the country.

The MVC games among Saint Louis University, Bradley, and Oklahoma A&M in the 1940s and into the early 1950s formed some of the best rivalries in college basketball—all in the same league. Eddie Hickey at Saint Louis University won the 1948 National Invitation Tournament with Ed Macauley. "We had three (MVC) teams ranked in the Top 10 most of my career," said Bradley's Gene Melchiorre. "Oklahoma A&M, Saint Louis, and us."

Stillwater's Gallagher Hall was a jumpin' place to play basketball, as was Bradley's Robertson Field House

and Saint Louis University's Kiel Auditorium in downtown St. Louis.

Oklahoma A&M went to Final Fours in 1949 and 1951, sandwiched around Bradley's runner-up finish to CCNY in 1950 when Melchiorre's Braves also finished second to the New York City school in the NIT. Oklahoma A&M finished second to Kentucky in 1949 in the NCAA Tournament, the third time in five years the Aggies were in the title game.

Moe Iba, Henry Iba's son, said his father, despite being one of the icons of the game, was probably more revered outside of Stillwater than in it. "It was really funny," Moe Iba said. "Stillwater is a very small town. I guess that is what they thought he was supposed to do was win national championships. He coached the (U.S.) Olympic team three times from a school and a town of 30,000 people. . . . This is the way he carried himself in that town. He didn't ask for anything. He went out and got his hair cut at the barbershop and shot the shit with the guys."

It was all a part of the MVC lore. Great coaches. Excellent basketball.

During the 1950s, Bradley played in two NCAA title games—also in 1954 when the Braves had left the league over the Johnny Bright incident. In 1955, Bradley was back in the MVC, and the first black athletes had arrived in Peoria, starting a gold rush through the mid-1960s to three NIT titles (1957, 1960, and 1964). At the time, the NIT championships were as prestigious as NCAA crowns.

In the early and mid-1950s, MVC schools such as Wichita State, Bradley, Cincinnati (joining the league in 1956), and Drake began embracing and recruiting the black athlete years before their counterparts in many places in the South and even in limited numbers in other conferences such as the Big Ten and Pacific 10.

The recruiting was making a huge impact nationally by the late 1950s. With the arrival of Oscar Robertson at Cincinnati on the freshman team in the fall of 1956, the talent level was turned up a notch. He was the first African American player on UC's varsity basketball team and literally became college basketball's biggest star before television was in vogue.

"At that particular time, that was the best basketball conference in America, but America didn't know it because of the cities: Memphis, Tulsa, Peoria, Wichita, Cincinnati," said Bob Ortegel, who played at Bradley, was head coach at Drake, and later was a television commentator for the MVC. "You didn't have any big media outlets, and of course, you didn't have television like you do now. You look at the records of those teams—nobody wanted to play those teams. That league was recruiting the black player as much if not more than any league in the country at that time. All you had to do was look at the rosters, and those black players did a tremendous job."

From 1959 to 1965, the Missouri Valley Conference had a team win the National Invitation Tournament or make the Final Four for seven straight seasons. From 1959 to 1963, Cincinnati made five straight Final Fours, won two NCAA titles, and finished second once. Bradley won the NIT in 1960 and 1964, and Wichita State was in the Final Four in 1965.

"It was a conference of All-America players—probably six or seven players made All-America status," said North Texas' coach during that era, Charles Johnson. "It was one of the top two or three conferences in the country."

TELEVISION STARTS
TO SPREAD THE WORD

The Big "O," Oscar Robertson, served as a magnet for other players, first on radio, and then briefly on television at the end of his college career as MVC games went on the tube for the first time in 1959–60 with a six-game package. "In Kentucky, you could pick up (UC) games on the radio," said Louisville's Butch Beard, who was drawn to the MVC because of Oscar. "My family was not blessed with a television. I would have to go over to the neighbors' house to see it on TV, but I would listen to UC games on the radio. And the reason why I wore 14, he wore 14. . . . Oscar Robertson was by far the best player at that time." Likewise, in 1960, Dave Stallworth says he saw Oscar Robertson play on television and was attracted to the MVC and wound up at Wichita State.

Soon, MVC games were being originated all over the country thanks to innovative Eddie Einhorn, who put together his first televised college game, Bradley–St. Bonaventure on Feb. 2, 1961, from Madison Square Garden in New York City. It was shown back to markets in Buffalo, N.Y., and Peoria, Ill. Einhorn did the color at halftime.

The following season, Einhorn produced Cincinnati, Wichita State, and Bradley road games for television. A decade later, Einhorn added the MVC Television Network to his TVS nationally syndicated package and took games all over the country. "They had good basketball in small markets and they were the best teams," Einhorn said of the MVC of the early 1960s. "My original concept was televising big road games back to their own markets."

Eddie Einhorn

The 1963–64 season ushered in the first year of the Missouri Valley Conference Network, which featured games each Saturday at noon. For the rest of the decade, the network had 20 to 30 stations all over the Midwest and into the Southwest. Einhorn stepped that even further with greater national exposure in 1969–70, when he took MVC games into the East with his TVS package.

In the meantime, Wichita State had arrived as a national power in the early 1960s with Ralph Miller and Dave Stallworth. Miller, like Iba before him in the East, was scheduling games in Chicago and Detroit for greater exposure. The Shockers' game against Cazzie Russell and top-ranked Michigan at Cobo Arena in Detroit remains as one of the great intersectional games of all time. Russell beat Wichita State, 87–85, on a half-court shot near the end of the game. "Gary Thompson and Ralph Miller

(Wichita State coaches) had a good relationship with George Ireland, and they would play double-headers in Chicago Stadium and then the team would return for a game here," said Ron Heller, a Wichita State player and assistant coach.

Bradley's Chuck Orsborn had started a series with Notre Dame in 1957–58 at Chicago Stadium. The Braves beat the Fighting Irish nine straight times in Chicago before losing there in 1968, the last game of the series.

That series provided just a glimpse of the MVC's overall basketball strength, which was constantly shifting with different teams winning the league championship. By the late 1960s, Louisville and Drake had supplanted Cincinnati and Wichita State as the MVC's top powers. "Wes Unseld and Beard at Louisville, Bingo Smith at Tulsa, Joe Allen at Bradley, Rich Roberson and Jim Ard at Cincinnati, Wichita State had Warren Armstrong—it was just a loaded, loaded league," said Drake's Willie McCarter. "I look back on it and laugh. They talk about Big 10 this and that. The MVC consisted of—add it all up, look it all up—of basketball traditions you have even today. You talk about Louisville and Cincinnati. All those teams used to be a part of the league, with only the first-place team going anywhere (as far as the NCAA Tournament)."

McCarter's point is well taken. The NCAA, before expanding the men's tournament field to 32 teams in 1975, allowed only one team per league (the conference champion) into its field. And consider the competitiveness of the MVC at that time. Had the current multiple same-conference berths been allowed, the MVC might have well ended up with multiple teams in the Final Four on several occasions.

From 1961–62 until 1971–72, the MVC had a total of six playoff games to determine five regular-season champions who annually received the league's lone NCAA slot. In 1962, Cincinnati beat Bradley in an MVC playoff game, and the Bearcats are still the only NCAA Division I men's basketball champions in history to have to win a conference playoff game to make the tournament.

"I thought from top to bottom, the MVC was the best conference outside of the ACC and those great UCLA teams," said Tom Hedrick, who was a frequent MVC play-by-play man. From 1969 to 1975, the MVC had four Final Four teams—Drake (1969), Louisville

By the late 1960s, Louisville and Drake had supplanted Cincinnati and Wichita State as the MVC's top powers.

Wichita State's Warren Armstrong showing tenacious defense

Jim Ard

Butch Beard

(1972), Memphis State (1973), and Louisville (1975). Each time the MVC team lost to eventual NCAA champion UCLA.

By the time an MVC team got to the NCAA Tournament in those days, it was always well tested. "The Valley was the single hardest place to play in America," said Lee Hunt, who was Gene Bartow's assistant at Memphis. "The tin roof at Bradley, talk about loud and home-court advantage. It was the hardest place to play. Some fans came out of the stands after Bartow after a game. It was a great league. There were so many super games."

CHANGING MEMBERSHIP

By the 1975–76 season, Louisville was gone. Cincinnati had become an independent after the 1969–70 season. And Memphis State left the MVC following the 1972–73 season. All three schools became members of the Metro Conference. Coincidentally, both Louisville and Memphis State made Final Four appearances in 1975 and 1973, respectively, and were out of the league by the following seasons.

"The reason the Valley was able to survive, it had such a strong core, with Bradley, Drake, Wichita State, and Tulsa," said Mickey Holmes, the MVC commissioner from

1972 to 1979. "When we expanded we brought in three strong institutions (Southern Illinois, Indiana State, and Creighton) that just completed that core perfectly. It gave it such inner strength, it continued to have vitality. There were strong leaders at the core of those institutions: strong faculty leadership, exceptionally strong presidential leadership. That was the real factor why that league was able to stay together. In the end, it flourished again."

The MVC admitted SIU in 1974; and Creighton and Indiana State came in 1976 to account for the defections.

Indiana State's addition proved to be particularly fortuitous, because the Sycamores, led by Larry Bird, fashioned an unbeaten regular season and advanced to the 1979 NCAA title game before losing to Magic Johnson and Michigan State.

Another school with a strong basketball program and midwestern stability—Illinois State—joined the league in 1980. Illinois State was the last MVC basketball addition for a decade. Ironically, Gene Smithson had built the Redbirds into a midwestern independent power, and he was the Wichita State coach when Illinois State actually joined the Missouri Valley

Conference. And Smithson's Shockers were the final MVC team in the 20th century to make an NCAA Regional final in 1981.

Clearly, Wichita State, Tulsa, and Bradley were the toast of the league from 1980 to 1988 when one of the three schools won or at least shared every regular-season title during that span and collected seven of the nine postseason tournament crowns.

Tulsa won the NIT in 1981, and Bradley claimed the NIT in 1982, years when both teams probably should have been in the NCAA Tournament. "Nolan Richardson (at Tulsa) had tremendous teams and several pros," said Wichita State's Smithson. "When I was at Wichita State, the Missouri Valley was loaded with NBA players." Smithson was in the MVC from 1978 to 1986, when future NBA players graced the league: Indiana State's Larry Bird, Wichita State's Cliff Levington, Antoine Carr, and Xavier McDaniel; West Texas State's Maurice Cheeks; Tulsa's Paul Pressey and Steve Harris; Bradley's Hersey Hawkins, Mitchell Anderson, and David Thirdkill; Drake's Lewis Lloyd; and Creighton's Benoit Benjamin.

At the same time coaches such as Randy Smithson, Nolan Richardson, Bradley's Dick Versace, New Mexico State's Ken Hayes, and Illinois State's Bob Donewald strongly influenced the tenor of the league and promoted it to a national audience. "Dick Versace was a showman," said Tony Barone, Versace's assistant at Bradley

Doug Elgin and Larry Bird hold the new Larry Bird MVC Player of the Year Trophy

Tulsa's Steve Harris

Bob Donewald

The State Farm MVC Tournament at Savvis Center

and later the head coach at Creighton. "He was good for the Valley. He promoted the Valley. I think that is when the Valley took a little bit of a turn. It was hard to maintain the level of excellence just with the players. . . . Part of the fun of the Missouri Valley was the coaches and the play-by-play."

ELGIN BECOMES THE MVC "SYSTEMS GUY"

One of the most significant developments during the latter part of the "MVC's First 100 Years" was the appointment of Doug Elgin as commissioner on May 17, 1988. Through 2006, Elgin already had the second-longest run of any commissioner in league history.

The former Virginia sports information director and Sun Belt Conference assistant commissioner is an architect of many of the MVC's current success stories. He initiated the movement of the men's postseason basketball tournament from campus sites to St. Louis in 1991; he oversaw the merging of the Gateway women's sports into the MVC in 1992; he brought in-house the league's television operation in 1993–94; he oversaw the addition of three teams to the league—Missouri State (1990), UNI (1991), and Evansville (1993). Missouri State had strong men's and women's basketball programs, UNI was well-rounded in several sports, and Evansville was a men's basketball power in the Midwestern Collegiate Conference before moving to the MVC.

For two seasons (1994–95 and 1995–96), the MVC operated as an 11-team men's basketball league before Tulsa departed for the Western Athletic Conference. During those two seasons, there were 18 conference games, so each MVC team played two selected opponents only once each during that season. "We didn't know Tulsa was going to leave, but we anticipated it," Elgin said of having a replacement to stay at 10 teams. The MVC has remained a 10-team league ever since, with a double-round-robin schedule in men's basketball.

In addition to mastering the membership equation, Elgin has been greatly influential in developing stringent men's basketball RPIs (Rating Percentage Index) in the Missouri Valley by implementing stronger requirements for non-conference basketball scheduling. He is one of the founding fathers of "Bracket Busters," a series in which schools from many of the so-called "mid-major" conferences pool their teams and come up with attractive late-season matchups for ESPN's family of networks.

St. Louis has also become a fixture on the NCAA men's and women's basketball tournament circuit. St. Louis and the MVC have played host to numerous men's regionals, the 2001 Women's Final Four, the 2005 Men's Final Four, and is scheduled to play host to another Women's Final Four in 2009.

Moreover, Elgin says he has built on the conference's great tradition and added new programs to enhance the MVC's brand. "There are a couple of things which make us different," Elgin said. "What makes us different is the people in our cities have generations of support for the local teams. . . . Look at Bradley. Back when Michael Jordan was with the Chicago Bulls, the Bradley University's program was an equivalent product in the eyes of Peorians. It has always been that way.

"We have always had great arenas. The average arena size is probably 9,000–10,000 seats in our conference. And our con-

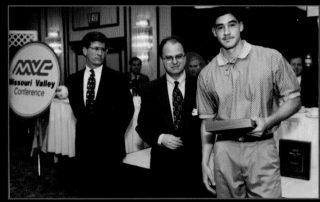

The MVC's Doug Elgin and Joe Mitch with Wichita State's Jason Perez

ference regular season and tournament average is always in the Top 10 (nationally). That really does make us different. That translates into interest from advertisers. Joe Mitch (associate commissioner) has done a sensational job overseeing our television ad sales over the last 15–16 years to the extent that you look through our tournament game program and the list of television advertisers, it looks like a who's who of regional and national corporations."

While the MVC hasn't had a team in a regional final since 1981 nor in the Final Four since 1979, it has consistently produced at least two NCAA Tournament teams each year since 1999, and on three occasions (1985, 1999, 2005) has had three teams in the field, with four teams being chosen in 2006.

The MVC has had Sweet 16 teams in 1994 (Tulsa), 1995 (Tulsa), Missouri State (1999), Southern Illinois (2002), and Bradley and Wichita State (2006). Creighton has pulled first-round upsets of Louisville (1999) and Florida (2002). Indiana State upset Oklahoma in the first round (2001). It may be just a matter of time before some MVC team bubbles to the top and makes a Final Four.

"I always felt it was the purest basketball league in the country," said former Wichita State player and assistant coach Randy Smithson. "It doesn't have football. I would love to see it get a national TV contract. It's a basketball league. I don't know if it ever will return (to the very top). Talk about straight up basketball. It was something else."

THE VALLEY

MISSOURI VALLEY CONFERENCE

MEN'S BASKETBALL YEARBOOK
2002-03

NCAA March Madness Begins at the Arch

$15.00

MVC TOURNAMENT

Missouri Valley Conference Commissioner Doug Elgin stood at a Savvis Center courtside entrance and watched the 2003 MVC Tournament final between Creighton and Southern Illinois unfold. "It was like an Ali–Frazier fight for us," Elgin remembers about a record MVC Tournament finals crowd of 14,991, which provided the perfect matchup for ESPN.

"He watched outside the entrance way like Moses looking into the Promised Land," MVC television voice Mitch Holthus recounted about the 2003 final. "The only difference is Doug got to go into the arena. . . . He is a visionary."

It certainly seems he is.

THE MVC MEN'S BASKETBALL TOURNAMENT

The MVC Tournament format and location is the brainchild of Elgin who urged conference leaders to move it to the Gateway City and away from campus sites in 1990.

Sixteen years later, the MVC Tournament's marriage with St. Louis is the second longest association between a city and a postseason conference tournament in Division I men's basketball. Only the Big East Conference's love affair with New York City and Madison Square Garden (since 1983) has more longevity.

Certainly don't expect a divorce between the MVC and St. Louis. Although the two parties enjoy one of the most successful ventures in postseason basketball, a few recent tweaks have enhanced the product.

The 2006 MVC Tournament final was moved from Monday night to Sunday afternoon and from ESPN to CBS for greater national exposure. The change from a Friday–Monday to a Thursday–Sunday tournament schedule resulted in a record crowd for the five

MVC basketball announcers, Mitch Holthus and Debbie Antonelli

Creighton celebrates the 1999 Men's Basketball Championship

Rich Herrin, Southern Illinois

sessions combined. The title game crowd of 13,969 was the second largest finals crowd in conference history. And the MVC walked away the following week with a record four NCAA Tournament bids (tournament winner Southern Illinois, Bradley, UNI, and regular-season champion Wichita State)—the four teams that reached the semifinals of the tournament.

"When I look at the "modern era" of the MVC, I think the most important decision we made as a conference was to bring the men's basketball tournament to St. Louis," Elgin said. "It helped us to stabilize the event, focus on corporate support and on promotion. It was important because St. Louis is the transportation hub of the region, and the home of the league office."

The 2007 MVC Tournament will return to the Savvis Center, and the final once again will be shown on CBS. The prospects of the tournament's growth continue to look good in St. Louis.

OVERCOMING HURDLES, MOVING TO ST. LOUIS

After regular-season champion SIU lost at Illinois State in the 1990 MVC Tournament final, there was a strong push by Salukis Coach Rich Herrin to move the tournament to a neutral site.

Despite 26 victories, SIU failed to get an at-large NCAA Tournament bid when Illinois State snared the league's automatic berth by winning the tournament. "Our president got after Doug to get the tournament off campus," Herrin said.

"We knew we had to minimize the home-court advantage," said Elgin, who also was aware that rotating the conference tournament among league schools provided the conference with only a revenue goal and no guaranteed revenue figure.

"As I looked at our budget, there was just no way we could operate without having a guaranteed figure for, at the time, our biggest revenue stream," Elgin said.

Wichita State took its 1991 MVC Tournament bid off the table, which allowed the conference office a chance to host the tournament in St. Louis for the first time. "I was at the table when there was divisiveness on whether or not it should go to the campuses," said Southern Illinois' former senior women's administrator Charlotte West. "One school was outbidding another school . . . and the rich got richer

Kiel Auditorium

and the poor got poorer. I think St. Louis is in a central location. I think it has had a demonstration of success there, and they have followed that up with getting sponsorships."

Before the big sponsorship era, however, the first tournament in St. Louis drew only 29,977 fans for seven games at the aging Kiel Auditorium. And the sound system went out during a press conference involving Indiana State Coach Tates Locke after he pounded his fist on the table. "He just got up at the press conference and just killed St. Louis, I mean killed it," said former Creighton Coach Tony Barone, whose team won the inaugural MVC Tourney in St. Louis. "He said, 'We are not having it here. This is ridiculous.' Then I got up afterward and said, 'Look, we need to give these people a chance.' Doug Elgin and Joe Mitch always said to me, 'Because of your support, we were able to keep this thing here.' And now, it is a very good tournament."

In 1992, the move to The Arena in St. Louis helped the tournament's playing conditions, and the fact that nearby Southern Illinois won three straight titles from 1993 to 1995 improved the crowds. "They said the St. Louis tournament was our second home," said Herrin of Salukis fans who had the shortest trip of all MVC fans to St. Louis.

Eventually Locke was proven wrong. The MVC Tournament did belong in St. Louis. Elgin's vision was correct. "Having leadership at the top makes a big difference," said Jack Watkins, MVC associate commissioner for marketing/television. "I am not sure other leagues would necessarily take the calculated risks that have been taken by this office that have worked out for us, like taking the tournament to a city with your closest school two hours away (SIU)."

"I was at the table when there was divisiveness on whether or not it should go to the campuses. One school was outbidding another . . . and the rich got richer and the poor got poorer."

Dr. Charlotte West, Southern Illinois

Although, before 2006, SIU had not won an MVC Tournament in a decade, its fans can't complain about losing on a lower-seeded team's home court any longer. "The history of our St. Louis event there have been very few (big) upsets," Elgin said. "If you take away the 4-5 matchup, there have been very few. The tournament has done exactly what the objective was and that is to advance our better teams on a neutral floor."

Tony Barone, Creighton

GREAT ARENA, GREAT GAMES, GREAT SPONSORSHIPS

The MVC Tournament grew as a 1990s sports building boom was occurring in St. Louis. The Savvis Center was completed in 1995 on the site of old Kiel Auditorium, and a year and a half later, the Trans World Dome (now the Edward Jones Dome), went up on the banks of the Mississippi as the Los Angeles Rams moved East to become the St. Louis Rams.

"There was a half-billion dollars of sports construction, and we were in a great position to capitalize on spectacular new facilities," said Elgin of gaining NCAA Tournament events as well as growing the MVC Tournament property at the Savvis Center.

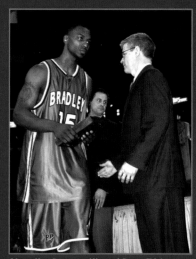

The MVC Tournament has a long list of presenting sponsors and corporate sponsors, including State Farm Insurance, the title sponsor. Elgin said once the MVC began hosting NCAA Tournament events, starting with the 1993 Midwest Regional, "I think that helped our visibility. I think that helped our sponsorship base here to understand we were here to stay. The growth of our men's tournament, I think, has been spectacular throughout the years."

Marcellus Sommerville and Doug Elgin

2006 State Farm MVC Tournament final

Since the 2003 MVC Tournament, large crowds have been the norm. In the 2006 semifinals, a single-session record crowd of 17,772 was established. The top four attendances for the entire MVC Tournaments have occurred the last four years: 63,739 in 2006; 62,007 in 2003; 53,342 in 2005; and 50,033 in 2004. "I think the strides that have been made the last three years and the number of fans who come to the tournament from our institutional communities have grown tremendously," said MVC associate commissioner and tournament director Joe Mitch. "But more importantly, we finally have captured the imagination and the attention of the people in St. Louis. I think we have a much better fan base here. I would like to think it is because our teams are fun to watch and we have 16 years of history and incredible, exciting games."

MEN'S MVC TOURNAMENT HISTORY HIGHLIGHTS

1977—Southern Illinois won the inaugural MVC Tour- nament over West Texas State, 82–69, in Wichita. SIU's Gary Wilson and Mike Glenn combined for 52 points. Maurice Cheeks scored just 12 for West Texas State. SIU would go 16 years before winning another MVC Tournament title in 1993.

Key players on SIUs 1976-77 basketball team, L to R: Kneeling: Mike Glenn, Corky Abrams. Standing: Gary Wilson, Al Grant, Wayne Abrams and Mit Huggins

1978—In the MVC title game at Creighton, the Bluejays' Rick Apke, brother of Head Coach Tom Apke, made an 18-foot shot as the buzzer sounded to give the hosts a 54–52 victory over Indiana State and superstar Larry Bird. Creighton held the ball for the final six minutes of the game with the scored tied. It was the first of nine Creighton MVC Tournament titles through 2005.

1981—Powerhouse Wichita State, which would go to the Elite Eight before losing to LSU, fell to Creighton, 70–64, in the MVC final in Wichita. The regular-season champion Shockers slipped to a No. 6 seed but rebounded to win three NCAA Tournament games. This was the last MVC team to advance to a regional final through the end of the millennium.

1983—Illinois State won its first MVC Tournament title and gained its first NCAA Tournament berth with an 84–64 victory over visiting Tulsa. The Redbirds' Rickie

Johnson scored 22 points before a frenzied crowd at Horton Field House.

1984—Tulsa beat Creighton, 70–68, in the first MVC title game that went into overtime. The Golden Hurricane's Ricky Ross made a jumper with two seconds left in overtime to give Tulsa the victory and offset a 12-for-13 shooting night by Creighton center Benoit Benjamin.

1985—Wichita State beat Tulsa, 84–82, in Tulsa and claimed its first of two MVC Tournament titles during a three-year period. Tulsa's Steve Harris outscored Wichita State's Xavier McDaniel 37–34, but Harris missed a shot in the closing seconds that would have sent the game into overtime.

1986—Tulsa, under first-year Coach J. D. Barnett, defeated Bradley, 74–58, in the tournament final played in Tulsa. The loss cost the Braves a better seed in the NCAA Tournament, which greatly affected their chances of advancing deep into the tournament. They lost in the second round to eventual NCAA champion Louisville.

1989—SIU Coach Rich Herrin was fuming because he believed Jerry Jones was fouled as time ran out in a 79–77 Creighton title-game victory in Wichita. No call was made. The game also featured a dunk by SIU's Freddie McSwain that was disallowed when it popped back out of the basket after going through the net. That basket and perhaps the no-call turned out to be the differences in the game.

1990—Regular-season champion Southern Illinois lost to Illinois State, 81–78, in Normal, Ill., in the title game. The Redbirds' Rickey Jackson was the tournament's most outstanding player during a week when his mother had died. The MVC regular-season champion Salukis, with 26 victories, failed to get an NCAA Tournament bid as an at-large team. As a result, the MVC Tournament was moved to St. Louis and a "neutral setting."

1991—With the move to St. Louis, the MVC played its first and only tournament at aging Kiel Auditorium. Indiana

State Coach Tates Locke had a famous post-game press conference (in which the sound system went out). He said the tournament should never have been moved to St. Louis. Creighton Coach Tony Barone, who won his second MVC Tournament title in three years, supported the move.

1992—With the tournament moving to The Arena in St. Louis, Missouri State made the MVC final for a second straight season and this time beat Tulsa, 71–68, with a little dose of "Spoonball." Missouri State Coach Charlie Spoonhour wowed them with his quips, courtside manner, and stingy defense.

1993—Illinois State defeated Drake, 60–59, in a semifinal game at The Arena, which was one of the weirdest in tournament history. The Redbirds trailed by eight points with 4:12 remaining, but they scored the last nine points of the game. Drake's William Celestine missed two free throws with 49 seconds to go and the first of a one-and-one with 11 seconds remaining. A bird distracted Celestine on one of the free throws. Drake Coach Rudy Washington cried foul after the game because the regular-season champion Redbirds were allowed an early warm-up on The Arena floor before the game and his team was not.

Tyler McKinney, Creighton

1993–1995—In 1993, SIU and Coach Rich Herrin started a run of three straight MVC Tournament titles, the only time one MVC school and/or one coach has accomplished the feat. The Salukis beat Illinois State (1993), UNI (1994), and Tulsa (1995) in consecutive finals. SIU guards Paul Lusk and Chris Carr were 9–0 in MVC Tournament games, the only players in league history to produce such records at the time.

1996—The most unusual game-ending shot in MVC Tournament history occurred in the semifinals of Bradley's 64–62 victory over Missouri State. Bradley's Deon Jackson grabbed a rebound and from near mid-court launched a turnaround three-point attempt that went in as the buzzer sounded. But Tulsa beat Bradley in the title game.

1997–1998—Illinois State became the first team in MVC history to win back-to-back regular-season and tournament titles in consecutive seasons. During an entire timeout late in the first half, an upset Coach Kevin Stallings stared down MVC referees in a 1997 semifinal against UNI. He was upset over a call that went against ISU. The Redbirds rallied to win, 69–65. It remains one of the tournament's most enduring moments.

2001—Indiana State won its second MVC Tournament title and first in 22 years when it defeated Bradley in the title game. The Sycamores, who had finished in a tie for fourth in the MVC regular season, then upset Oklahoma in the first round of the NCAA Tournament as a No. 13 seed.

2004—UNI advanced to the NCAA Tournament for the first time since it joined the league. The Panthers claimed their first MVC Tournament title in the first double-overtime title game against Missouri State (79–74). UNI guard Ben Jacobson was also the tournament's Most Outstanding Player.

1999–2005—Creighton made a run of five MVC Tourney titles in seven seasons, which is the best seven-year run of any team, and the Bluejays raised the school's total to a league-high nine tournament crowns. Creighton guard Tyler McKinney, who was injured and didn't play in the 2004 tournament, equaled the 9–0 tournament mark of SIU's Paul Lusk and Chris Carr when the Bluejays beat Missouri State in the 2005 final. With five MVC Tournament titles, Creighton Coach Dana Altman has won the tournament more times than any other coach in the history of the league.

2006—Southern Illinois ended a decade of frustration when it defeated Bradley, 59–46, in the MVC Tournament final. The No. 2-seeded Salukis won their first postseason crown since 1995. SIU Coach Chris Lowery, who was a member of SIU's 1993 and 1994 MVC Tournament title teams, became the first person to win an MVC Tournament championship as a head coach and as a player. The 2006 MVC Tournament final was televised by CBS after 20 straight years on ESPN (ESPN2 in 2002).

Deon Jackson

MOST EXCITING ENDING

In unison, MVC Commissioner Doug Elgin and Associate Commissioner Jack Watkins cite the single most exciting play in MVC Tournament history in St. Louis. It occurred in a 1996 semifinal game between Bradley and Missouri State. Bradley's Deon Jackson made a wild three-point shot to win the game, 64–62, on the final play.

"The greatest shot in the history of college basketball to win a game was in the 1996 Missouri Valley Conference Tournament," Elgin said.

A Bradley player took a shot, but he missed. The ball was tipped out and headed toward half court. Missouri State's Ben Kandlbinder just needed to knock the ball into the backcourt for the victory. But Kandlbinder stopped to celebrate and actually raised his arms in the victory pose.

"Bradley's Deon Jackson chases down the ball and with 3-2-1 seconds remaining, out past the top of the key and going towards half court and he shoots . . . ," Elgin said.

"That ball is going in!" exclaimed MVC Associate Commissioner Joe Mitch, who was sitting next to Watkins.

"It hit nothing but net," Watkins recalled.

"He looked like Jim Valvano running around the court."

DRAKE
BASKETBALL
14 BIG HOME GAMES
NEXT HOME GAME
KANSAS U. DEC. 18
GAMES START AT 8:15 PM

Drake Fieldhouse

SIU Arena

Freedom Hall

Horton Field House

THE FACTS, SIGHTS, SOUNDS, AND MEMORIES FROM SOME OF THE MVC'S LEGENDARY FIELD HOUSES

SIU ARENA (1964–PRESENT)

Perhaps the Salukis' biggest victory over a ranked team came three years after the SIU Arena opened and in the midst of a 30-game home-court winning streak. Although the Salukis were a decade away from becoming an MVC member, ironically, they beat MVC member Louisville, 53–50, on Jan. 11, 1967, when the Cardinals were ranked second in the country and featured Wes Unseld and Butch Beard. The Salukis' stars in that era were Walt Frazier and Dick Garrett. The Salukis won 33 straight home games from January 2004 through January 2006, which ranks as the longest home-court winning streak at the SIU Arena. The Salukis also won a record 42 straight MVC home games from January 2002 through January 2006.

A feature of the Salukis' original floor in the building was the timber that stood on end to make the floor particularly hard. "It was the butts of 2-by-4s," said Porter Moser, a Creighton player. "It was like playing on concrete. . . . It had no give. It was the worst basketball floor ever."

LOUISVILLE'S FREEDOM HALL

The Cardinals were MVC members from 1964 to 1975, and during that time the Final Four was held two times (1967 and 1969) at Freedom Hall, Louisville's home court. Drake, an MVC member, played in the 1969 Final Four at Freedom Hall. The two seasons prior to Louisville joining the MVC, Cincinnati, then a Valley member, played in the national title game in 1962 and 1963 at Freedom Hall, and in 1959 the Bearcats finished third there.

ILLINOIS STATE'S HORTON FIELD HOUSE (1963–1988)

One of the unique features of Illinois State's old field house was that the press box served both the basketball arena and the football field, which was located adjacent to the field house.

Although Illinois State was an independent at the time, Will Robinson became the first African American to be a head coach at a major-college basketball program when the Redbirds beat Bemidji State, 80–67, on Dec. 1, 1970, at Horton Field House.

TULSA'S CONVENTION CENTER

The Golden Hurricane, an MVC member from 1934 to 1996, started playing selected home games at the Convention Center in 1964, but they

Fairgrounds Pavilion

Armory Field House

Mid-South Coliseum

Hulman Center

didn't move all their home games there on a permanent basis until the 1977–78 season. During a 1977 game against Oral Roberts, after the game started, officials realized there was no mid-court stripe. The game was stopped and tape was laid down for the center stripe.

CINCINNATI GARDENS AND ARMORY FIELD HOUSE

Cincinnati competed as an MVC member from 1957 through 1970. At one time, the Bearcats played home games at the Armory Field House and Cincinnati Gardens, compiling a 90-game home winning streak at the two buildings over a seven-year period. The winning streak started with Oscar Robertson's sophomore season in 1957–58 (a 105–49 victory over Indiana State) and ended early in the 1963–64 season with a 51–47 loss to Kansas. In between, Cincinnati went to five Final Fours, won two NCAA titles, and won six MVC regular-season championships.

MEMPHIS MID-SOUTH COLISEUM

Memphis State competed as a member of the Missouri Valley Conference from 1967 to 1973. From 1970 to 1973 under Coach Gene Bartow, the Tigers compiled a 42–3 home record. Bartow lost only one MVC game at home during his tenure, 94–91, in double overtime to Tulsa during the 1970–71 season. The cornerstone players of those dominant MSU teams were three-time All-MVC selections Larry Finch and Ronnie Robinson, two local high school players who helped the Tigers more than double home attendance. The 11,381 average home attendance in 1972–73 was the highest in the 27 seasons the Tigers played at Mid-South Coliseum, ending in 1991.

INDIANA STATE'S HULMAN CENTER (1973–PRESENT)

When Indiana State was marching to the NCAA title game against Michigan State during the 1978–79 season, Indiana State students improvised making their confetti to celebrate the Sycamores' home victories. They removed toilet paper from the dorms and shredded it. The bathrooms were not always stocked.

Larry Bird's final regular-season home game, a nationally televised MVC game against Wichita State, almost didn't come off. A leak in the Hulman Center roof, which was caused by a snowstorm, had to be patched before Indiana State won, 109–84.

EVANSVILLE'S ROBERTS STADIUM (1956–PRESENT)

Opened in 1956, Roberts Stadium was renovated in 1990, four years before Evansville began competing in the MVC. Long before the Aces joined the MVC, Roberts Stadium housed five NCAA Division II championship teams under legendary Aces' Coach Arad McCutchan ('59, '60, '64, '65, '71). The first two years Evansville was in the MVC, the Aces led the league in home attendance (10,489 in 1995, and 10,457 in 1996).

WICHITA STATE'S ROUNDHOUSE, LEVITT, CHARLES KOCH (1955–PRESENT)

Unranked Wichita State defeated defending NCAA champion and

second-ranked Cincinnati, 52–51, on Dec. 18, 1961, on Lanny Van Eman's corner jump shot with three seconds remaining in Wichita. The WSU victory ended Cincinnati's 27-game winning streak and propelled Wichita State into the national spotlight. "For me it was really fun, too," Van Eman said. "My first child was born at 4–5 in the morning. I went to the hospital at 2 o'clock in the morning. I virtually had no sleep. Ralph (Miller) often said the shot was designed for another player—Gene Wiley. "For whatever reason, the screen to him didn't work well. By the time he came and got it, he was higher and further out—out of his comfort zone. He played very well four or five feet from the basket. He threw it back to me. I had the ball and was just as surprised as anyone else. I took one dribble and shot it from 18–20 feet out."

Roberts Stadium

Wichita State rallied for a 60–56 victory over Iowa in a 1981 NCAA Tournament second-round game in Wichita after trailing 40–25 with 18:50 to go. "The floor was just like on fire," Wichita State's Randy Smithson said of the second-half Shockers' rally. "It was electrifying."

On Wichita State fans' tradition of standing until the Shockers scored a basket in a half: "We played there once and their fans, in the first half or the second, they were known to stand and cheer until their team scored a bucket," said Bradley's Donald Reese. "It must have taken six, seven, eight minutes for them to get a bucket. To me that was fun. We said, 'Let's keep them standing up a little longer.'"

Koch Arena, formerly Levitt Arena

Cincinnati entered a game at Wichita State on Feb. 16, 1963, ranked No. 1 and was riding a 37-game winning streak. Dave Stallworth's 46 points overcame a six-point WSU deficit late in the game and propelled the Shockers to a pulsating 65–64 victory. Cincinnati Coach Ed Jucker said this was a tougher loss than their NCAA title game defeat to Loyola of Chicago. "Cincy had some harsh words to say about me," Stallworth said about a previous WSU loss that season to the Bearcats. "They said I wasn't the player people said I was and how their defense held me. I couldn't put it in the hole because I had looks all day long. I missed a layup. That's how things went. . . . They got to come back here. I got to hear all of this stuff, how great Cincinnati was, and they were going to do the same thing up there they did in Cincinnati. But I knew better. They didn't have anybody on their team who could hold me . . . I was doing the same thing here—but I was making the baskets."

Civic Auditorium

OMAHA'S CIVIC AUDITORIUM (1957–2003)
Creighton defeated Southern Illinois, 102–100, in overtime on Feb. 17, 1989, following an unlikely comeback in the final minute. "We were down a ton, and people were leaving," former Creighton Coach Tony Barone said of a six-point deficit with 45 seconds remaining. "The gym really started to get empty. And a kid by the name of Todd Eisner, he stepped back and made a three. He caught the ball in front of the three-point line and had the presence of mind to step back and make the three (to tie the game). His dad was a coach. He took one step back off the dribble and drained a

Veterans Memorial Stadium

Kiel Auditorium

Hammons Center

St. Louis Arena (Second MVC men's basketball tournament was played here after the MVC moved its tournament to St. Louis)

Robertson Field House

three right in front of our bench. It was an incredible shot. Then we won it in overtime and beat them when James Farr made a little bucket."

Creighton won the MVC Tournament title in 1978 on its home floor over Indiana State and Larry Bird. The Bluejays held the ball the final six minutes of the game, then Head Coach Tom Apke's brother, Rick, made an 18-foot jump shot to win the game, 54–52.

DRAKE'S VETERANS MEMORIAL AUDITORIUM (1962–1992)

Mike VandeGarde's two free throws with no time remaining lifted the Redbirds to a 76–75 victory at Drake on March 2, 1992. The fans at Drake's Veterans Memorial Auditorium were in a money-pitching mood. "There was no time left when they called a foul on the rebound," VandeGarde said. "The team (Drake) had run into the locker room, and they had to bring them out. Nobody was at the free throw line. The fans were throwing coins at me. I said, 'Hey, ref, they are throwing coins at me.' He said, 'You better shoot it now.' I made it. Then they started shaking the basket. And he repeated it."

Former Tulsa guard Mike Anderson remembers a game Drake won, 56–55, on Feb. 15, 1982, in Des Moines. "Drake was at the free-throw line," Anderson recalled. "They shoot a free throw. We go for the rebound. I think maybe we are down one point. Two guys go for the ball, it hits the floor and goes back in the basket. It hit the floor! It was on ESPN, as a matter of fact. It was one of those highlight bonuses."

SAINT LOUIS' KIEL AUDITORIUM

"It definitely had great ambiance," MVC Commissioner Doug Elgin said. "It had a stage at one end. There was a concert hall on the other side, and it was sound proof. . . . Kiel Auditorium was built during the Depression. It was such a fortress. It was a labyrinth of hallways and was constructed of marble and granite. The opera house is still there."

MISSOURI STATE'S HAMMONS CENTER (1976–Present)

"We (Elgin and Joe Mitch) were sitting at the game (Missouri State), and they had their Sugar Bears and their dance team, and 8,800 people stuck into their facility," Missouri Valley Conference Commissioner Doug Elgin said. "The Bears were playing Illinois State and Bob Donewald. Illinois State won the game (55–51). Joe Mitch leaned over to me and said, 'If I lived in Springfield, I would buy season tickets here.'" And we were both thinking the same thing. It was clear they had an atmosphere in their building that was ACC–like."

TULSA'S FAIRGROUNDS PAVILION (1950–1977)

"Birds would fly through there, but you couldn't see the roof," said former Tulsa Coach Ken Hayes. "Birds would be fly through as smoke (from fans' cigarettes) was ascending to the roof. The lights were bad, and the floor was terrible. In my 10 years there, I never took a recruit to see the Pavilion. It is located a mile or two away from campus. Structurally it is a very sound building. A lot of people have strong ties with it. It is kind of legendary in its own right like Robertson Field House."

Tulsa's high-scoring Willie Biles, who played at Tulsa's Fairgrounds Pavilion from 1971 to 1974, had no complaints about the surroundings. "To see a smooth surface, inside, with a roof . . . the only thing I saw was the rim. I was used to playing outside on concrete, and concrete was good. I started playing on dirt. To get a smooth surface was unbelievable."

Snake Pit

"A very unique place was the Fairgrounds," said Louisville's Butch Beard, who played from the Cardinals from 1966 to 1969. "At that particular time, they had a spotlight over the basket. And they had a player, Eldridge Webb, who could use that glass. And he could use that light, which was directly over the basket. He used to bank the shot."

BRADLEY'S ROBERTSON FIELD HOUSE (1949–1982)
"It was like being on a stage," said Joe Dalfonso, former Bradley sports information director. "The only lights were on the gym floor. The raised floor was different. It was two airport hangars put together. The Field House gave us a chance to win any game on any given night, and the best example of that was on Feb. 1, 1977, when we lost 107–106 to UNLV."

Gallagher-Iba Arena

Bradley was on the way to a 9–18 season. But against the Runnin' Rebels, who featured Reggie Theus and Eddie Owens, Bradley guard Roger Phegley scored 46 points. "Seven guys off that UNLV team were drafted in the NBA, not all in the same year, of course," Phegley said. "It was just one of those games. We caught them by surprise. The home-court advantage at the Field House was always tremendous. It was one of those games if the inferior team hangs around long enough, they think they can win. We played about as well as we probably could play. They struggled to guard me, and they (his teammates) were willing to give me the ball because I had the hot hand. It also would have been a better story had we won the game."

Amarillo Civic Center

"In this area, Robertson Field House was really a legendary place to play," Bradley's Paul Unruh (1946–50) said. "The players who played here really enjoyed it because you played on a stage. The floor was raised. It gave an excitement to the game that was totally different than playing on a level floor the same as people sitting there. The seats went up both sides of the floor into a metal building. The noise was just something unbelievable."

"They'd be yelling for you so hard. If you were tired, you actually gained energy," Bradley's Bobby Joe Mason (1956–60) said of the fans at Robertson. "Other teams hated to play here. . . . They were always hollerin' and yelling for you. The place would be rumbling with noise."

Bob Ortegel, a Bradley Brave (1958–62) and then Drake coach (1974–81), added: "I remember the first year we (Drake) played there, I

Savvis Center

An early MVC Tournament is held at Nebraska Basketball Arena, circa 1918

1907   2007

100 YEARS OF ATHLETICS EXCELLENCE

pointed out to the players, and it sounds silly, but that the floor was 94 feet long and 50 feet wide, and it was literally like playing on the biggest stage in the world. It was so electrifying. . . . When we (the Braves) would play Cincinnati somebody would always throw a black cat into the locker room—the black cat was bad luck—and the cat would then scoot out of the locker room."

Louisville's Butch Beard: "I guess a lot of people are afraid they would fall off (the floor) if they shot a layup. I had a career high my sophomore year up there, 41 points."

NORTH TEXAS STATE SNAKE PIT

North Texas State competed as a MVC member from 1957 to 1975 and more often than not finished in the second division, but North Texas State had one of the truly tough places in play in college basketball, complete with rowdy crowd, crowded sideline, and sight problems because of glaring sunlight. "It was a place when we got everybody in there, people were on the floor with us," said former North Texas State Coach Charlie Johnson (1959–65). "When we started pressing a team, it was sort of a sixth man for us, because fans were so close. I am sure it made it pretty tough to play there."

"We had a pretty good fight at North Texas . . . ," said Bob Ortegel, who played for Bradley (1958–62). "One of our players was tripped (by a fan) going down the sidelines. In order to take the ball out of bounds, they had to turn their legs for you to get in there."

"If a game started at 1 o'clock it bothered you for about the first 10–12 minutes, but after that the sun would move back and then it's OK," said Wichita State's Dave Stallworth. "When we went down there, we would usually try to practice about the same time we would play. So we would make sure we were going the other way (in the first half), because we would have the choice of baskets at the beginning of the game. The second half the sun was gone, and we were in good shape. Everybody complained about the sun in afternoon games."

"The floor was terrible," said former MVC official and supervisor Johnny Overby. "They would put a zone defense on, and they could beat the Boston Celtics on that floor. It was small. There was no room on the sidelines. It was a high school gymnasium with bleachers. . . . The bleachers were right up to the sidelines. It could seat only 4,000–5,000. It wasn't a basketball atmosphere compared to Bradley, Wichita, and Cincinnati. It was a Texas school. . . . They thought it was still football season."

OKLAHOMA A&M'S GALLAGHER ARENA

The Cowboys usually had MVC powerhouses during the Coach Henry Iba era (1934–57 in the Valley). Iba also made sure the Cowboys had one of the best basketball facilities. "Gallagher was the biggest on-campus basketball facility west of the Mississippi River (when it opened)," said Moe Iba, former Oklahoma A&M basketball player and son of the legendary Henry Iba. "Madison Square Garden was bigger. Chicago Stadium was bigger. And some of the other towns had bigger arenas, but this was the biggest (on campus) facility west of the Mississippi River."

"Dad built it," Moe Iba said. "He had been there maybe one or two years. He convinced the president (of Oklahoma A&M) that they needed a new arena. The place they played in, the old field house, was awful."

All-American Bob Kurland lived in a dorm room in Gallagher Arena in the mid-1940s. He would sweep out the arena and close the windows each day as part of his scholarship agreement. The floor was often dusty because there were waves of soldiers performing drills at the arena during World War II. "It is the same floor we have played on for 50 years," Kurland said.

WEST TEXAS STATE
(AMARILLO CIVIC CENTER)

West Texas State competed in MVC basketball from 1970 to 1986 and played games in Canyon and nearby Amarillo. Mike Anderson of Tulsa remembers when West Texas State beat Tulsa, 85–83, in overtime on Feb. 7, 1981. "Of course, in West Texas you have a lot of Cowboys," Anderson recalled. "And, as the game was winding down, you heard a BAM! And you thought the clock had gone off. And West Texas happened to have the ball. But it wasn't the clock. Somebody must have shot a cap gun or something. Then about four seconds later they hit a shot to win it or tie it. It was very, very strange."

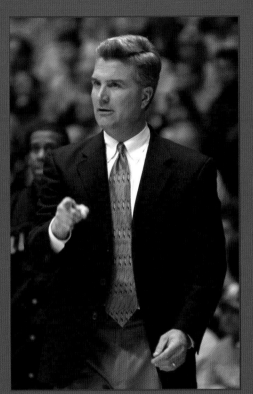

Bruce Weber, Southern Illinois

J. D. Barnett, Tulsa

B ruce Weber took Illinois to the national title game in 2005, a mere two years after he had coached Southern Illinois to the NCAA Tournament a second straight season. After five seasons, one NCAA Sweet 16 appearance (2002), one Missouri Valley Conference Coach of the Year award (2003), and two regular-season Missouri Valley Conference titles (2002 and 2003), it was time for Weber to leave Carbondale.

He became the latest in a long list of successful MVC coaches who have made the leap to other conferences and done well. Along with Tubby Smith and Nolan Richardson, Weber is the third former MVC coach to make the NCAA title game between 1994 and 2005 at another school. "The Valley breeds them," said Pooh Williamson, a former Tulsa player and Golden Hurricane assistant and interim head coach.

The MVC started to become a launching pad for coaching careers during the mid-1980s when the first of those former MVC coaches—Richardson—jumped from Tulsa to Arkansas. At Tulsa, Richardson won the National Invitation Tournament in 1981 and then followed with three NCAA Tournament appearances in four years. He built a strong resume and won the school's first outright regular-season MVC basketball title in 1985.

By the beginning of the next season, in 1985–86, Arkansas had snatched up Richardson to replace Coach Eddie Sutton, who had moved on to Kentucky. Tulsa had hired J. D. Barnett to replace Richardson, who eventually won an NCAA title at Arkansas in 1994 and was runner-up to UCLA in 1995.

The coaching carousel was beginning to spin at Tulsa. By the mid-1990s, Tulsa had hired two more coaches, Tubby Smith and Steve Robinson, who used the MVC for a stepping stone for jobs at Georgia and Florida State, respectively. Eventually, Smith wound up at Kentucky, where he, too, won an NCAA title in 1998. Three years before, at Tulsa, Smith didn't even have a parking space at his office in the shadows of the TU football stadium. "I remember the battles between Tulsa and Southern Illinois and Northern Iowa," Smith said. "We just had great coaches, J. D. Barnett, who I replaced, was an outstanding coach. Dana Altman at Creighton, Charlie Spoonhour at Missouri State, and Eldon Miller at UNI."

Losing coaches to bigger schools isn't something MVC officials look forward to, but they remain philosophical when it happens. "Any time we lost a coach, it was a temporary setback," said MVC Commissioner

Doug Elgin, who has been in the league since 1988. "But that's the strength of our league—our administrators are hiring the right people. Our presidents are funding compensation packages so we can keep people as long as we possibly can. It usually is not the finances, it is the bigger stage that entices people to leave more than anything else."

Elgin called it one of his darkest MVC days when the flamboyant Charlie Spoonhour left Missouri State for Saint Louis University following the Bears' 1992 NCAA Tournament appearance. "I was from a little bit different niche," Spoonhour said of other MVC coaches moving on to other leagues. "They were a little younger. They were kind of the young turks. They were very good. The league was little older (coaching) league when I was in it. I didn't fit their demographic. My hair was gray."

Missouri State Athletic Director Bill Rowe says Spoonhour's exposure in the MVC Tournament in St. Louis may have led Saint Louis University to hire him. Spoonhour coached in two MVC Tournament title games during his two seasons in the league, losing to Creighton in 1991 and beating Tulsa in 1992 in St. Louis. "We had an MVC luncheon at the Missouri Athletic Club in St. Louis," Rowe said. "Saint Louis U. was not doing well. Charlie spoke. And the whole place, he had them mesmerized. They were laughing and having fun. Of course, we were winning games. You could almost see, they (Saint Louis supporters) thinking the MSU people are having a lot of fun. And we are not. We may have overexposed him a little bit."

Rowe also had to replace Steve Alford, who went to Iowa after taking the 12th-seeded Bears to the NCAA Tournament's Sweet 16 in 1999. "A lot of fans can't seem to understand that (coaches leaving)," Rowe said. "You know the MVC is a developmental league. A lot of people ask, 'Why can't you keep him (Alford)? He has done all of this.' First of all, he wants to coach in the Big Ten."

From 1994 to 2006, led by many of the up-and-coming coaches, the MVC landed at least two teams in the NCAA Tournament 10 times, three teams twice (1999 and 2005), and four teams in 2006. Only in 1997 and 1998 did the MVC have a lone NCAA representative—Illinois State. This 13-year era has produced six Sweet 16 teams—Tulsa in 1994 and 1995, Missouri State in 1999, Southern Illinois in 2002, and Bradley and Wichita State in 2006.

Charlie Spoonhour, Missouri State

Tulsa's upset of UCLA and Oklahoma State in the 1994 NCAA Tournament drew great attention to the MVC, and when Smith's Golden Hurricane repeated the Sweet 16 feat in 1995, it earned Smith a parking spot at Georgia. "We had to play 11 a.m. games," Smith said of his MVC days. "We played 11 p.m. games in the league just to get on TV. We did whatever it took. That's what the Valley was like. Whenever they came to me, I would play them, and I think that is what helped our athletes "

All those Sweet 16 coaches are gone from the MVC now, including the latest, Weber, now at Illinois. But there's a major difference in the routes he took to the NCAA Tournament from Illinois and Southern Illinois. The Illini were the top seed in the 2005 tournament. He had to wait nervously on SIU's NCAA at-large selections in 2002 and 2003. His 2002 Salukis were seeded 11th, and his 2003 SIU team, which lost a controversial first-round, one-point decision to Missouri, was seeded 11th again. "They forget about us," said Weber, whose Salukis made the Sweet 16 in 2002 by beating Texas Tech and Georgia. "We get in the conference and we are not on TV (nationally). We get in the NCAA Tournament, and

Eddie Fogler, Wichita State

the early 1980s for violations under the previous two coaching regimes. "As soon as I met him, I thought he would be a great coach," Perkins said of Fogler. "He had great organization, he understood the game, and he had relationships. He was a perfect choice for us."

Fogler coached Wichita State to the NCAA Tournament his first season by winning the 1987 MVC Tournament. The following season, Fogler took the Shockers to the NCAA Tournament as an at-large entry—the last time they made the field in the 20th century.

A third straight postseason trip under Fogler—to the National Invitation Tournament—followed in 1988–89. "I brought in the true North Carolina system . . . and we are talking going to class, being on time," Fogler said. "Our first road game, we left our starting center Henry Carr behind. He was late for the bus—literally 15 seconds. He made it to airport on his own, and he ran for being late."

Three years after he arrived, Fogler was gone to Vanderbilt, taking a higher-paying job in the Southeastern Conference, and he eventually wound up at South Carolina, another SEC school.

TONY BARONE CARVED HIS NICHE AT CREIGHTON

Creighton Coach Tony Barone was a contemporary of Fogler's in the MVC and had even greater success by the time he left Omaha. He moved over from Dick Versace's staff at Bradley to coach the Bluejays in 1985–86. "He was the kind of coach, as a player you would run through the wall for him," said Illinois State Coach Porter Moser, who played for Barone at Creighton. "There wasn't a day ever he came into practice and you did not see him fired up and see him prepared. I have tried to emulate him as a coach. . . . He made enthusiasm and energy contagious."

It took Barone a little while, but once he recruited forwards Chad Gallagher and Bob Harstad, who scored nearly 4,100 points between them, the Bluejays were off and flying. Following the 1990–91 season, Barone, however, jumped to Texas A&M after taking the Bluejays to MVC regular-season and tournament crowns for the second time in three years.

"Looking back on everything, I should have stayed at Creighton," Barone said of his move to Texas A&M, which produced only one winning season in seven years. He's now working for the Memphis Grizzlies.

they say you are a surprise. We have been good all along. We are not a surprise."

After Weber collected two MVC regular-season titles and was hired at Illinois, the SIU coaching carousel was spinning, a la Tulsa. Matt Painter, an SIU assistant, replaced Weber, won one MVC regular-season title in 2004, and jumped to his alma mater, Purdue, where he spent one season as associate head coach and then became the head coach when Keady retired. Painter was replaced at SIU, by former Saluki Chris Lowery. He left Weber's Illinois staff after the 2003–04 season and became the third Salukis coach in three seasons, but the result was the same in 2004–05—a fourth straight regular-season MVC title for the Salukis under a third different coach.

WICHITA STATE'S EDDIE FOGLER GAVE SHOCKERS NEW IMAGE

After Wichita State fired Gene Smithson in 1986, Shockers' Athletic Director Lew Perkins needed a coach with a clean image and the proper pedigree. He went to Dean Smith's North Carolina staff and plucked Eddie Fogler. The Shockers had been penalized by the NCAA in

"Creighton offered all the things I enjoy in a basketball program: excellent academic institution, a smaller environment where the student body and fans can really become a part of your team," Barone said. "The community itself can become a part of your team."

ILLINOIS STATE'S DUO OF BENDER, STALLINGS MADE THINGS HAPPEN IN 1990s

In the 1980s, Coach Bob Knight disciple, Bob Donewald, had Illinois State in post-season play six times, three straight years in the NCAA Tournament (1983–85). But by 1989, the Redbirds had dropped to fifth in the league, and after a 13–17 overall record in 1988–89, the Donewald era ended in Normal, despite his overall 208–121 record. He became head coach at Western Michigan for 11 seasons.

Two young thoroughbred coaches—Bob Bender and Kevin Stallings—then piloted the Redbirds' program from 1989 to 1999 before moving on to other jobs. Bender's pedigree was Duke and Indiana; Stallings' was Purdue and Kansas. Benders' teams from 1989 to 1993 were basically no-frills, no-name clubs that relied on balanced scoring and defense—much like Donewald's. The Redbirds claimed the MVC Tournament in Bender's first season (1989–90) and regular-season MVC titles in his final two seasons (1991–92 and 1992–93) in Normal.

Bob Donewald, Illinois State

Bender failed to land a first-team All-MVC player during his four seasons in the league. "We were not the greatest athletes and the most talented team," said former Illinois State player Mike VandeGarde. "That belonged to Southern Illinois, and at times Creighton and Tulsa were probably the most talented teams. But as far as passion, hustle, and individual effort, our team could be matched against anybody."

VandeGarde remembers the turning point for Bender during the 1990–91 season, when the team started 0–13 and he was a freshman. "He took everything away from us. He took away our jerseys. He took away our sneakers. He sat down the entire team, he said, 'Guys, you are playing like crap.'" He thought if we were playing that bad, we were going to look that bad."

Bender gave the team white BVD V-necks—like undershirts from Wal-Mart. He gave the team members black magic markers and had them write their numbers on them. And he had the intramural staffers procure the smallest gray boy shorts they could find. He limited the players to one pair of shoes. They practiced in the auxiliary gym. "And, after we practiced, we had to wash all the gear ourselves," VandeGarde said. "We won three straight games."

More importantly, it set the stage for the next two seasons when the Redbirds won MVC regular-season titles. In 1993–94, Stallings took over for Bender, who left for Washington. After three upper division MVC finishes, Stallings won back-to-back MVC regular-season and tournament titles in 1997 and 1998, before taking the Vanderbilt job in 1999.

Stallings was able to recruit more talent than Bender procured, particularly Rico Hill, a 6-6 post player from Brother Rice High School in Chicago. Hill was the MVC Player of the Year in 1998 and the MVC Tournament MVP his junior season in 1997.

The other star under Stallings was 6-6 Dan Muller, the first player in MVC history to win the Defensive Player of the Year award two straight years, 1996 and 1997. Muller was also the MVC Tournament MVP in 1998.

Stallings, who played for Gene Keady at Purdue, recruited Muller out of West Lafayette, Ind., Central Catholic High School. Keady admitted later he made a mistake in not recruiting Muller in his own backyard. Not only did Stallings have an eye for talent, he was considered an excellent bench coach. "He's one of the best basketball minds I have ever been around," Illinois Coach Bruce Weber said of Stallings. "He's very creative and innovative and has a special feel for the game of basketball."

One thing Stallings inherited from Keady was "The Stare," and it was never more evident than during a 1997 MVC Tournament semifinal game against UNI in St. Louis. The Redbirds had won the MVC regular-season title that season but had lost to UNI twice. The Panthers'

Eldon Miller had taken MVC Coach of the Year honors and his star, Jason Daisy, was Player of the Year. Stallings was upset he was not named MVC Coach of the Year and didn't show up for the pre-tournament press conference. When the officiating didn't seem to be going Illinois State's way late in the first half, Stallings let his look talk during a media timeout. "Stallings doesn't huddle with his team," MVC Associate Commissioner Jack Watkins said. "His team is behind him. Ed Schumer, John Higgins and Eric Harmon (the game officials) are under the basket. He just glares at them. His arms are folded. That's what is known in the league as 'The Stare.' Illinois State came back and won the game and won the tournament."

Kevin Stallings, Illinois State

MVC SCHOOL	COACH	WHERE HE JUMPED
Tulsa	Nolan Richardson	Arkansas
Wichita State	Eddie Fogler	Vanderbilt (Later South Carolina)
Creighton	Tony Barone	Texas A&M
Illinois State	Bob Bender	Washington
Tulsa	Tubby Smith	Georgia (Later Kentucky)
Tulsa	Steve Robinson	Florida State
Missouri State	Charlie Spoonhour	Saint Louis (Later UNLV)
Illinois State	Kevin Stallings	Vanderbilt
Missouri State	Steve Alford	Iowa
Southern Illinois	Bruce Weber	Illinois
Southern Illinois	Matt Painter	Purdue
Northern Iowa	Greg McDermott	Iowa State

Oscar Robertson

"the Valley"

Missouri Valley Conference schools actively recruited African American players in the early and mid-1950s and integrated years before the all-white Southeastern and Atlantic Coast conferences broke the color barrier. By the early 1960s, the MVC had a greater number of black basketball players than the Big Ten, Pacific Eight, and Big Eight conferences. The infusion of these athletes made the MVC a giant force in college basketball.

That's not to say that the MVC's black basketball players in the 1950s through the early 1970s didn't encounter racism and hardship while traveling in the South and even to other league schools and on their own campuses. "You got spit on and drinks where thrown on you, and you would have to take it," said Wes Westfall, who played at Memphis State from 1971 to 1974. "Our satisfaction: we would go out and beat their butts."

THE MVC'S BLACK ATHLETE OFTEN IN THE EYE OF THE STORM

MVC schools Drake (1949), Wichita State (1951), and Saint Louis (1952) were among the forerunners in breaking the color barrier in college basketball, followed closely by Bradley (1955) and Cincinnati (1957).

By 1962, 11 years after the first African American played basketball in the MVC, Cincinnati Coach Ed Jucker started four black players in the NCAA title game against Ohio State. A year later when the MVC's Cincinnati played Loyola of Chicago for the 1963 NCAA title, the Bearcats had three black starters and the Ramblers four, three years before UTEP Coach Don Haskins started five black players in his historic upset of Kentucky in the 1966 NCAA title game. "We would have four blacks on our team," said Lanny Van Eman, who played and coached for Wichita State in the early 1960s. "George Ireland (coach of Loyola of Chicago) and Ralph Miller (Wichita State coach) were significant, not as significant as Haskins, but they would unabashedly play four black players. . . . What happened, virtually nobody was recruiting black players."

With segregation in the South being challenged and the civil rights movement of the 1950s and 1960s gaining momentum, the MVC juxtaposed athletics with social concerns.

It wasn't always a pretty sight, either. "I do remember a fan leaning over a railing when we were on the way to our locker room at Tulsa spitting at one of our players," said Bradley's Bob Ortegel, who played for the Braves from 1959 to 1962.

A riot, caused by a racial remark, broke out at a Drake–Louisville game in January 1969, at Freedom Hall. And the fans were involved as well. "One of the Louisville players called Al Williams (an African American Drake player) a nigger," said Dolph Pulliam, a Drake player, who is an African American. "I think there was just one police officer in the building. There were not that many black players on their team. . . . It was ugly. It was on Missouri Valley Conference TV."

Another Drake teammate, Rick Wanamaker, who was white, added: "Louisville had some black players (most notably Butch Beard), but it was still a Southern team. Someone made some racial comments and there were several fisticuffs. It was an all-out fight. Everybody joined in, not just the benches. They didn't like Drake anyway. They take basketball pretty seriously in Louisville."

Bobby Joe Mason

It was a guarded camp when the teams played again that season in Des Moines. "When we played at Drake that year, their students would throw chickens at us," said Louisville's Jerry King. "It was wild. We ended up losing (101–67). We had our state troopers, and they had the entire court lined with theirs.'"

BRIGHT, LITTLETON FIRST BLACK STARS
While Drake's Johnny Bright was the biggest African American football star in the postwar MVC, the first black basketball star was Wichita State's Cleo Littleton, who came with Miller to the Shockers from Wichita East High School in 1951.

Miller had broken the color line in the Kansas high school ranks, suiting up black players such as Littleton. It was at times a lonely road for Littleton in the college ranks. "In Oklahoma and Texas, I had to stay with families and take cabs to go to practice and then to the games," Littleton said at his MVC Hall of Fame induction in 2000. "It was not good for team spirit. You could imagine the harassment these guys got for playing ball with a black guy."

And when he was not allowed to eat in restaurants with his white teammates: "As much as I sat on the bus and ate, it hurt them just as bad as it did me," Littleton said. "Three

or four guys would say, 'I will stay on the bus with Cleo— and just bring me a ham sandwich.'"

Littleton remembers playing in a 1955 Wichita State game in St. Louis against the Saint Louis Billikens at Kiel Auditorium and fearing for his life. "We had lost . . . and as I was leaving the court, some little kid spit on me and I pushed him away," Littleton recalled. "I think 3,000 fans were on the floor after me. And Dick Boushka (a Saint Louis University player) came up to me and put his arm around me and said, 'Let me get you out of here where it is safe.' And he walked me up to the dressing room. If it had not been for Dick, I don't think I probably would have made it up there."

Racial taunting was a way of life, especially for the star players such as Cincinnati's Oscar Robertson and Wichita State's Dave Stallworth. Robertson broke the color barrier at Cincinnati in 1956.

MVC coaches, who were white, at times took their entire teams through the back door when the black players couldn't enter the front. Or, they just left the hotel altogether. "In Denton, Tex., in 1969, coach was handing out keys to players for the rooms and one player was white and one was black," Drake's Pulliam said. "So the manager at the hotel said you can't do that. So coach (Maury John) said, 'Guys, bring all the keys back.' We handed him all the keys. He gave the manager the keys, and we got in the cars. We went to Dallas and stayed in Dallas."

"In Houston, I think it was, we (black players) couldn't eat in the dining room, and we couldn't come through the front door," Bradley's Bobby Joe Mason said. "So the coach (Chuck Orsborn) said if they have to go in the back, the whole team has to go in the back. If they have to eat in the back, then the whole team has to eat back there."

While the MVC's black athletes were often treated like second-class citizens off the court, they were leading their teams to greatness on it.

The Bearcats won three MVC titles (1958–60) with Robertson and made two Final Fours (1959, 1960). Stallworth led Wichita State to national prominence and paved the way for two MVC titles (1964, 1965) and a Final Four. "He (Robertson) took a lot of harassment being black," remembers Johnny Overby, who was just coming up as an official. "In those days, a lot of blacks were playing in the conference, a lot more so than in other conferences. No, he never complained, never heard him complain."

Cincinnati's Ralph Davis was a white teammate of Oscar Robertson's and remembers when the Bearcats played at the Dixie Classic in North Carolina. "Anybody was on the floor, you could hear it all along press row—starting with the media—things you wouldn't want to repeat," Davis said. "It was bad. That was the first time I was ever in something where I had heard (racial) slurs. We had played all over the country, the East and Midwest. Down there we had that kind of a problem. But Oscar put on a show."

Stallworth grew up in the South, had encountered segregation, and had watched many great black basketball and football players go elsewhere to play because the Southwest Conference wasn't accepting black athletes in the early 1960s. "I went to an all-black school (in Dallas)," Stallworth said. "My elementary school was all black, my junior high was all black. I lived in an all-black neighborhood. The only time I had any mingling with white players and white coaches was when I got to Wichita State. . . . When we went down to North Texas State, the black players couldn't eat with the white players. When we went down there, my folks usually came over and got me. I went home. Living in Wichita wasn't too much different than living in the South. I got here in February 1961, and there were still some restaurants I couldn't go to in Wichita."

MEMPHIS STATE, DRAKE TEAMS HELPED WITH RACE RELATIONS

In the late 1960s, the MVC's Memphis State was the first team to take a black player into Starkville, Miss., when the Tigers played Mississippi State. "It was Herb Hilliard," said former Memphis State Coach Moe Iba, who broke the color barrier there. "He handled it pretty well. It was different because I thought we were going to be able to go down the night before and spend the night. We couldn't do it because there was no place to stay. We drove down the day of the game, played the game and came home. It was a changeover at Memphis State because they had never had any blacks. It went pretty smooth."

> *Memphis was a racially torn city in the early 1970s, but the Tiger basketball team brought it together. "After Finch and Robinson came to Memphis State, the whole city came together," said Lee Hunt, who was an assistant coach under Gene Bartow.*

"Bingo Smith had gone to Tulsa and Richard Jones to Illinois and a number of blacks in Memphis had gone to other schools," Iba added. "I went around and talked to the leaders of the community. . . . They were very skeptical about breaking the color barrier. But as time went on, everything worked out."

Memphis was a racially torn city in the early 1970s, but the Tiger basketball team brought it together. "After Finch and Robinson came to Memphis State, the whole city came together," said Lee Hunt, who was an assistant coach under Gene Bartow in the early 1970s. "Ronnie and Finch were great ambassadors. . . . Winning solves a lot of problems in a lot of areas."

In the case of the Drake basketball team, which made the Final Four in 1969, it was the blending of black and white players on a team in a very conservative city that made for a great story.

In 2004, the Des Moines branch of the NAACP honored the 1968–69 Drake team, which included four African American players and an African American assistant coach, the late Gus Guydon, who was generally considered to be the first in Division I. "The older I get, the more appreciate it," said former Drake player Willie McCarter. "The only thing white in my high school was the chalk. What happened was he (Maury John) convinced three blacks from Gary, Ind., from an inner-city school to go to Des Moines, Iowa. . . . And what he did, he wouldn't let us isolate ourselves. He integrated us with roommates. My best friend other than Dolph is Dale Teeter (who was white). . . . That whole environment made a difference in my total life. It has made a total difference in the way I live my life and think."

Official
PROGRAM
SEVENTEENTH ANNUAL

DRAKE RELAYS

DRAKE STADIUM
APRIL 23-24, 1926

PRICE 25 CENTS

DRAKE RELAYS

Really, it is a very impressive story. From a forgettable, misadventurous beginning, the Drake Relays grew in stature, size and prestige until it became one of America's top two annual track and field spectacles.

Long-time Drake Relays Director, Bob Ehrhart

A TRACK AND FIELD SPECTACLE

But, first things first. Born in a surprise blizzard in 1910 on the morning of the meet, the event was snowbound before a race was run. Many schools that were to participate couldn't get to Des Moines. Scrambling, meet officials filled out the field with a few athletes from area colleges and high schools, Drake University students, and runners from a Sunday School class at a church located near the campus. Spectators numbered a stone cold 100.

You've heard it said: What doesn't kill you, makes you stronger. Drake tried again in 1911 and saw success. And so . . . from Jesse Owens to Wilma Rudolph, from Al Oerter to Jim Ryun, from Jim Duncan to Clyde Duncan, the Relays have built a legacy that places them among the crown jewels of the Missouri Valley Conference.

Nowadays, the Relays simply laugh at the capricious swings of late-spring weather that can hit Des Moines on an April weekend. Why? Because like death and taxes, the show goes on, no matter what. If it rains, bring your umbrella. If the day dawns cold and raw, bundle up. But April in Des Moines means Drake Relays and this much is fact: Everybody is going to be there.

1911 Drake Relays

Ask Paul Morrison Drake's historian. To the Drake family, Morrison will always be the one who wears the "D." He saw his first Drake Relays in 1934 and he draws on decades of memories. In retrospect, he told the *Des Moines Register*: "The weather didn't stop the Drake Relays in 1910 and from then on, it was a great event."

The Relays are the state of Iowa's signature sports event. They share with the Penn Relays the lofty position as the nation's premier annual track and field carnivals. Beyond that, the Drake Relays are neatly and forever stitched into the fabric of Des Moines and Iowa. The West Coast long held forth as the mecca of track and field, but the Drake Relays own a certain charm—a comfortable Midwest feel—and spectators as well as athletes love it.

If you live in Iowa, you embrace the Relays for another reason. They signal that spring is stirring and it's time to put another winter to rest—happily, by the way. Winters in Iowa can turn harsh. Over the years, spectators have seen a roll-call of world and collegiate track and field greats, not to mention Iowa high school athletes and even an array of runners from Des Moines elementary schools. The 2006 Relays drew more than 8,000 athletes from 720 teams in 25 states who competed in 112 events. There were 78 foreign nations represented in the field.

Wilma Rudolph

In 1935, Jesse Owens, then a sophomore at Ohio State, made his only competitive appearance at Drake. He set an American long jump record of 26 feet 1 inches and the next day tied the Relays record in the 100 in 9.5 seconds. In those days, the 100 was run in yards, not meters as it is today. In 1936, the Olympic Games were staged in Berlin. They were to be Hitler's tour de force, but Owens ran circles around Hitler and emerged as a worldwide hero after he won the 100, the 200, and the long jump.

Drake welcomed another Olympic hero in 1961. It was tall and willowy Wilma Rudolph who, as Owens did in 1936, captured the world's hearts with a fantastic Olympics in Rome in 1960. At Drake, she ran an invitational 100 and, from the moment she stepped on the track in her blue sweats with USA in large red and white lettering on the front, all eyes were on her, and not just because she was about to become the first female to run at the Relays. She was a Tennessee State Tiger Belle and she was special. Morrison remembers it as though it were yesterday, how the packed stadium fell silent, almost solemn, as Wilma settled into the starting blocks.

"I've never heard it be as quiet as it was for the start of that race," says Morrison.

It was a neat moment in Relays history. Over time, many unforgettable moments were etched in the memories of spectators and athletes alike thanks to Professor Jim Duncan, who was the meet announcer from 1963 to 1988.

Duncan was perhaps the best track and field announcer in the country. He had an amazing memory for names, times, and distances and he knew the sport inside and out. Besides that, he was a pretty good quartermiler in his day, good enough that he won the MVC 440 title in 51.5 seconds as a junior at Drake University, where he was a Phi Beta Kappa scholar. For 31 years, he served as head of the school's radio department.

Perched on his wooden stand at the Relays near the finish line, microphone in his left hand and statistics and notes in his right hand, Duncan kept the crowd informed during races in his crisp, incisive voice about who and what they needed to know.

There was magic in the way he made the races come alive. As the runners hurried down the backstretch, around the final turn and into the homestretch, the crowd noise would rise. Duncan would pull people right out of their seats cheering and clapping with his soul-stirring play-by-play of a race. Athletes who competed at the Relays would talk years later about how they got chills hearing Duncan's voice when they ran and how they could feel the crowd and why, because of him, the Relays were their favorite event of the year.

THE OLYMPIC GAMES—IN COLOR

'DAY OF INFAMY' II: WAR BRINGS
HAVOC AND HEROISM TO PEARL HARBOR

LIFE

BOBBY MORROW, OLYMPIC SPRINT CHAMP

20 CENTS

DECEMBER 10, 1956

Jesse Owens

Clyde Duncan, not related to Jim Duncan, was a hotshot high school sprinter at Des Moines North who in 1964 stunned the crowd with a wind-aided 9.3 in the 100. He later ran at Texas Southern and is a member of the Relays Athletes Hall of Fame. Speaking of high schools, North made its mark in Relays archives with its relay teams and a quartet of runners nicknamed "The Flying Four."

No one who was on hand on a brisk, biting, rainy day in 1956 will ever forget the showdown at 100 yards, matching Abilene Christian's Bobby Morrow, the world's premier sprinter at the time, and Duke's Dave Sime. The track surface was cinders. Sime upset Morrow in 9.4 in what is still considered one of the great 100 duels of all time, anyplace, anywhere.

Morrow was unbeaten in 30 straight 100 races until he met Sime, who had gone to Duke on a baseball scholarship. A brilliant sprinter, Morrow was known as "the kid from the cotton patch" (his family lived on a cotton farm in the Rio Grande Valley in Texas). Later in 1956, at the Melbourne Olympics, Morrow won the 100, 200, and anchored the winning U.S. 4x100-yard relay team. An injury cost Sime a berth in the 1956 Olympics.

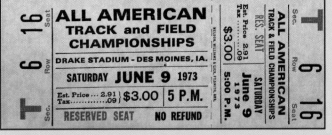

Sime was a silver medalist in the 100 at the 1960 Olympics in Rome. Both Morrow and Sime are enshrined in the Relays Athletes Hall of Fame.

If you look and listen, you'll discover the Relays ghosts and hear the echoes in every hallowed corner of Drake Stadium. There's Glenn Cunningham, Ralph Metcalfe, Harrison Dillard, Cornelius Warmerdam, Jackson Scholz, Ted Wheeler, Parry O'Brien, George Kerr, Ralph Boston, Bob Hayes, Bruce Jenner, Frank Shorter, Randy Wilson, Debbie Esser, Michael Johnson, J.W. Mashburn, Jim Lavery, Merlene Ottey, Mal Whitfield, Wes Santee, Fred Wolcott, Don Lash, Jeremy Wariner, Suzy Favor Hamilton, Joey Woody, Danny Harris, Holli Hyche, Don Laz, Al Feuerbach, Kenyan Mike Boit, Caesar Smith, Don Gerhmann, and so many more.

Four Southern Illinois University athletes are in the Hall of Fame: Ivory Crockett (100), Mike Franks (400), Bob Roggy (javelin), and Connie Price-Smith (shot and discus).

About those Relays ghosts and echoes: In 1970, Brigham Young's Ralph Mann won the 400 hurdles. Later that year,

April 28-29, 1978
Drake Stadium
Des Moines, Iowa
Two Dollars

Jim Duncan
Voice of the Relays
—See inside story—

Former Drake SID, Paul Morrison, 1938

Drake played host to the NCAA Championships and Mann won the event again, but faster yet in a world record clocking of 48.8 seconds. When he finished the race and heard his time, he dropped to the track and kissed it.

Jim Ryun, a Kansas sophomore in 1967, clocked a 3:59.1 anchor mile in the four-mile relay. It was the first sub-4-minute mile in 58 years of Relays competition.

In 1957, Wilt Chamberlain, already a basketball legend at Kansas, won the high jump at Drake. In 1979, Steve Scott fought through chilly wind gusts of 32 miles an hour to win the open mile in 3:55.2, a Relays record. And how about Carl Lewis? The day he was to run at the Relays, it sleeted. Olympic legends like Lewis could have said "no thanks, too dangerous to run." Instead, Lewis helped shovel the track and ran anyway, endearing himself to Relays fans. And how about this? The Relays provided a path to the White House for Ronald Reagan, who in 1934 broadcast live the event as a staff announcer at WHO radio in Des Moines. You can look it up.

In 2006, Drake unveiled a $17 million update of the stadium. The centerpiece is a $2.5 million Mondo rubberized track that is fast. The field was named for Drake football legend Johnny Bright. The renovation, careful to keep Relays history and tradition, was needed so that Drake can bid for NCAA and U.S. National meets and maybe even Olympic Trials.

What does the future hold? The Relays are in good hands. Brian Brown, one of the world's preeminent high jumpers in the late 1990s, was named Relays director in 2006, following in the footsteps of long-time meet director, Bob Ehrhart.

Brown's wife, Natasha Kaiser-Brown, a Des Moines product and twice an Olympian, is the Drake track and field coach. In 1989, she established an NCAA indoor record in the 400. In 1993, she was ranked second in the world in the 400. She competed in 16 Drake Relays.

—Dave Dorr

Jim Ryun, first runner to break the 4-minute mile, competes at the Drake Relays

Enter Thru SUBWAY

CONTESTANT
• DRAKE
BEWARE!
NON-TRANSFERABLE
DO NOT SELL OR TRANSFER THIS TICKET
Void if presented by anyone other than the bona-fide contestant to whom issued
• SAT., APRIL 24, 1948 •
No. 0808

ADMISSION
RELAYS •
FRIDAY
• APRIL 23, 1948 •

Enter Thru SUBWAY

DRAKE UNIVERSITY
1881-1981
Our 100th Year

April 24-25 • Drake Stadium • Des Moines, Iowa • Two Dollars

here we go
Bulldogs,
here we go..

DRAKE

Founded in 1881 by George T. Carpenter, a preacher, and Francis Marion Drake, a Civil War general, Drake has been a member of the Missouri Valley Conference since 1907, although they withdrew from the conference from 1951 to 1955 after the Johnny Bright incident—a deliberate on-field attack on Drake's star football player in a game at Oklahoma A&M that never led to consequences for the attacker. Drake moved to NCAA Division I-AA nonscholarship in football in 1996 and is now a member of the Pioneer Football League.

Bulldog basketball reached its zenith in the late 1960s, under the leadership of Coach Maury John. Drake's highly athletic team went toe-to-toe in the 1969 NCAA Final Four against a UCLA juggernaut led by Lew Alcindor.

THE MAURY JOHN YEARS AND THE 1969 NCAA RUN

For more than three decades, Drake's Al Williams has remembered those final, frantic seconds against UCLA and center Lew Alcindor in the 1969 NCAA Final Four semifinals at Louisville's Freedom Hall. "One or two plays here or there and we would have won the national championship," said Williams, a former 6-5 forward-center for the Bulldogs. "We weren't overachievers. We underachieved on the basis of one game. No one expected us to challenge UCLA like we did . . . but no one on our team was satisfied we played it close or were in the Final Four. We felt we should have won it all."

Drake was a heavy underdog and such an unknown that announcer Curt Gowdy called the Bulldogs "Duke" several times during the national telecast of the semifinal game. Had Drake pulled off the upset of the Bruins and eventually won the NCAA title, a Hollywood screenplay probably would have been written about this unlikely cast of characters. But the top-ranked Bruins prevailed, 85–82, after a dramatic Drake comeback from a nine-point deficit with less than two minutes remaining. Drake pulled within a point, 83–82, with seconds left when forward Dolph Pulliam, despite contact, put in a rebound basket off an errant Willie McCarter jump shot from the left corner. Years later, some Drake players say the score could have been tied and the game gone into overtime if a foul had been called.

"From my vantage point, he (Pulliam) was fouled," McCarter said. "I grabbed the ball and someone grabbed me," Pulliam said of his rebound basket. "But the ball went in. I fell. He (the official) says no foul. I have no idea who grabbed me.

John celebrates a victory

Maury John

Everything was moving so fast. I just wanted to get that shot up."

After Pulliam's basket, the ball was inbounded by the Bruins, and the Bulldogs quickly fouled Lynn Shackelford, who made two free throws as time ran out for the final margin.

Two days later, Drake overwhelmed North Carolina, 104–84, in the consolation game before UCLA thumped Purdue, 92–72, in the title game. UCLA's victory over the Boilermakers was so decisive Bruin fans began chanting during the game, "Drake's No. 2." Drake fans retorted, from across the way: "We're No. 1 1/2." Resourceful Coach Maury John had proven a point with a unique group of players at Drake, a small private MVC school in Des Moines. He would follow up the 1969 Final Four appearance with two NCAA regional final finishes in 1970 and 1971 before leaving to coach at nearby Iowa State.

Al Williams shoots a baseline jumper

Dolph Pulliam takes a charge

Through the 2005–06 season, John is still the only coach in Missouri Valley Conference history to be named the league's basketball coach of the year three straight seasons (1968–70).

JOHN BLENDED PLAYERS, ROLES

Formerly coach of Moberly (Mo.) Junior College, John blended black, inner-city recruits and Iowa's small-town white kids into a team. He was one of the first major-college coaches to utilize junior college players in his pressure defense and up-tempo style of game.

"He was a great Xs and Os guy," said his son, Dr. Maurice John. "He was creative. He was a great teacher and had to take players and make them better by the time they were finished. He had to be great at recruiting, conditioning, and motivating. His goal was to get it close the last few minutes and have a chance to win. . . . He lived for overtime."

Willie McCarter on the defense

When John took over the Drake program in 1958–59, one of his assistants coached baseball in the spring. The Drake basketball budget was so small, John initially had to stay at alumni homes when recruiting. Prior to John becoming coach, the Drake Bulldogs had never been to a postseason tournament, nor appeared on national television, nor made the Associated Press Top 10.

Five years later under John, Drake ended a 25-year drought and claimed a share of the MVC men's basketball title with a slow, plodding team uncharacteristic of the way John liked to coach. The Bulldogs lost a playoff game to MVC co-champion Wichita State but still went to the National Invitation Tournament and split two games.

By 1969, Drake was a good shooting team made up of small, quick, and athletic players. Coach John threw on a press even the fabled Bruins couldn't handle. Drake almost pushed the game into overtime. "UCLA had never seen a team as quick as we were," Pulliam said. "UCLA's press was known to destroy teams. They thought their press

Maury John during a Bulldog timeout

would break our spirits. But Willie Wise (also 6-5) and myself ruled the backboards and they hadn't seen a team press them. We hadn't received a lot of TV exposure. They didn't know a lot about us."

It was a close-knit group bent on winning, and they played under the radar of most media and national television.

In the late 1960s, John had created a family atmosphere among white and black players during a turbulent time in race relations in the United States. "It was the time of a lot of controversy across the country," said Williams, who was black. "Drake didn't have a lot of problems, not any on campus."

John recruited Pulliam out of the inner city of Gary, Ind., and Pulliam finally convinced John to take his fellow Roosevelt High School classmate, Willie McCarter, who was an undersized but talented sixth-man on the team. McCarter only received a scholarship from Drake his freshman season when another player from back East failed to qualify before school started. McCarter was headed to junior college. "We didn't even know there was a Missouri Valley Conference. No idea," said Pulliam. "I liked him

(John), and my brothers and sisters liked him. He said he would take care of me and I would graduate in four years with a degree I could use. My brothers and sisters said, 'You are going to Drake.'"

Back on the floor, John made sure all players, black or white, knew their roles. "He was able to sell his way of play and get people to buy into it," said another son, John John, who later played for his father at Iowa State. "He never had the greatest All-Americas. He was always scrambling to get the next tier of players and develop them. "It worked. He was a good judge of character, and they all knew their roles . . . cheerleader, captain of defense, captain of offense, captain of rebounding."

Pulliam was considered the captain of John's famed "belly-button defense." John had convinced a reluctant Pulliam to become the team's defensive stopper during his sophomore season, and down the stretch of the 1968–69 season, there was no better defensive player in college basketball. In a game against Louisville that season, Cardinals Coach John Dromo attempted to move All-American Butch

McCarter driving the lane against the Bruins

Beard from forward to guard to get him away from Pulliam. John countered by moving Pulliam outside. Pulliam remembers this exchange on the court. "Beard said, 'What are you doing out here?'" Pulliam recalled. "I said, 'I am guarding you tonight. Where you go, I go.'"

"There wasn't a player he couldn't cover," said Rick Wanamaker, a reserve center on the 1968–69 Drake team. "His shoes would tear apart. He would go through a pair in a game or less. He had big feet and big hands, and he just pounded the floor. He was not a glider."

McCarter, who later went on to play for the Los Angeles Lakers, was captain of the Drake offense, but he also improved as an all-around player in the drive to the 1969 Final Four. "He became a complete basketball player," John said during the 1968–69 season. "If Willie (McCarter) can't get a shot, he knows how to get it to somebody who can shoot."

Dolph Pulliam

Willie Wise, a 6-5 senior forward who also played in the ABA and NBA, was a captain of rebounding along with Williams. But he could do it all. "He was so well-rounded," Wanamaker said. "In my entire career I never blocked one of his shots, and I tried in practice every day. No defensive player had the patience to block his shot because he would fake until he got an opening."

There was even a captain of the bench, reserve Dale Teeter, who was responsible for cheerleading. "It was Coach John's way of giving all of us some value," McCarter said. "None of us was slighted in any way. . . . If we lost, we all had to look at our own areas to see what was going wrong."

MEETING TURNED 1968–69 SEASON AROUND

Drake was unranked most of the 1968–69 season and only rose to No. 11 in the final Associated Press poll. The Bulldogs basically faced a sudden-death situation in the MVC in late January after losing two straight league games and falling three games behind first-place Tulsa. "The likelihood of us going to the NCAA was not very good if we lost one more game," Pulliam said. In those days only the MVC's regular-season champion advanced to the NCAA Tournament.

Willie Wise lays it up

At a players-only meeting after a devastating 118–99 loss to North Texas State in Denton on Jan. 30, the season turned around. Drake won its next 12 games before losing to UCLA in the Final Four. "He (John) wasn't in the meeting," McCarter said. "We hammered each other harder than he ever did."

After the team meeting, the Bulldogs reversed road losses to Louisville and North Texas by beating the Cardinals by 34 points and the Eagles by 15 in Des Moines. Drake also won back-to-back-to-back road games at Bradley, Wichita State, and Tulsa.

During the winning streak, John moved Williams, who had greatly improved his defensive rebounding, into the starting lineup. It meant Drake had one of the shorter lineups in the Missouri Valley Conference with the 6-5 Wise moving to center replacing 6-8 Garry Odom, but what the Drake Bulldogs gave up in size they gained in quickness and athleticism.

Drake tied with Louisville for the MVC title. In order to go to the NCAA Tournament, the Bulldogs still had to beat Louisville again in a single-game playoff in Wichita.

Earlier in the season, a brawl with racial overtones had erupted in Louisville when the two teams played. Drake's Williams and Louisville's Marv Selvy scuffled in the closing minutes of Louisville's 84–79 victory. But for a second straight game between the two teams there were no incidents. With all five starters scoring in double figures, the Bulldogs responded with their 10th straight victory, 77–73. "We were in the mentality, we couldn't lose anyway," McCarter said.

Drake got past Texas A&M in the first round of the NCAA Tournament, 81–63, and then faced Colorado State in the regional final in Manhattan, Kan. John had announced to the team that if the Bulldogs beat Colorado State he would take care of ("all by himself") Lew Alcindor and UCLA, which was seeking its fifth NCAA title in six seasons. John's psychology worked. Drake defeated Colorado State, 84–77, to become the sixth MVC team in the decade to advance to the Final Four. When the Bulldogs showed up back in Des Moines for pre–Final Four practice, John got the team's attention when he showed up uncharacteristically in a suit and tie. "Gather round. I will tell you how we will defeat UCLA," John said. The Bulldogs would play their game, which was UCLA's game—run and press—and they wouldn't double- or triple-team Alcindor. They would play him straight up.

"We thought we were better than they were," Wanamaker said. "We were probably better. We were faster, better on defense, and usually better shooters than in that game. . . . But that was a good policy. Why take away our strength, running and defense. We played regular Drake basketball."

Drake very well could have won had two things not happened. The Bulldogs didn't figure UCLA guard John Vallely, an 11-point scorer, would manage 29 points, and the Bulldogs, who shot 46.7 percent on the season, missed 51 shots (32 for 83). "I have always felt I let the team down," McCarter said. "I missed an awful lot of shots (17). And that had nothing to do with Kareem (Alcindor). I was shooting jumpers."

Eleven points separated Drake from three straight Final Four appearances from 1969 to 1971.

MAKING TWO MORE RUNS
Drake was back in the NCAA Tournament the following season without McCarter, Pulliam, or Wise. In 1970, Drake won its first MVC outright men's basketball title in 61 years, as John revamped his offense and reloaded with several junior college players.

Six-foot guard Bobby Jones (Paducah, Ky.), 6-5 forward Jeff Halliburton (San Jacinto College, Tex.), and 6-7 Tom Bush (College of Southern Idaho) were the hub of Drake's 1-4 offense, which ran through Halliburton, the MVC's 1970 field goal percentage champion.

The Bulldogs, ranked No. 19 in the preseason, started the season 5–4 and finished sixth in the Rainbow Classic. But they won their first 10 MVC games and beat Cincinnati by two full games in the league race.

Drake fell one step short of the Final Four when it lost to Coach Lou Henson's New Mexico State team, led by eventual NBA players Sam Lacey, Jimmy Collins, and Charley Criss, 87–78, in the 1970 NCAA Midwest Regional final. "Coach John adjusted to his talent," Wanamaker said. "Things changed and we became more of a half-court team. Defense was still the emphasis, but we didn't run as much. Jeff Halliburton would go one-on-one through the whole defense and take them on."

Rick Wanamaker battles Lew Alcindor

1969 Drake Bulldogs

Front Row, Left to Right:
Dan Callahan, Maurice John,
Gus Guydon.
Middle Row, Left to Right:
Gary Zeller, Ron Gwin, Dolph Pulliam, Willie
McCarter, Al Sakys, Don Draper,
Bob Mast, Dave Wicklund.
Back Row, Left to Right:
Dale Teeter, Willie Wise, Jim Nordrum, Rick
Wanamaker, Larry Sharp,
Garry Odom, Jim O'Dea, Al Williams.

The Captains — Al Williams and Gary Zeller

DRAKE
BASKETBALL

Drake University Basketball Guide

A year later with basically the same team, Drake tied Louisville for the 1971 MVC crown, beat the Cardinals in a one-game playoff, and eventually fell to Kansas—by two points—in the 1971 Midwest Regional final.

A first-round 79–72 NCAA Tournament victory over Notre Dame in 1971 remains vivid in Maury John's son John John's mind. He still has a tape of that game in which the Fighting Irish's Austin Carr was held to 26 points. Carr, who had averaged 52.2 points in four previous NCAA games over two seasons, made only 11 of 27 shots with Jones covering his every move. "I remember Drake had three starters who fouled out," John John said. "We had three reserves in the game who were not recruited by anybody and we were still winning. I remember before the game, dad asked who would guard Carr, and Jones said he would. And he basically shut him down by denying him the ball. It was all about getting the right players who my dad convinced if they played hard, 'you will win, trust me.'"

John left several marks on the Drake program. He still has the top five winning

Rick Wanamaker and Lew Alcindor battle for a rebound

seasons in school history, the school's only three NCAA Tournament appearances, and the single Final Four trip. "My dad said that 1969 team was one of the greatest pleasures of his life," John John said. "It was easy to coach."

LEWIS LLOYD

Drake's Lewis Lloyd eventually became a two-time Missouri Valley Conference Player of the Year selection in 1980 and 1981, but in 1979, Drake Coach Bob Ortegel was told he would never land the 6-6, 215-pound Lloyd, a Philadelphian who was starring at New Mexico Military Institute. "Ted Owens of Kansas told me, 'Coach, there is no way you are going to get this kid,'" Ortegel recalled. 'You really need to concentrate on those kids you can get.' That just infuriated me."

While recruiting Lloyd, Ortegel traveled to Roswell, N.M., and watched him march around the track at 5:30 a.m. "And they'd go to breakfast and get this discipline stuff," Ortegel recalled. "There I was. . . . I wanted this kid to know I really wanted him."

Ortegel's persistence eventually won over Lewis Lloyd, who was an instant star in Des Moines. In his first major-college season, 1979–80, Lloyd finished second nationally with 30.2 points and 15.0 rebounds a contest.

"He (Lloyd) had such a great belief in himself," Ortegel said. "He had self-confidence without being an egomaniac. We were playing at Oral Roberts (his senior season) and we had the ball for the last shot. I knew where the ball was going. There wasn't any doubt in my mind when I took the time out. . . . He came over to me, and said, 'Hey coach.' I said, 'I know, Lewis, we are going to give you the ball, but I don't think they are going to let you get inside. They are going to run at you on the dribble.' So we made the pass inbounds, he just turned and took the shot and he followed the ball through the air. The ball went in the basket, and he ran right up the tunnel into the locker room."

Drake had beaten ORU, 97–95, in overtime during the 1980–81 season when Lloyd led the MVC in scoring (26.3 ppg, fourth nationally) and still averaged 10.0 rebounds a game.

Lewis Lloyd is one of only five players in MVC history to score 800 or more points in a season. Oscar

Lewis Lloyd

Robertson (1958–60) and Larry Bird (1977–79) did it three times each. Hersey Hawkins (1988) and Xavier McDaniel (1985) are the others.

JOHNNY BRIGHT: AN MVC PROFILE IN COURAGE

Drake's Johnny Bright dared to win the Heisman Trophy in 1951 and make history. It was a feat African Americans such as Bright, a native of Fort Wayne, Ind., had never dreamed possible growing up in a segregated sports society.

Bob Ortegel

However, Bright, a 6-foot, 215-pound senior in Drake's single-wing offense, was riding high going into a game against Oklahoma A&M on Oct. 20, 1951. Bright led the country in total offense as the unbeaten Bulldogs prepared to play the Aggies in a Missouri Valley Conference game in Stillwater, Okla.

Two seasons earlier, Bright, a marvelous all-around athlete who starred in track, basketball, football, and softball, was the first African American football player to play at Lewis Field. The 1949 game, when Bright was a sophomore, had been won by the Aggies without incident, 28–0.

This victory was before Bright had developed a reputation as a dazzling running back. He led the nation in total offense in 1949, with 1,950 yards (the first sophomore to do so), and again in 1950, with 2,400 yards. "We played the single wing. His hands were on the ball most plays," said Bright's Drake teammate, Nick Manloes. "We had tremendous respect for John. He was a great passer as well as a runner. He could run well right or left, and he could accelerate. He knew how to let the holes open in front of him."

The Oklahoma A&M defense was bent on stopping Bright from the first play in the game according to long-time Drake University historian and Sports Information Director Paul Morrison. "I was in the press box sitting next to Maury White, who was covering the game for *The Register*," said Morrison. "And to me it was very obvious from the start they were out to get John after the first two or three plays of the game. He had a bad habit of after getting rid of the ball, just standing there and watching the play develop, and he got slugged several times. In fact, right away I turned to Maury and said, 'Boy, they are really getting to John.'"

Other teammates noticed it as well. Bright was complaining when he came back to the huddle.

And well he should have been. On the very first play Bright's jaw had been broken when Oklahoma A&M lineman Wilbanks Smith delivered a forearm to Bright's face, which was not protected by a face mask in that era. Because the incident had occurred away from the play—Bright had stepped back after handing the ball to fullback Gene Macomber—the officials did not see the forearm shiver, and thus did not call a 15-yard penalty.

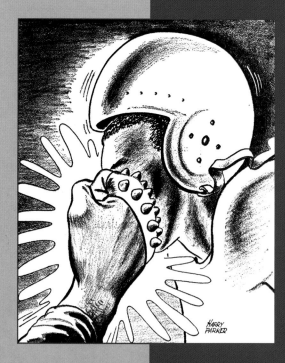

In fact, after picking himself off the ground, Bright threw a 61-yard touchdown pass on the next play. Two more times Smith knocked Bright to the ground after he had handed off the ball. When he was swarmed by a group of tacklers, Bright finally had to leave the game for good. Oklahoma A&M eventually won, 27–14.

"We did not know he was seriously hurt until halftime," said Drake teammate Keith Burgett. And no one might really have known what had happened had two *Des Moines Register* photographers, Don Ultang and John Robinson, not captured Smith's forearms to the jaw on film. The two had flown to Stillwater as an assignment for the "Big Peach" coverage of Saturday's college football games long before on-site transmission of photos.

Ultang actually was the pilot, and he was instructed to take pictures early in the game, hop into the plane, pilot it back to Des Moines, develop the pictures, and get them into the Sunday paper. Ultang and Robinson didn't even know what they had on the film as they traveled back to Des Moines from Stillwater. They only knew that Bright had been roughed up early in the game.

Bright at practice

"We went into our respective rooms," Ultang said of when they arrived at the paper. "The picture editor was leaning over my shoulder as the negative was clearing. I can see an elbow in Bright's jaw. That's the first we knew we had nailed it. . . . I just said to the picture editor, 'I think we got it.' Then he said, 'But do you have anything more?'"

Ultang and Robinson had enough to win a Pulitzer Prize for a sequence of pictures published in *The Register* on Oct. 21, 1951, which showed Smith stalking and eventually savagely hitting Bright.

Outrage ensued once the paper depicted the hit, which ended Bright's Heisman bid. Life ran the photos as well, and the story was picked up nationally. Bright had to have his jaw wired shut and eat through a straw. He played in only one more college game and finished fifth in the 1951 Heisman Trophy balloting.

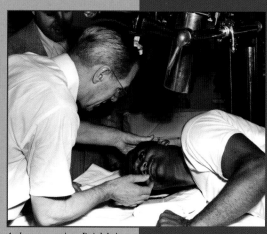

A doctor examines Bright's jaw

"We knew it was bad when he had to come out," Manoles said. "I had a feeling it was a combination of being both (being black and

Johnny Bright

a star). He was one of the first to play in the stadiums in the South. We had only three or four blacks on our team, and he was the star."

Manoles said Bright often had to stay in different quarters because of Jim Crow. "We would travel by train and some of the times he would have to stay at the porters' quarters at the top of the hotel," Manoles said. "We felt badly about it. He would say, 'Don't shed any tears for me. The porters will take care of me.' And he would get them tickets for the games."

Bright, who accounted for nearly 6,000 yards in his Drake career, was inducted into the College Football Hall of Fame posthumously in 1984. And the Heisman Trophy? An African American wouldn't win it until more than a decade after Bright played college football, in 1961, when Ernie Davis of Syracuse captured the trophy from the Downtown Athletic Club of New York City.

Burgett said Bright, who passed away in 1983 of a heart attack during elective knee surgery, told him he believed the hit was racially motivated. "He believed it," Burgett said. "And I believed it—it was racially motivated."

F. A. Dry, who was a center on the Oklahoma A&M team, disagreed. "They tried to make it a racial incident," Dry said. "But that was not on anybody's mind. I imagine a majority of Oklahoma A&M's kids were part Indian. We had full-bloods on the team. I don't think it ever entered anybody's mind. It didn't enter my mind."

Oklahoma A&M Coach J. B. Whitworth wrote letters of apology to both Bright and Drake Coach Warren Gaer, but he never took any disciplinary action against Smith, who has refused to talk about the incident in recent years. The MVC never took any action, either. The MVC's first commissioner, Arthur Eilers, actually was in the press box at the game in Stillwater. "And I laugh about it," Morrison said. "When he was asked about it, he said he was in the restroom. And he didn't see it."

In 1952, Drake dropped out of the MVC, and Bradley followed because the MVC took no action over the incident. Both schools rejoined the MVC in 1955 in sports other than football. Meanwhile, the NCAA Football Rules Committee instituted a new penalty after the Bright incident. The NCAA changed the penalty for striking with "forearm, elbow or locked hands or for flagrantly rough play or unsportsmanlike conduct from 15 yards to mandatory suspension."

Sequential images on right photographed by Des Moines Register *photographers John Robinson and Don Ultang. As quoted in the November 5, 1951 issue of* Life Magazine, *"What happened was that (Wilbanks) Smith smashed a right cross to Bright's jaw that broke it. "I knew it was broken the first play," says Bright. "I felt it bust." Knocked flat, Bright got up and on the next play threw a pass for a touchdown. First chance he got after Bright's touchdown pass, Smith came piling in again. Bright was 10 yards out of the play and, like the referree, was watching the ball carrier when Smith slugged him again. He got up, but on next play, had to be helped off the field. He could only last a total of 10 plays. Drake lost 27–14.*

Bright, Jaw Broken, Drake Streak Ends, 27-14

JOHNNY HURT ON FIRST PLAY, THEN HURLS SCORING PASS (STORY: PAGE 8)

OKLAHOMA A&M

OKLAHOMA A&M GLORY DAYS

A&M changed its name to
State in 1957. The school
ber of the Missouri Valley
e from 1925 to 1957 and was
use on the basketball court.
Coach Henry Iba brought
ck NCAA championships to
in 1945 and 1946 behind the
f 7-footer Bob Kurland.

COACH HENRY IBA & BOB KURLAND

In 1934, Oklahoma A&M may have made the coaching hire
of the 20th century. Little did officials know at the Missouri
Valley Conference school in Stillwater, Okla., the summon-
ing of Coach Henry Iba from the University of Colorado
helped shape the future of the league. Iba's man-to-man defense and
motion offense were years ahead of most other innovations in college
basketball and were the trademarks of Iba's teams that won or shared
six MVC championships between 1935 and 1942. Iba's basketball
knowledge, combined with his genuine personality and his down-to-
earth philosophy on life, made him an early giant of the game.

"He got the players to accept the way they would have to play to
win," said Moe Iba, his son, who played for his father and later

Henry Iba's 1946 Aggies team with 7-footer Bob Kurland in third row behind Iba

Henry Iba directs traffic on the court

Henry Iba, the elder statesman

"WELL --
Seven-foot Bob Kurland, star of the Oklahoma A and M cage team who makes split-second decisions on the floor, puzzles over an answer to Radio Announcer Larry Ray, of Kansas City, Mo., when interviewed after he had sparked the Aggies to a 44-29 victory over Baylor University in the Western NCAA playoffs at Kansas City March 22.

ASSOCIATED PRESS PHOTO

Bob Kurland gains national exposure

coached at Memphis, Nebraska, and TCU. "And then, I think, his basketball knowledge and what they did was probably a little ahead of its time. . . . The other thing was hard work. When he first started coaching you could coach kids year-round. He would bring in 40 to 50 players and just work, work, work and find out who would want to play. His communication with players and coaches was fantastic because he took the time to make you understand what you were trying to do basketball-wise."

Iba's teams were among the best defensive squads in the MVC and the most disciplined on offense. "He recruited players who enjoyed doing that," said Chuck Orsborn, a Bradley player in the late 1930s and later the Braves' coach.

With the addition of one towering recruit, Oklahoma A&M became nationally known in the mid-1940s. Iba's recruitment of gangly, 7-footer Robert Kurland in 1943 from Jennings, Mo., a suburb of St. Louis, resulted in Oklahoma A&M's back-to-back NCAA titles in 1945 and 1946. Kurland's development at Oklahoma A&M also created the establishment of goaltending rules in college basketball and paved the way for a new era of big men in the game.

Kurland's development at Oklahoma A&M also created the establishment of goaltending rules in college basketball and paved the way for a new era of big men in the game.

"He was unusual," said Oklahoma A&M teammate Sam Aubrey. "There were not many big guys in that age. I was a center at 6-4, 6-5 as a sophomore, then Bob came in." Later nicknamed "Foothills," Kurland was recruited with little fanfare, as Iba sent him only a couple of letters. Kurland was attracted to Oklahoma A&M for three reasons. His high school coach knew of Iba as coach at Maryville Teachers College (later Northwest Missouri State). Kurland liked Oklahoma A&M's engineering program, and he was fearful the two prominent MVC basketball programs recruiting him in his backyard, Saint Louis University and Washington University, might drop their programs as World War II heated up. Saint Louis University actually did in 1943–44. Oklahoma A&M had announced it would continue its program without interruption.

1907 2007

105

100 YEARS OF ATHLETICS EXCELLENCE

Iba invited Kurland to Stillwater for dinner and a tryout. "He never had seen anything like me before," said Kurland, who was only developing as a player and was too tall to be drafted into the armed forces. "But he liked my attitude and said if I would stay in school, stay eligible and come to practice, 'I can get you a deal here for room, board and tuition.'"

Iba said at the time he didn't know if Kurland could play college basketball. He had resisted recruiting tall players previously because they were usually clumsy. "When they recruited him, nobody thought there was going to be any way he could play," said Moe Iba. "The one thing I can remember during that era, and being six years old, we had a back fence. And he came over one day. And, of course, I am little. Instead of climbing over the fence, he just stepped over it. I realized how big he was."

Considered a freak by some opposing coaches, Kurland played sparingly during his first two college seasons and was used as a defensive shot blocker, which forced a change in goaltending rules.

"I learned the game of basketball," said Kurland, who credits older Oklahoma A&M teammate Floyd Burdette tutoring him in those early years. Kurland would jump rope after practice to improve his agility and foot speed. And Iba's teams always trained by running. "It was real tough for him to run up and down the court, but he improved and improved," said Aggies' teammate A. L. Bennett.

KURLAND'S TOUGH BEGINNING

Kansas Coach Phog Allen had called players such as Kurland "glandular goons" when Kurland enrolled at Oklahoma A&M in the fall of 1942. And, when Kurland's Oklahoma A&M team played at Kansas during his freshman season, Iba spared the young Kurland from any embarrassment during a 36–29 loss to Allen's team. Oklahoma A&M finished the game with four players on the floor, although Kurland was sitting on the Oklahoma A&M bench and available to play.

"He knew my going into the game would not cause the game to change," Kurland said. "Mr. Iba was a wise man in recognizing the soft spot in a kid's head. . . . It didn't bother me. I knew I would have gotten my block knocked off."

The A&M
College Magazine

APRIL
1945
—o—
STILLWATER,
OKLAHOMA

Vol. XVII   No. 7

Kurland's development into a three-time MVC All-American came slowly, but it came to fruition under unique living and practicing circumstances. Kurland eventually wound up living in a room in Gallagher Arena with a trainer and another player after military troops took over the school's dorms, which helped his development as a player and a student. He could study right up until 15 minutes before practice and shower directly afterward. "He had access to the floor at all hours," Aubrey said. "And he utilized it. He shot the ball a lot." As part of Kurland's scholarship agreement, once he moved out of the dorms, he received an extra $10–12 cash. But he had to lock every window and door of Gallagher Hall before he went to bed each night, and before each practice, he had to sweep the floor, which would be dusty from military exercises performed there every day. "I would take two of those average-sized mops and put one in each hand," Kurland recalled from his winter home in Sanibel Island off Florida's Gulf Coast. "I should have had it patented. We would be millionaires by now. I never

1945 Aggies basketball team, left to right: Blake Williams, Weldon Kern, Joe Halbert, J. L. Parks and Bob Kurland

thought a thing about it," Kurland added about his janitorial tasks. "Really, that was part of his (Iba's) discipline. . . . It was his way of keeping me in line." The 1940s truly were a different era, when the game's stars were not yet coddled. Television had yet to take hold. MVC teams traveled mostly by car and train. And teams were only beginning to engage in intersectional regular-season competition.

During Kurland's sophomore and junior seasons, the MVC suspended basketball competition because of World War II. Oklahoma A&M played a schedule laced with the names of such military teams as Enid Air School, Tinker Field, Will Rogers AAF, and Pentathlon Military.

Players were coming and going from the war, including those on Oklahoma A&M's roster. However, Kurland was the bedrock of the program. He caused quite a stir during his sophomore season in a 14–11 victory at Oklahoma, which lost seven of eight games to Oklahoma A&M during Kurland's career. "At the time, he could slap the ball out of there," Iba told Bob Hammel of Indiana's *Bloomington Herald-Times* in a 1988 article. "Really and truly, I never did like it. But we used a 1-1-3 zone and we had a lot of low scores because they couldn't shoot over Bob."

Oklahoma Coach Bruce Drake, who was livid over that low-scoring game, was a member of the Basketball Rules Committee. Drake even had an official placed on a platform above the basket to study Kurland's shot-blocking. Kurland could swat away any shot as long as it was not in the cylinder.

By the beginning of the 1944–45 season, the rule was changed to prohibit any player from blocking a shot on its downward flight with a possibility of going in the basket. Kurland, however, had developed his offensive skills, and Oklahoma A&M began a two-year domination of college basketball in 1945 and 1946.

The stage already had been set by Iba for the Aggies to capitalize on Kurland's presence. Long before Kurland arrived, Iba, who doubled as the school's athletic director, had successfully convinced the Oklahoma A&M president that the school needed a new arena. In 1938, the first game was played at the new showcase, Gallagher Hall, which accommodated more than 6,000 fans and was dubbed the "Madison Square Garden of the Plains."

The Gallagher Hall scene also included one of the first organized student sections. Iba had Oklahoma A&M students dress in identical orange coats, sit together, and ring cowbells. "Gallagher was the biggest on-campus basketball facility west of the Mississippi River (at the time)," Moe Iba said. "People would drive from Oklahoma City and Tulsa to come to the games, and if you left your seat at half time, you could never get back to it."

On the road, the Aggies were quite a show as well, especially during the Kurland years. "Every year we went back East in December. It was ritual," Sam Aubrey said, even before Kurland arrived on the scene. "We were gone quite a bit. Mr. Iba was a friend of a guy back East who ran Madison Square Garden, Ned Irish."

Added Kurland: "Mr Iba had the idea the Midwest deserved recognition. . . . He wanted to spread the good word for the game. And the time I was in school, I was a major attraction."

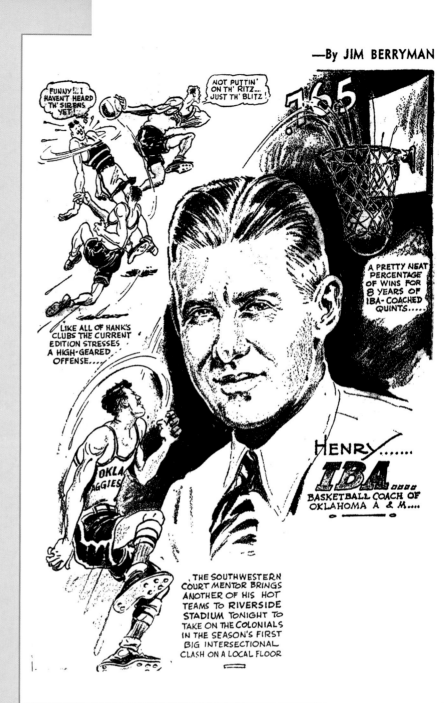

—By JIM BERRYMAN

FUNNY! I HAVEN'T HEARD TH' SIRENS YET!

NOT PUTTIN' ON TH' RITZ... JUST TH' BLITZ!

A PRETTY NEAT PERCENTAGE OF WINS FOR 8 YEARS OF IBA-COACHED QUINTS....

LIKE ALL OF HANK'S CLUBS THE CURRENT EDITION STRESSES A HIGH-GEARED OFFENSE...

HENRY....... IBA.... BASKETBALL COACH OF OKLAHOMA A & M....

OKLA. AGGIES

, THE SOUTHWESTERN COURT MENTOR BRINGS ANOTHER OF HIS HOT TEAMS TO RIVERSIDE STADIUM TONIGHT TO TAKE ON THE COLONIALS IN THE SEASON'S FIRST BIG INTERSECTIONAL CLASH ON A LOCAL FLOOR

AGGIES ON EASTERN SWINGS; KURLAND'S FIRST DUNK

During one of those swings East, Iba credited Kurland with the first dunk in a game during the mid-1940s against Temple in Philadelphia. Making the long treks East, traveling by rail, Kurland recalls rubbing elbows with the soldiers preparing to go to war. Some of those leaving were his own teammates and coaches: Aubrey (who was shot through the hip in Italy); A. L. Bennett (who fought in the Battle of the Bulge); and Floyd Burdette (an Air Force captain). "It was cramped and upsetting," Kurland said of the lengthy train rides. "Here we were 4-F, ineligible to be drafted and getting on a train with 500 soldiers who could get their butt shot off."

As World War II dragged on, more players were called up for military duty, and Kurland was Oklahoma A&M's only returning letterman in 1944–45. The Aggies, stout defensively, basically listened to Iba and rode the scoring of Kurland (17.1 ppg) and senior forward Cecil Hankins (13.3 ppg), who tripled as a track and football star.

"Mr. Iba was a difficult but brilliant teacher," Kurland said. "His secret for success was no secret at all. We were going to play the game his way. Players could have the wins. He would accept the losses. If we did it his way, we wouldn't lose many games. Iba convinced us in team sport the greatest sin was to fail to extend yourself to your full ability. . . . If I would wind up with 14–20 points, he (Iba) was tickled to death." Iba demanded balanced scoring, crisp passing, and no ball-hogging by individuals.

During Kurland's junior season, the Aggies lost just four games. One of those was a 48–46 February defeat at DePaul, which featured 6-10 skyscraper George Mikan, who was more of a scorer than Kurland. But that would be Oklahoma A&M's last loss of the 1944–45 season.

The Aggies, competing in their first NCAA Tournament in 1945, won three tournament games by allowing opposing teams an average of 41 points. Oklahoma A&M blew away defending NCAA champion Utah by 35 points in the first round and beat Arkansas, 68–41, for the third time in four seasonal meetings to reach the 1945 title game against New York University at Madison Square Garden. Bob Kurland out-dueled 16-year-old Dolph Schayes (22–6 in the scoring column) as Oklahoma A&M won, 49–45. Kurland claimed the first of two NCAA Tournament Most Outstanding Player awards by leading the tournament in scoring.

Two days following the 1945 NCAA title game, a special Red Cross Benefit Game at Madison Square Garden pitted Kurland against National Invitation Tournament champion DePaul and Mikan in a rematch of their regular-season game. This time Kurland got the better of Mikan, who fouled out after 14 minutes. Kurland outscored Mikan, 14–9, in the Aggies' 52–44 victory. Mikan and I were the two most prominent players in the United States," Kurland recalled. "The game, like most title games, was not worth a damn. Everybody was nervous and upset. And both of us, George and I, were tight. "They were calling a legitimate game. And George was a big strong guy who got away with whacking guys. George made mistakes. And I did, too. But I lasted longer than he did. And Cecil Hankins (scoring) saved our bacon."

The significance of Oklahoma A&M's victory was big because it established the NCAA champion on equal footing with the NIT titlist, which heretofore was considered superior. The win certainly helped shape the Kurland legacy. "I think (Kurland) was one of the greatest players to ever have played this game," said Saint Louis University and NBA star "Easy" Ed Macauley, comparing Kurland to Mikan. "Mikan's teams did not win the NCAA Tournament and he was not the leading scorer in the NCAA Tournament."

ANOTHER TITLE, 1946

Kurland said the 1945–46 Aggies were better than the previous year's edition, as several players, including Aubrey and Bennett returned after the war. The MVC

Coach Iba celebrates his first NCAA championship in 1945

resumed league competition, with Oklahoma A&M winning all 12 league games by double-digit margins. "Cecil Hankins was one of the best athletes to ever attend the university," Kurland said of one of the 1944–45 seniors. "Cecil, you could depend on for 12 to 15 points and the others would chip in 4-5-6-7 points. We had a good team my junior year. But my senior year, those guys you want to be in a foxhole with you. Those players left as boys and came back as men."

Certainly Aubrey had. He arrived back from Europe on crutches and could hardly walk, let alone run. But Iba kept his "scholarship" promise to Aubrey and the others who, along with Kurland, led Oklahoma A&M to a 31–2 overall record. "After our freshman seasons, Iba told those going off to war they would honor their scholarships," said Bennett, who played on the 1946 NCAA title team. "Well, looking back, it was kind of automatic after we came back."

Aubrey miraculously worked his way back into the lineup and wound up All-League. All five first-team All-MVC players (Kurland, Aubrey, J. L. Parks, Weldon Kern, Blake Williams) were from Oklahoma A&M. That is the only time one school has comprised the entire All-MVC first team.

Oklahoma A&M's only losses in 1945–46 were an early season 46–42 defeat to Mikan's DePaul team in Stillwater and to Bowling Green, 48–37, in Chicago, a day after the Aggies beat DePaul in a rematch. Kurland said several players became ill before the Bowling Green loss after eating some bad sauerkraut and pork chops.

Despite sailing through the MVC with a 12–0 record, Oklahoma A&M had to meet a 19–1 Kansas team and Coach Phog Allen in a district playoff game at Municipal Auditorium in Kansas City to qualify for the NCAA Tournament. Allen's earlier remarks about Kurland came back into play, although Kurland admits years later they became friends when Kurland was on the 1952 U.S. Olympic team

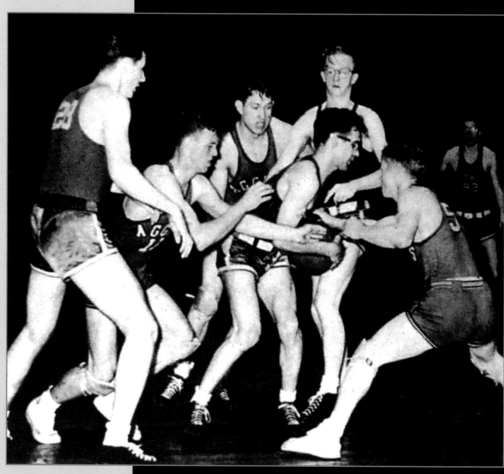

DePaul and Oklahoma A&M players staged a tug-of-war for the ball in mid-court during the game at Madison Square Garden, New York, March 29, 1945. L to R: Gene LaRochelle (#28), DePaul; J. L. Parks (#11), Oklahoma; Joe Halbert, Oklahoma; Ernie DeBemedetto (holding ball), DePaul; White Kachan (behind DeBemedetto), DePaul; and Weldon Kern, Oklahoma. Oklahoma won the game, 52–44, to capture the unofficial National Championship.

N·C·A·A
Western Championship Finals

MUNICIPAL AUDITORIUM
KANSAS CITY, MISSOURI
MARCH 23-24, 1945

OFFICIAL
25¢
PROGRAM

and Allen was an assistant coach. "I thought it was my obligation to whip his ass, if I could," Kurland remembers of that game in which he scored 28 points and Oklahoma A&M prevailed, 49–38. "Let's say I played with extra motivation."

Once in the NCAA Tournament, Oklahoma A&M was even more dominant in 1946 than it was the previous year. The Aggies allowed only 34.6 points in three games. Kurland averaged 24 points in the NCAA Tournament, while Oklahoma A&M managed only a 46.3-point average as a team.

Kurland's final collegiate game was a tight one in the NCAA final at Madison Square Garden. The Aggies defeated North Carolina, led by star 6-6 Bones McKinney, 43–40. McKinney harassed Kurland verbally the entire game, so much so the Tar Heel star only scored five points. Kurland quipped: "As the game wore on, he didn't have the size or strength against a guy my

size. . . . He tried to gain an advantage and thought we would fold. He was outsized and outclassed. But Dillon almost beat our butt."

North Carolina's 6-4 forward, James Dillon, scored 16 points and led a second-half charge before Kurland scored seven straight Aggie points to put the game out of reach. "My job was to rebound," Aubrey said. "(Dillon) had this hook shot. That sucker could hit the upper corner of the board with that shot. Bingo it would come right down through the hole. It is one of those things you remember."

Oklahoma A&M became the first team to win back-to-back NCAA titles, and Kurland was the first player to win two Most Outstanding Player Awards in the NCAA Tournament. Even without Kurland, who went on to work for Phillips Petroleum and play for the company's AAU team, Oklahoma A&M remained a national power well into the late 1950s.

Iba and the Aggies receive the 1946 NCAA championship trophy

america's best

NATIONAL COLLEGIATE ATHLETIC ASSOCIATION
BASKETBALL TOURNAMENT · EAST-WEST FINALS

MADISON SQUARE GARDEN   MARCH 27, 1945   SOUVENIR PROGRAM 15c

Oklahoma A&M left the MVC following the 1956–57 season and became Oklahoma State. The Aggies have never again had an era such as Iba's in the MVC, which included 14 undisputed or shared MVC titles, the NCAA titles, and four trips to the Final Four. The Aggies also finished second in the NCAA Tournament to Adolph Rupp's Kentucky team in 1949.

Coaches of the current era certainly have recognized Henry Iba and have drawn upon his wizardry displayed in those glory years. "Our defensive principles have not changed," said current-day Oklahoma State Coach Eddie Sutton, who played for Iba from 1956–58. "Ninety percent of the things we do on defense were given to me by Mr. Iba. Mr. Iba gave me so much. And he gave a lot of other people a lot."

It was not unusual in his later years for such coaches as Bob Knight, Mike Krzyzewski, and Dean Smith to seek out the three-time U.S. Olympic team coach. Iba was in Los Angeles at Knight's side as a consultant when the United States won gold at the 1984 Olympics. "People outside of the area probably thought more of him than they did right there in Stillwater," Moe Iba said. "He went out and got his hair cut at the barber shop and shot the shit with the guys. He told me one day that he would really feel successful if he made $100 a day. He probably never made more than $45,000 in a year." The U.S. Basketball Writers Association named its annual Coach of the Year award in honor of Iba.

INDIANA
UNIVERSITY

DEPARTMENT OF INTERCOLLEGIATE ATHLETICS   ASSEMBLY HALL   BLOOMINGTON, INDIANA 47405   PH 812 332 2794

February 22, 1985

Ms. Doris Dellinger
2912 Crescent Drive
Stillwater, Oklahoma 74074

Dear Doris:

The following are some thoughts on Coach Iba relative to the 1984 Olympics Team. You can paraphrase them or add to them as you see fit.

During the entire selection and training process for the 1984 U.S. Olympics Team no one was more in evidence than Henry Iba. Coach Iba had been the head coach of the United States' teams in 1964, 1968 and 1972. There is no man ever associated withe the game of basketball for whom I have more respect than Mr. Iba and it was because of this that I had asked him to help us all the way through the selection and training of our 1984 team.

The Coach didn't miss a single session or practice beginning with the first day of selection on April 16th. He was there to ask us questions while at the same time answer questions we had for him. He did a fantastic job of evaluating players from beginning to end and worked with many of the players that eventually made up our gold medal team. There is No man ever associated with the game of basketball who should be placed in a more revered position than Henry Iba. It was a tremendous thrill for all of us to have him as a very integral and important part of our planning, training and play with the 1984 U.S. Olympic Team. His contributions from beginning to end were exceptional and each of us that was part of the 1984 U.S. Olympic Team will first and foremost remember the tremendous enthusiasm that he brought to the team above all else when we think of our association with this particular basketball team.

Sincerely yours,

Bob Knight
Basketball Coach

BK:md

Kyle Korver

HICKEY GOT HIS START WITH CREIGHTON

Creighton University was founded in Omaha, Neb., in 1878 by Mary Lucretia Creighton in memory of her husband Edward. The school was immediately transferred to the bishop of Omaha, who enlisted the Jesuits to operate the institution.

Creighton University first became a member of the Missouri Valley Conference in 1928 and withdrew in 1947 before rejoining the league in 1976.

Legendary coach Eddie Hickey, a Creighton graduate, got his start in the Missouri Valley Conference with Creighton in 1935. Hickey's Bluejay squads battled Oklahoma A&M and the Aggies' great coach Henry Iba for Missouri Valley Conference supremacy for more than a decade. "They were rivals," Saint Louis University star Ed Macauley said. "Henry Iba was a great gentleman of basketball. He would beat your brains out, but as far as taking care of people and respecting people, he was a great man, as was Hickey. They had two of the best coaches in the same

In 1999, Rodney Buford led Creighton to the first of two straight MVC tournament championships for the Bluejays and five overall in a seven-year span (1999-2005)

Eddie Hickey coached at Creighton from 1935 to 1945

Benoit Benjamin

class all the way, as was Hickey," said Saint Louis University star D. C. Wilcutt. "They were very close friends. It was just a contrast in styles. Iba would pass the ball 10 times before anybody shot, and Hickey would just throw it out and go on down and score."

CREIGHTON'S BIG BEN

The best big man in Creighton's history is undoubtedly behemoth 7-foot, 250-pound center Benoit Benjamin. Selected No. 3 overall by the Los Angeles Clippers in the 1985 NBA Draft, Benjamin is the Bluejays' highest draft pick.

The Bluejays never finished above fourth in the Missouri Valley Conference during Benjamin's three seasons under Coach Willis Reed, but Benjamin was a dominant big man in the MVC, scoring 1,575 points, collecting 1,005 rebounds, and blocking 411 shots. Benjamin (1982–85) had three triple-doubles (points, rebounds, blocked shots) during his Creighton career and is still the career blocks leader in school history. In MVC history, only Wichita State's Gene Wiley had more triple-doubles of that variety (points, rebounds, blocks), with four in the early 1960s. Benjamin went on to a 15-year career in the NBA.

THE BOB AND CHAD SHOW

Clearly, the Tony Barone coaching era at Creighton from 1985 to 1991 was buoyed by two recruits—Bob Harstad and Chad Gallagher. The "Dynamic Duo" finished among the school's top-five career scorers and rebounders. From 1987 to 1991, Gallagher and Harstad led Creighton to two MVC Tournament crowns (1989, 1991), two regular-season titles (1989, 1991), two NCAA Tournaments (1989, 1991), and one NIT berth (1990).

conference." The diminutive Hickey, who was nicknamed the "Little General," won three straight MVC titles at Creighton from 1941 to 1943 and competed in two National Invitation Tournaments and one NCAA Tournament during that span. From 1935 to 1947, he posted an overall 127–71 record at Creighton, 73–35 in MVC play.

When Hickey was lured to St. Louis and became head coach for the Billikens in 1947–48, the coaching rivalry with Iba continued for another decade. "Iba was first-

Harstad, at 6-5, was a ferocious rebounder, but he was not a sure-bet Division I player because he was not a big scorer in high school in Colorado. The first time Barone saw Harstad, he was wearing a Mohawk haircut and no socks. Harstad also was a soccer goalie and loved to sky-

CREIGHTON'S DYNAMIC DUO

CHAD GALLAGHER

BOB HARSTAD

Bob Harstad

recruited player who everybody thought was a little bit of a flake. . . . We became enthralled with Chad because he could score the basketball. He was a priority recruit for us."

Once the two players landed at Creighton they meshed into a scoring-rebounding machine. They produced more than 3,000 points and 2,000 rebounds during a four-year period. "They became two guys who worked off each other," Barone said. "Gallagher had an

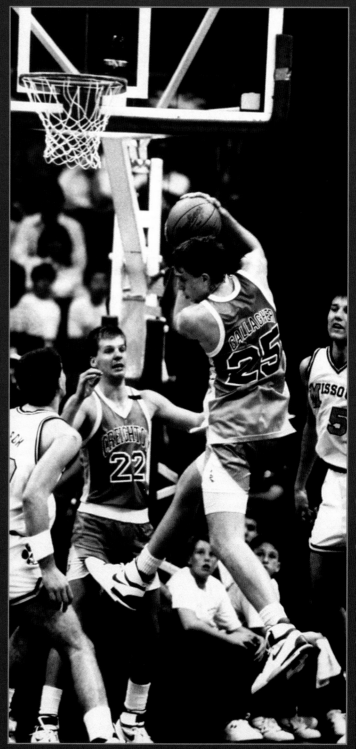

Chad Gallagher

dive off mountains. "At 6-5, 230 pounds, he had the quickness to get across the soccer goal," Barone said. "So, we said, 'Hey we are going to take a chance on him.' He wound up being one of the hardest working kids we ever had. He was one of the toughest kids we have ever had."

"Chad was a completely different story," Barone said of the 6-11 post player from Illinois. "He was a highly

Tony Barone celebrates a conference championship

Tony Barone

unbelievable scoring touch," said Porter Moser, a former Creighton teammate. "Chad, I wouldn't say he was the toughest kid coming in. By the time he left, he was tough. Bobby was just naturally mean. If everybody else was tough, Chad fell in line. Bobby was a weight-lifting partner of Chad's, and he would not let him do seven reps, if he was supposed to do 10."

DANA ALTMAN: MVC TOURNEY KING

Creighton Coach Dana Altman, dean of Missouri Valley Conference coaches, has had several chances to leave the friendly confines of Omaha during his tenure with the Bluejays, but he has stayed in Nebraska, his home state, since the 1994–95 season. Illinois, Clemson, Miami, Penn State, and Minnesota have shown interest in Altman in the past, but he hasn't budged while other MVC coaches have come and gone during the last

decade. Altman may be the top coach in Division I who hasn't bitten on the lure of one of the glamour conferences. Maybe it's because he already has been there—head coach at Kansas State from 1990 to 1994.

He also may be comfortable with his record at Creighton. Altman is the most successful MVC Tournament coach in history in terms of titles (five), from 1999 to 2005. He entered the 2006–07 season third among coaches in MVC victories with 135 behind only Oklahoma A&M's Henry Iba (187), Creighton and Saint Louis' Eddie Hickey (163),

Altman has laid down a tradition at the Jesuit school near downtown Omaha. In 2005, Creighton stood at 15–10 after a close loss at Southern Illinois on Feb. 12 and appeared to be going nowhere. "I think the main thing after the loss, I think coach challenged us," said Creighton forward Jimmy Motz. "He challenged everybody and just wanted to get a reaction and a response. We responded well, obviously, winning eight in a row."

The Bluejays finished the 2004–05 season with 23 victories and another MVC Tournament title. "We set a

2000 Missouri Valley Conference champions

conference record by winning at least 10 games in the conference nine years in a row, and this will be our eighth postseason in a row, and we've had seven 20-victory seasons in a row," Altman said. "But at that 15–10 mark we were 7–7 in the conference. I didn't think we were going to hit any of our marks. And I think that was kind of the thing that brought it home to them. That's where the unselfishness of the guys I think really came into play." Altman's eight straight 20-victory seasons are the most in MVC history, surpassing six by Cincinnati (1958 to 1963), Bradley (1957 to 1962), and Oklahoma A&M (1944 to 1949).

Altman has utilized red-shirting and kept players for five full seasons. Fifth-year seniors often play for the Bluejays. "It gets our players in our system one more year," Altman said. "It helps to know each other and what to expect from the coaching staff. My assistants have been with me all 11 years. We play guys as freshmen and keep them in the rotation. . . . It helps us to compete with larger schools who may have bigger players. Red-shirted players can take advantage of our

Johnny Mathies, 2005 MVC Tournament MVP

weight program. We are in it for the long haul. We don't lose anybody early to the NBA Draft."

So far, the Bluejays' biggest NCAA moment under Altman was a last-second win over Florida in 2002's first round. The Bluejays won in double overtime, 83–82, on Terrell Taylor's three-point basket with 0.2 seconds remaining. But they fell to Illinois in the second round.

ALTMAN'S MVC TOURNAMENT RUN

YEAR	SCORE–TITLE GAME	CREIGHTON'S TOURNEY MOP
1999	Creighton defeats Evansville, 70–61	Rodney Buford
2000	Creighton defeats Missouri State, 57–45	Ryan Sears
2002	Creighton defeats Southern Illinois, 84–76	Kyle Korver
2003	Creighton defeats Southern Illinois, 80–56	Kyle Korver
2005	Creighton defeats Missouri State, 75–57	Johnny Mathies

Dana Altman

In NCAA tournament play under Altman (through 2006), Creighton is 2–6. "We haven't had the success Gonzaga has had in the NCAA Tournament," said Altman. "We have to take that next step."

KYLE KORVER

Creighton's Kyle Korver took great pride in being named the Missouri Valley Conference Player of the Year twice in 2002 and 2003, and when people refer to the MVC as a "mid-major" conference, Korver bristles. "I just hate it," the 6-7, 210-pound Korver said. "I think we should be judged by our wins and losses and not by the size of the school or how much money you have or if you have a football team. We just go out there and play and hopefully change people's minds."

In 2003, Korver became the sixth player in MVC history to be named Player of the Year twice. He joined Indiana State's Larry Bird, Drake's Lewis Lloyd, Louisville's Junior Bridgeman, Wichita State's Xavier McDaniel, and Bradley's Hersey Hawkins in that select class. In 2005, Southern Illinois' Darren Brooks became the seventh MVC player to win the award twice.

Few big-time recruiters predicted that Korver, from Pella, Ia., would become the career MVC three-point basket leader. Korver finished his career with 371 three-

Kyle Korver

Qwest Center OMAHA™ exterior

pointers, ranking sixth in NCAA Division I history at the time. "Kyle was under-recruited," Altman said. "He came from a small school in central Iowa. Coming out of high school, at 6-7, he had a nice stroke. We signed him early. . . . The recruiting battle was not that fierce."

Korver finished as a 45.3 percent career three-point shooter, and he improved his game enough each year to wind up in the National Basketball Association. He was drafted in the second round in 2003 by New Jersey, the 51st pick overall. The Philadelphia 76ers then acquired his rights. "He made himself a good player," Altman said. "He's definitely highly skilled. He shoots it and passes and started to put the ball on the floor (as a senior). Each year, he made himself a better shooter, passer, and ball-handler."

The lanky, shaggy-haired wing player worked during his senior year to put the ball on the floor and to create his shot. "When I came in as a freshman, they said I was just a shooter," Korver said. "They put a label on me . . . and that made me mad. I hated being called one dimensional."

Qwest Center OMAHA™ interior

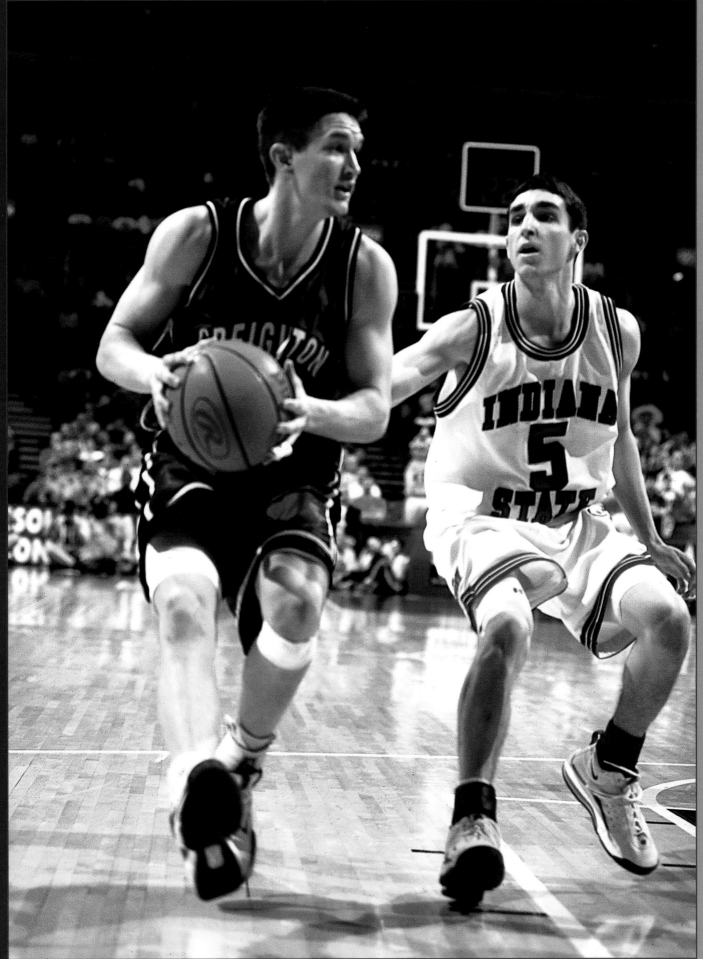

Creighton's Ryan Sears and Indiana State's Michael Menser

TULSA

The University of Tulsa was originally founded in 1882 as the Presbyterian school for Indian Schools by Alice Mary Robertson. Originally located in Muskogee, Okla., the college moved to Tulsa in 1907 and gained university status in 1920. Tulsa was a member of the Missouri Valley Conference° from 1934 to 1996. The Golden Hurricane was a powerhouse both on the court and on the gridiron during their MVC days. Basketball coaches such as Tubby Smith, J. D. Barnett, and Nolan Richardson held the reins of the Hurricane.

Bobby "Bingo" Smith

BINGO WAS THE BEST

Who was the best athlete to ever play for Tulsa? It may have been guard Bobby "Bingo" Smith, who, out of high school, turned down a bonus to play for the Pittsburgh Pirates as a pitcher and a chance to play football at UCLA. Smith got his nickname "Bingo" from a Tulsa basketball radio play-by-play man who would describe his looping, high-arching wing shot going in as, "bingo!"

"Many people have asked me who is the best basketball player I have coached," said former Tulsa and New Mexico State Coach Ken Hayes. "I'd say I don't know, but Bingo Smith was the best athlete I have ever coached. He was just an awesome athlete." Hayes remembers Smith once finished basketball practice and then went over to the track pit and high-jumped 6-8 in sweat clothes and tennis shoes. He also could catch any pass thrown in his direction. At one time, Smith had a 2-handicap in golf, Hayes said. "He (Smith) didn't pursue football, and our football coach never forgave him for not continuing football," Hayes said. "I wasn't excited about him being an all-sport guy. His heart was in basketball."

Smith, a 6-5, 195-pounder from Memphis, played basketball for Tulsa from 1965 to 1969. The Golden Hurricane rose to a No. 7 ranking and an 18–2 record his senior season in 1968–69 (Hayes' first season as head coach) before losing six of their last seven games. Smith led the Missouri Valley Conference in scoring that season (24.5 ppg) and wound up as the league's MVP.

Smith was a draft selection of the San Diego Rockets of the American Basketball Association, but he was later selected by the expansion Cleveland Cavaliers and played 11 seasons in the NBA and scored 10,882 points during his professional career.

THE NOLAN RICHARDSON ERA

Nolan Richardson blazed into Tulsa from Western Texas Junior College in the spring of 1980 with polka-dot shirts, full-court pressure, and a national junior college title on his resume. The Missouri Valley Conference had never seen anything like the flamboyant Richardson, a former Texas Western (now Texas–El Paso) star under Don Haskins in the early 1960s. The muscular Richardson, with his open collar and short-sleeved shirts, still looked like he could suit up and play power forward.

He quickly became a marquee coach in the MVC and challenged the league's top coaches and programs of the early 1980s—Wichita State and Gene Smithson, Bradley and Dick Versace, and Illinois State and Bob Donewald.

Richardson took Haskins' half-court defensive pressure the entire 94 feet of the floor and used it to create a frenetic offensive pace. That style led to the 1981 National Invitation Tournament title during his first season at Tulsa, and 13 years later an NCAA title when he was coach at Arkansas.

Through the end of the 20th century, Richardson was the only coach in college basketball history who had won the NJCAA title, the NIT title, and the NCAA title during his career.

Richardson, an African American, grew up in the poor section of El Paso and was raised by his grandmother, but he overcame his humble beginnings to become an all-sport star at El Paso's Bowie High School and later at UTEP.

He then transferred that athletic drive to the bench, first in high school and then at the college level. His 1979–80 Western Texas Junior College team completed a 37–0 record and won the NJCAA title, prompting his hiring at Tulsa, which had suffered through five straight losing seasons and had not had a 20-victory season since 1955—prior to his arrival.

"FORTY MINUTES OF HELL"

Richardson's "40 Minutes of Hell" basketball transformed Tulsa into an instant winner. Bringing four of his starters from the Western Texas Junior College team to Tulsa, Richardson posted a 26–7 record in his first season and beat Syracuse in the NIT final in Madison Square Garden to give the MVC its fifth NIT title. "What I did was take the philosophy of defense, which is pressure, and also took another philosophy I wanted on offense," Richardson said. "Let's get it on for 40 minutes."

Mike Anderson, the point guard on Jefferson State (Ala.), the team that Western Texas Junior College beat in the 1980 NJCAA final, was the fifth starter for Richardson's first Tulsa team. "He was a driven coach," Anderson recalled years later. "You talk about '40 Minutes of Hell.' . . . Our practices were wars. We went 50 minutes before we even touched the ball. We would run and do situps and pushups. We would sit on the wall and then run some more.

"But I remember beating Louisville," said Anderson, later a Richardson assistant coach at Arkansas and head coach at UAB and now Missouri. "And that was the game that put Tulsa on the map." Louisville, the defending 1980 NCAA champion, had lost Darrell Griffith, but still had Scooter and Rodney McCray. Tulsa won, 68–60, in Richardson's third home game at the Tulsa Convention Center, which became a temple of doom for opponents. Tulsa also won non-conference games against Oklahoma State and Purdue there in Richardson's first season as head coach.

In fact, Richardson won his first 35 games at the Convention Center in downtown Tulsa before losing to Oklahoma State in his third season, and Tulsa started drawing fans and creating interest in the program for the first time in many years. "I started (the running, pressing style) in junior college and when I got to Tulsa, I still had the good players, and the fans enjoyed it so much more," Richardson said. "We had to draw the everyday Joe to come out to the game. And that kind of basketball was exciting to people."

Golden Hurricane basketball became a happening. Attendance for Tulsa home games was 3,766 in 1979–80, the season before Richardson became head coach, but home crowds zoomed to more than 8,000 a game by his second season at the commuter school.

Almost from the start, Richardson became a lightning rod for attention and developed an MVC coaching rivalry with Versace and Illinois State's Donewald, who once called Richardson a "thug in polka-dots."

"The uniforms stood out," Anderson said of the gaudy striped jerseys. "Whether it was good or bad, it drew attention. That was coach's way of doing it. They knew who Tulsa was. The interesting thing about it, it just kind of went all over the state. You saw people with these striped uniforms. It caught on."

Joe Dalfonso, Bradley's former sports information director, recalls the first game between Richardson's Tulsa team and Bradley in Peoria in January 1981, won by Bradley, 70–63. "Richardson was yelling at the refs," Dalfonso said. "Dick yells something. Nolan told Dick, 'I'm doing the talking here.' Dick countered, 'Just coach your team, you freshman rookie.'"

Scott Edgar, one of Richardson's assistant coaches at Tulsa and later at Arkansas, remembers that stressful MVC rivalry. "The rivalry was as heated as any I have been involved with in 25 years of coaching," Edgar said. "It was the personalities and the magnitude of the teams."

"Nolan's teams were a lot like ours," said former Bradley guard Donald Reese. "They competed and they didn't have 7-footers. . . . But they had guys who would bust their tails and work hard for their coach and gave it 150 percent every time they step out on the court. Wichita, but also Tulsa, would rank as the games you really looked forward to playing."

FLAMBOYANT RICHARDSON STOOD OUT

Richardson eventually became one of the most controversial coaching figures in MVC history with his flamboyant and imposing sideline manner and criticism of MVC officials. "He drew attention not only to Tulsa but to the conference and turned it around overnight," said former MVC publicist Jeff Hurd. "They used to have classic battles. Nolan was strong-willed and usually had a few things to say. It was not unusual for Nolan to come over (to the league office). They would close John's (Overby, MVC supervisor of officials' door) and would get into some classic shouting matches over officiating issues. I know they respected each other, but Nolan would not back down." In 1981–82, Richardson accused MVC officials of being out to get him after he received seven technical fouls in the opening part of the season, a fact Overby denied.

Regardless of Richardson's bench theatrics, Tulsa imposed its style on MVC teams and created a quick pace with the press. During Richardson's five seasons in the MVC, the Golden Hurricane finished tied for second twice, won the school's first outright MVC regular-season title in 1985, and tied for another in 1984. "I don't think they ever adjusted," Edgar said. "If it is unusual now, what do you think it was like years ago to play against . . . the 1-3-1 and full-court press and half-court traps."

Tulsa beat MVC favorite Wichita State twice during the 1981 MVC regular season, including a thrilling 74–72 double-overtime decision in Wichita. Led by Antoine Carr and Cliff Levingston, the Shockers won the 1981 MVC regular-season title by one game over Tulsa and Creighton. Bradley finished two games back.

While the Shockers advanced to the Elite Eight of the NCAA Tournament before losing to LSU, Tulsa also grabbed season-ending headlines and added to Richardson's aura by winning the NIT. "As you look back, people didn't know anything about us," Edgar said.

Tulsa won NIT games over UT–Pan American, UTEP, and South Alabama at Oral Roberts' Mabee Center in

Richardson on the sidelines

Tulsa by a total of 16 points. The Golden Hurricane then faced West Virginia in the semifinals at Madison Square Garden.

Paul Pressey, the "Rubber-Band Man," had his national coming out party in an 89–87 victory over West Virginia. He scored 20 points, handed out nine assists, and made seven steals. He also connected on three straight jump shots late in the game to push Tulsa ahead to stay. "He can play a great game when he only scores two points because he plays both ends of the floor," Richardson said after the NIT semifinal victory. "He's a phenomenal player, and he's a clever player. He plays with his eyes, his feet, and his mind. He was all over the court on defense."

Paul Pressey (right)

Tulsa's victory over West Virginia set up the NIT title game against Syracuse in front of a heavily partisan instate Orangemen crowd. "Fan support will be for them," Richardson said before the title game. "But I think the Missouri Valley Conference has prepared us well. It's a great conference. Top Valley teams can play anybody, anywhere."

Notre Dame Coach Digger Phelps, who served as a television analyst for the game, predicted Syracuse would beat Tulsa, but the Golden Hurricane backed up Richardson's statements. With Tulsa up by two points, Anderson missed the front end of a one-and-one free throw situation with eight seconds remaining. The Orangemen's Erich Santifer tied the score to send the game into overtime, but Tulsa prevailed in the extra period.

Tulsa's 6-9 center-forward Greg Stewart, a fourth-round NBA Draft pick a year later, scored on a twisting layup with 30 seconds remaining in overtime to beat the Orangemen, 86–84. NIT MVP Stewart scored 23 points in the title game. "I will never forget the parade they had for us," Anderson said. "It was a celebration they had downtown at the square. There were over 10,000 people throwing confetti. . . . That city embraced us."

PAUL PRESSEY: TULSA'S JEWEL

With five starters returning, Tulsa entered the 1981–82 season with hopes of making a big run in the NCAA Tournament. Pressey had established himself as one of the top players in college basketball and would wind up becoming a first-round draft pick in 1982 by the Milwaukee Bucks. "(Pressey was the) only one I know quick enough to play tennis with himself," quipped former TCU Coach Jim Killingsworth after his Horned Frogs fell to Tulsa during the 1981–82 season.

Early in the season, Tulsa lost at eventual 1982 NCAA champion North Carolina and an MVC road game at New Mexico State, but the Golden Hurricane made amends for those losses when it played host to Wichita State in a rare CBS national television game in mid-January.

Tulsa (11–2) was ranked 18th; Wichita State (12–3) 16th in the Associated Press poll. It was a showcase game for the MVC on a bitterly cold day in Tulsa. "That was a historical game for the city of Tulsa," Edgar said. Falling behind 23–8, the Golden Hurricane appeared to be out of the game, but then Pressey again began showing why he was nicknamed the "Rubber-Band Man." He wound up with seven steals in the game to go along with 20 points, seven assists, and seven rebounds.

"Coach Nolan said his arms grew," Anderson remembered.

"I have been around a lot of good players," Edgar said. "But he could guard a guard. He could guard a forward. And he could guard a center at times."

By halftime, Tulsa had the momentum, trailing only 38–32, and eventually won, 99–88. Stewart and Anderson each scored 26 points, and Tulsa's press ground up the Shockers.

The MVC regular-season crown eluded the Golden Hurricane again. Bradley won the 1982 title when it defeated the Golden Hurricane, 82–79, in overtime in Peoria in the final game of the regular season. Tulsa, however, rebounded to win the MVC Tournament on its home floor and gained the school's first NCAA Tournament berth in 27 years.

Tulsa caught a break again when it got to play at Oral Roberts' Mabee Center in the Midwest Regional. Third-seeded Tulsa received a first-round bye and waited on the winner of Alcorn State–Houston. Later, Richardson admitted the experience of the first-round game might have aided lower-seeded Houston, because he said his team looked "rusty."

Little was known about the Houston team, which featured Clyde Drexler, Michael Young, Rob Williams, and Larry Micheaux. Akeem (later Hakeem) Olajuwon wasn't even starting at that point as a first-year player on the collegiate level, but the legend of Phi Slama Jama was about to be born at the expense of the Golden Hurricane.

Tulsa played without inspirational leader and resourceful scorer David Brown, who was out with a knee injury. The Golden Hurricane led only once, 1–0, in the second-round NCAA Tournament game and eventually lost, 78–74, despite having a rabid fan following at the game on the Oral Roberts University campus. Thus ended Richardson's attempt to win the national junior college, NIT, and NCAA tournaments in consecutive years.

"Houston did a tremendous job of handling our press," Richardson said after the loss to the Cougars. "They spread us out and kept our traps from working. They also did a good job of keeping Pressey from handling the ball. . . . We have not played a team with forwards who could move like Drexler and Young. All their big people have tremendous quickness."

Flashy Houston guard Rob Williams poured in 26 points against Tulsa and fed the Cougars' aggressive big men. Williams took Guy Lewis' Houston team all the way to the 1982 Final Four, where the Cougars lost to North Carolina.

The Houston loss signaled the end of the seniors' two-year run from Western Texas Junior College to major-college basketball, but in two years, the group had won 50 games and put Richardson and Tulsa basketball on the radar screen. "When I took this job, I made a few statements to the community that the University of Tulsa no longer would be a second division basketball program," Richardson told the *Tulsa Tribune* on the eve of claiming a piece of the MVC regular-season title in 1984. "I said it would be a program the school and the community could be proud of. . . . And when you are up there, you always have a chance to win."

RICHARDSON'S NEW ERA

Sophomores Steve Harris, Vince Williams, and Herbert Johnson ushered in a new players' leadership era at Tulsa in 1982–83 after the departure of Coach Nolan Richardson's core group from Western Texas Junior College. During their sophomore through senior seasons, they played in three MVC Tournament title games (winning in 1982) and claimed two regular-season titles in

Tubby Smith

Coach Tubby Smith's four-year stay in Tulsa had one of the weirdest turn of events in recent college basketball memory.

Smith's Golden Hurricane basketball team was barred from postseason play during his second season (1992–93) because of NCAA violations in the school's track and field program. "I think it was the only time in the history of the NCAA an entire athletic program was put on probation because of the track team," said Smith. "We didn't compete that year in the Missouri Valley Conference Tournament."

Tulsa had failed to meet the minimum sports sponsorship criteria (minimum number of contests with the minimum number of athletes). TU officials earlier had overstated the number of track athletes competing for the school. "I was upset because I did not know they were going to do that," Smith said. "But God works in crazy ways and made me stay there and we had two great years."

Having arrived only a year before from Kentucky where he was an assistant coach for Rick Pitino's Wildcats, Smith was stunned at the development. Regardless, he landed enough players to get the Golden Hurricane back to the NCAA Tournament in 1994 when the school was off "probation."

The big catch for Smith was Tulsa's homegrown Shea Seals, a talented 6-5 forward who, as a freshman, catapulted the Golden Hurricane and the MVC into the NCAA Tournament spotlight during the 1993–94 season. "He was the breakthrough recruit," said Alvin "Pooh" Williamson, a guard on that team and later a Golden Hurricane assistant and interim head coach. "His final two teams were Seton Hall and Tulsa, and when he turned down Seton Hall to stay at Tulsa, he was the recruit that turned the tide."

"Shea was a real homebody kid, and we were very, very fortunate to get him," Smith said. "That kind of catapulted us, and Pooh, too, all of our players. One thing about Tulsa . . . you can recruit that region and never leave there."

1984 (tie) and 1985. Kansas transfer Ricky Ross also was a key part of the 1983 and 1984 Tulsa teams.

The unquestionable leader from 1982 to 1985 was Harris, from Blue Springs, Mo. He was nicknamed "Silk" by Richardson because of the effortless way he played. The 6-5 Harris, a first-round NBA Draft pick in 1985, wound up with 2,272 career points at Tulsa and was a three-time first-team All-MVC selection. He held the Tulsa career scoring record for 12 years until it was broken by Shea Seals in 1997.

Harris and his teammates continued Richardson's pressing, defensive pressure-oriented style. "They came after me," said Bradley point guard Jim Les, who played for the Braves from 1984 to 1986. "They had a good press and would try and get the ball out of my hands. They would run three or four guys at me . . . I remember wondering how many guys does he have over there? They would have a lot of energy and more lip. They would talk a lot and make sure I would know things wouldn't be easy."

Shea Seals

SEALS MAKES IMMEDIATE IMPACT

Seals scored 33 points in his first collegiate game against Houston Baptist, sinking seven three-point field goals. "Shea was averaging close to 30 points his first four games as a freshman, before he tore his knee up and had to have his knee scoped," Smith said. "Then he missed a few games before he came back against Oklahoma in the All-College Tournament. . . . Shea Seals could do all things. He could shoot with range. He could play point. He could defend. He was tenacious. He played strong and physical. He reminded you of a Ron Artest, but he was just a little more fluid. He was a combination of Artest and Paul Pressey (former Tulsa star), but he was stockier at 6-5."

With the injury, Seals missed Tulsa's home losses to powerhouses Oklahoma State and eventual NCAA champion Arkansas, a 93–91 overtime affair, which was one of the best college games of the entire season.

"They were happy because they played them close," Smith said of his players after the loss to the Razorbacks. "I said, 'We are not here to play games close. We should have won this game. We were better than they are.' . . . I just went off: 'I am not going to tolerate anything but your best. We are going to be better.' . . . That was a great tool for me. It was a great motivating game. I just felt like we should have won that game. Had we won it, it would have been a major upset, but losing it probably did as much for us as winning because it made our guys realize we could compete with anybody in the country."

Tulsa won the 1994 MVC regular season by a game over Bradley and Southern Illinois. It was a clean sweep for the Golden Hurricane in the MVC individual honors department as well. Shea Seals was MVC Freshman of the Year. Gary Collier was MVC Player of the Year. Lou Dawkins was Defensive Player of the Year. And Smith was MVC Coach of the Year, for the first of two straight seasons.

Yet the Golden Hurricane had to watch nervously on NCAA Tournament Selection Sunday because they were upset in the semifinals of the MVC Tournament in St. Louis by UNI and failed to get the league's automatic bid. "We were the first Valley team to get in the NCAA as an at-large team in six years," Smith said. "The Valley was only getting one team in (postseason tournament champion). I knew that."

By virtue of its tough non-conference schedule, Tulsa was selected at-large and was a 12 seed and sent to Oklahoma City to play fifth-seeded UCLA. Tulsa was one of the last teams selected for the NCAA Tournament.

MVC BACK ON THE NCAA MAP

UCLA forwards Ed and Charles O'Bannon and guard Tyus Edney told the media before the favored Bruins met the Golden Hurricane in the first round of the 1994 NCAA Tournament that they didn't know where Tulsa was located. "I don't know anything about them," Ed O'Bannon said. "I didn't even know Tulsa was in Oklahoma."

"Tubby Smith confided later that during the pre-tournament meeting in Oklahoma City, Jim Harrick (UCLA coach) saddled up to him and said, 'I hate to ask you this, but can I get the Oklahoma State tape from your regular-season game?'" Elgin recalled. Oklahoma State likely would be the opponent in the second round, playing the UCLA–Tulsa winner.

Tulsa was 0-for-6 in first-round NCAA Tournament games before meeting the Bruins. UCLA had won 10 NCAA titles at that point. Mismatch all the way? Wrong. "UCLA underestimated us," Smith said. "They really didn't know much about us. That helped. Us being an at-large (selection), and not getting the automatic bid, I think all of those things set the stage."

Tulsa jumped on UCLA for a 29-point lead, 46–17, with 6:19 left in the first half on the way to a stunning 112–102 victory. "We got out to a quick start," Williamson said. "They missed a shot. We went down on the fast break and scored. We didn't feel tight. We had nothing to lose. We wanted to prove a point we belonged in the tournament. . . . The next thing you know it was out of control."

Smith was as dazed as the Bruins were when he looked at the stat sheet at intermission. Tulsa led 63–38. "I didn't recognize the score until halftime," Smith said. "I asked my staff, 'Is that score right?' They hadn't seen anyone like us press the way we did. They let you score. They wouldn't guard you closely." Collier led Tulsa with 34 points, and Seals and Williamson each chipped in 20, as UCLA gave up a record number of points in an NCAA Tournament game.

Harrick approached Smith at the 1994 Final Four in Charlotte and asked what he had seen that would allow his team to dominate the Bruins. "I said, 'I thought we could score on you, and your kids wouldn't fight through screens,'" Smith said. "He took that to heart . . . I told him the truth. 'I will just tell you your kids seemed soft.' We were basically very physical and aggressive, and I said by the time your kids got aggressive in the second half, the game was over because we had such a big lead. I

Lou Dawkins

Defensively they were a much tougher team." And the Bruins won the 1995 NCAA title with that lesson learned.

In 1994, Collier wound up as the leading scorer (average) in the NCAA Tournament (31.3 average in three NCAA Tournament games), and Williamson played flawlessly at point guard.

They continued to sparkle in the second round when Tulsa reversed its earlier loss to Oklahoma State and beat the Cowboys, 82–80. Seals played in the second Oklahoma State game. OSU forward Fred Burley, who held Collier scoreless from behind the three-point arc in the earlier game, didn't play in the NCAA Tournament rematch because of curfew violation. Collier scored 25 points in the rematch and acted like a man on a mission.

"They were up by 11 at halftime," Smith said. "Brooks Thompson was killing us, and he made a half-court shot right before halftime. Brooks followed the shot and handed the ball to Gary. I will never forget it. Gary comes into the locker room, and he never says a lot. He was talking to the team. He was crying, and he was upset. I didn't know why he was so upset. . . . He gave the whole. 'Win One for the Gipper' speech. Everyone was fired up. We had never seen him so emotionally charged up. . . . I go back and watch the film the night after the game and am evaluating it. And I say, 'You see what he (Thompson) did to Gary?' That in itself, Gary must have said something to the players."

Gary Collier

Bryant Reeves had 19 points in the first half, but Tulsa limited him to 12 hard-earned points in the second half. Lou Dawkins made a three-point shot from the corner with nine seconds left to put the Golden Hurricane up by four points.

Tulsa became the first MVC team to make the Sweet 16 since Wichita State was in the Elite Eight in 1981—a drought of 13 years. "Joe Mitch and I were standing on the concourse," Elgin said. "We didn't have seats. . . . I just remember going backstage and celebrating with Joe. It was one of the

Tubby Smith

The emotional victory over Oklahoma State set up a Sweet 16 meeting against Arkansas at Reunion Arena in Dallas. This was the same Arkansas team that had beaten Tulsa by two points without Seals. "They'd make a run, we'd make a run, and then they would stop it," Smith said. "We never gave up. We were down 17–18 points, we'd cut it to nine. We'd get down 15–17 cut it to 10. We just never could sustain it. It was just the difference in their ability, the talent they had and we had. We just didn't have an answer for their inside game."

Arkansas went on to win the 1994 NCAA title. In fact, Tulsa played three of the teams that made the Final Four in 1995—UCLA, Oklahoma State, and Arkansas (again). "That game (Arkansas) put us back in the national spotlight," Elgin said.

Smith always has wondered if the Golden Hurricane had not had to play Arkansas so early what might have happened. "That Tulsa team could have beaten a lot of teams I coached here at Kentucky and at Georgia," Smith said. "I reminisce about that team all the time."

ANOTHER SWEET 16 ENTRY: 1995
Smith had to change his coaching philosophy in 1994–95 with the loss of Dawkins and Collier. The Golden Hurricane went from being an athletic, up-tempo, full-court team to a more defensive-oriented, half-court team that featured more size. "We won those games (in 1994–95), by locking people down," Williamson said. "That was to Coach Smith's credit. He saw what we had. The previous year, we would run and outscore people. This year we would stop guys and ground it out on offense."

"We were much bigger," Smith said. "We went from being the smallest team in the Valley to being the tallest team. . . . We had to adapt to those guys. We weren't as quick. We weren't pressing as much or running as much, and Pooh

made that adjustment. He was a big key to that. We had a lot of young guys. So he shot more. He had to do so much more that year."

Smith said he grew up as a coach as well. "Pooh Williamson used to tell me this. 'Coach, when things are tight, lighten up,'" Smith said. "I remember he came back to practice and we were honoring him. I would be in guy's faces and all over them in practice. Even now (when it) is gravy time (tournament time) I lighten up."

Williamson and Smith both remember an MVC road trip to the state of Illinois when the Golden Hurricane played poorly in a 95–79 loss at Illinois State. Williamson said the team expected Smith to scold them severely after the defeat, but he didn't. And the team came back and won at Bradley two days later going away, 73–53.

Bradley was a key road victory on the way to Tulsa's second-straight undisputed MVC regular-season title. "We came back and played an unbelievable game (at Bradley)," Smith said. "They had one of the longest (home-court) winning streaks in the country. I will never forget how great Alvin played in that game."

Tulsa was upset in the MVC title game by Southern Illinois, but it had a high enough power rating to make the NCAA Tournament field at-large. The Golden Hurricane beat Illinois and Old Dominion before losing to UMass and Marcus Camby in the Sweet 16. It was Smith's final game at Tulsa before leaving for Georgia.

"He was intense and paid attention to detail," Williamson said. "He wanted you to do everything right. . . . His Kentucky teams play the same way. . . . He had a great work ethic. We used to practice at 6 a.m. He would have us shoot 100 free throws at 6 a.m. just because he wanted us to get out of bed."

TULSA'S PASSING FANCY

Glenn Dobbs, a former Golden Hurricane gridiron player in the 1940s, returned to Tulsa as head coach in 1961 and unleashed an aerial attack that befuddled most opponents and led major-college football in passing offense from 1962 to 1966.

His pro-style passing system allowed two Golden Hurricane players—quarterback Jerry Rhome in 1964 and receiver Howard Twilley in 1965—to finish runners-up in the Heisman Trophy balloting in those respective years. "Rhome was as good a competitor as you would ever want," said F. A. Dry, who was an assistant on the late Dobbs' Tulsa staff in the 1960s. "He was a smart kid. He loved to throw the football, and he was extremely accurate. He didn't have the great arm like some of the real throwers. I went to pro football right after that and coached. But he could throw on the run, and throw on the run to his left."

Twilley, a smallish, lightly recruited player from Galena Park, Tex., set a gaggle of pass reception records spanning his three-year career in which he caught from Rhome in 1963 and 1964 and quarterback Billy Guy Anderson his final season in 1965. "In 1965, we averaged 65 passes a game," Dry said. "Now they (college teams) are doing that, but they platoon. We were the only passing team in the country at the time. . . . When we took over the club, we were not equipped for that. We went out and got a quarterback who could throw it and receivers who could catch it. Our first real catch was John Simmons (an end in the early 1960s). In 1964, he broke his arm and Twilley got his first start."

That's all the chance Twilley needed. A 5-10, 180-pounder who Dry described as "a real tenacious receiver without great speed, had good quickness, and was really a hard worker, he could catch anything you threw to him."

By the time he left Tulsa, Twilley had set the NCAA record bar for pass receivers. Entering the 2005 season, the former All-Pro with the Miami Dolphins still held an NCAA record for most catches per game in a season (13.4) in 1965—a remarkable fact considering it was 40 years after the fact. "I was one of those guys who knew I didn't have great natural talent, so I worked for everything I got," Twilley once told the now-defunct *Tulsa Tribune*. "Things didn't always come easy for me." Twilley revealed only one other school recruited him besides Tulsa–Tarleton State in Stephenville, Tex.

Rhome, who was a redshirt after transferring from SMU, remembers when Twilley broke into the Tulsa scene as a freshman when he was not eligible to play for the Varsity. "Dobbs would line up the Varsity to play the freshmen and redshirts in a scrimmage," Rhome recalled. "We played six quarters and the Varsity was still behind. Dobbs told the Varsity, 'If you don't beat them, you cannot leave the field.' They could not beat us. . . .

"There was this little guy catching the ball all over the field (from Rhome). It was some guy name Howard. I didn't know if that was his first or last name. It was some guy from Houston. My team had all these transfers and junior college guys, and they couldn't beat us. The

Glenn Dobbs starred for Tulsa in the 1940s, and returned as head coach in 1961

scrimmage started at noon, and they let us off the field at 6 p.m."

That was the beginning of the quarterback–receiver relationship between Rhome and Twilley, and by the 1964 season when Twilley was a full-time starter, it really took off.

Given the chance, Twilley led major-college football in receiving yards in both 1964 and 1965. "What he was, he was Steve Largent," Rhome said of another of Tulsa's receivers in the mid-1970s. "He came a long later. I coached Steve Largent at Tulsa and in the NFL, and they were just alike. Twilley was not even drafted and he went down to Miami and they went 17–0. Houston drafted Largent and cut him. I was at Seattle and we picked him off waivers."

Rhome said Dobbs took a different approach. He handpicked players such as Rhome and Twilley to fit into a system that was dominated by big linemen, good receivers and quarterbacks who could pass. This flashy passing attack helped draw attention and fans to a small private school such as Tulsa.

Dobbs even took Tulsa on a spring barnstorming tour around the state playing colleges in scrimmages to heighten interest. "Before the 1964 season, he wrote every sportswriter in America and projected we would break all the passing records," said Rhome. "He called the shots. And he put us on the line where everybody in the country was watching. And it started happening. . . . We didn't have a P.R. office. That was our P.R."

Dobbs recruited mainly junior college players and transfers who were older and more mature, anybody he could get really, while the major powers such as Oklahoma and Texas would take freshmen blue-chip players and try to dominate with the running game. Tulsa was referred to as Transfer U.

Furthermore, Dobbs surrounded himself with good coaches who knew the passing game: Dry, later a head college coach and an assistant in the pros, and the legendary Sammy Baugh of TCU were big aids to Dobbs during that era. "I worked with Sammy Baugh a year and half," Rhome said. "It was pretty big for the program. I would visit him late at night for chalk talk my junior and senior years. He later became head coach of the Oilers. Glenn set the stage of what he wanted to play and F. A. Dry was the man behind it all."

After Rhome finished his senior season with 2,870 yards passing and 32 touchdowns in 1964, Anderson came in and passed for an NCAA–leading 3,464 yards the following season when Twilley was a senior. Four times during the 1965 season, Anderson passed for more than 450 yards in a game, including a school- and then NCAA-record 502 yards in a 48–20 victory over Colorado State. "Anderson was taller and more of a classic drop-

Jerry Rhome

Howard Twilley

back passer," Dry said. "He was not as versatile as Jerry was. He was an older kid. He had gone through junior college. He was a backup to Rhome his junior year. We threw a lot more with Anderson than Rhome because our running game was not as good."

Dry had the unique perspective of coaching both Twilley (1963–65), when he was an assistant, and Largent (1972–75), when he was the head coach, at Tulsa. Both were two-time All-MVC selections. Twilley was a 12th-round NFL Draft choice by the Miami Dolphins in 1966 and Largent was a fourth-round selection by the Houston Oilers a decade later, but made his professional name with the Seattle Seahawks. "Largent had more speed than Howard," Dry said of Largent, the Pro Football Hall of Famer. "But Howard had extremely quick feet and was real tough inside the 20."

POLKA-DOT CONTROVERSY

Illinois State Coach Bob Donewald and Tulsa Coach Nolan Richardson were at odds in the early 1980s. During a 61–55 Illinois State victory over Tulsa at Illinois State in January 1983, Richardson separated a fight between a player from each team.

During the same altercation, Richardson was bumped by another Illinois State player and threatened a lawsuit. He claimed that Donewald "smirked" at him after the game, according to a report in the *Tulsa Tribune*. The hard feelings actually started the previous March when Tulsa beat Illinois State in the 1982 MVC title game, and Richardson believed Paul Pressey had been undercut. "They ought to do something about that thug in the polka-dot shirt," Bob Donewald was quoted as saying a couple days later after the January 1983 game.

Later, the two coaches developed a healthy respect for each other despite their contrasting styles of play. Donewald, a former Bob Knight assistant at Indiana, preferred a half-court, slower-paced game, but his team still tied Tulsa for the 1984 MVC regular-season title and won the MVC Tournament in 1983 with a victory over the Golden Hurricane.

Nolan Richardson wearing a polka-dot shirt was a familiar sight at the TU games

BILES' REMARKABLE TURNAROUND

Tulsa Coach John Phillips uses Golden Hurricane All-American Willie Biles (1973–74 and 1974–75) as an example of a player who can blossom as a junior and senior. "I told our players about Willie Biles," Phillips said. "When he was a freshman and sophomore, he maybe averaged three or four minutes a game, and his junior year averages 30 points a game. I saw him that year torch some really good teams in the Valley. He came out of nowhere. Nobody knew anything about him."

Biles averaged 30.3 points as a junior and 24.7 as a senior. He was the first MVC player to average 30 or more points since Cincinnati's Oscar Robertson in 1959–60. Biles led the MVC in scoring as a junior and senior.

TULSA'S FIRST ALL-AMERICAN

Tulsa Coach Clarence Iba (1949–60) recruited Bob Patterson in the early 1950s, never believing he would be a big scorer. By Patterson's senior year in 1954–55, however, he led the MVC in scoring and the Golden Hurricane to a piece of its first MVC title. "He said he would be a great rebounder, but he can't shoot," said Gene Iba, Clarence's son who played for him in the late 1950s at Tulsa. "Bob Patterson worked on his shot every day, and he wound up being one of the leading scorers (tied for sixth) in the country."

In 1954–55, Patterson averaged 27.6 points and 13.2 rebounds. He had eight 30-plus scoring games as the Golden Hurricane tied Saint Louis for the regular-season MVC title. Patterson was the first Tulsa player taken in the NBA Draft.

Bob Patterson

Macauley celebrates the 1948 NIT championship

SAINT LOUIS U.

Founded in 1818, Saint Louis University is the oldest university west of the Mississippi River. The Jesuit institution was a member of the Missouri Valley Conference from 1937 to 1974. In those years, the Billikens were a soccer power-house, winning 10 national titles, the most in NCAA history. SLU won one national championship while in the Valley—the NIT in 1948—led by Hall of Famer Ed Macauley.

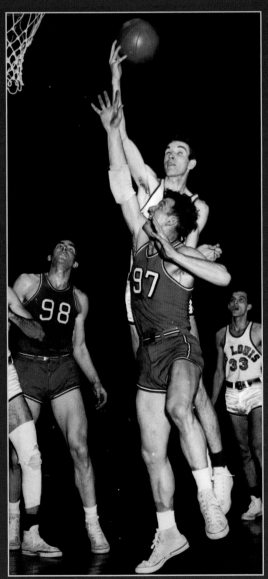

Macauley rises above his competition

THE ED MACAULEY YEARS:
WINNING MVC'S FIRST NIT TITLE

Many members of Saint Louis University's 1948 National Invitation Tournament title team grew up in nearby neighborhoods. They attended St. Louis–area high schools such as McBride, Beaumont, Soldan, Cleveland, and Saint Louis University High. Some were innocent high school boys who hadn't traveled much past the Mississippi and Missouri Rivers and were too young for war. Others were grown men. They were hardened World War II veterans who were happy to still be alive after spending time in combat. The boys and men bonded as a team.

These homegrown Billikens began filling Kiel Auditorium to the brim in the late 1940s, won the school's first Missouri Valley Conference title in 1947, and became the toast of St. Louis after beating New York University in the 1948 NIT title game at Madison Square Garden. That was the MVC's first NIT title.

More than 50 years later, many of them still gathered. The titular head of the clan, star center Ed Macauley, led the reunions into the 21st century. "The team is like a family almost," said Macauley, who starred with the old St. Louis Hawks and the Boston Celtics after his career at Saint Louis University. "We have all stayed together. . . . We all know each other's children. It's a very, very unique team. It started in the high schools of St. Louis and it kept going through college. . . . They (some of the players) fought in the war and were shot at," Macauley added. "They were happy to be alive after the war and the other half of the team was kids just out of high school. We blended well because of the character of the men on the team."

Macauley was one of the kids back in the 1940s. Fresh out of Saint Louis University High in 1945, Macauley was recruited by such powers as Boston College, Notre Dame, Kentucky, and nearby Missouri. He opted to stay in his hometown. His mother wanted him close to home because his father was an invalid.

Contrast Macauley with Billikens' teammate, guard Dan Miller, who returned from Europe in 1945–46 after flying 35 missions over Germany. "I guess every time I got in the airplane, I thought, 'What the hell, I am going to come back,'" Miller said of his World War II experiences. "We're going to make it. All of a sudden, you get a positive attitude about the way you want to do things, and that's the way I came out of the service."

Billikens 1948 NIT championship team

Macauley said he hadn't *even* flown on an airplane until the team took a charter from Drake his freshman year. Nervously, Macauley fidgeted before takeoff from Drake. Miller, the captain on the team, told him to watch the propeller all the way back and if it stopped, come get him. Macauley gripped his seat and hung on for dear life. "I watched that damn propeller all the way home," the 6-8 Macauley said with a chuckle.

"I think all of us coming out of high school looked up to these guys and what they did," Macauley added. And they gradually blended their talents together under new coach John Flanigan.

MACAULEY HAD SOME TOUGH MOMENTS
In his freshman season of 1945–46, Macauley had some other shaky moments on the road. He gave up 58 points in a head-to-head matchup in Stillwater against Oklahoma A&M's great center Bob Kurland. The Billikens struggled to a 13–11 record in Flanigan's first year. Macauley still was named second-team All-Missouri Valley Conference.

The next year, Kurland was gone, Flanigan had matured as a coach, and Macauley became a big star. The Billikens defeated Oklahoma A&M twice and won the MVC title with an 11–1 record. Their only league loss was to Eddie Hickey's Creighton team.

Macauley led the MVC in scoring average in conference games (14.0) his sophomore season. He had developed by working out against his teammate Jim Cullen and the young coach, the 6-4 Flanigan, who had been an excellent player in the old Amateur Athletic Union League.

Macauley became prodigious shooting with either hand, just to get shots off against those two in practice or scrimmages. "I learned more about basketball from him (Flanigan) and was forced to make moves to try and score on him and became accustomed to being pounded," Macauley said.

The modest Flanigan deferred to Cullen: "I always said one of the reasons Ed became great was because Jim Cullen worked against him in scrimmages."

Macauley made All-MVC his final three seasons, All-America his final two seasons, and was the Associated Press National Player of the Year as a senior in 1948–49. To some of his war-veteran teammates, though, he was just a kid until they actually saw him play.

Saint Louis guard D. C. Wilcutt had been an infantryman in the South Pacific during World War II, while Macauley was a star at Saint Louis University High. "I really had never heard of Ed until we got down to Saint Louis University," said Wilcutt, who later became a highly successful coach at Christian Brothers College (CBC) High School. "But he was everything they said he was. He had a great hook shot, and he did shoot the ball right handed or left-handed, which was unusual to come back with the left-handed hook. It is hardly in the game anymore. For our team, he was a good rebounder."

FLANIGAN, THEN HICKEY

Despite the budding offensive stardom of Macauley, the Bills played a conservative brand of defensive basketball under Flanigan. Flanigan, however, lasted as the Bills' head coach only two seasons, despite compiling a 2–2 record against Oklahoma A&M Coach Henry Iba, the "Iron Duke," who was considered one of the top defensive coaches in college basketball.

In the next-to-last meeting between the two coaches, Flanigan's Billikens held the Oklahoma A&M Aggies to 20 points on their home floor in Stillwater (38–20). The 20 points is still a Saint Louis University record for fewest allowed an opponent in a game. "That was one of the worst defeats Iba had ever suffered in Stillwater," Flanigan said. "Don Shields, the Temple coach, told me Iba was hell-bent on winning that second game up here. We won (31–29). Dan Miller made the last basket." That was Flanigan's last Oklahoma A&M game before he returned full time to the insurance business in St. Louis.

The Billikens lost to Oklahoma, 47–41, in an NCAA play-in game in Kansas City in the 1946–47 finale. Flanigan got into a dispute with the school president during the game. "He was fired," Macauley said of Flanigan. "We had a president of the school who was a great fan, but sometimes he did not control his emotions at the game. Flanigan and Father (Patrick J.) Holloran during the game got into it. Father Holloran was trying to tell John how to coach, and John did not appreciate that."

Hickey, the highly successful Creighton coach, replaced Flanigan before the next season, and at his first team meeting, he boldly predicted great success with Macauley and a

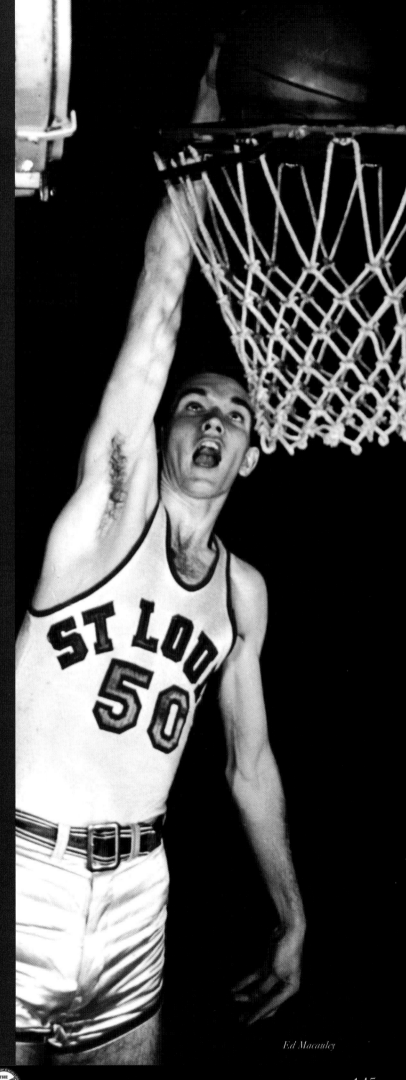

Ed Macauley

*The 1948 Billikens enjoy a victory parade at Union Station in
St. Louis following their NIT championship*

Eddie HICKEY

AS A PLAYER AND COACH THE VETERAN ATHLETIC
DIRECTOR AND HEAD COACH OF ST. LOUIS U.
HAS COMPILED AN ENVIABLE RECORD IN
HIS LONG CAREER. IN HIS FIRST YEAR
AS HEAD BASKETBALL COACH AT ST.
LOUIS IN '47 HIS BILLIKEN TEAM
TURNED IN A 24-3 RECORD AND
CAME HOME WITH THE COVETED
N.I.T. CHAMPIONSHIP! IN HIS PREP
DAYS AT TRINITY IN SIOUX CITY
EDDIE WAS A STANDOUT IN FOOT-
BALL, BASKETBALL, AND BASEBALL
AND CAPTAINED EACH OF THE
TEAMS. HE WAS AN ALL-NORTH
CENTRAL CONFERENCE BACK AT
CREIGHTON U. AND PLAYED TWO
YEARS ON THE BLUEJAY BASKET-
BALL TEAM. AT 53 YEARS OF AGE
EDDIE HAS COACHED 29 YEARS.

WOW! HOW
ABOUT THAT
RECORD?

SINCE COACHING THE N.I.T. CHAMPS IN '47-'48
HICKEY'S BILLIKENS HAVE WON THE SUGAR
BOWL TITLE TWICE, THE COTTON BOWL TITLE,
PLAYED IN THE N.I.T. FIVE MORE TIMES AND THE
N.C.A.A. ONCE! HIS ST. LOUIS TEAMS HAVE WON
158, LOST 63. AT CREIGHTON PREP 1926-34
HIS TEAMS WON 115, LOST 26, AND AT CREIGHTON
U. 1935-'46 THE RECORD WAS 132 WON, 72 LOST!

J.F. Goff

veteran team returning. Hickey never lacked confidence, but it might have been to compensate for his size. Eddie Hickey was a stubby 5-5, 11 inches shorter than the lanky Flanigan, and nicknamed "The Little General" and "Little Napoleon."

"He said we are going to play so many games here," Wilcutt remembered. "And then we are going to New York and the NIT. . . . I thought, 'Who is this guy?'" Wilcutt soon found out.

Hickey brought a fast-breaking style to St. Louis that season that clicked with the fans, the players, and the NIT selection committee. It suited Macauley's game as well. "He just opened the game up for us," Miller said. "The fast break was the best thing that ever happened to our team. It just suited us. We had big guys and we had fast little guys who could really move the ball."

Hickey's fast break featured no dribbling, just passing the ball down the floor. It was a unique style not seen much in the 1940s, and it made the Billikens fan favorites everywhere they played, including Madison Square Garden. Hickey called that team the "Paddycake Boys. . . . They hummed the ball around so fast, folks thought they were playing paddycake."

Macauley was tremendous in Hickey's system, because he was an active big man who could get the ball off the boards and ignite the fast break. "Primarily the job of the big men like Ed was to get the rebound and then throw the outlet pass," said Lou Lehman, a Saint Louis University guard. "These big men would hit the outside man and then everybody would fill in the lanes, and it was strictly pass it back and forth down the floor as fast as you could run."

Hickey's fast-paced style was in stark contrast to Iba's defensive-oriented half-court game that dominated the MVC in the 1940s and early 1950s. Iba got the better of Hickey, posting a 15–7 record against the former World War II Navy lieutenant. "They were rivals,"

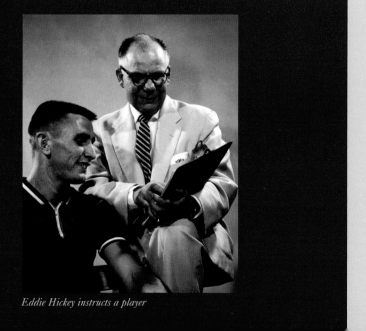

Eddie Hickey instructs a player

Macauley said. "Henry Iba was a great gentleman of basketball. He would beat your brains out, but as far as taking care of people and respecting people, he was a great man, as was Hickey. They had two of the best coaches in the same conference."

Only two teams beat Hickey's attack during the 1947–48 season, Oklahoma A&M twice and DePaul. A highlight of the 1947–48 regular season was Saint Louis breaking rival Notre Dame's 38-game home-court winning streak. With a 21–3 regular-season record, Saint Louis, the MVC runnerup to the Aggies, accepted an NIT bid.

NIT CHAMPS IN 1948

Part of Hickey's success was based on attention to details and strong discipline. Wilcutt could have lost his starting spot because he adhered to neither. Wilcutt remembers the train ride to New York City for the NIT. The long train ride was stuffy and hot during an early spring day in March. Wilcutt didn't have a coat and tie on when a photographer hopped aboard the train in Indianapolis to take a picture of the Billikens' starting five. Hickey told Wilcutt, who had been a starting forward all season, to step out of the picture because he was not wearing the required attire.

"Somebody else get in the picture," Hickey commanded. "That's how disciplined he was," Wilcutt said. "When we got to New York, I wore a tie with my pajamas the rest of the trip. I didn't know if I was going to start in the NIT, but I did."

Once they made it to the Big Apple, fast-breaking Saint Louis faced stubborn opposition, but they rolled past Bowling Green, 69–53, and then Western Kentucky, 60–53, to make the final against hometown New York University and its center, Dolph Schayes. "The tougher game was against Western Kentucky," Lehman said. "They had a bunch of guys who had come out of the service. They had an outstanding ball club, and they thought they were going to win the whole thing."

Macauley scored 19 points in the semifinals against Western Kentucky, came back with a 24-point title game against the Violets, and collected NIT Most Outstanding Player honors after the Billikens' 65–52 victory. "I think that after we were going to celebrate," Wilcutt said of the Billikens, who were a little awestruck in the Big Apple. "I think we went bowling. We didn't know what to do."

When the Billikens arrived back in St. Louis, a crowd of 15,000 was waiting for the team at Union Station. Saint Louis' strong finish set up potentially bigger things for Macauley as a senior in 1948–49.

The Billikens won their first 11 games, including a 42–40 victory over eventual NCAA champion Kentucky in the Sugar Bowl Tournament in New Orleans in late December. The Wildcats went on to win a second-straight NCAA title three months later. Lehman sparked Saint Louis in the final moments of the victory over the Wildcats, but he was in awe of Kentucky's Fabulous Five, who were coached by Adolph Rupp and led by Ralph Beard and Alex Groza. The next day, when Groza asked Lehman what time it was during the Sugar Bowl football game, Lehman called him, "sir." Macauley winced. "I respected them," Lehman said.

MACAULEY ERA LEFT MARK ON PROGRAM

By virtue of the victory over the defending NCAA champion Wildcats, the Billikens were the top-ranked team in the first Associated Press college basketball poll in history in January 1949. After rising to the top spot, the Billikens lost the next game to Oklahoma A&M, 29–27. It was the first of two losses that season to the Aggies, who won the MVC title and claimed an NCAA Tournament berth.

Saint Louis finished second in the MVC and went to the NIT, but they lost in the opening game to Bowling Green, 80–74, in Macauley's final collegiate appearance. During Saint Louis' 22–4 1948–49 season, Macauley led the nation in field goal percentage (52.4 percent) and was named the Associated Press National Player of the Year.

In a January 1949 article in *This Week Magazine* in the *Des Moines Sunday Register*, Hickey was quoted on Macauley: "They don't call him 'Easy' Ed Macauley for nothing. His unusual muscular coordination and a rhythm more than made up for his lack of heft. I have never seen a smoother player. He handles a basketball as gracefully as Fritz Kreisler does a violin."

A first-round draft pick by the St. Louis Bombers, Macauley became a seven-time NBA All-Star with the Boston Celtics and his hometown team, the St. Louis Hawks.

After Macauley left, Hickey's Saint Louis teams continued to battle Oklahoma A&M and Bradley for MVC supremacy. Hickey won MVC titles in 1952, 1955 (tie with Tulsa), and 1957 before he left to coach at Marquette. In 11 seasons in St. Louis, Hickey failed to finish either first or second in the MVC only twice. But Hickey's greatest moment occurred in his first season at Saint Louis University, when Macauley's local boys hoisted the NIT trophy in old Madison Square Garden in 1948.

The team and school passed on an opportunity to go back to New York City for an Olympic qualifying tournament later that year to determine which team would represent the United States in the 1948 Olympics in London. Several players already had seen those sights during World War II and didn't particularly want to relive the memories, and at least one of the players' wives was expecting a child that summer of 1948. "We decided not to go to the qualifying tournament because our whole team couldn't go," Macauley said. "That was the kind of team it was."

HOW "EASY" ED GOT HIS NICKNAME

Ed Macauley picked up his nickname "Easy" Ed early in his career at Saint Louis University when he was named captain for the first time. He prematurely thought the game was about to begin. At Saint Louis University's old West Pine Gym, Macauley climbed a spiral staircase from the locker rooms in the basement and pushed open a closed door and ran onto the floor. He took a couple of dribbles and took a shot at the basket, but none of his teammates followed him. The National Anthem was being played.

"When I realized it, I stopped," Macauley remembered. "And everybody said, 'Take it Easy, Ed! the game hasn't started yet. And the publicity guy liked that. . . . It was the greatest thing that ever happened to me, to have a nickname. It was because of my stupidity, not because of my ability."

ST, LOUIS THROUGH AND THROUGH

Saint Louis University's 1947–48 National Invitation Tournament champions was comprised entirely of players from St. Louis–area high schools.

Lou Lehman	– Beaumont
Bob Schmidt	– Cleveland
Joe Schmidt	– Cleveland
Danny Miller	– McBride
D. C. Wilcutt	– Normandy
Joe Ossola	– Collinsville (Ill.)
Ed Macauley	– Saint Louis U. High
Hank Raymonds	– Saint Louis U. High
Jack Wrape	– Saint Louis U. High
Clayton Cary	– Saint Louis U. High
Marvin Schatzman	– Soldan
John Cordia	– Saint Louis U. High

Jim Bain

BAIN RECEIVED HIS OFFICIATING START IN SAINT LOUIS UNIVERSITY GAME AT KIEL

Jim Bain, long-time Missouri Valley, Big Eight, and Big Ten basketball official and later supervisor of MVC officials, got his Division I officiating start in St. Louis on Dec. 17, 1964, in a game between Saint Louis University and Princeton at Kiel Auditorium. Saint Louis University coach John Benington's "Karate Defense" was focused on Princeton's Bill Bradley, a Crystal City, Mo., star who had shunned instate schools to go to the Ivy League. Bain, who had been a high school official, and veteran Big Ten and MVC official Red Strothers called 61 fouls and several technical fouls. Bradley scored 34 points but was constantly hacked, scoring 20 of his points on free throws.

Bain recounts that the next day that legendary *St. Louis Globe-Democrat* columnist Bob Burnes wrote: "Red Strothers, a veteran official in the Big Ten and the Missouri Valley, should have done better. And Jim Bain, officiating his first Division I game, should obviously return to high school."

Bain was further chastised by Big Ten supervisor of officials Bill Haarlow, who had a son on the Princeton team. He told Bain he would never

Dick Boushka

officiate a game in his league. "The thought ran through my mind, if this is what Division I is all about, I don't know if I want to take all the verbal abuse," Bain remembered. Of course, Bain went on to officiate games in the Big Ten as well as the Big Eight and Missouri Valley conferences. He officiated in the Final Four in 1970 and in 1973 was a Final Four standby official.

BILLIKENS' 1950s STAR: "DEADEYE DICK" BOUSHKA

Swingman Dick Boushka, a three-time MVC selection from 1953 to 1955, was the Billikens' top star of the 1950s, but he never played in the NBA because he went into private business after graduation and starred on Amateur Athletic Union teams for Vickers Petroleum Co. "He would have been a great player in the NBA because of his ability to score," Saint Louis center Ed Macauley said. "He was an extremely athletic individual. He could have been good in other sports. But he chose a better career path. He was gaining experience in business while in the industrial (AAU) league."

Boushka averaged 19.2 points during his career at Saint Louis University. He became president of Vickers Oil Co. in 1963 at age 29.

Al McGuire with Hank Raymonds and Rick Majerus

RAYMONDS A BILLIKEN

Hank Raymonds, who later served as assistant and head coach at Marquette, was a member of Saint Louis University's 1948 NIT title team. He played for Saint Louis University's High School before becoming a Billiken. "Hank couldn't score or shoot, but he was tough," Macauley said.

Raymonds was a Marquette assistant coach first under Eddie Hickey and then Al McGuire and was on the bench when Marquette won the NCAA title in 1977. He succeeded McGuire as head coach at Marquette from 1977 to 1983 and compiled a 126–50 record.

Xavier McDaniel

WICHITA STATE

Founded as Fairmont College in 1895, and known as the Municipal University of Wichita from 1926 to 1964, Wichita State University has been a member of the Missouri Valley Conference since 1945. Shocker basketball has a storied tradition that continues to the present, with a Sweet 16 appearance in the 2006 NCAA Tournament. Home court is at Charles Koch Arena, formerly known as the Roundhouse and Levitt Arena. Named after a prominent Wichita businessman, the arena was remodeled in 2003.

The Shockers are also known for their baseball, churning out major leaguers with regularity. Coach Gene Stephenson brought WSU baseball to prominence with sheer willpower and determination, starting the program from scratch in 1978. WSU owns more all-sports trophies (15) than any other Valley institution.

DAVE STALLWORTH, RALPH MILLER, AND A FINAL FOUR WITHOUT 'EM BOTH

Lanny Van Eman remembers the day Dave Stallworth showed up at the Wichita State basketball offices in the winter of 1961. It was hardly a grand arrival for a player who would wind up as the school's greatest basketball player.

"He came to Wichita on a bus, with tennis shoes tied together and hung over his shoulders," said Van Eman, a guard at Wichita State from 1958–62 and later an assistant coach for the Shockers. "He also had a gym bag and a good-sized shopping bag. Those were his worldly possessions at the time. He was a very shy sort of guy." Four years later, the 6-7 Stallworth left with 18 Wichita State basketball records, legendary status in the Missouri Valley Conference, and some of the greatest individual clutch performances ever seen in the Midwest, earning his nickname "The Rave."

In high school, Stallworth was an unknown during an era when recruiting was done by word of mouth, telephone calls, and newspaper clippings. Coming from an all-black high school in Dallas hindered recruiters from discovering Stallworth. His Madison High School's game scores barely rated agate, let alone stories, in the Dallas dailies in the racially segregated South of the late 1950s and early 1960s. "You got to realize what basketball meant to Texas. You are second rate when you talk about any sport other than football," said Stallworth, who played end for Madison High School's football team and consid-

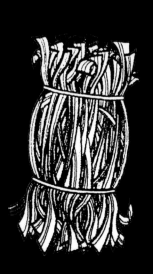

Henry Levitt Arena

ered historically black Grambling his top college choice before visiting Wichita. "I only played basketball to stay in shape for football. Then I learned to like it a lot."

From his humble beginnings in South Oak Cliff's Trinity River area in Texas, Stallworth became a first-round pick (No. 3 overall) in the 1965 NBA Draft by the New York Knicks. He logged 10 seasons in professional basketball and played for the Knicks' 1970 NBA championship team. Stallworth, an All-American and three-time All-MVC player, was part of the MVC's inaugural Hall-of-Fame Class in 1997.

"He was like Oscar Robertson," said Ron Heller, a Wichita State player from 1958 to 1961 and later a Wichita State assistant coach. "He could play any position on the court. . . . His attitude, his approach to the game . . . A basketball went out of play in a drill, he would go shag it. He just loved to play the game. It wasn't what he said, it was what he did."

Stallworth just as easily could have slipped though Wichita State's recruiting net. He recounted how a friend of Wichita State Coach Ralph Miller was on a flight and spoke with sprinter Stone Johnson. Johnson, who attended the same high school as Stallworth, was returning from the 1960 Rome Olympics. "Stone was saying he knew a guy who could really play the game of basketball," Stallworth remembered. "And they (Wichita State) came down to Dallas and saw me play. Stone knew I played a different brand of basketball than everybody else. I was pretty good at a pretty young age." The Shockers scouted a high school game that featured Nate Bowman, a 6-10 center from Fort Worth, against Stallworth. Wichita State landed Stallworth and Bowman, both of whom ended up as teammates with the New York Knicks.

Recruiting in the late 1950s and early 1960s was an inexact science at best. "He (Miller) found some people who could play the game in some funny places in our country," said Gary Thompson, who played for Miller, was an assistant coach for him, and later became Wichita State's head coach from 1964 to 1971. "I think he felt he

had to. He couldn't compete (in recruiting) with Kansas, Kansas State, and Oklahoma State. We didn't have the reputation, and it forced us to do that type of recruiting. He was very good at it."

Miller recruited players who had played little or had checkered high school basketball success, such as center Gene Wiley, forwards Ron Heller and Sam Smith, and guard Jerry Kittiko. He developed recruiting bases in Texas and Pennsylvania, particularly McKeesport in the latter state.

By far, Stallworth was Miller's greatest recruiting story at Wichita State. "When Ralph recruited him out of Dallas, he said to the people in Wichita, 'I have a player who can be just as good as Oscar Robertson,'" remembers Johnny Overby, an MVC game official and later supervisor of league officials. "Stallworth moved and reacted like a 5-10 guy," Thompson said. "He had all the size and all the agility in one lump sum."

Miller, in his own right, ranks as a legend and is a member of the National Basketball Hall of Fame.

GETTING IT STARTED IN WICHITA

A multi-sport star from Chanute, Kan., Miller studied under James Naismith and played for Coach Phog Allen at Kansas. At Wichita East High School and then at Wichita State, Iowa, and Oregon State, Miller coached strict discipline, precise offense, and passing. He coached Wichita State from 1951 to 1964.

"What he did was very simplistic," Van Eman said. "He would not allow for any slippage. He maybe was best known early on for not permitting a bounce pass. His philosophy had this genesis: His teams played in a lot of large arenas in the MVC, which also had hockey, and they also played at Chicago Stadium and Madison Square Garden, which had portable courts. One or two turnovers (with bad bounces) could be the difference. He was really adamant about minimizing turnovers, eliminating second shots, and playing defense."

Miller—inducted into the MVC Hall of Fame posthumously in 2001—was among the first college coaches to utilize the full-court zone press. He ran the triangle and

> *Stallworth ended his college career with 18 Wichita State basketball records, legendary status in the Missouri Valley Conference, and some of the greatest individual clutch performanes ever seen in the Midwest.*

Dave Stallworth

1-4 offenses. "He got a lot of teasing and questions from the press because he was bringing it (the zone press) from high school," Thompson said. "They said it would never work because of the good ball-handlers in college. It was solid. What propelled him into stardom was the full-court zone press."

Miller had the nickname "Rawhide" because of his pockmarked face. He also was nicknamed "The Ripper" for his stern demeanor. Wichita State's career scoring leader, Cleo Littleton (1951–54), played for Miller in both high school and college, as did Thompson. "You could say Bobby Knight was my coach for seven years," Littleton quipped during his MVC Hall of Fame induction in 2000. "Ralph was very strict. During high school, you missed a layup, you got a swat, you missed again, you got another swat. If you had two or three swats, he would give you an opportunity to run 30 layups or get another swat."

With star players such as Littleton, who was black, Miller helped break the color line in Kansas high school basketball by winning the state title in 1951. He also coached numerous black players at Wichita State, including Littleton, Stallworth, Bowman, Ernie Moore, and Kelly Pete during an era when several major conferences didn't have any black players on their teams. "All the things said about him, he had a willingness to step out on the fringe with black players," Van Eman said of the reluctance of many schools, particularly in the South, to give black players scholarships.

Still, there were roadblocks for Miller in Wichita.

The school's downtown gym, the Forum, was cramped, and few students attended the games. Miller believed he needed a new on-campus arena to attract top players consistently from outside the area and to become a power. He got his wish.

The Roundhouse was the 10,400-seat arena that Miller urged school and city officials to build in the mid-1950s at a cost of $1.4 million. But it was the arena Stallworth, not Miller, finally filled, as the team became a national power in the 1960s and rose to a No. 1 ranking early in the 1964–65 season.

From 1961 to 1964, Wichita State defeated 10 straight ranked teams at home. The string of victories at the Roundhouse started shortly before

Stallworth was eligible, on Dec. 18, 1961, when Van Eman's shot with three seconds remaining upended the defending national champion Cincinnati Bearcats and ended their 27-game winning streak, 52–51.

Van Eman, a transfer from North Carolina State, used up his eligibility at the end of the first semester several weeks later, but Stallworth and another guard, Leonard Kelley, joined the team for the last eight games of the season and the Shockers became a hot ticket. Wichita State finished the 1961–62 season in the National Invitation Tournament but lost in the first round to Dayton.

The decision to play Stallworth also meant that he would be ineligible the second semester of the 1964–65 season when he would be a senior and the Shockers had a real shot at winning the NCAA title. "The decision Ralph made was lousy," Thompson said, chuckling. "I wish he hadn't made it. In some regards, Dave wishes the same thing. He wishes he could have played games our final year. It was a good ball club, and we had a shot at it."

But that was much later.

STALLWORTH'S STAR RISES
By the 1962–63 season (his second), Stallworth was even more of a force. He increased his scoring from 19.8 to 22.8 points per game. He could play any position, pass, and rebound, and he led the Wichita State fast break by grabbing rebounds,

Ralph Miller

turning and finding teammates streaking down the floor, or just doing it all himself.

He was a taller and faster yet less powerful and explosive version of Oscar Robertson, who already was in the NBA. "I was doing things people just didn't see 6-7 guys do," Stallworth said. "I could dribble the ball. I could play the guard, the small forward. That was my natural position. Or, I could play the power forward or the center. And I had some speed."

Early in the 1962–63 season, No. 2-ranked Ohio State fell to Wichita State, 71–54, before the largest crowd (11,375) in the history of the Roundhouse, now known as Charles Koch Arena. Stallworth scored 22 points against the Buckeyes, who were coming off an NCAA runner-up finish the previous season. "It was the game that almost wasn't," Stallworth said. "They had over 11,000 in there. The fire marshal said we are not going to let you play this game. There would have been a riot. He allowed the game to be played only after the aisles were cleared. Everybody sucked in their breath and scooted to the center of the bench seats."

At a slightly less packed Roundhouse six weeks later (Feb. 16, 1963), Stallworth displayed all his talents with a Wichita State career-high 46-point outburst in a 65–64 victory over Cincinnati. Despite vomiting orange juice at halftime, he scored the last seven points of the game, wiped out a six-point UC lead with four minutes remaining, and ended the Bearcats' 37-game winning streak. The Shockers still finished a distant second to eventual NCAA runner-up Cincinnati in the MVC regular-season race and were first-round losers in the NIT again, this time by one point to Villanova, but the Cincinnati game took on a legendary status in Wichita State basketball history. Stallworth clinched All-America for the first of three straight seasons with his exhilarating performance against the Bearcats. "He made almost every shot in the books," Miller told the *Dallas Times Herald*. "You name it. He made it. And some of the moves were fantastic. I even saw movies of the game, and I still don't believe it."

A year later, in 1963–64, with Stallworth averaging 26.5 points, Bowman chipping in solid board play, and several guards contributing, the Shockers had a close brush with the Final Four. A surprising 62–59 win over Cincinnati at the Roundhouse, when the Shockers rallied in the final minute behind Stallworth, proved to be a key victory in late January. Wichita State won its first MVC basketball title, but the Shockers had to beat Drake in a one-game playoff in Lawrence, Kan., of all places, to go to the NCAA Tournament.

It was all set up for Wichita State to go to its first Final Four in Kansas City, Mo., because the NCAA Midwest Regional was being held at the Roundhouse. However, after a routine victory over Creighton and Paul Silas, 84–68, the Shockers were upset by Kansas State, 94–86. Van Eman, then an assistant coach for Miller, said Kansas State Coach Tex Winter devised a way to keep Stallworth from getting the ball and halted the Wichita State fast break.

Thompson believed that the team wasn't mentally prepared going into the regional final game. Years later, Miller labeled the loss "a tremendous disappointment": "I think we were good enough to make some waves," Miller said in 1989. "In the big games, you have to be prepared mentally as well as physically," Thompson said. "We were healthy. We had no one hurt and were on our home court. It didn't look like anything that could happen to us could be bad. We played poorly. Kansas State played great. And that's disaster for any team."

Following the 1963–64 season, Miller resigned at Wichita State and became the coach at Iowa. Gary Thompson, Miller's long-time assistant and former player, was named the Shockers' new coach.

THAT FINAL FOUR SEASON

Ironically, Wichita State went to the 1965 Final Four in Portland, but neither Miller nor Stallworth, the main actors who put Shocker basketball on the national stage, were there.

Thompson, the Shockers' rookie head coach, knew he had Stallworth for just 16 games during the 1964–65 season because of

Stallworth's deadly jumper

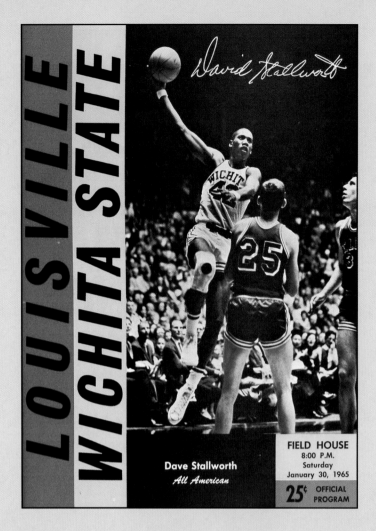

FIELD HOUSE
8:00 P.M.
Saturday
January 30, 1965

Dave Stallworth
All American

25¢ OFFICIAL PROGRAM

Stallworth claims ownership of the boards

Miller's decision to play the star midway through the 1961–62 season. What Thompson didn't know was that center Nate Bowman became academically ineligible at nearly the same time Stallworth's three years of eligibility were exhausted.

Stallworth's farewell was memorable at the Roundhouse. He scored 40 points in his final game against Louisville on Jan. 30, 1965, and had 45 points against Loyola of Chicago the day before on the same floor.

Once Stallworth's jumpers and Bowman's rebounding were gone, WSU could have folded. "One day in practice, Gary Thompson had to try his starting five's tallest player who was 6-5," said 6-4 forward Jamie Thompson, who became a solid starter in place of Stallworth. "He just decided to play his best players. We didn't make any turnovers, played solid defense, and we were all good shooters. We would work the ball around and get a good shot. Gary Thompson gets 90 percent of the credit making a change."

Added Gary Thompson: "We scored 80 to 90 points the first semester. But to win, we had to cut it down to 50–60–70 points a game to give us a chance at it. We had to do it by controlling the ball much longer before we put the ball in the air. We slowed the game down and took minutes off the clock."

Wichita State predictably struggled down the stretch and lost three MVC games. Still, the Shockers hung on to win their first outright MVC title and made the NCAA Tournament. Wichita State beat an outmatched SMU team, 86–81, in the first round of the tournament, and then the Shockers topped Coach Henry Iba and Oklahoma A&M, 54–46, in the Midwest Regional final. Thompson beat Iba in a half-court game in which Wichita State actually took the ball to mid-court line, controlled it for long stretches, and then repeatedly hit the A&M defense for layups. "We shot more layups in that game than most college teams shoot in 10 games," Gary Thompson said.

This same strategy backfired against a more athletic UCLA team in the Final Four semifinals, as the Shockers fell 108–89. In the third-place game, Princeton's Bill Bradley set a Final Four individual scoring record by ripping the Shockers for 58 points in a 118–82 throttling.

The Shockers can only imagine what might have been with Stallworth and Bowman in the Final Four. Michigan and Cazzie Russell, which lost to UCLA, 91–80, in the NCAA title game, barely beat the Shockers, 87–85, in December at Cobo Hall in Detroit. "If Stallworth and Bowman would have been in the same starting lineup, (the UCLA game) would have been a totally different game—we would have gotten to the finals," Jamie Thompson said. "We could have played with UCLA. We could have played with anybody. It would have been a totally different deal."

Upon returning to the hotel after the loss to Princeton, Heller, then an assistant coach for Thompson, remembers his depressed head coach receiving a pep talk from one of the game's giants. "(Kentucky coach) Adolph Rupp says to Gary, 'Hey, come here a minute. Get your head up. A lot of guys never have been here and never will be,'" Heller recalled. "Gary says, 'Thank you, Mr. Rupp.' Gary felt bad we gave up so many points. Those were the best words at the right moment."

CLEO LITTLETON

Freshmen were eligible for varsity competition in 1951 in college basketball, and Cleo Littleton from Wichita East High School took advantage of it, making All-Missouri Valley Conference his first season at Wichita State. Littleton collected three more all-conference awards and is still the only four-time All-MVC first-team basketball player in the 100-year history of the conference.

Littleton was born in Oklahoma but moved to Wichita when he was three years old. He came from a very religious family and went to church several times a week. He gravitated toward basketball, and at 6-4 was a big man for that era, but he also could handle the ball.

Littleton played for Coach Ralph Miller and won a state title at Wichita East. He then moved with Miller to Wichita State, where he became the first player west of the Mississippi River to score 2,000 points in his college career. He is still the Wichita State career scoring leader with 2,164 points, 12 more than Xavier McDaniel, who played for the Shockers from 1981 to 1985.

In 2000, Littleton was inducted into the MVC Hall of Fame. "I have no business with those guys, but I accept it anyway," Littleton said at the time. He is one of five Shockers to have his number (13) retired: McDaniel (34), Dave Stallworth (42), Antoine Carr (35), and Cliff Levingston (54).

Littleton competed during an era when black athletes weren't welcome during some road trips. Segregation

Gary Thompson

was still a way of American life in the 1950s in some parts of the country. "I was not allowed to go restaurants to eat or to use restrooms . . . I had to stay on the bus," Littleton said during his induction. "That was not good for the team concept."

THE SMITHSON YEARS
BRING INVIGORATION, PROBATION

Gene Smithson was ready to move on from Illinois State in 1978 after the Redbirds had posted three straight 20-victory seasons. As a Division I independent in that era, Illinois State had failed to receive an at-large bid to the NCAA Tournament. So Smithson jumped to Wichita State of the Missouri Valley Conference starting with the 1978–79 season, where he could make an NCAA Tournament run. "We were in the NIT," Smithson said of his final season at Illinois State. "We had good teams which could have competed in the NCAA . . . I was frustrated. Other programs started talking to me. I wanted to get where I could compete in the NCAA and improve my financial situation."

By the early 1980s, Smithson had taken Wichita State to the Elite Eight of the NCAA Tournament and also embroiled the Shockers in an NCAA probation.

Smithson built Wichita State into a national power with a collection of athletes rivaling anything the MVC had seen in years.

In a period of a half-dozen years, his Wichita State teams featured such future NBA players as Ozell Jones, Antoine Carr, Cliff Levingston, Xavier McDaniel, and Greg Dreiling. Smithson's athletic and emotionally charged teams packed Henry Levitt Arena, where crowds rose above 10,000 again and gave rise to the cheer, "We're Going to Beat the Hell Out of You."

Black was in vogue. Fans wore it. The arena was dominated by the color, giving way to a dark feeling of a dungeon. His teams played a highly entertaining full-court game, which began to gain notice nationally. "We were the rebels," said Wichita State's Carr. "We wore black uniforms and black shoes and nobody wanted to play us."

Smithson, the former Argo (Ill.) High School coach, demanded Mental Toughness Extra Effort (MTXE) from his players. "I told my assistant coaches, 'Don't bring me a soft player, look for a hard player who will take a hit and get up and get on with it,'" Smithson said. "We looked for size with quickness, and we were fortunate to have big guys extremely athletic. . . . We ran a controlled fast break and played a quick-tempo type game. Defensively, we were pressing and it matched our philosophy. And it blended in with my personality."

Smithson said the key recruit was the 6-9 Carr out of Wichita Heights High School, which had produced star KU guard Darnell Valentine. Carr appeared headed to KU, but Gene Smithson connected with him when he went into his home and ate heaps of chitlins. "I had a friend named Darnell Valentine playing at KU," Carr said. "He always said I would be a Jayhawker. I said no, there will be an end to that era. It is time for the Shockers to show up. And we did every night." "Antoine Carr was an incredible athlete—probably one of the best 6-9 athletes in the country at that time," Smithson said.

Before playing a game for the Shockers, Carr played in the McDonald's High School All-Star Game and helped convince the two Californians, Levingston and Jones, to sign with Wichita State. Levingston and Carr became

Cleo Littleton

known as the "bookend" forwards, although their style of play differed. "I had no idea how good Cliff would be when he got here," said Wichita State's 6-7 Jay Jackson, a defensive specialist on that team. "He was pretty raw. At first, he could hardly make a left-handed layup. He was a hard worker in practice. He was the fastest guy on the team. He could run up and down the court all day long. Once he got offensive skills, it was all there."

MAKING THE BREAKTHROUGH IN 1981
Smithson's first season at Wichita State (14–14 in 1978–79) was hardly a prelude of things to come, but his

Antoine Carr

"*I passed the ball to him against Bradley. I was giving it to him to dunk. He gave it back to me for a layup. He said, 'Don't do it again. That's what I do. I share the ball.'*"

second season (17–12 and an NIT berth) showed what the promising freshmen—Levingston, Carr, and Jones—were capable of delivering. Add a backcourt of Illinois transfer 6-5 sophomore Mike Jones and Illinois State and 6-3 junior college transfer Randy Smithson, son of the coach, then even former Marquette Coach Al McGuire took notice. "When those guys (Carr, Levingston, and Ozell Jones) were freshmen, Al came down and spoke at the arena," Smithson said. "We had an exhibition game against Russia and beat Russia. He got out in middle of floor. He told WSU fans, 'Remember this is going to be a great team, remember.'"

True to McGuire's word, Wichita State won 19 of its first 21 games in 1980–81, with Carr and the 6-8 Levingston combining to average more than 34 points and exactly 16 rebounds a game. The 6-11 Ozell Jones fit in between them as a shot-blocking center who could step out and make a 15-foot jump shot as well as run the court. "I accused Cliff of missing my passes to pad his rebounding stats," Randy Smithson said. "He was a great defender and could run all day. Cliff could run like a deer. He got out to run five-minute miles like it was nothing in 95-degree heat. They called him 'Good News.' He had a lot of charisma."

"Antoine Carr was as gifted a player as I ever played with," Randy Smithson stated. "Maybe one of the most gifted to play the game. He was unselfish. I tell this story. I loved playing with him. I passed the ball to him against Bradley. I was giving it to him to dunk. He gave it back to me for a layup. He said, 'Don't do it again. That's what I do. I share the ball.' I was a junior and senior when they came in. My job was to mold them and shape them. I was a little like Steve Nash. I am not saying I was that good. I distributed the ball and made athletes look

Wichita State won the 1981 MVC regular-season title, only the Shockers' second since 1965. That was despite two losses to second-place Tulsa, which would go on to win the National Invitation Tournament in Coach Nolan Richardson's first season at the school. Because the Shockers lost to Creighton in the MVC title game in Wichita, they were an NCAA at-large selection, but they still got to play the first two NCAA rounds in Wichita.

While reeling from the loss to Creighton, Wichita State was informed by the NCAA that Jones, the Shockers' starting sophomore center, had lost all appeals to be eligible for the NCAA Tournament. His high school P.E. courses could not be counted toward his initial

The Smithsons: Gene, the father (above) and Randy, the son (below)

eligibility requirements in college because his high school did not count them for other students. "His transcript had been on file for two years," Gene Smithson said. "We kind of fought it but lost the decision." The Creighton game turned out to be Jones' final as a Shocker.

Even without Jones, the Shockers swept by Southern University, 95–70, in the first round and then encountered third-seeded Iowa in the second round before a packed house at Henry Levitt Arena. Coach Lute Olson's Hawkeyes had been to the Final Four the previous season and had lost to eventual NCAA champion Louisville in the semifinals. Much of that Iowa team returned.

Early in the second half, Wichita State trailed, 40–25. The Shockers' season appeared to be coming to an end. "In the huddle, Antoine Carr said, 'It is my time now, and I want the ball,'" Randy Smithson said. "He also took their 7-footers out of the game."

Wichita State scored 15 straight points to tie the score. "The crowd had a big part of the game," Jay Jackson said. "They (the band) just kept playing over, 'We are going to beat the hell out of you.' The crowd was going nuts and nuts about them (Iowa) not scoring."

After Wichita State climbed back into the game, both teams traded baskets until the score was tied at 56 with 17 seconds left in the game after Carr scored on a layup. Iowa called its final timeout to set up a last play, but missed a shot with under 10 seconds left. Carr rebounded and was fouled.

Iowa's Bob Hansen called a sixth timeout, which resulted in a technical foul on the Hawkeyes. With the score still tied at 56, Carr missed the front end of a one-and-one on the personal foul on Iowa, and he appeared to be ready to shoot the technical foul shots, which could still win the game. "I said, 'No, this one is mine,'" Randy Smithson said. "I am going to make the free throws."

He did for a 58–56 Wichita State lead. Carr made two more when he was fouled again on the inbounds pass, and those free throws provided Wichita State with a trip to New Orleans to face arch-rival Kansas in the Sweet 16. The Jayhawks and Shockers had not played since the 1955–56 season.

It was a classic matchup of the blue-blood Jayhawks, who had refused to schedule the upstart Shockers from the MVC. Randy Smithson already had provided bulletin board material for the game when he popped off to the *Wichita Eagle-Beacon* earlier in the season when Wichita State had gotten off to a fast start. "I said, 'It's a joke KU is rated and we are not in the Top

20,'" Smithson recalled. "The next day in the headlines: 'Smithson Says KU a Joke.' I walked into the office. My dad ripped me a new one. I said, 'I didn't say that.' He said, 'Yeah, you are always running your mouth to reporters. Watch what you say.' They had that on their bulletin board. But what's the odds we would be playing them in the tournament? . . . Within two minutes they are up four, the joke is on me."

Wichita State guard Mike Jones, however, had other ideas near the end of "The Battle of New Orleans." Kansas appeared to be on the way to victory with just under a minute to play. The Jayhawks were ahead by three points and KU guard Darnell Valentine, the Wichita native who led all scorers with 21 points, was at the free-throw line shooting the front end of a one-and-one. He missed the front end. Wichita State closed to within one point on Jones's 25-foot jumper. Then after a KU timeout, Valentine missed an easy layup on the other end of the floor, which would have restored the lead to three points.

Jones made the game winner from nearly the same spot on the floor with two seconds remaining to ultimately send the Shockers to a 66–65 victory and into the regional title game against LSU. "I always knew I could do something like that," Jones told the *Wichita Eagle-Beacon* years later. "I was so excited for our fans."

Mike Jones

One frantic sequence remained. On the KU inbounds play with two seconds remaining, Valentine nearly redeemed himself when he set a pick near the baseline and the Shockers' Jackson ran into him. "I was following the ball," Jackson said. "I felt like the biggest goat in the history of Wichita. But it was a no call. The referee said in *SI (Sports Illustrated)* he didn't make the call because I didn't run through him (Valentine). I stopped and made contact. They called another timeout. Ted (Owens, KU coach) was screaming at the refs, and Gene was chewing my ass. "I told him I didn't see him. After that, I got back off the ball when they threw it in. I don't think they got a shot off."

"It could have gone both ways," Gene Smithson said. "It was a no-call situation. . . . In those kind of situations, you don't decide a game like that on a call. It was a no-call."

As electrifying a finish as it was for Wichita State fans, it was devastating for often-under-fire Kansas Coach Ted Owens. It would be the final NCAA Tournament appearance of his KU career and last winning season in Lawrence.

"That ball game just took the starch out of Ted," said Tom Hedrick, long-time Kansas and MVC broadcaster. "I don't think he was ever the same. There was big time pressure. It was the game Wichita talked about, and it finally came to fruition. . . . The Shockers simply knocked down the shots in the last five minutes and KU didn't. I remember walking out there, and I never thought I had seen him lower. It was a political game. Wichita State beat big brother. You would have thought they had won the national title game."

Cliff Levingston

The Shockers defeated Kansas without point guard Tony Martin, who was out for the season with a back injury, which he suffered the previous game against Iowa. This meant that both Jones and Jackson, the top two reserves, saw more playing time. "People didn't realize how good we were," Randy Smithson said. "Ozell was ineligible and Tony Martin, our point guard, goes down with a back injury against Iowa and we still go all the way to the Final Eight without two starters. . . . But then we have to play LSU. They are 30–3 and we are playing in the Superdome, and more than 30,000 fans are yelling. 'Tiger Bait, Tiger Bait' and we are without two starters."

LSU won, 96–85. "It (injuries) hurt us in the LSU game," Gene Smithson said. "Antoine got into foul trouble, and that really hurt us. Had we had all of our players, we could have protected him more. We thought we had an excellent chance of winning the NCAA title if we had had everybody intact. Losing Ozell and losing Tony Martin weakened our bench of course and our talent level."

SHOCKERS LEARN THEY CAN'T GO TO NCAAs
Although an NCAA investigation had been on-going into the Wichita State basketball program during the 1980–81 season, the findings and probation didn't occur until during the middle of 1981–82.

Anticipation for the upcoming season was still great in Wichita during the fall of 1981 because five of the top seven players, including the "Bookends" returned from a 26–7 Elite Eight team. Plus, the Shockers were welcoming another outstanding freshman class, which included two Wichita high school standouts, shooter 6-4 Aubrey Sherrod (Wichita Heights) and big man, 7-1 Greg Dreiling (Kapaun–Mt. Carmel).

Although Wichita State fans were most familiar with these two local high school stars, the best of the lot turned out to be another freshman, 6-7 Xavier McDaniel from Columbia, S.C. "When I told my mother and high school coach I was going to (Wichita) Kansas, everybody said, 'Wo, they have Antoine and Cliff,'" McDaniel said when he was inducted into the MVC Hall of Fame in 1998. "I said as along as they are running and jumping, I am all right."

McDaniel averaged only 5.8 points per game his freshman year. He considered transferring, but he decided to stay and eventually became the first player in Division I history to lead the country in both rebounding and scoring during his senior season in 1984–85. "I brought him off the bench," Gene Smithson said of the 1981–82 season. "I thought I would lose him at the semester of his freshman year. He questioned whether he was going to get playing time. I assured him he would be fine."

The fact that a future NBA star was on the Shockers' bench should indicate the talent level that season. Wichita State won its first

the "BATTLE of NEW ORLEANS"

WICHITA STATE – 66

KANSAS UNIVERSITY – 65

N.C.A.A. MIDWEST REGIONALS
BASKETBALL CHAMPIONSHIPS
MARCH 20, 1981

SUPERDOME – NEW ORLEANS
Largest Crowd Ever for
NCAA Tournament Game
34,036

1st Meeting of Two Teams
in *26* Years
Last Time at Wichita State
Dec. 7, 1955

Winning Shot - Wichita State reserve Mike Jones launches his game-winning 25-foot shot against Kansas in the NCAA Midwest Regional semifinal contest at New Orleans. Jones scored Wichita State's last four points, pumping in two long shots in the final minute, as the Shockers came from three points behind to upset the Jayhawks.

eight games and rose to a No. 2 ranking nationally before dropping games to North Carolina State and San Francisco in Honolulu.

The real hammer fell a couple of weeks later when Wichita State was placed on a three-year NCAA probation. On Jan. 11, 1982, the NCAA announced 44 violations in the WSU basketball program, 32 under the previous coach, Harry Miller, and 12 under the current coach, Gene Smithson. The Shockers were banned from postseason play for two seasons, 1981–82 and 1982–83. "It took two or three weeks for us to get back our chemistry," Gene Smithson said. "Those kids were hurt over it."

The Shockers finished in a tie for second in the MVC regular-season race, dropping two games to a Tulsa team, which was led by Paul Pressey. "Tulsa was our nemesis," said Randy Smithson, who was an assistant coach for the Shockers after completing his eligibility in 1980–81. "They gave us prob-lems. They were all great games. Their style was trap and jump and that messed with us. We could out play them for 36 minutes and then have a four-minute let down, they would make up 15 points. . . . It seemed like it was who had the last spurt who would win, and it seemed like they always got it."

Randy Smithson was the Shockers' head coach from 1996-2000

Wichita State won its final seven games, including a 66–65 victory over LSU in Baton Rouge, to finish with a 23–6 record. There was no MVC Tournament for Wichita State, either. "I don't know that we took things as seriously as we would have if we had had a chance to win it all," said Jackson, who was a senior. "We were all frustrated. We had a great team, and we couldn't do anything."

LEVINGSTON, DREILING LEAVE;
CARR STAYS, MCDANIEL STARS

Levingston declared for the NBA Draft after the 1981–82 season. Dreiling decided to transfer to Kansas. Carr stayed for his senior season, and McDaniel—the X-Man—starred as a sophomore.

That was the backdrop for a second-straight season when Wichita State would stay home from the MVC and NCAA Tournaments because of the NCAA-imposed sanctions. To add to the frustrations, Carr missed the first six games of the season with a stress fracture in his leg, and the Shockers dropped their opener at New Orleans, 96–82, which would be only one of three losses all season.

"I think it was difficult," said Randy Smithson. "What motivated us was we said we have the best team in the country and we wanted to prove that every game. Every game was our NCAA Tournament. Not many teams could keep it going through probation and would be able to do that. I would say we would have won the NCAA Tournament hands down. I say to this day that was the best team we ever had at Wichita State (1982–83)."

The 1982–83 team looked quite different from the previous two Wichita State teams. Carr was the leader, and McDaniel had become a starter and the other bookend. Six-10 Yugoslovian Zarko Durisic was the man in the middle, and Sherrod, a sopho-more, was one of the league's top outside shooters.

The Shockers (25–3 overall) finished 17–1 in MVC play. Only a one-point loss at Illinois State marred the Shockers' conference record, which was four games better than any other team.

Carr was the MVC's leading scorer. "Antoine Carr was a man among boys. He was so big and so strong," said Bradley guard Jim Les. "Nobody in the league could stop him." McDaniel was the nation's leading rebounder. "Xavier had incredible will and incredible focus, to think he could accomplish anything," Gene Smithson said.

In the final two games of the 1982–83 season, McDaniel and Carr showed why they were inducted into the MVC Hall of Fame a year apart in the late 1990s. McDaniel had 34 points and 20 rebounds in Wichita State's 97–96

Xavier McDaniel

double-overtime victory at Bradley. The X-Man had put up big rebounding numbers in a previous Bradley game in Wichita, and Bradley Coach Dick Versace had accused the Wichita State stat crew of padding his rebounds. This time, the Braves' statisticians kept the books, and during the game McDaniel gave it to the Bradley bench. "He (Xavier) looks over at us and says, 'Is that O.K. now? Do you know I can rebound?'" remembered Tony Barone, who was an assistant coach at Bradley at the time.

Carr's moment came a few days later when he finished his career at Wichita State with a school-record 47 points against Southern Illinois. Before the game Randy Smithson relayed of Carr, "He said, 'Duke—that's what my dad called me—Duke, I am going to show all these people if I had been selfish what I could have done.'" Carr's 47-point total has an asterisk beside it, because one of his baskets was a three-pointer. Given that the MVC was experimenting with the three-point line that season, the three-pointer allowed him to break Dave Stallworth's previous WSU record of 46 points. Nevertheless Carr's jersey joined Stallworth's and was retired by the school after the game. Carr told reporters, "If ever you have a feeling you didn't want to leave a place, that's the feeling I have. And I don't want to leave yet."

After Carr left and became a first-round NBA Draft pick of the Detroit Pistons, Wichita State basketball was never quite the same, despite the presence of McDaniel.

The next three years, Wichita State failed to win 20 games in any one season, but they nonetheless made the NCAA Tournament in 1985.

During a season in which "X" became the first player to lead Division I in rebounding and scoring the same year, Wichita State rebounded to win the 1985 MVC Tournament despite a 12-loss regular season. The Shockers lost in the first round of the NCAA Tournament in 1985 to Georgia.

Gene Smithson, now retired, still loves to talk about the old days, although a hint of sadness tinges his voice when the NCAA sanctions are mentioned. He, his son Randy, and the rest of the staff were fired in 1986 after a 14–14 season. He later coached in the Puerto Rico Professional League and at Central Florida Community College. "My philosophy is that you have got to move on," Gene Smithson said

WSU's All-American trio (L to R): Cliff Levingston, Xavier McDaniel and Antoine Carr

lead Division I in rebounding. The bald-headed McDaniel's high-arching turnaround jump shot—along with fierce defense—was his offensive trademark during his basketball career, which included 10 solid years in the NBA.

"What a freak of nature," said Randy Smithson, who was an assistant coach at WSU when McDaniel was a player. "He would go over you, through you, and by you to get a rebound. He would rebound the ball, throw an outlet pass, and get behind the defense for an alley-oop and dunk it—all on the same play."

In 1984–85 at Wichita State, McDaniel provided fans with a statistical anomaly at the time. He was the first player in Division I history to lead the country in both rebounding (14.8) and scoring (27.2) during the same season. McDaniel also led the country in rebounding as a sophomore (14.4) in 1982–83, although much taller and bigger centers—Houston's Akeem Olajuwon, Virginia's Ralph Sampson, and Georgetown's Patrick Ewing—were playing college basketball concurrently.

McDaniel, the MVC Player of the Year in 1984 and 1985, was a three-time All-MVC first-team selection and was inducted into the league's Hall of Fame in 1998. "I knew one thing, the guy was tenacious," Gene Smithson said. "I would have to protect other players from him in practice. It was just a war. He got inside the lines and he commanded attention. He was such a competitor that he expected everybody around him to be as competitive as he would be. He was up all the time. He would rather get a rebound than a basket."

"There's no doubt I was disappointed and I was hurt (by the NCAA sanctions). But at the same time I am not a quitter. I put that behind us. We came back in 1985 to go back to the NCAAs."

"He is at peace, although it has been tough on him," said son Randy, now a junior college coach. "It was probably a deal where he was black-balled (to get other Division I jobs). He knows he had great players and great teams. Naturally, he would like to be respected like others."

THE X-MAN COMETH

The most aggressive basketball player in MVC history may have been Wichita State's 6-7 Xavier McDaniel. Known as the "X-Man" or "X," McDaniel was to the MVC what Michael Jordan was to the Atlantic Coast Conference during that era. The X-Man was a Shocker from 1981 to 1985.

McDaniel, wiry and quick enough to parlay an assortment of scoring moves into becoming the nation's leading scorer as a senior, also was strong enough to twice

Wichita State basketball's good fortune was the fact that the Shocker head football coach at the time, Jeff Jeffries, had a WSU assistant who had lived across the street from McDaniel's family in Columbia, S.C. McDaniel played basketball at A.C. Flora High School in Columbia, and one of his high school teammates was Tyrone Corbin, who later played at DePaul and in the NBA. "We thought there might be some reluctance for him to come," Gene Smithson said. "Carr (Antoine) and Levingston (Cliff) were juniors. We thought that might intimidate the X-Man. He wasn't intimidated. One day, after one of the many heated practices, Antoine and Cliff were riding him. He chased them down and said, 'You two Playboy All-Americans, one day, I will have one of your jobs. They will know the X-Man was here.'"

Former Bradley guard Jim Les remembers once when he ran into McDaniel in the lane. "Early in the game, he uses up a foul to lay me out. He shows me this is his area and real estate and he didn't like me being in there. I had my eye on him the rest of the game. . . . Some guys had physical skills. He had those and he combined them with a mental approach."

BASKETBALL RESURGENCE

The current Wichita State basketball resurgence started with the hiring of Dr. Donald L. Beggs as president on Jan. 1, 1999, followed by the naming of Jim Schaus as athletic director a little more than five months later. Together, they produced the foundation for the Shockers' return to the nation's elite in college basketball.

Dedication ceremony for Charles Koch Arena

The first step came in the overhaul of the Shocker's basketball facility known as "Roundhouse Renaissance," which was announced in October of 2000. After intitial pledges of nearly $13 million, including $6 million by Charles Koch, the eventual $25 million project began in March 2002. The inaugural game at the reconstructed Charles Koch Arena was on Nov. 19, 2003.

The second step was the hiring of Mark Turgeon as basketball coach with the 2000-01 season. In his fourth year, Turgeon posted the first of three straight 20-victory seasons and in 2006, brought the Shockers their first Missouri Valley Conference regular-season men's basketball title since 1983. Turgeon is the only men's basketball coach in Wichita State history to improve the school's win total five straight seasons through 2005–06.

WSU President Don Beggs

Athletic Director Jim Schaus

ARCHITECT OF A SUPERPOWER: SHOCKERS' GENE STEPHENSON

Martin Perline remembers becoming Wichita State's faculty representative more than a quarter of a century ago. He was making a trip to the NCAA Convention in 1977. At the time, then WSU Athletic Director Ted Bredehoft made a startling revelation to him. "He said we were going to hire a baseball coach," Perline recalled. "I said, 'We don't play baseball, Ted.' 'We are going to,' he said. He hired Gene (Stephenson) at that meeting. . . . The next thing you know we have a coach around and we are playing baseball. And we are playing in a lot down here in northeast Wichita."

Bredehoft was known to do the unpredictable and the flamboyant. He had a feeling baseball just might work, for

Coach Mark Turgeon

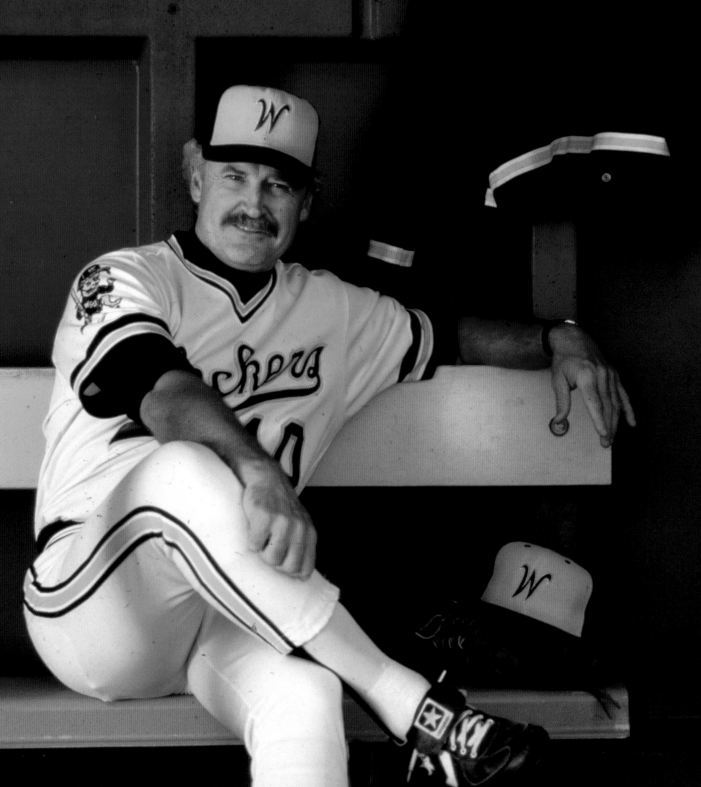

Gene Stephenson

whatever reason, and he hired Oklahoman Gene Stephenson, then an eager young assistant coach on Enos Semore's University of Oklahoma baseball staff who had just helped the Sooners to five straight College World Series berths.

Wichita State discontinued baseball after the 1970 season because of financial reasons and the lack of a permanent field. Eight years later baseball was back, on a shoestring budget and with no promise of success. "I was just young enough and strong enough and bull-headed enough. I never saw the failure, the potential disaster," said Stephenson one day recently in his modern offices overlooking WSU's state-of-the-art Eck Stadium. "I always saw nothing but opportunity. And here's a great chance to build something from nothing. I always said to myself, 'One day when we build this, what a wonderful thing it will be to look back on this, and we started this absolutely from ground zero—nothing. How many programs can rise to national prominence when they actually started from nothing? We didn't even have a baseball."

Perline said few people believed Wichita State could become the dominant baseball program in the MVC. Since baseball's re-establishment at WSU, the Shockers have participated in the College World Series eight times through 2006, won the 1989 NCAA Championship, and have cranked out All-Americans and major-league baseball draftees like a factory.

"To say Gene built the program, Gene built the program," Perline said. "If you had said to me when they hired Gene, and playing in this little lot down here, and he was going to go to the College World Series numerous times and win it once, I'd say you are pipe-dreaming. 'You are smoking something guy, it won't happen.' First of all, we are playing in the Midwest. When you are playing baseball you are in the Southeast, it's the West because of the weather. They start early. How are you going to recruit in the middle of Kansas? He did it. He deserves credit."

Stephenson took a pay cut upon leaving Oklahoma. He had no job security at WSU, and little or no budget to travel or to recruit. He had to use car and van pools to travel to away games, and even to get to games in Wichita the first season.

In 1978, the Shockers shared a park with a high school, and often had to cut doubleheaders short so the high school games could be played. Once on campus, seating for fans was atop a flatbed truck. The field was cordoned off by a chain-link fence so Stephenson could charge admission to the games. "From that humble beginning, the second year of 1979, we actually won 65 games," Stephenson said of

Gene Stephenson early in his career at WSU

WSU Faculty Respresentative Martin Perline and his wife, Donna, cheer for the Shockers

Phil Stephenson (R) and his brother, Gene, share a congratulatory hug

ing any favoritism. That made me a better player. My freshman year, we played 80 games and I played in 67 of them and hit .443. That proved to everybody I could play."

By Gene Stephenson's third season, 1980, Wichita State had won its first MVC Tournament and advanced to its first NCAA Tournament, still playing on a field, now on campus, that lacked permanent bleachers, dugouts, dressing rooms, and every other standard amenity. But that was about to change.

Phil Stephenson, who played first base and the outfield, put together an NCAA-record 47-game hitting streak in 1981 when the Shockers had one of their best teams. Wichita State had dugouts put in that season after Gene Stephenson raised money for the project. The Shockers made another NCAA Tournament appearance but lost in the 1981 NCAA Regionals.

overcoming the obvious lack of facilities and budget. "I have been one who has always said and has believed it with all my heart, it is about good people who attract other good people."

Stephenson had a talent for working with what he had, or didn't have, in the early years at WSU, but recruiting was one aspect of collegiate sports where Stephenson truly shined. He recruited future major-league star Joe Carter out of Oklahoma City and got the football team to pay for the scholarship, because Carter doubled up in sports the first year. Stephenson had scouts who told him about prospects coast-to-coast and everywhere in between. He worked the Watts-Line at night at a local company making recruiting calls to save money. His work ethic made up for lack of resources.

Gene's brother, Phil, who was 15 years younger, was one of the top high school baseball players in the state of Oklahoma. At first, the elder Stephenson wasn't sure he wanted to coach his brother but then relented, and the younger Stephenson came to Wichita. "The first year (1979) was pretty difficult," said Phil Stephenson, who eventually finished as WSU's career leader in hits, runs scored, RBIs, total bases, stolen bases, and walks. "He was a lot tougher on me, he had to be, so he wasn't show-

In 1982, during Phil Stephenson's senior season, the Shockers made their first College World Series appearance despite the loss of several major-league draft picks from the previous season, including Carter. Don Heinkel became the winningest pitcher (51 victories) in NCAA history, and the Shockers won an NCAA-record 73 games. "We started out 4–6," said Phil Stephenson, who was named the Player of the Year in college baseball in 1982 by *All-America Baseball News*. "I was moved to center field the first 10 games. They decided I needed to move back to first. We played some lesser teams after the start and then when we started playing better competition, we were on a roll." Wichita State fell to Miami, 4–3, in the second game in Omaha and then lost to the Hurricanes, 9–3, in the title game. Nevertheless, the Shockers had produced four first-team All-Americans, two of them pitchers—Heinkel and Bryan Oelkers—along with Stephenson and catcher Charlie O'Brien. Gene Stephenson was recognized as National Coach of the Year by *All-America Baseball News*, and the Shockers had their first No. 1 ranking by *Baseball America*.

Now in 1983 we have seating for the first time that is not on a flatbed trailer," Stephenson said of bleachers donated by a philanthropist. "And it was permanent. We still had no place to shower or dress. We did changing in the car. I had an office down at Levitt (Basketball) Arena. That stayed that way until 1985. Everybody thinks you have this fancy facility and everything. All this was blood, sweat, and tears for a long time. And now. Most of my fund-raising every year was trying to cover operations. In 1987, 10 years after I came here, I was still only making $28,000."

In 1985, however, Wichita State had opened Eck Stadium, named after Wichita businessman Randy Eck. The stadium was fitted for just more than 3,000 grandstand seats, along with locker rooms, baseball offices, and a press box.

Wichita State returned to the College World Series in 1988 by defeating No.1-ranked Oklahoma State twice in the regionals. The Shockers came close to winning it all but lost to Arizona State, 4–3, in 10 innings and then were blasted by the Sun Devils, 19–1, in a second game in the double-elimination tournament. Improvements were made to Eck Stadium in 1988 as well: a rubberized warning track, new astroturf, and 292 box seats. Wichita State baseball was the recipient of a $4 million endowment program in the name of Ron Tyler, a Wichita businessman.

Stephenson eventually managed to put the entire package together for the MVC's first national baseball title in 1989. "Winning it all 1989, I think it goes back to 1988," Stephenson said. "We go to the College World Series. We are within one pitch three times of going to the championship game. It was heartbreaking." In 1989, the Shockers didn't flinch when they got close. Wichita State was faced with elimination seven times during the NCAA Regionals and College World Series and the Shockers won every time. "There was a perseverance," Stephenson said of a team dogged by injuries. "I was down to like 11 players, and the championship night, when we won the thing, I was down to 10. That's all I had as position players. I had some pitchers. We were so depleted, yet came back and won the thing. We have had better teams since then and gotten to the championship game and not won."

Pitcher Greg Brummett, a future major leaguer, was named the 1989 College World Series Most Valuable Player after ending his college career on a 13-game

Gene Stephenson with the 1989 National Championship Trophy

winning streak. Brummett had three victories in the College World Series, in which star shortstop Mike Lansing, another future major leaguer, didn't play because of a back injury.

In 1989, Wichita State had to fight its way back through the loser's bracket after dropping its second game in Omaha to Florida State, but the Shockers bounced back to beat Arkansas, Florida State twice, and then Texas, 5–3, in the title game.

After Stephenson won the NCAA title, Oklahoma offered him a job when Semore retired. "There was something about this place (Wichita State), I wanted to finish," said Stephenson, who again turned down the Sooners 15 years later in the summer of 2005. "I felt like we could win more national championships. I felt like we were the sport on campus. And at OU, we would never be that."

Under Stephenson (through 2006), the Shockers also have claimed 14 MVC Tournament titles, and they have been fixtures in the NCAA Tournament, qualifying in all but five seasons since 1978.

From 1982 to 1996, Stephenson made seven trips to the College World Series. Besides 1982 and 1989 final-game appearances, Wichita State also advanced to the 1991 and 1993 title games, where the Shockers lost to LSU twice. High standards were set by Stephenson at Wichita State. "It was healthy," said former Shocker pitching ace Travis Wyckoff (1993–96). "There was a pressure, but it was a healthy pressure. Expectations were high. Guys raised their level or they didn't make it there."

"It was the emphasis he put on baseball, because when he first started in the late 1970s and early 1980s, he did more than just recruit players. He was a fundraiser, too," said Gene's brother, Phil Stephenson. "A lot of schools didn't put emphasis on it until the mid-1990s. He was 15 to 20 years ahead of them."

Stephenson provided a launching pad for major-league careers for players such as Carter, O'Brien, Stephenson, Heinkel, Brummett, Lansing, Russ Morman, Rick Wrona, Eric Wedge, David Haas, Tyler Green, Pat Meares, Darren Dreifort, Doug Mirabelli, Braden Looper, Casey Blake, and several others.

"I think the first thing that sticks out about Gene, he is big-time driven," Wyckoff said. "He wants to have

"He did more than just recruit players. He was a fundraiser, too. A lot of schools didn't put emphasis on it until the mid-1990s. He was 15 or 20 years ahead of them."

Eck Stadium

the best and biggest (facilities). He has done a very good job of recruiting. And there's his competitiveness . . . He has an idea where he wants to be and goes and gets it done."

JOE CARTER EXEMPLIFYING SHOCKER SUCCESS ON THE DIAMOND

Joe Carter (1979–81) was Wichita State's first great baseball star under Coach Gene Stephenson and the first baseball player elected to the MVC Hall of Fame in 1999. At his induction in St. Louis, he revealed that he always had a dream as a youngster growing up in Oklahoma City. "It started with a dream by a kid, one day hitting a home run in the bottom of the ninth of the World Series to help his team win the championship," Carter said. "And it came true."

Sure enough, Carter hit the game-winning home run for the Toronto Blue Jays in the sixth and final game of the 1993 Major League World Series when his three-run blast in the bottom of the ninth beat Philadelphia, 8–6. Carter played 16 years in the major leagues with the Chicago Cubs, Cleveland Indians, San Diego Padres, Toronto Blue Jays, Baltimore Orioles, and San Francisco Giants.

The 6-3, 215-pound Carter was a three-time college All-American and two-time All-MVC Player of the Year. In 1981, his junior and final college season, he was named College Player of the Year by the Sporting News and All-America Baseball News. Drafted by the Chicago Cubs in the first round as the No. 2 overall pick, Carter left college baseball with the NCAA single-season marks for doubles (34), total bases (229), and RBIs (120).

Regardless of his prowess on the diamond, Carter was a football and basketball player first and foremost coming out of high school, and he was on a football scholarship at Wichita State in the fall of 1979. Major league scouts knew of his tremendous baseball potential as did Wichita State Coach Gene Stephenson. "I look back and my career almost never got started at Wichita State," Carter said. "I was in two-a-days practicing football and a scout from the Boston Red Sox called my father and said, 'Look, we want to make you an offer, will you consider it?' I thought about it long and hard." Carter's father came and picked him up at Wichita State for a meeting with the scout back in Oklahoma City.

Joe Carter

"All the time we were in the car, I kept thinking, 'Do I want this guy to make me an offer? I loved baseball. Baseball was going to be my sport I was going to play. We got about half way, and I thought, you know what, I gave my word. I told Jim Wright (Wichita State football coach) I would come to Wichita State and play football. Another one of the quarterbacks they had recruited said he was not going to play football, and was only going to play baseball, and I said, 'Wow, I can't leave these guys with just two quarterbacks.' I got all the way home and I called the scout, and I said, 'Look, I appreciate you

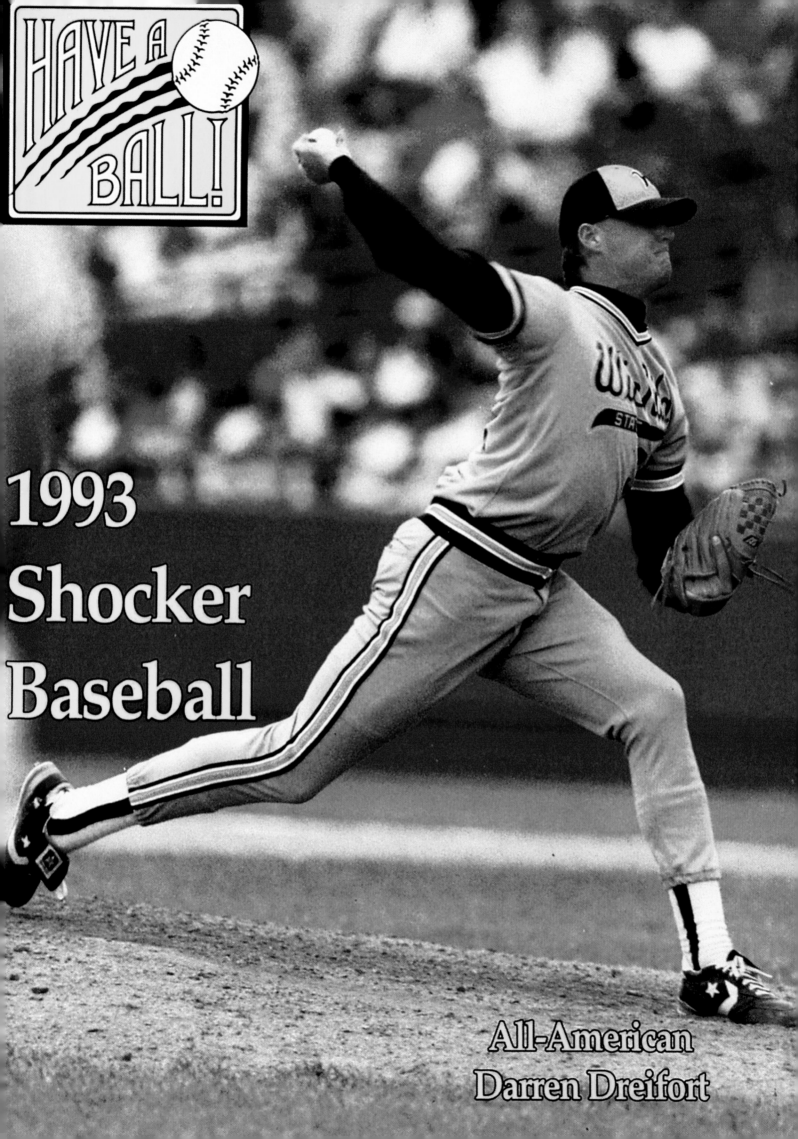

HAVE A BALL!

1993
Shocker
Baseball

All-American
Darren Dreifort

Shockers baseball team honors George H. W. Bush with a jersey

guys wanting to sign me and making an offer, but I gave my word to Wichita State and I am going to go back there. And I am going to start something I was really missing.' And I am glad I made that decision."

Carter thanks Stephenson for recruiting him. He played one season of football and led the Shockers in punt returns. Then he played three seasons of baseball and hit .450 as a freshman, .432 as a sophomore, and .411 as a junior. "I want to thank him, because not only did he recruit me, he talked Jim Wright into giving me a football scholarship, so he didn't have to pay for it," Carter said. "That was the only way I could play two sports. I came to Wichita State really a diamond in the rough. A lot of people told me a lot of things I couldn't do. But I knew I could do it. And I am glad I gave myself that chance."

WSU PLANE CRASH LEAVES LASTING MARK
On Oct. 2, 1970, a plane carrying part of the Wichita State football team en route to a game at Utah State crashed near Silver Plume, Colo. Thirty-one people died in the crash.

For more than 35 years now, those associated in some way with the Wichita State plane crash have come to the campus to pay their respects on the anniversary of the crash. Some, once in their youth, are well into middle age now as they watch officials place a wreath on the memorial sculpture located on Alumni Drive.

The names of the passengers who perished, including WSU administrators, coaches, and 14 players, are listed on the memorial. Among those who died in the crash were Head Coach Ben Wilson and the school's athletic director Bert Katzenmeyer. The Memorial '70 Structure, located near 18th and Hillside, consists of two large white concrete structures. One symbolizes the plane that crashed. The other one, tall and rectangular, symbolizes the hope and future of the people on the other plane that didn't crash.

Early October is always a time for reflection, especially for the survivors of the plane crash. "The other guy next to me didn't make it out of the plane and I did," said Randy Jackson, one of eight WSU players who survived the crash along with the co-pilot. "Why did I? I try to forget . . . but something like that you always remember." It was a clear afternoon in the Colorado Rockies, when the aspen had turned a beautiful yellow. The slopes of Mount Trelease, 30 miles west of Denver, lay ahead, but the chartered, twin-engine Martin 404 heading for Logan, Utah, veered too close to the mountainside and crashed.

The National Transportation Board ruled that pilot error was the official reason for the crash. The board also said the chartered plane was overweight by at least 2,000 pounds. Following the crash, Golden Eagle Aviation ceased operations after it lost its license. "Sometimes the memory fades, but it shouldn't," said another survivor, Rick Stephens on the 10th anniversary of the crash. "Maybe the attitude of the transportation of athletes changed. I know it changed the way Wichita State handled that part of its program."

Martin Perline, a member of the Wichita State faculty then and the school's faculty representative later, remembers the day vividly. "It was tragic," Perline said. "The news comes across on the radio, and initially you don't know what happened. We lost the plane. . . . Did it crash? There was a certain amount of consternation, almost panic."

Perline touches on the ramifications: "There was a huge benefit on campus to raise money for the crash victims. Bill Cosby was there. Monte Hall was there. It was very tragic and we are not really talking to what it did to the football program. That was sort of incidental to the loss of life."

Wichita State's remaining players and coaches elected to carry on the season, but they finished 0–9. The Shockers took a 45-man traveling roster to Arkansas (a 62–0 loss), the first game back after the crash. The traveling squad consisted of 20 freshmen, including quarterback Tom Owen, who later played in the National Football League. "We have to go on, as hard as that was, the team was decimated," Perline said.

In that era, the NCAA did not allow freshmen to play on the varsity teams, but the association waived the rule in 1970 for Wichita State so the team could continue its "Second Season" of six games with 43 freshmen, 23 sophomores, 6 juniors, and 3 seniors. "I think we wanted to play, but we didn't know what was ahead of us," Owen said years later. "It (the Arkansas) game opened our eyes to the level of competition we would play. When I went in to play against Arkansas that year, I had never played before that many people. . . . Everybody knew we were just out to get experience. The odds of us winning would have been real tough."

Bob Seaman, who had been the offensive coordinator on Wilson's staff and was on the plane that didn't crash, took over the head coaching reins of the team, which lost its final six games. "He put things back together," said Jackson, a running back who was seriously injured in the crash and didn't play until the 1971 season. "He did the best job anybody could do under the circumstances. I will always have a lot of praise for him."

The Missouri Valley Conference designated Oct. 31, 1970, as Wichita State Day and urged conference members to accept donations at games on their campuses for the Wichita State Fund. It raised money for items not covered by insurance: football equipment lost in the crash, expenses incurred by the families of the players in the crash, and the loss of revenue for two games cancelled immediately after the crash.

"The other guy next to me didn't make it out of the plane and I did," said Randy Jackson, one of eight WSU players who survived the crash. "Why did I? I try to forget . . . but something like that, you always remember."

"I don't think it had a lasting effect in terms of the football program," Perline said. "It had a lasting effect on the people. We have a memorial here, and the people still remember it every year. I don't think it affected the program to the extent that is why it was dispensed with." After the crash, Wichita State had only two winning seasons in the next 17 years. The program was discontinued after the 1986 season because of mounting red ink in the athletic department budget.

After taking over the team, Seaman received a three-year contract. He took the freshmen and sophomores of 1970, and when they were juniors and seniors, posted a 6–5 record. He was fired after the team went 4–7 in 1973, the final year of his contract. Coach Willie Jeffries produced the other winning record (8–3) in 1982.

Seaman said on the 10th anniversary of the crash that he would remember it every day of his life because he had a reminder in his life—a daughter. "My wife was coming home from the doctor's office, and she had learned she was pregnant with her," Seaman said. "My wife had heard on the radio that the plane went down, but she didn't know which plane I was on. I look at that little girl every day of my life and think of the crash."

A lasting memorial to Wichita State plane crash victims is at the crash site

Memorial at Wichita State campus

Wreckage can still be seen at the Colorado crash site

Hersey Hawkins: All-time career scoring leader in MVC history

BRADLEY

Bradley University is located in Peoria, Ill., and was founded in 1897 as Bradley Polytechnic Institute by philanthropist Lydia Moss Bradley. The school became a four-year college in 1927 and became a university in 1930. In 2006, the Braves revived the tradition of the men's basketball program with a Sweet 16 appearance, their first since the 1950s, when they appeared in the Final Four twice.

Bradley first joined the Missouri Valley Conference in 1949. Its men's basketball team plays in the Carver Arena, which opened in 1982. Previously, the legendary and unique Robertson Memorial Field House hosted games. Robertson Field House was built from two airplane hangers, with a court raised on a stage, offering a distinct playing and viewing experience.

A FABULOUS MVC START

More than a half century after he played for Bradley, basketball star Paul Unruh was inducted into the Missouri Valley Conference Hall of Fame in March 2004. He graciously thanked the MVC for inviting the Bradley Braves to join the league as a basketball-playing member in 1948.

Bradley's glorious men's basketball era began in the late 1930s, with a history of three trips to the NIT (1938, 1939, and 1947). Bradley discontinued intercollegiate sports during WWII, and returned as an independent in 1945.

Bradley's entrance into the MVC coincided with the death—in the fall of 1948—of the legendary A. J. Robertson, the former Bradley basketball–baseball–football coach and athletic director who held the multiple positions for more than 30 years. Bradley had hired a new basketball coach, Forddy Anderson, from Drake the previous spring, and the basketball team began playing in a new facility, the 6,753-seat A. J. Robertson Memorial Field

A. J. Robertson

House, built in 1949 for the cost of $400,000. "Was there any way Forddy Anderson would have become our coach unless we would have been a part of the MVC?" asked Unruh, who played for the Braves from 1946 to 1950. "I would like to thank the Missouri Valley on behalf of myself and Bradley."

The late Robertson had hoped Bradley, after posting a 28–3 record in 1947–48, would receive a bid to the National Invitation Tournament at Madison Square Garden in New York City. However, Robertson's final season as coach ended in disappointment. No invitation came for Bradley, which played 26 of its 31 games at home that season. It was indeed time to join a league

Robertson Field House

such as the MVC, which could enhance the school's profile.

JOINING THE MVC

"Robbie (Robertson) was concerned about our fan base and would have loved to get a lot of money to build a field house," Unruh recalled. "It (the NIT bid) never came in 1948. It was devastating. We were counting on it so much, and it never came. My point is this. Out of that came a blessing. The next year we were in the MVC."

Bradley placed third in its first season in the MVC (1949), but the following year, the Braves won their first MVC title and finished second in both the NCAA and NIT tournaments. They tied for second in the MVC in 1951. The Braves won 27 games in their inaugural MVC season and posted 32 victories in the two following years. "Forddy Anderson was brilliant . . . his tactics, bench work, and handling of the players," said Unruh, one of two Bradley players to lead the team in scoring four straight seasons. "He was just a young guy. He was hardly older than some of our players who were veterans, yet he commanded great respect."

Gene Melchiorre

The backcourt Billy Mann and Gene "Squeaky" Melchiorre reported as grizzled freshmen in 1947 from Fort Sheridan in Chicago. The Melchiorre–Mann backcourt, along with Unruh, a 6-4 forward, were staples of the early MVC Bradley teams. Anderson inherited these players from Robertson, and he won his first 12 games in 1948–49.

"Forddy's style was new," said Joe Stowell, a Bradley player on that team and later an assistant and head coach for the Braves. "He ran and pressed a lot more than teams at that time."

Unruh, a two-time All-MVC player and an All-American his senior season, fit into Anderson's up-tempo scheme because he held the school's record in the quarter-mile. Unruh also had perfected a turnaround jump shot, which was just making the scene in college basketball. "Back then he was a pioneer," said Gene Morse, a Bradley star in the 1950s.

Melchiorre, on the other hand, was unique for any era. "There wasn't a player before or since like him," Stowell said of Bradley's

Bradley Fieldhouse in the early 1950s

BRADLEY
vs. DRAKE

OFFICIAL
PROGRAM
25c

PEORIA STADIUM

OCTOBER 1, 1949 • 8:00 P. M.

three-time All-MVC selection and two-time All-American. "He could make passes left-handed or over his head and it was not for show. He and Billy Mann played really well together. They always knew exactly what each other was going to do."

Paul Unruh

The 5-8 Melchiorre also could play in the post against taller players. His fakes and feints and quick moves to the basket made him one of college basketball's most unorthodox scorers. "I think we all developed post moves at Bradley because we weren't very tall," Melchiorre said. "When I would go into the post, our biggest guy was 6-4 and he would go outside and take the big man out of the middle. So that really opened up the area for us all the time."

Bradley's breakthrough game during that first season in the MVC was a 35–31 victory over third-ranked Oklahoma A&M on Feb. 28, 1949, in front of a standing-room-only crowd at the old armory in Peoria. Anderson went against his coaching grain and decided to beat Oklahoma A&M Coach Henry Iba at Iba's slower, defensive-oriented game. The victory over the Aggies helped vault Bradley to a No. 7 ranking and a berth in the NIT where the Braves split four games at Madison Square Garden.

MOVING INTO THE 1950s

The following season, 1949–50, stood out as one of the most intriguing in Bradley history, and it was against a backdrop of great changes occurring in college basketball. The MVC, for instance, for the fourth straight season had a different membership makeup for basketball, as members were coming and going during the post–World War II years. "You are talking about a time when everything was in transition," said Unruh, a Bradley senior in 1949–50. "Television was on its way, but it wasn't there yet. Airplanes were being used for travel, but still trains and buses were preferred. During my career we saw the TWA Constellation appear, which made coast-to-coast travel very comfortable. And we were part of that. It was basketball without tattoos, without long hair, without fancy passing, without dunks. And the rims were sacred. You broke one and the game was over. A lot of things were totally different than they are today."

Bradley's second-place 1950 NCAA trophy

In 1949–50, Bradley finished as the No. 1-ranked team in the country and won the seven-team MVC race with an 11–1 record.

Forddy Anderson and team, 1954

Bradley and CCNY are the only two schools in college basketball history to play each other in the NIT and NCAA Championship games in the same year (1950).

The Braves' one loss was a road game to first-year MVC member Detroit.

Since major conference champions were not guaranteed spots in the NCAA Tournament until a year later when the field was expanded from 8 to 16 teams, Bradley accepted an NIT bid first. "The NIT had as much prestige or more," Stowell said. "They passed out the bids (NIT). You accepted that first because you were not sure you were going to the NCAA Tournament. We then got the NCAA bid."

The Braves played in both. For the only time in college basketball history, two teams—Bradley and CCNY—played each other in both the NIT and NCAA title games. CCNY, the first NCAA champion with black players in its starting lineup, beat the Braves twice and became the only team to collect the two titles in the same season.

Three years later, a new NCAA rule was passed, and teams were allowed to play in just one postseason tournament each season, which made it impossible for any school to pull off Bradley and CCNY's dual title-game feat again. "What a grind it was to move from city to city to play in those games," Unruh said. "And yet we were doing something that hadn't been done and wouldn't be done again. We were determined. I thought we had the teams and recognition to go all the way in both tournaments."

During a period of 15 days, Bradley played seven post-season games. The Braves traveled from Peoria, Ill., to New York City to play in the NIT, then back to Kansas City for the NCAA Tournament before returning to New York City for a rematch against CCNY in the NCAA title game. Meanwhile, CCNY never left New York City to play any of the postseason games and was well rested.

CCNY beat Bradley, 69–61, in the NIT final on March 18. The Bradley–CCNY rematch 10 days later in the NCAA final was a more intense game, which still stirs strong emotions among former Bradley players. Three Braves, including Unruh, fouled out of the game, which CCNY eventually won, 71–68. "I wish I could see the foul they called on me because it is still upsetting," Unruh said of his fifth foul. "I was on the perimeter and we had the ball, and yet they managed to call a blocking foul on me, and put me on the bench." Still, Bradley trailed only 69–68 with 20 seconds remaining when the resourceful Melchiorre, who led all scorers with 16 points, drove to the basket and collided with 6-4 CCNY center-forward Irwin Dambrot, the NCAA Tournament's MVP.

Melchiorre fell to the floor after contact with Dambrot, but no foul was called. Dambrot picked up the ball and threw a length-of-the-floor pass to teammate Norm Mager for the final points. "Of course, he was hammered," said Unruh, who was watching from the bench. "There was no question about it."

"These two officials had never worked together before," Melchiorre recalled in November 2003. "One was from

Bradley's All-American Bob Carney

the Midwest; the other was from the East. One guy was under the basket. And the other fellow was out past the free-throw line in the center. I think when the foul occurred, the one fellow thought it was the other fellow's call, so that's why neither of them called it."

The NCAA title game against CCNY was Unruh's last Bradley game. He graduated in 1950, but Melchiorre and Mann, along with center Elmer Behnke, returned to lead the Braves to a 32–6 overall record in 1950–51 and a tie for second in the MVC behind Oklahoma A&M.

After failing to make the NCAAs and instead of going to the NIT, Bradley opted to participate in a tournament in Hawaii, where it finished second to Oregon State. The Braves then hosted the National Campus Basketball Tournament and invited seven other top teams from across the country. Bradley finished second to Syracuse during the event, which also included lectures, dinners, oratory contests, book reviews, and tours of Peoria for the teams.

RETURNING TO THE MVC: ORSBORN'S NIT TITLES AND CHET "THE JET"

In the early 1950s, Bradley temporarily became an independent again following an incident that had nothing to do with basketball, but everything to do with race relations. The Braves' basketball team was temporarily denied a conference basketball schedule following the 1950–51 season, when Bradley withdrew from the Missouri Valley as a result of the fallout surrounding the Drake–Oklahoma A&M football controversy. Drake's black running back Johnny Bright suffered a broken jaw when he was savagely tackled by Oklahoma A&M's defensive tackle Wilbanks Smith in a 1951 game. Bradley, in sympathy for its fellow conference member, joined Drake and left the league when no action was taken by the MVC against Smith or Oklahoma A&M.

During Bradley's four-year MVC absence, a Braves team led by All-American Bob Carney lost to LaSalle and Tom Gola in the 1954 NCAA final after losing 12 games in a rugged schedule during the regular season. But the 1954 season isn't credited to the MVC record, because of the Braves "independent" status.

By 1955–56, animosity over the Bright incident had dissipated, and Bradley rejoined the MVC. By the following season, the Braves had their third coach in four years—Chuck "Ozzie" Orsborn, who played on Bradley's "Famous Five" teams of 1936–39. Orsborn, Bradley's assistant and freshman coach, replaced Bob Vanatta, who had departed for Memphis State after two seasons.

ORSBORN–MASON INFLUENCE GREAT

Orsborn led the Braves back to national prominence quickly by winning the National Invitation Tournament in his first season as head coach. In nine years, he carved out the best winning percentage (77.6) of any Bradley men's basketball coach during the 20th century by posting a 194–56 record.

Paul Unruh

Like Forddy Anderson, who had left to coach at Michigan State following Bradley's highly successful 1953–54 season that included a trip to the NCAA Final Four, Orsborn preferred pressing defenses and an up-tempo game, which fit Bradley's personnel. He was a great fast-break coach and innovator," Bradley's All-America forward Chet Walker said. "Ozzie could adjust his system to the players. He would analyze your strong points, where you could shoot from on the court. He could adjust his game plan to your strengths and your weaknesses. "He had a system he would run, with two players fanning out to the side, and a trailer coming down the middle. It was the trailer concept of the fast break, with the forward, small forward, and sometimes the center. I was involved in the trailer thing."

Orsborn had one other very good trait: he was color-blind. There's little wonder Bradley officials sided with Drake in the Bright incident. It would have been hypocritical if they had not, given their recruiting practices of that era. Orsborn and Assistant Coach Joe Stowell made a living recruiting black players at a time when most Southern schools were shunning them. With the infusion of athleticism from those players, Orsborn created an electric atmosphere on the court in central Illinois.

The 1950–51 season ushered out Bradley's inaugural MVC era. Unruh and Melchiorre were remembered for establishing a strong foundation for Bradley during its formative years in the league. "We had some really great coaches that era," Melchiorre said of the Missouri Valley. "And we had some great teams in the Valley. We had three teams ranked in the Top 10 most of my career: St. Louis, Oklahoma A&M, and us. We didn't have many 6-8, 7-footers who could run and play ball well. Now, everybody who is 6-6 and 6-8 seems to be able to do it all in comparison."

Gene Melchiorre

The first black players at Bradley, recruited in 1955 when Vanatta was still head coach, were 6-5 Shellie McMillon and Curley Johnson from powerhouse DuSable High School in Chicago. They both played on Bradley's first NIT title team in 1956–57 during Orsborn's first season as head coach.

The recruitment of McMillon and Johnson started a stream of black stars migrating to Peoria from Chicago, downstate Illinois, and points south down into Florida. Among the new stars were flashy guard Bobby Joe Mason from Centralia, Ill., coming a year after McMillon and Johnson arrived, and in the early 1960s, swingman Levern

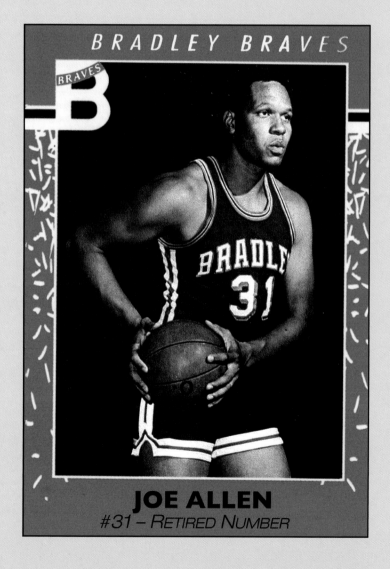

BRADLEY BRAVES

JOE ALLEN
#31 – RETIRED NUMBER

Tart and center Joe Strawder from Florida. The racism these players faced as they played MVC games in the South, at such places as Houston and North Texas State, was rampant. "They tried to spit on us coming out and going to the dressing room," Mason said. "We still beat them. It didn't matter." Bradley was developing a definite talent advantage over many MVC schools with the forward-thinking recruiting philosophy.

Chuck "Ozzie" Orsborn

Forddy Anderson

"I will tell you he (McMillon) was one of the most fierce type of players," said Gene Morse, a Bradley player from 1956–59. "He would announce to the other players that (the space around the basket) was his territory at the beginning of the game. . . . He could go back up for the ball as quick as anybody I would ever see. He might get three rebounds on the same play."

The other inside scoring-rebounding staple on Orsborn's first team was white, 6-7 Barney Cable, from Rochester, Pa. Cable still holds the Bradley record of 28 rebounds in a game (twice). Both he and McMillon played in the NBA after completing their Bradley careers. "Cable was tall and he could shoot outside," Morse said, "He had a beautiful outside shot. And when he wanted to, he could do it all."

When Mason, who later played 15 seasons for the Harlem Globetrotters, became academically eligible during the middle of the 1956–57 season, Bradley had a powerhouse team. The 19th-ranked Braves finished second in the MVC to Saint Louis and went to the NIT, where Mason was a sophomore star. "Bobby Joe Mason was the most effective basketball player that I ever coached," Orsborn said. "He could penetrate a zone defense. It was usually poor coaching to allow any player to do that, but he was adept enough that he could penetrate and draw two or three players to him and still be capable enough to pass the ball to one of his teammates for a shot."

Mason led one of the most amazing comebacks in NIT history during his first season with the Braves. In the quarterfinal round of the 1957 NIT, Bradley defeated Xavier (Ohio), 116–81, with a rousing second-half comeback that produced 72 points, still an NIT record. The Braves had been booed off the court at half time, but the sophisticated Madison Square Garden fans fell in love with the rallying Braves in the second half, as Mason led the Bradley press. "It (the press) was pretty effective," Orsborn said. "In those days it was not unheard of, but it wasn't used as much. . . . It just depends if you have the personnel to execute it."

The Braves pounded Temple, 94–66, in the semifinals, then faced previous Bradley coach Vanatta's Memphis team in the NIT final. In a nationally televised game before an estimated eight million people, Bradley won, 84–83, when McMillon converted a three-point play off an offensive rebound with 29 seconds remaining. Mason chipped in 22 points. "We took great delight in beating him (Vanatta)," Morse said. "He recruits us and you expect him to stay. To be honest with you that gave us a little more incentive. . . . It was one of the most physical games I had ever played in."

In three 1957 NIT games, Bradley averaged 98 points with its pressing, quick-hitting attack. It was a style Orsborn would use for years to come, including the following season, with Cable, McMillon, and Mason returning.

"We played the same type of ball at Centralia," Mason said of his southern Illinois roots. "So playing for Ozzie was really easy for me. . . . It was just fact if Mike Owens and I came down on the fast break, we were going to score."

THE CINCINNATI ROADBLOCK

As the 1957–58 season began, Bradley was labeled an NCAA title contender with a No. 4 ranking in the first Associated Press poll. But the Braves didn't deliver at the end of the season and lost in the quarterfinals of the NIT against Xavier (Ohio). Bradley lost seven games that year, and two defeats in the MVC were enough to cost the Braves (12–2) the league championship as Cincinnati (13–1) and sophomore sensation Oscar Robertson began their domination.

One of the highlights of the 1957–58 season was Bradley's 79–73 victory over Cincinnati in Peoria, where Robertson was 0–3 during his college career. Morse limited Robertson to 14 points, which was the "Big O's" second-lowest scoring total (he had 13 in two other games) in college competition. "I was a more physical player," Morse said. "Once he got the ball, I more or less went belly-up to him. I think I prevented him from getting shots he could get and then harassed him. I was 6-3

Pope Paul VI lays his hand on Joe Allen's shoulder

and a fairly strong player, and I bothered him a little bit."

The "Big O" wasn't alone in facing problems at Bradley's Robertson Field House. Under Orsborn, the Braves had a 91.1 percent winning percentage (123–12) at their home court.

Overall, Orsborn's Braves won 72.9 percent of their MVC contests (86–32), which ranked fifth all-time among coaches in the league. However, during Orsborn's nine seasons (1957 through 1965), the Braves failed to win an undisputed MVC crown, and none of Orsborn's teams went to the NCAA Tournament, which included only league champions in those days along with selected independents.

Orsborn's biggest MVC problem was Cincinnati. The "Big O" led the Bearcats to three MVC titles from 1958–60. Later, a core group of Paul Hogue, Tom Thacker, and Ron Bonham won three more MVC championships for the Bearcats (1961–63). Orsborn's closest brush with making the NCAA Tournament was in 1962 when Bradley and Cincinnati tied for the MVC title, but the Bearcats won a one-game playoff in Evansville, Ind., to snare the NCAA berth. "At that time, the Missouri Valley was rated among the top three conferences in the country," said Stowell, who was Orsborn's assistant. "Cincinnati was so strong. We were strong. Saint Louis was always good. Wichita State was always good."

Bobby Joe Mason

During that span, Cincinnati advanced to five Final Fours, won two NCAA titles, and finished second once. Instead of going to the NCAA Tournament, the Braves were invited to seven NITs in Orsborn's nine seasons, winning three of them and finishing second in another.

WALKER BECOMES BRADLEY'S STAR

In the late 1950s and early 1960s, forward Chet "The Jet" Walker, from Benton Harbor, Mich., had much to do with the Braves at least posing a challenge to Cincinnati's six-year MVC championship run. The 6-7 Walker was on his way to Nebraska when Stowell intercepted him in Benton Harbor and had associates whisk him away to Peoria in a recruiting coup in 1958 they still talk about at Bradley.

Walker was so certain he would play for the Cornhuskers, he already had his clothes shipped to Lincoln. Then came Stowell's recruiting trip north, and everything changed. "Two weeks, I was wearing the same thing every day," Walker recounted in 2004 about his arrival in Peoria. "Once I got there and started playing and met the students, I thought I might as well stay there. Finally, when I called my mother (and told her where he was), she was really mad. She was a nervous wreck. She thought the plane had crashed."

"We all threw in some stuff for him to wear," added teammate Bob Ortegel. "I remember Joe Stowell saying, 'Hey we need to get some stuff for him to wear.' You couldn't give him shoes, because you had to give him the exact size. . . . He was the most unassuming All-American I have ever seen. He just never acted like an All-American."

Walker led the Bradley freshmen to a 15–0 record in 1958–59, while the varsity, paced by Mason, went 25–4 and finished second to Cincinnati in the MVC. The Braves compiled a 15–0 home record and lost only three games before falling to St. John's, 76–71, in the final of the NIT.

With Walker becoming a sophomore and eligible for the varsity in 1959–60, anticipation was high in Peoria, and he didn't disappoint.

Joe Stowell

Orsborn and Assistant Coach Joe Stowell made a living recruiting black players at a time when most Southern schools were shunning them.

In his first game against Abilene Christian, Walker, with his patented baseline jump shot, scored 44 points and broke the Bradley single-game scoring record at the time.

"I only got to play a half season with Chet," Mason said. "But Chet was somebody you knew you had to get the ball to. All you had to do was get the ball to him, and the rest would take care of itself." Mason was only eligible the first 19 games of the 1959–60 season because he started his three years of varsity competition midway through the 1956–57 season. Mason was still around to team up with fellow guard Mike Owens to upset top-ranked Cincinnati, 91–90, on Jan. 16, 1960.

The upset was voted the "Greatest Game in Bradley History" by fans during the 2002–03 season in celebration of the school's first century of basketball. Roberston scored 46 points and grabbed 10 rebounds in his final appearance in Peoria. Walker countered with 28 points and 12 rebounds, forward Al Saunders had 22 points, and Mason 21 before 100 writers and a standing-room-only crowd in the double airport-hangar setting. The key call came late in the game when Robertson's basket was disallowed after he was whistled for stepping out of bounds.

"Playing against him (Robertson) was challenging," Walker said. "You hear so much about some of these people you don't know if they are that good or not. He was better than expected. . . . When I was a sophomore, we had a really good team around me. We were not very tall. But we had the two guards, Michael Owens and Bobby Joe Mason, who were excellent players. They were able to penetrate and draw the defense away from me and I was able to shoot layups the whole game."

Without Mason, Bradley lost a late-season MVC game at Houston. The loss cost Bradley the league title, which was claimed by Cincinnati, but the Braves, who rallied for several victories that season with their patented press, made their third NIT final in four seasons and won their second championship.

Walker, as usual, became a key figure in the drive to the NIT title. After the Braves defeated

Some of the greatest games in Bradley history were with Cincinnati and the "Big O"

Dayton, 78–64, in the NIT quarterfinals, Walker was relaxing in his New York City hotel room when there was a knock at his door. A person in a bellman's uniform said Coach Orsborn had sent orange juice to his room for refreshment. "Someone tried to poison me," Walker said. "He brought some tainted orange juice. My roommate Al Saunders didn't touch his. I didn't drink the rest of mine. The coach didn't send any juice down there. . . . I started having stomach cramps and diarrhea. I was really sick." Walker said he believed gamblers were trying to alter the score in the game by taking him out.

Even with a sick Walker, Bradley defeated St. Bonaventure in the semifinals, 82–71. In the final, Walker was still ailing but managed to help lead a comeback from 12 points down with 10 minutes left to beat Lenny Wilkens and Providence, 88–72. Bradley's Mack Herndon, 6-5 forward from Chicago DuSable and normally a defensive stopper, scored 26 points in the title game.

Walker made All-America three straight seasons and posted 54 double-doubles out of the 81 games he played at Bradley. With Walker in the lineup, the Braves finished ranked in the AP poll Top 10 in each of his three seasons: No. 4 in 1960, No. 6 in 1961, and No. 5 in his final season. Walker averaged 21.7 points per game as a sophomore, 25.2 points as a junior, and 26.4 points as a senior.

Walker's greatest skill was taking the ball outside and scoring on bigger players. He patterned his play after Hall of Famers Maurice Stokes and Elgin Baylor. "I was a center in college, at 6-6, 6-7," Walker said. "Because of my versatility I would take these big guys away from the basket. They were not very versatile compared to the guys today. I would take them outside and use my outside game to my advantage."

In Walker's junior season, the Braves won their first 12 games, but they struggled midseason, saw their 46-game home-court winning streak snapped by Drake, and lost the MVC race to eventual 1961 NCAA champion Cincinnati.

With the addition of two recruits from Florida, 6-2 Lavern Tart and 6-9 Joe Strawder, Bradley tied Cincinnati for the 1962 MVC title, but the Bearcats won the playoff for the league championship and went on to win the NCAA title for a second straight year. Walker's last college game was actually a humbling, quarterfinal NIT loss to Duquesne.

Walker hits two of his 28 points during the Cincinnati upset

1959–60 Bradley Braves

Chet Walker with the Chicago Bulls

ORSBORN'S THIRD NIT TITLE

Tart and Strawder led Bradley back to Madison Square Garden two years later and won Orsborn's third NIT title. The Braves actually dropped to third in the MVC in 1963–64 behind co-champions Wichita State and Drake.

The Braves lost six games that season by a total of 20 points and barely got past St. Joseph's, 83–81, in the NIT quarterfinals. They easily dispatched Army in the semifinals, setting up a title game matchup against New Mexico, which had beaten Drake earlier in the NIT. "New Mexico had led the nation in defense during the season," Orsborn said. "And their coach (Bob King) was telling about how great a defense they had, and I got tired of hearing about it."

The game pitted Bradley center Joe Strawder against New Mexico center Ira Harge. When Harge got into early foul trouble, Bradley took the lead and kept it. "In the first half they fiddled with the ball like Oklahoma State used to do," Orsborn said. "They made 14 passes before they would shoot. But in the second half, they couldn't do that because they were behind."

Behind Tart, who became the NIT MVP with an 18-point scoring average in three games, the Braves crushed New Mexico, 86–58. "He was the MVP, but it was unusual they gave it to (a player on) the winning team," Orsborn chuckled with a hint of sarcasm. In Bradley's previous two championship years, the NIT MVPs came from Memphis and Providence, teams the Braves beat for the title. Memphis' Win Wilfong was the MVP in 1957 and Providence's Lenny Wilkens was the MVP in 1960.

Orsborn left a legacy at Bradley of fast-paced basketball, NIT success, and recruiting the black athlete. And the man who eventually would succeed him as head coach in 1965, Stowell, was a driving force on the bench and behind the scenes. "Joe was probably the best practice coach I have ever seen," said former Bradley player Ortegel (1959–62), who later was the head coach at Drake. "Enthusiasm, intensity, energy . . . Stowell would go out on the floor and play with you," Ortegel said. "Practice would be over and if he wanted to get extra work with you three-on-three, he would keep five guys. And he was talking all the time. And he was getting after you all the time. The combination of those two (Orsborn and Stowell) was a big reason for the success during that era. We did some things offensively and defensively, I still see today."

ROGER PHEGLEY

Roger Phegley was a standout pitcher for East Peoria High School in 1974. He could either sign with the Cincinnati Reds or accept a baseball scholarship to Bradley. "The Reds were in my parents' living room Sunday night, and I had signed a letter of intent to go to Bradley and had my books," Phegley said. "The minor league contract they offered me there was a $5,000 signing bonus. They were going to send me to Billings, Mont., and I needed $10,000 for a car. They wouldn't come up to that."

So, Phegley went to Bradley on a baseball scholarship. To get in shape for baseball during the fall, he first started playing pick-up games with Bradley basketball players. "When the pick-up basketball games were over and they started practice, I didn't know I wasn't supposed to be there, and I kept going back," Phegley said. And he made the team. At 6-5, 175 pounds in high school, Phegley started maturing and growing as a basketball player. He still pitched three seasons for the

Roger Phegley

Braves' baseball team, but he became one of the Missouri Valley Conference basketball stars and was the league's Player of the Year in 1977. "I played guard my last two years," Phegley said. "What gave me a chance to score back in the late 1970s, there were not a lot of teams who had a 6-7 guard who could take a smaller guy inside and still shoot from the perimeter."

Phegley eventually finished as the MVC's third all-time leading basketball scorer, trailing only University of Cincinnati's Oscar Robertson and Wichita State's Cleo Littleton at the time. He was the first Bradley player to score more than 2,000 points in his career.

"Versatile, effective, and consistent, that's the only way to describe Roger," Bradley's coach at the time, Joe Stowell, said. "He has the size to play forward and the ball-handling ability to be an effective guard. He has even played some center for us."

Phegley was the 14th player selected overall by the Washington Bullets in the 1978 NBA Draft and played six seasons in the league. As a rookie, he was a member of the Bullets' NBA finals team in 1979.

FLAMBOYANT DICK VERSACE; HIGH-SCORING HERSEY HAWKINS

Creighton guard Porter Moser earned a starting spot late in the 1986–87 season and was feeling pretty good about himself until Bluejays Coach Tony Barone told him his next defensive assignment was Bradley's Hersey Hawkins. Moser, a former walk-on, gulped, rolled his eyes, and prepared all week to face the Missouri Valley Conference's most prolific scorer in history. "The first possession I deflected a pass on the baseline," Moser said. "The second possession I got a finger on his jump shot, blocked it and it fell short. The third possession I deflected a pass. Then he had 11 points in the next 90 seconds. Well, that was that. I don't think coach could get me out of there fast enough."

Dick Versace

and never stopped working on offense. He would get an offensive rebound every time, and he would go out and run the lanes."

Preparing for Hawkins and Bradley during his senior season was like trying to get off the tracks with the proverbial freight train coming. Just anticipating the impending collision of styles sometimes made coaches nervous, even if they eventually won. "Bradley came into Wichita State and for two days I talked about controlled play and keeping it in the 60s, and we beat them 116–92," said former Shocker Coach Eddie Fogler of a 1988 game in which Hawkins scored 37 points.

Hawkins was recruited out of Chicago by Bradley Head Coach Dick Versace and Assistant Coach Tony Barone. Versace was skeptical of his size because he had always been an inside player. Once Versace was convinced Hawkins could make the switch to guard, "the Hawk" showed up on campus and became the top scorer in Bradley history. He led the Braves to MVC regular-season and tournament titles in 1986 under Versace and 1988 under Coach Stan Albeck.

The 6-3 Hawkins wound up scoring 38 points in a 101–77 Bradley victory. Three games later, the Braves lost to Louisville in the second round of the NCAA Tournament, and Hawkins finished with 3,008 points during his four-year stint in Peoria.

Hawkins, who was actually a center at Chicago's Westinghouse High School, moved to guard at Bradley and notched 37 games of 30 or more points, including the all-time individual MVC scoring mark of 63 points vs. Detroit in 1988. He was a two-time MVC Player of the Year and a national player of the year in the 1987–88 season, when he led the country in scoring (36.3 points a game) as a senior.

"Hersey could score in bunches," said Moser, who became Illinois State's head coach in 2003. "He could post up and shoot the three. He had a mid-range game

"Hersey was always ready," said Donald Reese, Bradley player from 1979–82. "He knew what he had to do to give his team a chance to win. And if there was a big shot to be taken, he would step up. . . . He never struck me as a person who would run away from the opportunity of the big shot."

Hawkins was the MVC's final first-team All-America of the 20th century, and he still ranked as the NCAA Division I's seventh all-time scorer 18 years later. Hawkins claimed that his experience at the center position in high school helped him become a prolific scorer all over the court. "I think it was a direct reflection of playing inside three years of high school," Hawkins said. "I could jump pretty high, and I was comfortable inside slashing to the basket. I elevated my game being able to shoot the jump shot, and I was always able to keep the defense off balance with my ability to drive to the hole and finish. I had more of a complete game."

IT BEGAN WITH VERSACE

Six years before Hawkins arrived, Versace, a highly successful Chicago-area high school coach, took over a slumbering Bradley basketball program. In 1978–79, his first season, Versace failed to win a road game in the MVC, and the Braves staggered to a 3–13 league record and tied with West Texas State for last place.

Versace, however, left his mark on the road his first season when he took his team off the floor following an altercation with a fan sitting behind the Braves' bench in a game at Tulsa. "That was the game some fan threw something at Dick, like a program," said Jeff Hurd, who was a publicist for the Missouri Valley Conference at the time. "Dick went up into the stands during the game. They stopped the game and cleared the floor, and Dick took the team to the locker room and was not going to play." It took Barone's persuasion and better security near the Braves' bench for the combustible Versace to return from the locker room after a half-hour delay. Tulsa ended up winning, 82–79, in overtime.

The next season, Versace reversed that conference record, moved from worst to first in the MVC regular season, and finished four games ahead of three teams tied for second place. The Braves not only won their first MVC regular-season title since 1962, but they also claimed their first MVC Tournament title and went to the NCAA Tournament for the first time since 1955 and lost to Texas A&M in the first round. "Right from the start, Dick knew he had to recruit to be successful," Barone said. "He was one of the best at it."

"I marketed my ability to move anywhere and be recognized," Versace said. "So if you recognized me, you recognized Bradley. I had the wild hairdos. I liked the fact I could walk into any gym anywhere in the continental United States and people would know who I was."

"I can remember when we [the Valley] went on road games," said Jim Les, a Bradley player from 1983 to 1986 and currently the Braves' head coach. "He would have that weird hairdo and everybody would pull out their cotton wigs and their big white wigs. We had great personalities as coaches. It in itself was a show other than the game, watching these guys compete against each other."

Versace re-established Bradley's Chicago pipeline, once active in the 1950s and 1960s, by signing high-scoring Mitchell Anderson, a 6-7 forward from Metro High School in the spring of 1978. Anderson led the Braves in

Hersey Hawkins

1974–75 Bradley Braves

Mitchell Anderson

scoring four straight seasons and was the school's all-time leading scorer before Hawkins happened upon the scene.

"We got him and it helped us get other players," Versace said of Chicago players such as Reese, Les, Hawkins, Voise Winters, Anthony Manual, and Mike Williams. "He (Anderson) was a prolific scorer. He had a gift. He had a knack. He averaged 44 points a game as a high school senior. I almost lost him to Michigan State. Magic Johnson stepped in and tried to get him to play with him, but he made a commitment to me and Bradley and he kept that commitment."

By the 1981–82 season, Anderson's senior year, Versace had Bradley on the verge of making a splash in the NCAA Tournament. Versace dipped into the junior college ranks and added defensive specialist St. Louisan David Thirdkill, nicknamed "The Sheriff" because he usually locked up the opposition's best scorer.

Bradley played in six overtime games that season, including the longest game in NCAA Division I history, an incredible 75–73 seven-overtime loss to Cincinnati. "After about the third overtime, I looked down at Ed Badger (Cincinnati coach) and he looked over at me and shrugged," Versace said. "I said, 'Tell one of your guys to make a shot.' If you had a tie game, you held the ball until you took the last shot (no shot clock in those days). . . . One of his guys made a shot and that was the end of it."

Another memorable movement that season involved Versace on the sidelines during the first round of the Rainbow Classic in Hawaii, an 87–82 loss to San Francisco. Dave Snell, the Braves' long-time radio play-by-play announcer, remembers the game like it was yesterday. Bradley was leading late but came unraveled during a series of poor officiating incidents. "They (the Dons) pushed Donald Reese out of bounds and called him for traveling," Snell said. "Then, as the game was tied, a Bradley player was stripped and he is called for blocking. Dick goes over to Larry Yamashita (a game official) and rips the whistle off his neck and throws it into the stands. Caught, I believe, by the athletic director's wife of North Carolina State."

"We had a couple of technicals," Barone said. "And we eventually lost the game. That is a classic on the Islands."

Despite three straight losses in Hawaii, Bradley regrouped to win the MVC regular-season title and appeared headed to the NCAA Tournament, but the Braves fell in double

vertime, 55–50, to Illinois State in the semifinals of the
MVC Tournament.

The Braves failed to get an NCAA at-large berth, the first
time an outright MVC regular-season champion didn't
make the field. Versace, who was openly critical of the
NCAA Tournament Committee, was angry because he
believed the Braves were good enough to make the Final
Four. So they went out and won Bradley's fourth National
Invitation Tournament title (1957, 1960, 1964, 1982), winning its five NIT games by an average of 15.2 points per
game. Anderson was named the Most Valuable Player of
the NIT in his final collegiate appearance.

"We were robbed actually," Reese said of the NCAA
snub. "You could pout and bitch about it or step up and
do the best with the hand you were dealt. We had a
meeting of the team before we met with the coaching
staff. 'Hey, we didn't get the bid. Now what do we do,
complain or move on?' Our point was to prove them
wrong. . . . And we walked through the NIT."

HERSEY BECOMES A BRAVE

Versace had to be convinced to take Hawkins. He
actually went to Chicago to see him play in a private
practice arranged by Westinghouse High School's
head coach. "I said, 'I tell you what, you really think
he can play guard? . . . I will drive to Chicago and
watch him play guard,'" Versace said. "I walk in, there
is a single chair at half court. He had all of his players
there and coaches and no one else. He said, 'Sit
down.'" I sit down and watch Hersey Hawkins play
guard for two hours. . . . And I said, 'Frank, I apolo-
gize. He can play.'"

At Bradley, "the Hawk" averaged 14.6 points as a
freshman in 1984–85, as the Braves posted a 17-13
record and lost to Marquette in the first round of
the NIT. "The one thing that was a highlight of my
freshman year, we ran an offense, the 'Low 1-4',"
Hawkins said. "We had a shooter in one corner, and
another shooter in the other corner, and two big men
inside. It was the third or fourth game, and Coach
Versace said, 'When you get it in this corner, shoot it.
And if you don't shoot it, you will be sitting next to me.'
I thought he had confidence for me to make the shot.
That was a turning point for me."

Jim Les became eligible during the 1983–84 season after
his transfer from Cleveland State and paired up with
Hawkins in the Braves' back court. Jim Les was a ball
boy for Bradley and longed to follow his older brother,

Tom. "Early on, you could see how tremendously talented he was his freshman season," Les said of Hawkins.
"But he was more concerned about fitting in and not
ruffling feathers."

Hawkins' sophomore season, 1985–86, was his coming
out party, as it was for Bradley on the national scene.
The Braves lost only one game during the regular
season, a first-round 81–76 Rainbow Classic defeat to
Clemson. Hawkins scored only about four more points a
game (18.7 ppg) that season, but his crucial baskets in
the last minutes of games—six either won or tied
games—were spectacular. Twice in back-to-back games
on the road, Hawkins made last-second shots.

First, the Braves beat Drake, 69–67, on an airborne-
Hawkins' five-footer. Two days later, Hawkins sent the
Dayton game into overtime with a 23-footer on the same
play. Bradley eventually won, 79–77. Both times, Versace sta-
tioned 6-8 Mike Williams at the free-throw line and
Hawkins near the basket. Les threw a lob or line-drive pass

Anthony Manual

Versace and assistant Tony Barone (left) pace the sidelines

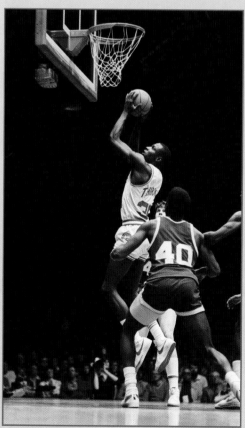

David Thirdkill

and Williams stepped out of the way an[d] cleared the lane for Hawkins, who caught th[e] ball and shot.

"I can't really explain them other than wi[th] the word 'confidence,'" Hawkins told *Vall[ey] Basketball*. "Because if my teammates hav[e] that much confidence in me, I feel I can't l[et] them down. I do it for them more than doin[g] it for myself. Of course, I don't think about i[t,] I just do it. It's just reaction some of the time[.]"

Les also pulled out several games (Marquett[e,] Villanova, and SIU) in the closing minutes b[y] making free throws. That allowed the Braves [to] finish 16–0 in MVC play, one of only two team[s] to go undefeated in the MVC since 1948. India[na] State in 1979 with Larry Bird was the other.

Once again, however, Bradley's season wa[s] marred in the MVC Tournament when th[e] Braves lost to host Tulsa in the title gam[e] 74–58. "It was the first year the (MVC) tour[]nament went to one site, and that was [a] tremendous advantage for Tulsa," Les sai[d.] "We were ranked in the Top 10 in the count[ry] and went through the Valley undefeated, an[d] this team was playing us at (their) home for [a] third time. I remember thinking how difficult the road we were given t[o] try and make a run. . . . Our first game was against UTEP, and we wer[e] the two highest ranked teams playing each other as 8–9 seeds."

In the NCAA Tournament, Bradley beat UTEP in the first round, then fell t[o] eventual champion Louisville in the second. Les speculated that Bradle[y] had been sent a message by the NCAA—Versace's complaining fou[r] years before about not making the field was not appreciated. "It wa[s] disappointing," Hawkins said. "I played on a couple of teams good enoug[h] to go pretty deep in the tournament, and we never got past the secon[d] round."

FOLLOWING VERSACE: ALBECK

Before the 1986–87 season, Versace resigned as the NCAA slappe[d] sanctions on the Braves for recruiting violations. Former Bradley playe[r] and NBA coach Stan Albeck took over the Braves' program, an[d] Hawkins nearly transferred to Villanova.

"When Dick Versace left, I wasn't excited about playing for anothe[r] coach," Hawkins said. "The NCAA sanctions were not real serious. Bu[t] it wasn't a good situation at the time. It was best I get out of it . . . Rolli[e] Massimino was the Villanova coach at the time. He and Dick Versace ha[d] always been friends. And Tommy Massimino had been one of the assis[]tants at Bradley. Villanova had just come off the national championshi[p] in 1985 [at the Rainbow Classic where Bradley defeated Villanova and began a 22-game winning streak.] I had actually told them I was coming and leaving Bradley." With the three-point line coming into play in college basketball that season and Bradley going to an up-tempo game, Albeck convinced Hawkins to stay for his junior year, although the Braves would be ineligible for postseason play. In 1986–87, Hawkins' scoring average soared to 27.2 points a game, which was fifth best in Division I.

"We had a couple of meetings and he changed my mind," Hawkins said. "It was, of course, we were going to run and gun. He was coming from Chicago (Bulls) where he had Michael Jordan, and he said they would run the same offense around me and I would get 25 shots a night. I would play the same position offensively and they would take advantage of my talents. I said, 'That sounds good.'

"That summer before Dick left, he asked me if I could average 25 points a game. He told me I think you can. It may have happened anyway, but I think Stan's offense helped out." During his junior and senior seasons, Hawkins also had the luxury of playing with point guard Anthony Manual, who replaced Les and wound up becoming the MVC's all-time assist king.

Hawkins led Division I in scoring from the beginning of his senior season, scoring 42 points in the Braves' opening victory over New Orleans. That season, he scored more than 50 points twice, and more than 40 points nine times. And his scoring average of 36.3 points was the best in MVC history, surpassing Oscar Robertson's 35.1 average in 1957–58.

For the second time in three years, the Braves won an outright MVC title and then claimed their second MVC Tournament title with an 83–59 victory over Illinois State in Peoria. "I remember Tom Lamonica (Illinois State's sports information director) sitting at the scorer's table before the game," said former Bradley SID Joe Dalfonso. "Lamonica said, 'When I saw the look in Hersey's eyes, I knew we didn't have a chance.'"

Hawkins capped off his MVC career by scoring 29 points against the Redbirds. He was named the 1988 tournament's Most Outstanding Player. "I think it is probably an overused term, he was a silent assassin, but he was a very unassuming guy," Les said. "He was so well liked, it helped him. He was such a team player. Guys relished setting a better screen for him."

Jim Les

Stan Albeck

Ed Jucker

CINCINNATI

The University of Cincinnati was founded in 1819 and was a member of the Missouri Valley Conference from 1957 to 1969. Bearcats basketball was organized at the start of the 20th century and climaxed as a part of the MVC, reaching the Final Four in five straight seasons from 1959 to 1963, winning the NCAA Tournament in 1961 and 1962. College basketball's Player of the Century, Oscar Robertson, played for the Bearcats from 1958 to 1960 and led them to third-place finishes in the NCAA tournament his junior and senior years.

THE OSCAR ROBERTSON YEARS

Early in 1957–58, Wichita State Coach Ralph Miller dispatched Assistant Coach Gary Thompson to Cincinnati. Thompson returned to Wichita with a blank scouting report on 6-5 sophomore Oscar Robertson. "I didn't write a thing," Thompson said of his initial foray into scouting. "I said we could play him with a single player and give him 50. Or, we could double or triple him and give the other guys 25–30 a piece. Coach Miller chuckled. After he saw him play, he understood."

The incomparable Oscar Robertson still inspires memories from former Purdue Coach Gene Keady more than four decades after the "Big O" was the toast of the Missouri Valley Conference. Kansas State and Cincinnati played twice in the NCAA Tournament in the late 1950s. "He would play guard and hit five or six jumpers," said Keady, then a Kansas State student athlete. "Then he would move to forward and make five or six. Then he would go to center and make some post moves. . . . This guy could really play."

At 6-5, Robertson was the prototype Michael Jordan, before Jordan was even born. Or, maybe it's the reverse. Jordan is just a mimic of the granddaddy great—OSCAR.

Veteran college basketball writer Dave Dorr, who covered literally hundreds of college and professional basketball games during his stint at the *St. Louis Post-Dispatch*, put it this way: "If I had to pick one player to take one shot to win a big game, it would be Oscar . . . the Big O."

In the new millennium, the Big O's legacy is immortalized in a bronzed statue of his spread-eagled rebound in a 1958 NCAA Tournament game against Kansas State and Bob Boozer. The United States Basketball Writers Association annually awards the Oscar Robertson Trophy to college basketball's best player.

That's exactly what Robertson was from 1958 to 1960—college basketball's consensus top player—although his NBA stardom with the Cincinnati Royals and Milwaukee Bucks somewhat overshadowed his standout college career. "We'd just go play," Robertson said decades later of his MVC days. "We didn't have a lot of fanfare."

In just three seasons (freshmen were ineligible for varsity competition in those days), Robertson rose swiftly above the college basketball stratosphere, setting the NCAA Division I career scoring record at the time and creating the triple-double statistic: double figures in points,

rebounds, and assists in one game. The Big O had 10 triple-doubles at Cincinnati and would have had more, but the school didn't keep assists his sophomore season.

Mainly, though, the Big O was going to receive the passes. His teammates knew who the main man was. "I threw a hard pass—he never once fumbled a pass from me," said UC guard Ralph Davis, who played with Robertson for five years, including one with the Cincinnati Royals. "I knew where he was going, and he would anticipate it. . . .

He had the greatest hands I have ever seen. . . . I didn't mind giving the ball up to him. I still was a member of the 1,000-point club and an All-American. He was the best, so you helped the best."

The Big O led Division I in scoring three straight seasons (1958 through 1960) with scoring averages of 35.1, 32.6, and 33.7 points. He was the first player in Division I history to do so. LSU's Pete Maravich from 1968 to 1970, is the only other Division I player to lead the nation in scoring three straight seasons.

Oscar Robertson goes spread eagle on a rebound

"I find it difficult to this day arbitrarily to admit Michael Jordan is the greatest player who has played," said former Wichita State guard Lanny Van Eman, later an assistant and head college coach. "I played high school basketball against Wilt Chamberlain, and four games (in college) against Oscar. . . . Cincinnati created a position no one had ever heard of, the ball-handling point forward. Everything went through him. He was used on all the fast breaks. He dribbled out. Someone got a rebound, and he came to middle of the court and he pushed the break down the floor. None of our big men were accustomed to guarding a forward playing the wing in the middle of the court."

Robertson led the Bearcats to three straight MVC regular-season titles, three straight NCAA Tournaments, and two Final Fours in 1959 and 1960 (finishing third twice).

Even with limited television and media exposure of the era, the Big O served as a magnet to the MVC all the way into Texas. Dave Stallworth, a student at Dallas' Madison High School, watched Cincinnati play on a black-and-white television on the brink of deciding which college to attend. Wichita State won out because it was a member of the MVC, along with Cincinnati. "The only thing we had seen was Southwest Conference basketball, which was so-so," Stallworth said. "I saw Bradley and Cincinnati play on TV, and Oscar was playing for Cincinnati. I said it a thousand times: 'He was the greatest basketball player I have ever seen.' . . . Michael Jordan could do all these physical things, but when you watched Oscar play, it was like reading a book. He handled the ball like it was on a string. I played against the man about six years in the pros (never in college). I never saw anybody take the ball away from him—never. You watch him, he was teaching people how to play."

Years later, Robertson says he was oblivious to the effect he was having on recruiting in the MVC. He was focused on two things: getting an education and playing basketball at a very high level—one never seen before.

"Even during his freshman season, you could tell he was destined for greatness," said Tay Baker, former Cincinnati player, assistant coach, and head coach. "He was so fundamentally sound. He played for one of the great high school coaches of all time. Oscar was a stickler for fundamentals and was proficient in every phase of the game."

BREAKING THE COLOR BARRIER

Robertson was born in Tennessee to parents who never completed education past the eighth grade. His family moved to Indianapolis where he was a legend at Crispus Attucks High School, which was the first all-black high school team to win the Indiana state title. He then broke the color barrier on the Cincinnati men's basketball team the first year the school was in the MVC.

Shy and reluctant to talk to the media, Robertson had seldom been around white people in the rural South. Fitting into a mostly white student body at UC wasn't always easy, either.

Racism, he knew about. It existed at Cincinnati, just like it did in the Deep South, and he encountered it on road trips to Texas and North Carolina during his college playing days. Even on campus, professors at UC weren't always fair to black students, and blacks weren't always welcome at certain places in and around campus where white players hung out, all of which Robertson relates in his book, *Oscar Robertson: The Big O.*

"When you are born in the South, like I was in Tennessee, you grew up knowing the lay of the land, and what is going on in a racial basis in the land," Robertson said. "Being a black kid, those things don't bother you a whole lot. It just rolls off your back because you know in your life this happens a lot.

"It didn't bother me. I was aware of it. And I wanted other people to know, 'Hey, are you aware of this. If you are on my team and you say we are all the same, and we try to win together, you shouldn't condone this.'"

The Big O had the extra burden of being black *and* a superstar, but he carried himself well, from the day he put on a Cincinnati uniform. In his first varsity game against Indiana State, Robertson scored 28 points in 28 minutes and away he went. By the end of the 1957–58 season, Robertson set Cincinnati season records for total points, most field goals, most free throws, best field-goal percentage and scoring average despite often playing under difficult circumstances on the road. "He took a lot of harassment being black," said Johnny Overby, who was coming up as an official. "In those days in the MVC, a lot of blacks were playing in the conference, a lot more so than in other conferences. But no, he never complained."

Cincinnati lost just two regular-season games in 1957–58—at Bradley and at Oklahoma State, each when 6-10 center Connie Dierking was out with a broken bone in his foot. Then the Bearcats won 16 straight games and fin ished with a 13–1 record in the MVC.

While Robertson was a handful every outing, two gam stand out during his sophomore season. His coming o party nationally was against Seton Hall at Madison Squa Garden when he scored 56 points in only his 11th colleg game. That outburst broke the Cincinnati single-gam scoring record of 49 points held by Jack Twyman. "On national basis, playing in New York, and doing well, that the way you have to do it," Robertson said. "I didn't rea ize the importance of the game to be honest, the impo tance of the scoring (that night), until much, much late probably after I got out of school."

Later in the season, Robertson exploded for 50 points i an 86–82 victory in a much more difficult environmen Wichita State's Roundhouse. Fans were throwing peanu shells, paper cups, and ice at Robertson, who scored 23 o Cincinnati's last 27 points, including the last six on fre throws. "Every time Cincinnati got him the ball, the fa were lambasting him," said Overby, who had officiated th freshman game. "They threw objects at him. Ralp (Miller) went to the P.A. system, and he informed the peo ple in the stands, if they treat players like that, he will tak Wichita State off the floor and forfeit to the University Cincinnati. There came a hush. . . . That's when the MV came up with the rule if you threw objects on the floor an they had to be cleaned up by the home team, there was possibility of a technical foul on the home team."

The Wichita State victory had great significance. It gav the Bearcats the first of six straight regular-season MVC titles (five outright). The Bearcats, in winning their firs MVC crown in their first year in the league, edged Bradle by one game in the standings.

Cincinnati eventually lost to Kansas State, 83–80, in over time in the NCAA Midwest Regional semifinals Robertson still remembers missing a free throw near th end of regulation, which could have won the game. A team mate believed Robertson was going to go over the tim limit and yelled at him to shoot it quickly. Robertson did n't go through his entire routine. "I was inexperienced, Robertson said. "What I should have done was thrown th ball back to them (official). In the game, Kansas State play ers were taking 16 seconds, more than 10 seconds. Nothin was ever done about it, although that is the rule."

Robertson scored 30 points against the Wildcats bu fouled out in overtime, the only time his sophomore sea son he was disqualified from a game. Miffed by the end

Robertson clears the lane

ing of that game, Robertson scored 56 in a Midwest Regional consolation game victory over Arkansas.

"Our sophomore year might have been our best team," Davis said.

GETTING TO, BUT
LOSING IN THE FINAL FOUR

Before Robertson's junior season, Cincinnati Head Coach George Smith, who was the MVC's Coach of the Year in 1958 and 1959, fretted about the loss of his inside defensive pivot men, Dierking and Wayne Stevens. "He (Robertson) should be even better than last season," said Smith, a former football player. "We hope our offense to be nearly equal of last season. . . . Defensing some of the giant pivot men we will face this season will probably be the toughest problem we have to overcome."

Although Cincinnati's frontline was small, the Bearcats won another MVC title with a 13–1 record, losing only at Bradley again. The Bearcats' other regular-season losses were back-to-back against North Carolina and North Carolina State in the Dixie Classic on the road in late December. Racial epithets were hurled at Robertson from press row in North Carolina. "It was bad," Davis said. "That was the first time I was ever in something and had heard slurs. We had played all over the country, the East and Midwest. But down there we had that kind of a problem. Oscar Robertson put on a show (with 29 points in each game)."

His supporting cast sometimes let Robertson down. "He didn't have a lot of great players around him," said Moe Iba, son of legendary Oklahoma State Hank Iba and a player at the school from 1960 to 1962. "If they had had a couple of more players, they probably would have won the national championship."

The Big O, nearly a half-century later, looks back and agrees. "We had some guys I don't know how they even got them on our team," Robertson said. "Some couldn't play. Some could play. The thing about basketball is you have to have people who can perform and can make plays.

Robertson as a Royal

. . . I know some criticized me. I heard some of the guys on the team criticized me, this wasn't a one-man team. It wasn't a one-man team when I was there, either. We passed the ball around and did different things. But if a guy can't do anything, it was foolish to throw him the ball."

Heading into the 1959 NCAA Tournament, the Bearcats were without their third-leading scorer, guard Mike Mendenall who had exhausted his eligibility after the regular season. Still, Davis contends Cincinnati should have won the NCAA title in 1959 and then again in 1960 when Robertson was a senior.

California's stifling defense, ranked No. 1 in the country, slowed down Cincinnati's high-flying offense in both NCAA semifinals, winning 64–58 in 1959 and 77–69 in 1960. California center Darrall Imhoff scored 22 points in each game.

In the two Final Fours against California, Robertson was held to a total of 37 points and made only 9 of 32 shots. Robertson never got to play in an NCAA title game.

"Both years we were the best team in the country and got beat," Davis said. "Pete Newell (California coach) concocted stuff and he beat us two years in a row. It was all Pete Newell. They slowed it down and worked Imhoff. We didn't stop him. We had players. It was one of those things. They had our number. . . . They played exceptional defense two years and frustrated us."

Robertson and the Bearcats get a welcome at the airport

SENIOR YEAR:
BIG O BECOMES THE TOP SCORER

Despite his three UC teams failing to win the NCAA title, the Big O left his legacy in the Missouri Valley Conference. The Bearcats, in Robertson's three seasons, compiled a 39–3 MVC record and won three league championships. They lost only to Bradley three times, all at Robertson Field House in Peoria, Ill.

The greatest of those games was the Big O's senior season, when Bradley won, 91–90. Fans voted that game as the greatest in 100 years of Braves' basketball. Bradley won only after a late basket by Robertson was disallowed when his right foot was planted on the baseline. He scored 46 points that night. No other Bearcat had more than 16 points. "It was impossible to stop him," said Bradley guard Bobby Joe Mason, who later was a member of the Harlem Globetrotters. "I remember that was what the coach told us. Oscar is going to get his. Stop those other four guys from scoring. You stop those other four guys we can win the ballgame. We only beat them by one point that year, but we wound up beating them every time they played here."

The Big O's "Kodak Moments" in his senior season were numerous. Playing at one of his favorite haunts, Madison Square Garden in the Holiday Festival, he scored 47 against St. Bonaventure, 25 vs. St.

Pete Newell

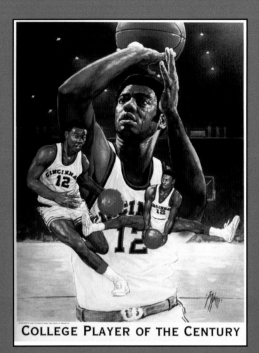

COLLEGE PLAYER OF THE CENTURY

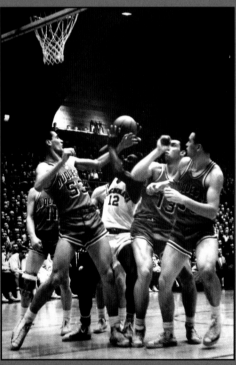

Robertson draws a team of defenders

Joseph's, and 50 against Iowa. He averaged more than 40 points in the three games.

Nine minutes into the Iowa game, however, Cincinnati trailed by 11 points. Smith called a timeout, and his instructions were explicit according to Davis. Give the ball to Oscar, step out of the way, and "let him work." In 11 minutes, Robertson scored 28 points, and the Bearcats were on their way to a 96–83 victory.

He set the then MVC single-game scoring record with 62 points against North Texas in 1960, and he became the NCAA career scoring leader that season, topping the previous record of Furman's Frank Selvy. He literally rewrote the MVC books in nearly every offensive statistical category and set 14 NCAA records.

He would be the all-time Cincinnati assist leader if the school had kept assists his sophomore year. He still has more rebounds than any Bearcat in history, and he shot 53.5 percent from the field and 78 percent from the line.

It was not just his scoring, his passing, or rebounding, it was his style. Gene Iba, a sophomore reserve for Tulsa, remembers the Big O's last game at the Cincinnati Field House, which was so crowded that the Tulsa team couldn't even get to its locker room at halftime. And the Golden Hurricane players stayed right on the bench during a 110–64 loss. "We had a guy named Bill Lucas covering Oscar," Iba said. "Bill was like 6-3, 185. Nobody meant to foul Oscar hard (but Bill did). I remember Oscar shook his head. . . . I remember four Cincinnati guys went over in the corner and stood, and he scored over five (Tulsa) guys." It was one of those unforgettable moments from an unforgettable player.

POST-OSCAR: QUITE AN ENCORE

The composition of the UC Bearcats changed dramatically once Oscar Robertson headed to Cincinnati Gardens on a permanent basis to play for the NBA Royals in the fall of 1960. Cincinnati was left to figure out how to replace its legendary star. The Bearcats didn't really replace the "Big O," however. They changed the way they played the game under first-year Head Coach Ed Jucker, who had been an assistant for Head Coach George Smith during the Robertson era.

The Bearcats won even bigger under Jucker and, oddly enough, without Robertson, who was revolutionary in how he could dominate the game from a position other than center.

With Robertson, UC went to two Final Fours in 1959 and 1960 but never won the NCAA title. Without Robertson, Cincinnati won the NCAA titles in 1961 and 1962 and nearly won a third straight in 1963 when it finished second. "Not that he was selfish, not that he dominated the ball," said Gary Thompson, a Wichita State assistant and player under Ralph Miller and later head coach of the Shockers. "But ne man, it has been proven through the years, does not make a team. What better illustration than the Oscar Robertson years at Cincinnati. Here's the greatest player of the decade at least, and they had to win it after he left. The word 'team' is key."

Others say if Oscar Robertson had not starred three seasons and led the country in scoring on the banks of the Ohio during that time, UC never would have won an NCAA title after he left. "Even though Oscar was not on the winning teams (NCAA titles), give him credit," said former North Texas State Coach Charles Johnson, who coached in the MVC during that era. "He influenced players who wanted to come to Cincinnati. He was not on the winning teams, but I still attribute their success at those times to him."

One of the players who came to Cincinnati because of Robertson was 6-9 center Paul Hogue, who played one season with Robertson as a sophomore, and then was one of the mainstays on the Bearcats' NCAA title teams in 1961 and 1962 after Robertson had departed. In each of his three varsity seasons, Hogue, a former high school tackle from Knoxville, Tenn., averaged in double figures in both scoring and rebounding. He was the only sophomore in the starting lineup Robertson's final season when the "Big O" ran the show.

Hogue, as a rugged inside player, proved to be valuable as the Bearcats changed tactics under Jucker in 1960–61. "We started out very slow Juck's (Jucker's) first year," said Tay Baker, who was the late Jucker's assistant coach then. "I had Tom Thacker and Tony Yates on the freshman team the year before. Tony Yates had been in the service, and Thacker was a year older when he had graduated from high school. We went the first few games, and it didn't work. We had kind of sensed Yates (point guard) and Thacker (6-2 forward) would be in the lineup."

After three early losses by a total of 44 points—the first two MVC games by double-digits on the road—the two sophomores were in there by the ninth game of the season, and they would remain there through three NCAA title games from 1961 to 1963.

The late Jucker eventually called the Air Force veteran Yates "the best defensive

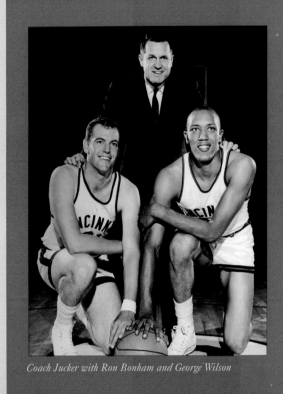
Coach Jucker with Ron Bonham and George Wilson

Coach Jucker and Paul Hogue

Armory Field House in Cincinnati

player in the country and the most underrated." Thacker, despite his size, was one of the best rebounding small forwards–big guards in college basketball. He never averaged less than 8.5 rebounds a season.

"We were an individually dominated team with Oscar," Baker continued. "(We then) became a five-man team with balanced scoring, defense, rebounding, and controlled tempo. It probably related to Pete Newell (the California head coach). We had lost to Cal twice in the Final Four, to a team that played controlled tempo. With the ingredients of the team we had, we could have tried to run up and down the floor to please people. But it would be best if we control tempo, play defense, get boards, and have balanced scoring."

In the ninth game of the 1960–61 season against Dayton, the Bearcats started a winning streak that extended into the next season and eventually reached 27 games. Hogue was at the forefront of it. Rebounding from a technical foul at the beginning of the second half of the Dayton game for throwing the ball into the stands, Hogue finished with 21 points and 15 rebounds in a victory over the Flyers. Hogue was later quoted as saying: "I didn't like losing by those big scores (19 to Bradley and 17 to Saint Louis), but I knew our time would come later in the season. Truthfully, I never dreamed it would be as big as it turned out."

The 1960–61 Cincinnati team wound up winning the MVC regular-season title by a game over second-place Bradley. It took the Bearcats all they had to hold off third-ranked Bradley in Cincinnati, 73–72, in late January, avenging an earlier 19-point loss in Peoria when the Braves were ranked No. 2.

Following a 77–60 victory over No. 6 Iowa at Chicago Stadium in early February, the Bearcats jumped back into the rankings and remained in the Top 10 through the middle of the 1963–64 season.

The Bearcats' only other real scare the rest of the 1960–61 regular season was a 67–64 victory over Wichita State in Cincinnati when Hogue dropped in 26 points and grabbed 18 rebounds. Cincinnati won the outright MVC title, when Bradley lost its last regular-season game to Saint Louis.

In the 1961 NCAA Tournament, the Bearcats beat Texas Tech and Kansas State to advance to their third straight Final Four. This time, the Bearcats didn't falter in the semifinals as they had done the previous two seasons against California. They bounced Utah by allowing the Utes only eight field goals in the first half. That prompted Utah Coach Jack Gardner to predict: "I think they will give Ohio State a good run for it tomorrow night. The key to the game, of course, ll be how well they defense Lucas (All-American rry Lucas)."

hio State was ranked No. 1 in the country and entered e NCAA title game at Kansas City's Municipal iditorium with a 27–0 record, it the Buckeyes, who aver- ed 85.1 points a game, were owed down by the defen- ve-minded Bearcats. It was e first time in NCAA ournament history two teams om the same state had met in e championship game.

ou felt the pressure, every ass, every defensive play, every bound," said Tom Hedrick ho was doing radio at court- de. Increasing the building of nsion for the title game, St. oseph's and Utah battled hrough a marathon four-over- me consolation final won by .. Joseph's, 127–120, delaying ne start of the final. Once the hampionship game partici- ants finally hit the floor, Ohio tate led 39–38 at halftime. ucas finished with 27 points nd 12 rebounds, but his uckeye running mate John avlicek was held to four oints.

Paul Hogue shoots a jumper

he Bearcats' balance (four layers in double figures) and defense proved to be too nuch for the Buckeyes, who were held to 26 points in the econd half. "We've got no All-Americas on this club," icker said after the game. But he singled out Yates' efense on the perimeter and guard Carl Bouldin's five- raight jump shots in the second half (16 points in the ame) that allowed UC to win. Reliable and intense for- vard Bob Wiesenhahn added 17 points and a team-high ine rebounds for the Bearcats.

hacker's short jump shot gave Cincinnati a 61–59 lead, ut future coach Bob Knight's only points of the game vith 1:41 left tied the score for Ohio State and sent the ame into overtime. There, Cincinnati outscored the uckeyes 9–4. Hogue, a poor free throw shooter, made vo foul shots to put the Bearcats ahead to stay.

Jucker became the first coach to win an NCAA title in his first full season as head coach at a school. He's the only coach in NCAA history to do it after losing a three-time NCAA scoring champion (Oscar Robertson) from the previous season.

Bouldin is still the only player to lead his team in scoring in the Final Four in the spring and then in the same calendar year play in the major leagues. He pitched in two games for the Washington Senators later that year.

The Bearcats fit perfectly together in that spring of 1961. "Hogue was a very strong guy," Baker said. "Wiesenhahn was an intense rebounder. Bouldin was a per- fect second guard. Thacker could play any place. And Yates, in my own personal opinion—and I am probably going out on a limb saying this—he didn't have the sta- tistics a lot of the players at UC had, but the importance of him to our program, I don't think there was a more impor- tant player in (the school's) history other than Oscar."

Coach Jucker called Yates, who later would become Cincinnati's head basketball coach, "His coach on the floor."

"That unity," Baker continued, "we only had because of Tony. He could have scored more if he had been on differ- ent teams, but his job was to run the show. He was a stick- ler on defense. He would get right in the face of a guy (teammate) loafing. Coaches didn't have to say anything to the players."

AN INSTANT REPLAY, DURING 1961–62 SEASON
Ohio State and Cincinnati would tread water and hold their positions among college basketball's elite for another season.

With 10 lettermen and three starters returning from the 1961 NCAA champs, the Bearcats lost only Bouldin and

Wiesenhahn. They lost some physical play of Wiesenhahn, but added more offensive firepower with jump shooter Ron Bonham and athleticism with leaper George Wilson at the forwards. Jucker moved Thacker to guard, which enhanced the team's rebounding. "Cincinnati was a better rebounding team after Oscar left," said Bob Ortegel, who played at Bradley during that era. "And Thacker was an incredible athlete. He played both ends of the floor. He could get so much done defensively, and he was such an outstanding rebounder."

The Bearcats entered the 1961–62 season with a 22-game winning streak and claimed their first five games before going to Wichita State on Dec. 18. But the UC winning streak ended at 27 games when a little Wichita State guard named Lanny Van Eman sank a shot heard around the country at Henry Levitt Arena. His corner jumper with three seconds remaining lifted the Shockers to a pulsating 52–51 victory over the defending national champions. "Cincinnati had a three-point lead with 40 seconds to go," said Van Eman, of the era without a shot clock or the three-point line. "It is different now. . . . Somehow, we managed to come back."

Tom Thacker

Cincinnati lost only one other game all season, a 70–68 overtime decision at Bradley, which was enough for the Braves and Bearcats to tie for the regular season MVC title and force a one-game playoff in Evansville, won rather easily by the Bearcats, 61–46.

NCAA Tournament victories in the first two rounds were even easier over Creighton (an independent at the time), 66–46, and Colorado, 73–46. Cincinnati made it to the Final Four for the fourth straight season, this time at Louisville's Freedom Hall.

Since the midseason loss at Bradley, Cincinnati had won 16 straight games heading into a semifinal meeting against UCLA. The Bruins, under Coach John Wooden, were in their first Final Four, and they served notice they were a program on the rise.

The score was tied at halftime, despite the Bearcats jumping to an 18–4 lead to start the game. In the second half, Cincinnati could never pull away from the pesky Bruins, who had two of their future head coaches in the lineup, Gary Cunningham and Walt Hazzard.

The score was tied, 70–70, with 10 seconds remainin when UC's senior guard Tom Sizer took the ball out bounds. Sizer couldn't get it to Hogue and tossed it Thacker, who sank a 25-footer to win the game. UCL called timeout with one second left, but Hazzard threw length-of-the-court pass that was deflected out of bound "That was it, baby," Thacker said of his basket. It was th exclamation point on Hogue's big game (36 points and 2 rebounds). Except for Thacker's basket, Hogue scored 1 of UC's last 17 points against the Bruins.

The victory over UCLA set up a rematch against Ohi State in the final, and this time, Cincinnati proved it was better team once again in a game that wasn't as close as th previous year's final.

Hogue grabbed Final Four MVP honors with his defens on Ohio State's Lucas, as well for a 22-point, 19-reboun performance against the Buckeyes. Although Lucas wa bothered with a knee injury suffered in the semifinal vic tory over Wake Forest, Ohio State coach Fred Taylo offered no excuses when he finished with just 11 points i Cincinnati's 71–59 victory.

Ed Jucker celebrates the 1960–61 NCAA championship with Singleton, Calhoun, and Sizer

As good as Hogue was, Jucker was equally complimentary of Thacker, who scored 21 points and grabbed six rebounds for the Bearcats, who finished the season with an 18-game winning streak. "Tom Thacker was like five men out there," Jucker said after the game. "He was all over the place, feeding, jumping, and rebounding. He played a very powerful game, and I cannot say enough about him."

The back-to-back Cincinnati–Ohio State finals were the only times during the 20th century two teams from the same state met in the NCAA final.

NEARLY A THREE-PEAT

The Bearcats lost Hogue to graduation and the NBA, but they returned the rest of the team and went into the 1962–63 season as the No. 1-ranked team in college basketball. Cincinnati had a great shot at becoming the first team in NCAA history to win three straight titles. Oklahoma A&M, as an MVC member, had won two straight in 1945 and 1946, and the great San Francisco teams, led by Bill Russell, collected consecutive titles in 1955 and 1956.

Jucker moved George Wilson to center and Thacker back to forward without missing a beat. The Bearcats held the No. 1 ranking all season and posted 19 straight victories to raise their winning streak to 37 games heading into mid-February.

Tay Baker

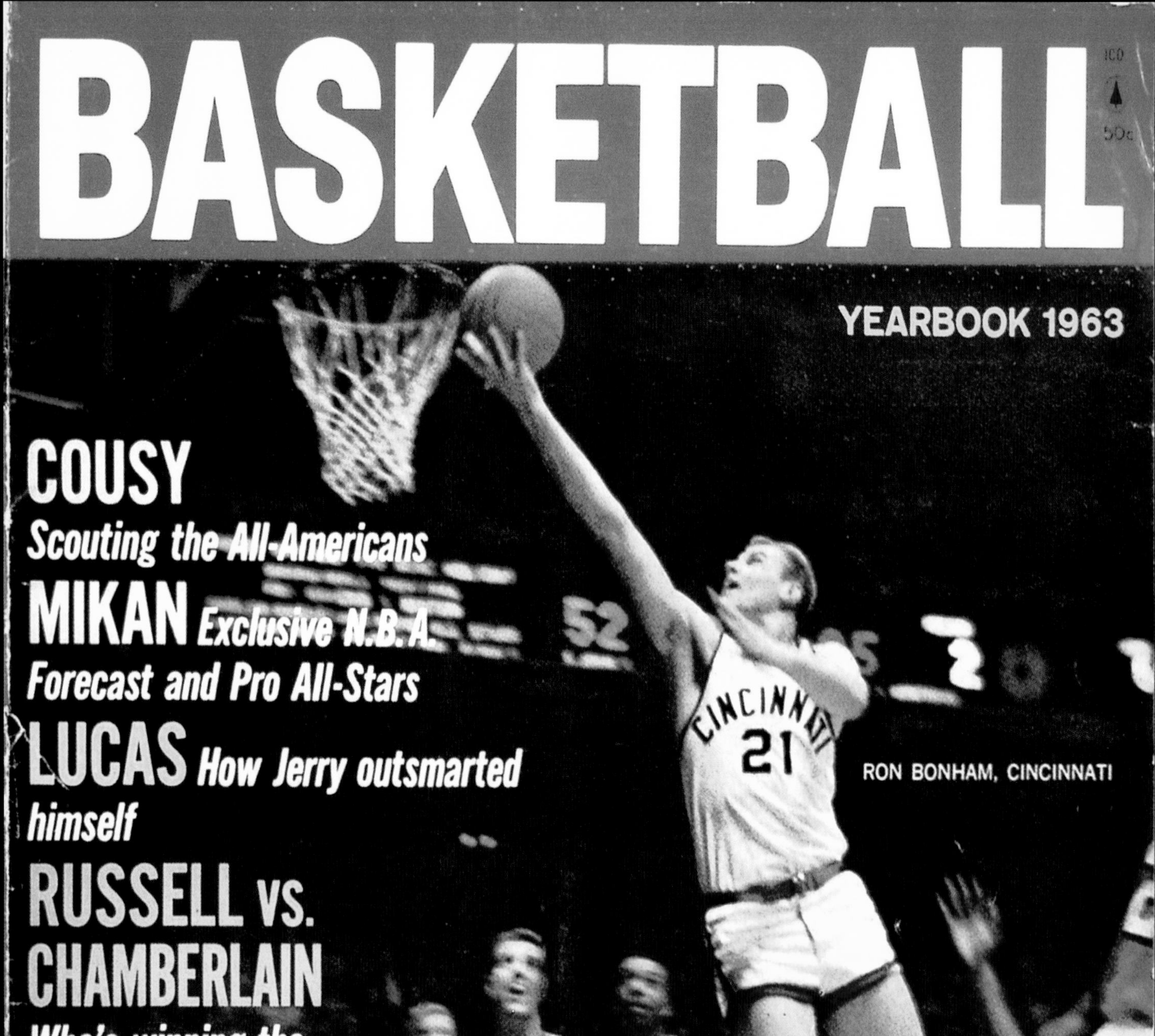
BASKETBALL
50¢
YEARBOOK 1963
COUSY
Scouting the All-Americans
MIKAN Exclusive N.B.A.
Forecast and Pro All-Stars
LUCAS How Jerry outsmarted
himself
RUSSELL vs.
CHAMBERLAIN
Who's winning the
war of the Giants?
Inside reports on 200
Colleges Sophs to watch
High school basketball
preview Complete
schedules.
CINCINNATI
21
22
RON BONHAM, CINCINNATI

Paul Hogue in the 1962 NCAA Finals

Then a strikingly reminiscent event occurred. For a second straight year they lost at Wichita State by one point, 65–64, when Dave Stallworth put on a show and led an energized comeback in the final minute. Years later, Jucker confided to Van Eman, later an assistant coach for the Shockers, that was the most hurtful loss of his entire career.

Nevertheless, the Bearcats recovered and won the MVC by four games over the Shockers, a fifth straight league title. This time, without Ohio State to block their path, it appeared there would be no stopping the top-rated Bearcats in the NCAA Tournament.

Still, after trailing both Texas and Colorado at halftime of the first two NCAA games, the Bearcats rallied to win close games over both teams. The Bearcats blew out Oregon State and Mel Counts in the NCAA semifinals, 80–46, after leading by just three at halftime. The OSU victory set up an NCAA final of teams with contrasting styles. Cincinnati led the nation in defense, allowing just 52.9 points a game, and Loyola of Chicago, coached by George Ireland, led the nation in scoring with 91.8 points a game. Something had to give.

The game was played more at Cincinnati's tempo and liking. The Bearcats took a 29–21 halftime lead, and the Ramblers appeared to be in trouble. But their press took over in the second half, forcing 16 UC turnovers in the game. Cincinnati went to a delay game, which didn't work, to protect several key players with fouls.

Loyola wound up tying the game in regulation, at 54–54, and Cincinnati gave up the winning basket on a rebound putback by Vic Rouse over Thacker with one second remaining in overtime, 60–58.

"This isn't just sour grapes," Baker said. "That game was one of the most poorly officiated games in the history of

The Bearcats celebrate their 1961 NCAA championship

college basketball. If you look at the films at this thing, the calls that were missed and calls that were made, it just makes you shudder. We said, 'Hey, let's run the clock, if we get a chance to score, do that.' It broke the momentum of the game. All of a sudden, we were fighting for our lives. We made a mistake in a rebounding situation late in the game, and they scored."

The NCAA title game in 1963 was remarkable for several reasons. It was the only NCAA title game of the 20th century in which one team (Loyola) never substituted, even with the overtime. The Ramblers won despite making only 27 percent of their shots, but they took 39 more shots than Cincinnati. Also, it was the first time in the history of the NCAA Tournament that more than half the starters (seven) in the title game were African American.

Following the 1963 NCAA Tournament, the Missouri Valley had the best winning percentage (68.3) of any conference, boosted mostly by Cincinnati's 18–4 record over a six-year period from 1958 to 1963. "I think the consensus at that time, it absolutely was the strongest basketball conference in the country,"

Baker said. "The rankings and record certainly help bare that out."

Cincinnati became the first team to make four straight Final Fours when it advanced to five in a row (1959–63). UCLA then made 10 straight from 1967 to 1976. In the 20th century, Duke was the only other team with five straight Final Four berths (1988–92).

Jucker finished his coaching career with an 11–1 NCAA Tournament record, losing only the one game to Loyola. He never returned to the NCAA Tournament after the 1963 season and retired two years later.

Wes Unseld

LOUISVILLE

The University of Louisville was founded in 1798 and was a member of the Missouri Valley Conference from 1964 to 1975. Men's basketball at Louisville thrived in the MVC with the Cardinals' greatest teams coming in 1972 and 1975 when Denny Crum led them to the NCAA Final Four both years.

WES UNSELD, DENNY CRUM MAKE CARDINALS A FORCE IN MVC

The University of Louisville broke the basketball color barrier in the state of Kentucky when the Cardinals played Wade Houston, Sam Smith, and Eddie Whitehead during the 1963–64 season. Those recruits didn't win the Cardinals any championships, but two years later they served as a major reason Louisville landed standout center Wes Unseld, the most important U of L recruit of the decade. "Unseld is to us what Oscar Robertson was to Cincinnati and Jerry Lucas was to Ohio State," the late Louisville Coach Peck Hickman predicted before Unseld ever played a varsity game.

Wes Unseld shooting his patented hook shot as Louisville defeats Kansas State 93–63 for regional third place, March 16, 1968 at Wichita State

Unseld and another African American Kentucky high school basketball star, guard Butch Beard, both picked U of L over the then all-white University of Kentucky basketball program, which didn't suit up its first black basketball player until center Tom Payne in 1970. "We were both recruited by Kentucky," said Beard, a year behind Unseld in school. "I never thought Coach Rupp (Adolph, of Kentucky) wanted a black player at that time. I will leave it that way."

Unseld starred for the Louisville freshman team in 1964–65, and the frosh beat the varsity, 87–86, in a preseason scrimmage. Hickman called Unseld the most "complete player" he had ever coached. By the beginning of the 1965–66 season, Unseld, then a sophomore, was eligible to play for the Louisville varsity in the school's second season competing for the Missouri Valley Conference title. The eventual three-time All-MVC selection immediately became one of the league's most dominant big men, as well as one of the best rebounders ever.

In his first MVC season, the 6-8 Unseld averaged 19.4 rebounds and 19.9 points a game. The 19.4 rebounds a game, which ranked second nationally that season, is still the best individual seasonal average in MVC history. "I had never played against a player of his size and his ability," said Beard, who teamed with Unseld for two seasons at Louisville. "At that time, he was one of the best rebounders for his size. His ability to throw the outlet pass was as good as anybody who played the game."

Unseld, later a 13-year star with the Baltimore/ Washington Bullets in the National Basketball Association, was among the inaugural members inducted into the MVC Hall of Fame in 1997. "I had been around kids at Texas Western, so I had seen some good players," said Moe Iba, who coached in the MVC at Memphis State from 1966 to 1970. "But he was so much bigger and stronger. The thing I remember about him, he could outlet the ball. And he could just turn and shoot."

In Unseld's sophomore season (1965–66), the Cardinals finished with the same conference record as the season before (8–6). But because of Unseld's star quality, Louisville, with a 16–9 record, was invited to play in the 1966 National Invitation Tournament in New York City. In a blockbuster first-round NIT game, Coach Bob Cousy's Boston College team defeated Louisville, 96–90, in triple overtime. By the time Unseld fouled out with 4:05 to play in the third overtime, he had 25 points and 26 rebounds. The New York media got an eyeful.

BEARD JOINS UNSELD

By the next season (1966–67), Beard became eligible to play for the varsity, and, as a sophomore, the flashy Beard led the Cardinals in scoring with a 20.5 points per game to Unseld's 18.7. The Cardinals lost only three road games during the regular season and won the first of seven MVC titles in nine years.

Unseld again was a rebounding force, averaging 19 a game (third nationally). Normally, he was the king of the hill around the basket, except when Wichita State's high-flying Warren Armstrong, a deluxe leaper at 6-2, was in the game. "I remember him (Armstrong) dunking the ball," Beard said. "I was guarding him and he got past me, and he was going in to dunk and was parallel with the basket. And I yelled at Wes, who was on the weak side, to let him go. I was afraid Wes would get his hand up there and he (Armstrong) would break it."

With Beard and Unseld together, Louisville rose to 23–3 before entering the NCAA Tournament. The only losses, by a total of 10 points, were road games at Southern Illinois, which had Walt Frazier and would win the National Invitation Tournament that season; at Wichita State; and at Cincinnati. Louisville's 1966–67 season ended suddenly in Lawrence, Kan., when SMU upset Louisville in the NCAA Midwest Regional semifinals. Louisville only needed to win two games to return home to play in the 1967 Final Four at Freedom Hall, but the Cardinals didn't make it.

The SMU–Louisville score was tied 81–81 in the closing seconds when the Cardinals' Fred Holden was tied up by SMU's Charles Beasley, who spiked the ball down the floor on the ensuing jump ball. "It was a freak game," said Jerry King, a Louisville forward on that team. "There was a jump ball at mid-court. We had a breakdown. We didn't put a guy under our goal. This SMU guy (jumping at center-court) . . . got up so high, he took a volleyball slam and hits the ball to a guy (Denny Holman) streaking outside who lays it up and in. The game was over. It was diagrammed. You don't normally outjump some guy by a foot."

Louisville lost to Kansas in the 1967 NCAA Midwest Regional consolation game, which turned out to be the final game for Coach Hickman, who retired after 23 years at Louisville without posting a losing season. "Hickman was a very good coach, and he didn't get the notoriety he should have gotten for his ability to coach," Beard said. "He really put Louisville on the map. He started the tradition. Denny Crum enhanced it."

Crum, however, wouldn't happen upon the scene for four more years. Louisville officials promoted Hickman assistant John Dromo to coach the team and he continued the winning tradition. In Unseld's final season, the Cardinals won the MVC title by two games over Bradley.

Dromo moved Beard from forward to guard. Beard fought the move at first but later realized it would prepare him better for an NBA career, which would span nine seasons with five different teams. The position switch also allowed Beard to better feed Unseld, who had another monster year.

Unseld set the Louisville scoring record by tossing in 45 points against Georgetown (Ky.) College in the 1967–68 season opener. He followed the next game, a 57–51 victory at Kansas, with 20 points and 14 rebounds, as Dromo's 1-3-1 zone stifled KU's star, Jo Jo White. "He (Unseld) had a nice, quiet demeanor, but when he hit the court he would go to war," King said. "I remember how he would communicate with the rest of us. It was with his intensity and the way he would look at you. He had a way of letting you know you needed to give a little bit more. He was a very, very good-natured person."

"What a lot of people don't realize is that he was a prototype power forward, but he played at center," King continued. "He was only pushing 6-7, but he was all muscle. He could very easily stand under the goal and two-hand dunk. He had a lot of lift. He would take a rebound and almost as he would come down, he was turning—and the ball was at mid-court, and he would trigger the fast break with the outlet pass."

Butch Beard

Beard twisting and turning

Wes Unseld

needed to do. He was really the missing link. After him and Unseld, we were real small. And when we would go against somebody like Houston or Kansas, they went 6-10 across the front line."

The Cardinals entered the NCAA Tournament on a 12-game winning streak but had to face top-ranked and unbeaten Houston, a former MVC member, in the Midwest Regional semifinals in Wichita, Kan. The Cougars' Elvin Hayes and Don Chaney spurred a 26–4 first-half scoring streak against Louisville that resulted in a 37–17 lead. Game over. Dromo's comment: "Hayes (35 points, 24 rebounds) was the best he had ever seen and Chaney (17 points) took us apart."

Unseld closed out his storied career in a 93–63 NCAA consolation game victory over Kansas State. Because he played only three varsity seasons, Unseld, in 1968, stood as the school's second all-time leading scorer and rebounder behind Charlie Tyra.

Unseld was class all the way. "Unseld was the team captain," said Johnny Overby, who was an MVC referee during that era. "He treated everybody with respect. He never asked for anything. He never wanted anything given to him. He was just a great person."

CRUM TAKES OVER LOUISVILLE HELM
In Dromo's next three seasons, the Cardinals failed to make the NCAA Tournament again. They went to three

Kansas avenged its loss in Lawrence by beating Louisville at Freedom Hall, 84–76, in double overtime. The Cardinals lost only two MVC games in 1968, back-to-back contests in January at Bradley and at Cincinnati. They were building for a chance at the NCAA title.

Louisville had taken a transfer from South Carolina, 6-9 Mike Grosso, who had been considered one of the top high school big men on the East Coast. Grosso had a sore right knee and wasn't that much of a factor during the 1967–68 season. "They had recruited him to be the bookend forward, and I would have been the shooting forward," King said. "On paper they knew what they

Unseld directs the team on the court

NITs but were MVC co-champions with Drake in 1969 when the Bulldogs won a playoff game in Wichita and again in 1971 when they lost another playoff game against Drake.

Dromo stepped down during the latter part of the 1970–71 season because of a heart attack. Interim Coach Howard Stacey, a Dromo assistant, was rumored to be on his way to Drake to replace Maury John. And he did wind up there, paving the way for UCLA assistant Denny Crum to become the Cardinals' next coach.

The youthful Crum, who had a West Coast background, in one season did what all the previous coaches failed to do—take the Cardinals to the Final Four. It helped that he had five starters returning, all seniors, including 6-2 star guard Jim Price, from a team that had won 20 games and tied for the 1971 MVC title.

Louisville lost its first game of the 1971–72 season at Florida by a point, a game Crum figured the overconfident team would lose because of its cocky attitude going into Gainesville. Crum had the Cardinals' attention after the loss. They won 15 straight before the first of two regular-season losses to Memphis State.

The key to the season, Crum was told when he arrived, was controlling the temperamental Price. "Jimmy came

Denny Crum

Crum issuing orders with his signature rolled-up program in hand

into my office when I first got there," Crum said. "And he said, 'Coach I just want you to know I am looking forward to playing for you.' And I never had one problem with him. I don't know what transpired before." Price finished his senior season with a flourish, leading the NCAA Tournament in scoring (27.7 ppg) and tossing in 30 against defending NCAA champion UCLA, Crum's old team, in the Final Four.

Crum did tinker with the returning starting lineup and inserted 6-9 Mike Lawhon in place of 6-foot guard Larry Carter and made 6-3 Henry Bacon a big guard. Lawhon was good at taking charges, screening off the boards, and despite his size, was a good outside shooter. He was the final piece to the puzzle against everybody except Memphis State.

Louisville's chance to go to the NCAA Tournament came down to reversing the two previous losses to the Tigers. In those games, Memphis State's 1-2-2

Jim Price drives the lane

zone had stifled the Cardinals. Enter 27-year-old center Ken Bradley, who had 13 points and nine rebounds in the third game against Gene Bartow's Tigers. "I devised an offense that mismatched them and screened their baseline man so he couldn't get out on the shooter," Crum said. "Ken Bradley was screening, and Mike Lawhon would make the shot. Or we would pump fake, and the baseline defender would come flying out to get the shooter, and Bradley would slide in and get the layup. We ended up beating them and wound up going to the Final Four."

Louisville beat Southwestern Louisiana and the nation's leading scorer Bo Lamar and then took care of Kansas State from the Big Eight. The Cardinals then ran into top-ranked UCLA and center Bill Walton in the Final Four. A 96–77 loss to the Bruins didn't dim Louisville's future under Crum.

Crum established his Louisville program on speed, big guards, and recruiting several athletes from the South and transforming them into basketball players. "We wanted to get good athletes who could run and jump," Crum said. "Then we thought we could teach them about what they needed to know about playing basketball. We made a living for years on kids just like that—kids who were really good athletes. Sure I would have liked to have had a 7-foot center, but there weren't any around that I could recruit."

One of those good athletes was Allen Murphy, who was recruited out of Birmingham, Ala., shortly after Crum arrived. Murphy was part of the same recruited class that included 6-5 Junior Bridgeman from East Chicago (Washington), Ind. They were well-rounded players, who could play multiple positions and could defend. "I always thought the guys from Louisville were pretty tough defensively," Tulsa's Willie Biles said. "All teams had their defensive stopper, and I remember guys Coach Denny Crum had—Junior Bridgeman. I remember him."

By the time the two were seniors, Crum had recruited a team capable of winning the NCAA title. He had added forward Wesley Cox, from Louisville; guard Phillip Bond; and a 6-10 freshman center Ricky Gallon from Tampa.

Bridgeman was the star, a converted guard from a high school forward, who Crum would post-up on smaller guards inside on offense and still play at forward on defense. The 6-5 Murphy was a high school high jumper and played forward on offense and went back to guard on defense because he was quicker laterally than Bridgeman.

"They were absolutely awesome," said Ken Hayes, who was coaching Tulsa at the time. "We beat them in Tulsa (82–77 in 1974–75), when they had Bridgeman and all those guys. Two weeks later, they are practicing at Freedom Hall and we have a shoot around. I walked right out on the floor and said, 'Hope you guys play hard. We are tired of beating you all.'" Louisville thumped Tulsa by 25 in the return game and finished the 1974–75 regular season with a 24–2 record. The Cardinals won their seventh and final MVC title.

Louisville's only other loss during the 1974–75 regular season was at Bradley, 65–59, three weeks after the Cardinals had barely escaped with an 82–80 overtime decision over the Braves at Freedom Hall. "We held the ball and had them asleep," said Bradley star Roger Phegley, then just a freshman. "There was no three-point shot, no shot clock. We just sat on it most of the game and had them dead in the water. I went to the free-throw line in the closing seconds, and I was a much better than average free-throw shooter."

With Bradley up by two points, Phegley missed the front end of a one-and-one. Murphy took Louisville's last shot to tie the game. "It hit the back of the rim and went straight up in the air," Phegley recalled. "Time was suspended. Everybody looked to see if it would fall in or out. It (went in and) put it into over-time. Their place went bonkers. We ended up getting beat in overtime."

Louisville beat three ranked teams on the way to the Final Four—No. 15 Rutgers, No. 12 Cincinnati, and in the regional finals, No. 4 Maryland, whose team included John Lucas, Brad Davis, and Owen Brown. Crum will never forget while walking off the floor what Maryland Coach Lefty Driesell said to him following the Cardinals' 96–82 victory. "He said, 'Damn,' and stomped his foot," Crum recalled. "He said, 'You didn't even have a single player who could start on my team.' . . . I don't know if that was true . . . but he didn't think so. They weren't highly recruited like his kids were. . . . They may have had individuals who were better (than our players), but they didn't play as well as we did together."

Allen Murphy

Phillip Bond

UCLA was the roadblock again in the Final Four, but this was a much closer game than the 1972 semifinal against the Bruins. Cox had suffered a torn hamstring two weeks before the season was over, but despite not practicing he held his own against the Bruins' big men. Murphy was sensational with a game-high 33 points.

In what turned out to be UCLA Coach John Wooden's next-to-last game, it came down to the wire. Louisville couldn't hang on to a 59–53 lead late, and the game went into overtime tied, 65–65. Louisville had a chance to go up by three points with 20 seconds left in overtime, but reserve guard Terry Howard, who was 28-for-28 from the line during the season, missed the front end of a one-and-one. UCLA grabbed the rebound and Richard Washington put in the game winner, a 12-footer from the baseline in a 75–74 victory. "Terry had not missed a free throw all year," Hayes still remembers. "If Terry hits that free throw. . . . That was one of our best teams. You couldn't find a better team. . . . Bridgeman was so unselfish. He could do a lot of things."

> "If Terry hits that free throw. . . . That was one of our best teams. You couldn't find a better team. . . . Bridgeman was so unselfish. He could do a lot of things."

The next season, Louisville was gone from the MVC and had joined the Metro Conference, but the 1974–75 season was quite a sendoff. Crum just wishes his team could have beaten UCLA to make the NCAA title game in 1975 where instate and arch-rival Kentucky awaited and eventually lost to the Bruins. "I had made comments I wouldn't trade Ricky Gallon for Rick Robey or Mike Phillips and all of those (Kentucky guys)," Crum said. "Of course, the press around here made a big deal of that. Then here we are both in the Final Four. We had a good chance to prove the kids we have the Bridgemans, Murphys, Gallons . . . those kids were as good as Kentucky's players, and we didn't get a chance to play them."

Junior Bridgeman

Memphis State's Billy Buford battling UCLA in the 1973 NCAA Final Four in St. Louis at the St. Louis Arena

MEMPHIS STATE

Founded in 1912 as West Tennessee State Normal School, the school was known as Memphis State University from 1941 to 1994, when it became the University of Memphis. The Tigers were a part of the Missouri Valley Conference from 1967 to 1973.

THE TIGERS MAKE NATIONAL SPLASH

At the beginning of the 1972–73 basketball season, the sports publicist for Memphis State already had set a high bar for the Tigers: Bill Grogan's slogan: "Meet Me in St. Louis, Wooden."

Grogan's take from the famous movie *Meet Me in St. Louis*, was an obvious reference to the fact the 1973 NCAA Final Four was being played in that city and six-time defending champion UCLA and Coach John Wooden would be there. Little did anyone know that Missouri Valley Conference champion Memphis State also would be in the Final Four for the first time in school history.

Going into the 1972–73 season, Memphis State (now University of Memphis) had never won an NCAA Tournament game. "He turned out to be quite a prognosticator," said Gene Bartow, who coached the Tigers then. "But I thought he was a nut."

The slogan was splashed around on Memphis State publicity materials and even showed up on some plastic glasses. And why not? By the end of the season, "Clean Gene" Bartow's Tigers were the toast of the city.

For the only time in school history, the Tigers won an outright MVC title in 1973 behind guard Larry Finch, forward Ronnie Robinson, and center Larry Kenon. Then the Tigers made an improbable run to meet the mighty Bruins in the NCAA title game in St. Louis. Bartow accomplished all this by inheriting Finch and Robinson, two of the city's top high school players who had been recruited by previous

---

TEAM OUTLOOK FOR 1972-73: 'Tiger's Can Do It!'

"MEET ME IN ST. LOUIS...."

By Bill Grogan
Sports Information Director

When Kerry Mills and Andrew Sterling got together back in 1904 and came up with the song "Meet Me In St. Louis, Louis," little did they know that the phrase would become so important—not only to St. Louis, to Broadway, and to Hollywood—but to Memphis State's 1972-73 basketball outlook.

Seldom does a team's prospectus dare to step out as boldly as does this one. For tht matter, though, seldom does a team, a program and a city, as talented, as dedicated to one aim, and as enthusiastic as these come along. **MEMPHIS STATE'S CHANCES IN 1972-73 ARE AS GOOD AS ANY OF THE MAJOR TEAM'S IN THE NATION WITH BUT POSSIBLY ONE EXCEPTION.** Only Coach Wooden and his UCLA Bruins appear, on paper, to be possibly stronger than the Tigers. And both, might just find each other at the NCAA finals in St. Louis.

Tiger SID Bill Grogan was prophetic in MSU media guide

Larry Finch, Gene Bartow, and Ronnie Robinson

Memphis State Coach Moe Iba, and by signing three junior college stars—Kenon (Amarillo College), Bobby Buford (Paducah, Ky., Community College), and forward Wes Westfall (Trinidad Co. State Junior College).

The main catch was Kenon, "Special K," who went on to a successful professional career with the New York Nets of the American Basketball Association and later the San Antonio Spurs and Chicago Bulls in the National Basketball Association. "Gene came by my office and said I am going to a (junior college) tournament and I am going to find my center," said Al Brown, a former Memphis baseball coach and now director of Memphis' M Club. "He said. 'We have Finch and Robinson, but you have to have three real players to win the NCAA. You can't do it with one or two.' And they came as close as you can come to doing it."

Memphis State lost to the Bruins, 87–66, in the 1973 NCAA title game, when Walton scored 44 points and made 21 of 22 shots in one of the greatest individual final-game performances in NCAA history.

To this day, some Memphis State players believe the officiating was very one-sided, although Bartow has been quoted as saying it was the greatest performance he had ever seen. "He got some favorable calls," Westfall said. "It was unreal. I am not saying he was not a great player, but he got some favorable calls. And they called some real ticky-tack fouls on us real quick."

FROM IBA TO BARTOW

Moe Iba, son of the legendary Oklahoma A&M Coach Henry Iba, became coach of the Tigers in 1966 after serving as an assistant coach on Texas Western's NCAA title team. Memphis State was an independent in Iba's first season and then moved into the MVC beginning in 1967–68.

Iba had helped coach a Texas Western team that started five black players and beat all-white Kentucky in the 1966 NCAA title game. Those Miners, under Don Haskins, helped revolutionize college basketball and usher in the black athlete into Southern colleges. "When I got there, it

Larry Kenon °

(Memphis State) had no scholarship black players," Iba said. "The only (black) player that was on the team was a walk-on, a young man named Herb Hilliard, and we immediately put him on scholarship. I knew going into the Valley that they were going to have to recruit some black kids to compete."

Most of the MVC schools had been recruiting black athletes for years. Memphis State's first two recruited black players were Joe Proctor from Knoxville, Tenn., and James Douglas from Nashville, Tenn., in 1968. The breakthrough with black high school recruits in Memphis came with Finch and Robinson from Melrose High School a year later. "I knew Larry was going to be a great player," Iba said. "There were three players in the city at that time who were great basketball players: Johnny Neumann, who went to Ole Miss, Finch, and Robinson. Finch committed

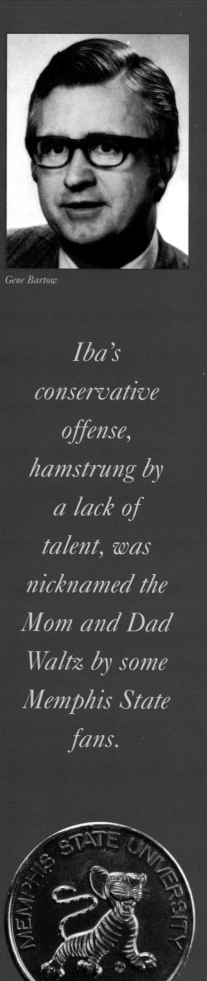

Gene Bartow

Iba's conservative offense, hamstrung by a lack of talent, was nicknamed the Mom and Dad Waltz by some Memphis State fans.

Coach Moe Iba and star guard Mike Butler prepare for Tigers' entry into Missouri Valley Conference

first (to Memphis State) and then Robinson."

Finch and Robinson, however, never played a varsity game for Iba. Under NCAA rules, they were ineligible to play for the varsity as freshmen during Iba's last season in 1969–70, when the varsity Tigers finished 6–20.

Iba's conservative offense, hamstrung by a lack of talent, was nicknamed the "Mom and Dad Waltz" by some Memphis State fans. Iba's tenure ended after four years, during which the Tigers were 3–45 in their first three MVC seasons. "We lost twice to Union University," said former Memphis State radio play-by-play man Jack Eaton. "After that, Moe was out of here."

Memphis State Athletic Director Billy Murphy bought into the fact that Bartow allegedly told him, "If they had a 10-second clock, it would never go off when we had the ball." A small college coach from Valparaiso needed some kind of gimmick to get the attention of Memphis State officials. "I think one of the reasons he got hired, they thought if a guy could win at Valparaiso without any scholarships, he might really do OK at a school that did have scholarships,"

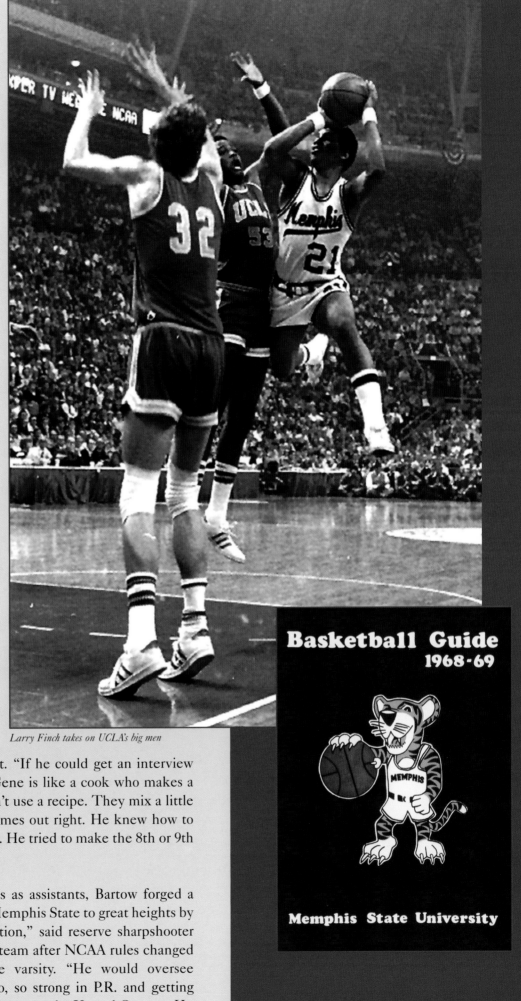

Larry Finch takes on UCLA's big men

Basketball Guide
1968-69

Memphis State University

said former Bartow assistant Lee Hunt. "If he could get an interview any place, he could sell himself. . . . Gene is like a cook who makes a cake or makes anything when they don't use a recipe. They mix a little of this and a little of that, and it all comes out right. He knew how to push the right buttons at the right time. He tried to make the 8th or 9th guy feel just as important as a starter."

By bringing in Hunt and Wayne Yates as assistants, Bartow forged a great coaching chemistry, which took Memphis State to great heights by 1973. "He had a really great combination," said reserve sharpshooter Bill Cook, a freshman on the 1972–73 team after NCAA rules changed permitting freshmen to play on the varsity. "He would oversee everything. He really was the maestro, so strong in P.R. and getting everybody on the same page. Coach Hunt was the Xs and Os man. He

Standing (L to R): Bill Grogan, Sports Information Director; Gene Bartow, Head Basketball Coach; Doug McKinney, Jim Liss, Jerry Tetzlaff, Ken Andrews, Wes Westfall, Larry Kenon, Wayne Yates, Assistant Coach; Charles DuVall, Ronnie Robinson, Billy Buford, LarryTrosper, Shannon Kennedy, Larry Finch, Bill Laurie, LeRoy Hunt, Assistant Coach; Norman McCoy, Assistant Sports Information Director. Kneeling (L to R): David Kimmel, Ed DeSchepper, Bill Cook, Ed Wilson, Eddie Young, Assistant Freshman Coach; John Tunstall, John Washington, Clarence Jones, Ted Turnipseed, Equipment Manager.

knew all the strategy and knew what to do. . . . Yates' specialty was finding the great players and getting them to sign."

With the new coaches, a fresh free-wheeling offensive approach, and Finch and Robinson eligible, Bartow's first Memphis State team finished 18–8 overall and 8–6 in the MVC in 1970–71. In the following season, the Tigers tied for the MVC title with Louisville. After losing to Saint Louis on Feb. 10, 1972, the Tigers won their last seven regular-season games and forced a playoff with 1972 co-champion Louisville in Nashville. Bartow did not believe the game should have been played, because the Tigers had beaten the Cardinals twice during the regular season. "The night after we beat them the second time, the athletic directors from Louisville and Denny (Crum) and I were in a room trying to decide if it had to be played," Bartow said. "The conference office was changing commissioners and nobody from the league office was there. I will always think my athletic director went along with Louisville and created great revenue from that game."

The last of six MVC championship playoff games (five different years) was quite a spectacle at Vanderbilt, because one side of the arena was filled with Louisville fans and the other half packed with Memphis State supporters. "The locker rooms were down in the basement," Crum said. "And two hours before the game, you could hear the absolute pandemonium that was going on in that place. You could hear it two levels down. Their fans would give some kind of cheer or yell. Then our fans would. I went upstairs to see it, and it was unbelievable."

Ronnie Robinson

Louisville reversed the two earlier decisions that season, with an 83–72 victory over the Tigers. The Cardinals went to the Final Four before falling to eventual NCAA champion UCLA in the semifinals. Memphis State lost in the first round of the NIT to Oral Roberts and had to wait another season to make an impression nationally.

JELLING AFTER SLOW START IN 1972–73

The 1972–73 season did not start off like a championship year. The Tigers, trying to work in the new junior college recruits, including Kenon, stumbled to a 5–3 start, losing games at LSU and at Marquette and a home game to Texas.

Some early injuries hurt, Bartow said, but developing chemistry was the main part of the problem. "It was the old story with jucos," Hunt said. "You let them down and rebuild them. Sometimes it takes to January for them to realize what to do. They found out their role and what they were supposed to do and it fell into place."

Kenon started slowly as well. "He was very introverted when he got here, " Hunt said. "He was real quiet, shy and was not fundamentally sound when we got him. The first day of practice, we did a pivoting drill, and he couldn't pivot."

"He (Kenon) got better and better as the season went along," Bartow said. "He and Robinson were our 1–2 rebounders, and our four guards (including Bill Laurie) were very solid. Larry Finch was an All-American. . . . Finch was just a great overall talent. Had we had the three-point line then, he probably would have led the nation in scoring. He guarded people and he was a good passer. He got upset with me because I thought he should go inside to Kenon and Robinson more."

Memphis State's breakthrough was on a three-game road trip when the Tigers won games at Vanderbilt (74–71), at Drake (97–92 in double overtime), and at Bradley (76–74). Those victories were part of a 14-game Memphis State winning streak.

At Vanderbilt, Bartow, unhappy with the way the officiating was going, appeared to motion his team off the floor, maybe as a way to make a point with the officials. The benches were on the baseline at Vanderbilt and, with the action at the opposite end of the benches, Bartow sprinted to the middle of the floor. "He was wanting to take us off the floor," Cook said. "I don't know if it was a strategic move to make his point with

the referees. If it was a bluff, it was a very good one. It seemed to have some type of an effect. We won."

"I asked Bartow after the game about it," Eaton said, "And he said, 'Anyone who would take his team off the court should be fired.'"

At Drake, one of the junior college players, Buford, was instrumental in the victory when he scored 10 of 13 points in the second overtime to key the Memphis State victory. Buford's performance followed Memphis State reserve guard Doug McKinney's miraculous 17-foot shot

Billy Buford hauls in a rebound

Memphis State University MSU

Basketball
1973-74 Guide

with one second remaining in the first overtime that tied the score, 84–84, and sent the game into another overtime. "He (McKinney) was a left-hander and shot a knuckleball," Hunt recalled. "He drove to the top of the key and rocked back with his left hand, shot it and it split the chords. He was somebody on our team least likely to take the critical shot."

At Bradley, two days later, Bartow was at the center of a controversy again when he was punched in the stomach by a fan while he was leaving the floor after Memphis State's hard-fought 76–74 victory. "I was standing right next to him," Westfall said. "We just got him off the floor immediately."

Later, the Tigers wrapped up the undisputed MVC title with a pulsating 54–53 victory at New Mexico State. Eaton recalls a sequence when Kenon made the key rebound of his career near the end of the game. "He was just awesome," Eaton said. "Their center had inside position and we were one point ahead. If super John Williamson hit the shot, we would have lost, but he missed. Their kid had the inside position, but Larry got the rebound."

Kenon's 501 rebounds and 273 field goals in 1972–73 are still Memphis single-season records more than 30 years later. "Larry Kenon looked like he had six fingers," Brown said. "He could catch the ball with one hand. He was probably the best player we ever had."

ON TO ST. LOUIS
TO MEET THE BRUINS

The MVC champion Tigers received a first-round bye in the 1973 NCAA Tournament and would play the winner of the South Carolina–Texas Tech game in the Midwest Region semifinals. The winner of the Southwestern Louisiana–Houston first-round game also fed into Midwest Regional to play Kansas State. "The (first-round) games were played in Wichita, Kan.," Eaton said of a radio broadcast his station decided to do. "And we took Gene Bartow along as a commentator. He asked me after the games, 'Jack what do you think?' I said I think we could beat Southwestern Louisiana in the morning and the other team in afternoon. He said, 'Oh don't say that.' He thought I would jinx him. I said we would wipe them out."

In Houston, Memphis State won its first NCAA Tournament game in history, 90–76, over South Carolina. Kenon and Finch combined for 59 points as the Tigers registered a school-record 60 rebounds against a Gamecocks team that included Mike Dunleavy and Alex English.

Bill Laurie

> *"They were beating us and the tide started turning,"* Westfall said. *"I looked at Kenon and told him, 'Marvin Barnes, he quit, Larry, he doesn't want to play anymore.'"*

The Midwest Regional championship game was even more lopsided. Memphis State clobbered Big Eight champion Kansas State, 92–72, behind Finch's 32 points and Robinson's 16 rebounds. This rout sent Memphis State up the Mississippi River to St. Louis and a Final Four semifinal game against Providence, coached by Dave Gavitt and starring guard Ernie DiGregorio and center Marvin Barnes.

UCLA held off Bob Knight's first Final Four team, 70–59, in one semifinal. The Memphis State–Providence game was one of the stranger semifinal games. The Friars bolted to an early big lead and led 49–40 at half, but Barnes had suffered what was described as a dislocated left knee cap in the first half. "They were beating us and the tide started turning," Westfall said. "I looked at Kenon and told him, 'Marvin Barnes, he quit, Larry, he doesn't want to play anymore.' He couldn't stand the pounding anymore. We were all 6-8 and 6-9. Most teams didn't have that size. I told Marvin Barnes he quit on the floor. 'You don't want to play.'"

"Tom" the Tiger, Memphis State's mascot

Wes Westfall

Bartow reacting to an official's call

1970-71 TIGER BASKETBALL GUIDE

memphis state university

"WHERE GOOD BASKETBALL IS A TRADITION"

Barnes returned with just under six minutes left in the game, and the Friars trailing. Providence couldn't overcome the bigger Tigers, who hauled in 54 rebounds. Kenon had 22 rebounds and Robinson 16, and the two combined for 52 points in Memphis State's 98–85 victory.

Presto, "Meet Me in St. Louis, Wooden," was going to occur.

Thank you very much, Bill Grogan.

Just facing the seemingly invincible Bruins wasn't enough though. Westfall, a St. Louis high school standout returning to his hometown for the big game, made another revelation. He and his buddies and Missouri natives, Iowa State players Martinez Denmon and Clinton Harris, watched the Indiana–UCLA semifinal in the stands. "They said, 'Man you guys could beat them,'" Westfall said. "That made me feel good. They were undefeated, and everybody laid down for them. They were like Notre Dame then in football, which was, they were up by 20 when they walked out of the locker room."

Memphis State players certainly weren't scared by the letters U-C-L-A initially. After a brilliant first half in the 1973 NCAA title game, the score was tied 39–39. Then, UCLA eventually broke away for a convincing 87–66 victory for its seventh straight NCAA title and 75th straight victory overall. "We led, 41–39, after making the first basket of the second half and never led again," Bartow said. "We had a lot of foul trouble in the first 10 minutes of the game—Kenon, Westfall, and Robinson. We had to juggle our big people and tried to use some zone. Any way you look at it, he (Walton) had a spectacular night. Had he had a normal night and had we not been in foul trouble, it could have been a game that had gone right to the wire.

"I have kidded Bill Walton a time or two," Bartow said. "I was in San Diego and we had lunch two or three times. I told him I might have been famous had he not been in that game. He said, 'Naw, Swen Nater (UCLA's backup center) would have scored 50 on you.'"

Gene Bartow and John Wooden meet before the 1973 NCAA championship game

Actually, it appeared easy. Walton was scoring on lob passes from guard Greg Lee, two of which put UCLA up to stay in the second half. "He would catch it and kind of drop it in," Hunt said. "Some people think it was dunking (illegal then)."

When Cook was asked what he would have liked to have seen differently during the game, he responded: "Bill Walton would have fouled out in the first half, but that didn't happen. There was a stretch when he had gotten his third and fourth fouls (61–55), we should have gone inside more—and put extra heat on him. We didn't go inside when he got in foul trouble."

Thoughts of what may have been for a most special MVC team lingers more than 30 years later. "That bunch of guys we had think until this day yet, we should have won the game and if we had played a seven-game series we would have beaten them," Hunt said. "UCLA was really good. I am not sure how it would come out in a seven-game series."

Slab Jones

NMSU was founded in 1888 in Las Cruces as an agricultural college. The Aggies were a member of the Missouri Valley Conference from 1970 to 1983.

COMING BACK FROM 28–0

New Mexico State trailed Bradley, 28–0, in Peoria, Ill., but came back to beat the Braves, 117–109, on Jan. 27, 1977, in one of the all-time great comebacks in college basketball history. "Nothing would go in, and then it totally reversed," New Mexico State Coach Ken Hayes said.

New Mexico State had encountered travel problems getting into snowy Chicago and then finding hotel rooms in Peoria where snow covered cars on the streets. The Aggies circled several times in a prop plane before finally landing in Peoria about 2 a.m. the day of the game only to find several of their hotel rooms occupied when they arrived. "Nobody had moved for two days," Hayes said. "Everybody was paralyzed."

No one could blame the Aggies for being a little tired when the game began. Falling behind 28–0 on the road normally would be too deep of a hole to escape, but New Mexico State did. "That was just one of those times they shot poorly, we came out and played well," said Bradley's Roger Phegley. "What gets lost in that game as good a run as we had (28–0), the halftime score was (close). They had made almost as good a comeback in the first half as what we took off at the beginning of the game."

SLAB JONES

New Mexico State center Slab Jones, from Houston, led his team in scoring three straight seasons from 1978 to 1980, and by the time he was finished, Jones had collected three All-Missouri Valley Conference first-team selections. "Slab was an impact player," former New Mexico State Coach Ken Hayes said. "He was physically strong and could jump well. His picture hanging in the rotunda of the Pan-American Center sums it up."

Jones also led the Aggies in rebounding with 11 a game his senior season in 1979–80 and shot 54.1 percent during his career in Las Cruces, but he was never known for his hands. "He talked real slow and in a deep base voice," Hayes said. "We were running a wing drill one day. He did have mediocre hands—at best. I fired a pass to him and it went through his hands into the chairs. I yelled at him, 'If it wasn't for me, you would have the worst hands in the building!' I threw it back to him like a baseball and he makes this thunderous dunk. He came back by me and said, 'If it wasn't for me, you wouldn't have a job.'"

When powerhouse UNC–Charlotte (now Charlotte) beat New Mexico State, 85–81, during the 1976–77 season, the resourceful Jones knew when to fake an injury late in the game. "Slab was a freshman, and we were playing UNC–Charlotte in our Roadrunner Classic," Hayes said. "We always wanted to play the weakest team in the first round. All I knew about Charlotte was my good friend, Lee Rose, was coaching them. They had a guy named Cornbread Maxwell. . . . We were down by two points with a minute or so left in the game and we are going to press. Guess who brings it down? Cornbread. Slab is covering him. Cornbread is looking at him, and he puts a move on Slab, and Slab falls flat on the floor. He was a smart guy. He grabbed his ankle like he had sprained it."

"Slab was an impact player. He was physically strong and could jump well. His picture hanging in the rotunda of the Pan-American Center sums it up."

New Mexico State coach Ken Hayes

Maurice Cheeks

West Texas State is now known as West Texas A&M University. West Texas State, founded in 1910 in Canyon, Tex., was a member of the Missouri Valley Conference from 1972 to 1985.

Maurice Cheeks

MAURICE CHEEKS

West Texas State guard Maurice Cheeks wasn't the only star on his Chicago DuSable High School team in 1974. The Buffaloes were recruiting one of his DuSable teammates when Cheeks sparked their interest.

Once he got to the Texas Panhandle, Cheeks became a two-time first-team All-MVC selection and a one-time second-team player. He was one of the most dreaded ball-handlers in the league because he could control a game. "If they had the lead—there was no shot clock back then—you were chasing him the rest of the night," said former New Mexico State and Tulsa Coach Ken Hayes. "That wasn't fun."

"He just got the job done," Indiana State's Bob Heaton remembered. "He was a point guard–playmaker kind of player. He created his own shot and had a big Afro. I remember that. He could do it."

The 6-1, 180-pound Cheeks played for West Texas State Coach Ron Ekker, who coached a conservative game and even had Cheeks running North Carolina Coach Dean Smith's "Four Corners" offense. "Ekker's offensive style complemented his ability," said Jerry Schaeffer, a West Texas State teammate of Cheeks. "Conservative, methodical, meticulous, passing game. . . . Maurice cultivated his methodical decision-making and basketball ability. It paid off as a professional player and now as a coach."

Despite playing for a poor team that was on NCAA probation his senior season, Cheeks was a star. "His senior year, we were 8–19," Schaeffer said. "We met Larry Bird and Indiana State for the third time. The last game we were down by 30. Cheeks had about six steals and five layups, and he showed his true character."

After the season, West Texas State fans had all-night parties, and Pizza Hut owners stuffed the ballot boxes in Amarillo and Canyon, Tex., in an effort to get Cheeks a spot in the pizza company's All-Star Game. It worked. He got in the game in Las Vegas, played great, and became a No. 1 draft pick in 1978 by the Philadelphia 76ers.

He was a four-time NBA All-Star during a 15-year professional career, 11 of those seasons in Philadelphia. He then went on to an NBA head coaching career in Portland and then back to the 76ers. "Cheeks was one of those guys who was a good college player and turned out to be a tremendous pro," Bradley's Roger Phegley said.

Coach Rich Herrin and Chris Lowery

SOUTHERN ILLINOIS

Founded as Southern Illinois Normal University in 1869, Southern Illinois University is the largest of the current Missouri Valley Conference membership institutions. SIU has been a member of the MVC since 1975. Located in Carbondale, Ill., SIU has a sister campus in Edwardsville, across the Mississippi River from St. Louis.

Under the leadership of Bruce Weber, Matt Painter, and Chris Lowery, the Saluki basketball program has made the NCAA Tournament for the past five seasons (2002–2006), a feat shared by only 14 other teams. Highlighting this run was a trip to the Sweet 16 in 2002.

Eight years before joining the MVC, SIU graduated its most famous player, Walt Frazier, who led the Salukis to the NIT championship in 1967.

HERRIN TAKES SIU FROM BOTTOM TO SEVEN-YEAR POSTSEASON RUN

By 1985, Southern Illinois had been in the Missouri Valley Conference for a decade, but its men's basketball program was in shambles.

Benton (Ill.) Coach Rich Herrin was hired from the Southern Illinois high school ranks and given the job of resurrecting Saluki basketball. Herrin inherited a slumping program that had only one winning record in the previous six seasons. He also had no previous college coaching experience. "You have to realize, when he came in, the situation was in dire straits," said Paul Lusk, an SIU guard from 1992 to 1995. "It was pitiful."

Although he had been a high school coaching legend at Benton and a solid coach at Okawville, Ill., Herrin, the son of a Methodist minister, nearly had second thoughts about taking the major-college position during his first collegiate game. "We were down (14 at half time) and I could see us getting beat by 35," Herrin remembered about the 1985–86 season opener against Chicago State in Carbondale.

"I thought, 'We have to play Nebraska and Arkansas that weekend. And I am getting beat to death by Chicago State.' I said, 'I don't have any business in Division I.' But Chicago State kind of played into our hands.

Rich Herrin

They'd take a shot and miss, and we'd come back and score. We gradually got back into it." SIU won Herrin's opener, 58–56, in a brief respite during an 8–20 rookie college season.

"When you look back, the program was in such bad shape, you weren't going to attract any big-time coach," said Rick Shipley, a Centralia, Ill., star who played for Herrin at SIU from 1987–91. "At the time he was the right hire. He had more local recognition."

The questions were twofold: Could Herrin adapt his coaching to the college level and also recruit the black athlete? The answers were yes and yes. "I didn't think there was that much difference," said Herrin, whose record in 13 seasons at SIU was 225–174. "Everybody tried to get me to say how much difference there was. . . . See, I had never coached a black player (as a high school coach), but I got along with black players. My dad was a preacher, and I was raised to treat people right."

HERRIN: SMALL TOWN RECRUITING, OFFENSIVE SUCCESS

Herrin's recruiting across the board was successful, although his greatest successes centered in the small towns of Illinois and Missouri. "I got players where I could get them," Herrin said. "But most of them were from small towns. I worked the city, but you bring a kid to Carbondale, you could see the atmosphere was different."

In his first season, Herrin won just four MVC games, but one of those victories was a miracle comeback against Wichita State from 11 points down with 1:48 remaining to win, 72–71. That offensive burst seemed to demonstrate that anything was possible under Herrin, even if it took two more seasons to break through with his first winning record. "It took him three years to get it going," said long-time SIU radio voice Mike Reis. "But I have heard Weber (Bruce, SIU coach from 1998–2003) say that a lot of what SIU was able to accomplish later, Herrin set up."

The turnaround occurred when SIU made four straight National Invitation Tournaments (1989–92). A stream of excellent athletes enrolled at SIU. . . . Freddie McSwain, Tony Harvey, Ashraf Amaya, Jerry Jones. "Rich allowed good players to play, particularly offensively," said Shipley, who was the MVC's leading rebounder in 1990–91. "He didn't put reins on guys who had good individual skills. . . . They said he just rolled the ball out there. . . . That was not the case."

Ashraf Amaya

"I am a great believer you make the game fun and exciting," Herrin said, "I am probably not as good a defensive coach as some other coaches. John Wooden at UCLA was probably as good a defensive coach as there was, but his teams would score 95 on the other team. I know I could coach defense. But we would shoot it quick and have some fun playing the game."

SIU almost made Herrin's first NCAA Tournament in 1989, but Creighton beat the Salukis, 79–77, in the MVC Tournament final in Wichita. A controversial ending still has Herrin seething years later because he believes Saluki Jerry Jones was fouled by Creighton's Chad Gallagher after a long pass downcourt from Shipley in the closing seconds. Two free throws could have sent the game into overtime, but SIU wound up the loser and then was blown out by Saint Louis, 87–54, in the first round of the NIT.

A year later, SIU was back in the MVC title game and lost to Illinois State, 81–78, in Normal, after winning the 1990 Missouri Valley Conference regular-season title. Herrin was so frustrated when the Salukis, with 26 victories, were snubbed by the NCAA Tournament Committee as an at-large entry that he lashed out in an

interview on ESPN. "I blasted the NCAA Committee pretty hard," Herrin said. "I thought it was very unfair. . . . The team that didn't get a bid was the best team. . . . I really think the Valley officials thought we had a bid and we would get two bids if Illinois State won." Herrin said he was told SIU's strength of schedule was the reason it did not get an at-large bid. Three years later, Herrin would make the NCAA breakthrough.

The arrival in the early 1990s of such small-town stars as guard Chris Carr (Pilot Knob, Mo.), Marcus Timmons (Haywood City, Mo.), and Paul Lusk (New Baden, Ill.) signaled the beginning of SIU's three-year MVC Tournament championship run from 1993 to 1995. Through the end of the 20th century, it was the only time an MVC school won three straight men's tournament titles.

TIMMONS, CARR, LUSK FORM SIU'S BASE
The 6-8 Timmons started for all of those teams and is generally regarded as the best player Herrin recruited to SIU. Timmons led the MVC in rebounding (9.8) in 1994 and finished among the Top 10 in several SIU career statistical categories. SIU Coach Chris Lowery, who played guard at SIU from 1990 to 1994 and took over the reins of the program in the spring of 2004, said of Timmons: "Marcus could do anything. Marcus could dribble. He could pass. He could shoot. He could defend a point guard. He could defend a center. He was 6-8 with long arms and super athletic."

"Timmons committed to Missouri," Herrin said. "But they didn't think he would qualify and they backed off him. . . . I could never exactly understand why he couldn't make it in the NBA.

Unlike Timmons, Carr eventually did develop into a solid NBA player despite less than an auspicious beginning in Carbondale. "Carr, my first year (1992–93), came off the bench," Lusk said of the player who became the MVC's leading scorer and MVC Tournament and regular-season Most Outstanding Player in 1995. "He was 6-5, a good rebounder and passer, but not that good a shooter. He developed an outside game. Carr came out of nowhere."

Lusk was the final piece to SIU's MVC Tournament title run. After playing at Iowa for a

Chris Carr

Marcus Timmons

Paul Lusk

season, he transferred to SIU and collected three MVC Tournament title rings. Lusk had rebuffed the Salukis earlier for the Big 10 school, and Saluki players tested him when he first arrived on campus. They wanted to know why he didn't come there in the first place, but he showed his new teammates why he was coveted by a lot of schools. "Paul could score, but he wasn't just a shooter," Lowery said. "He could score off the dribble. He could score on pull-up jumpers, and he was big. He was nearly 6-4. But we both wanted to win more than anything."

When Lusk arrived, Lowery moved to point guard and led the Salukis to a second-place MVC regular-season finish in 1993. Then, the Salukis beat Bradley (63–61 in overtime), Missouri State (76–68), and regular-season champion Illinois State (70–59). Amaya capped off a strong Saluki career by being named the Most Outstanding Player of the 1993 MVC Tournament at The Arena in St. Louis.

"I remember a big sigh of relief," Lowery said of SIU snaring the MVC's automatic berth and making its first NCAA appearance since 1977. "We had been to four straight NITs, and that became not enough. It became where he (Herrin) had too much talent and he didn't know what to do with it. After he got to the NCAA Tournament, it kind of validated him."

A 105–70 loss to Duke in the 1993 NCAA opening round hurt. "You know what Duke did to me in the first half?" Herrin said. "They shot threes and made 73 percent of them. They annihilated us. They didn't try to run the score up. We played very poorly."

Paul could score, but he wasn't just a shooter. He could score off the dribble. He could score on pull-up jumpers, and he was big.

Chris Carr celebrates an MVC championship in 1995

TWO MORE MVC TITLES FOR HERRIN

The Salukis roared back the following March for another MVC Tournament title and Herrin and SIU became the first coach and team to win consecutive MVC Tournament championships. Timmons, Carr, Lusk, and Lowery all scored in double figures in the 1994 MVC title-game victory over Northern Iowa, 77–74, at The Arena in St. Louis. They offset a hot-shooting night by the 1994 Tournament Outstanding Player, Cam Johnson of Northern Iowa.

Lowery was sensational down the stretch of the title game. He made two free throws and a steal to wrap up the victory. A 74–60 loss to Minnesota in the first round of the NCAA Tournament ended the season again. "We wanted to win," Lusk said of the NCAA Tournament. "We weren't excited just being there. We played

Minnesota well. We got down early, but we were always in the game."

SIU made it a three-peat in the MVC Tournament in 1995. The tournament shifted to downtown St Louis and the (Savvis) Kiel Center. The Salukis blasted MVC regular-season champion Tulsa, 77–62 in the title game.

The decisiveness of the Salukis' tournament title-game victory over Tulsa was surprising because SIU and Tulsa had split two regular-season games, which were decided by a total of three points. "There wasn't a soul who gave us a chance to win," Herrin said. "I had a guard named Jaratio Tucker from Arkansas, and he guarded Tulsa's Pooh Williamson and held him to three points (1-for-9 from the field). And we played behind their big 7-foote and made him shoot over us. They couldn't lob it into him and he couldn't get any offensive rebounds."

Carr and Lusk completed a three-year MVC Tournament run with a 9–0 record after the upset of the Golden Hurricane.

Although SIU took Syracuse to the wire before losing in the 1995 NCAA Tournament's first round, 96–92, SIU never won an NCAA Tournament game under Herrin, who was a solid coach. "He believed in fundamentals, discipline, and conditioning . . . all the things you used to talk about," said former Drake coach and Bradley player Bob Ortegel, and later the Dallas Mavericks announcer. "All you hear them talk about today is athleticism."

HERRIN'S LASTING LEGACY

In 2002, SIU won two games in the NCAA Tournament and advanced to the Sweet 16, but Herrin was long gone by then. He was forced to resign in 1998 following three straight losing seasons. After Carr elected to leave for the NBA Draft following the 1994–95 season, SIU slumped to an 11–18 record the next year and never recovered to finish in the MVC's first division during Herrin's final three seasons. "I didn't blame him (for going hardship)," Herrin said. "But we couldn't afford to lose a player like Carr. If we had had Carr the next year (1995–96) we would have won 20 games."

After his SIU career was over, Herrin could not get coaching out of his system and eventually went back to the high school ranks to coach at Marion, Ill. His former SIU players still remember him fondly. "He was a player's coach," Lowery said. "He really cared if you were happy or not. He not only cared about our success, but

SIUs Chris Lowery

1993 Salukis

your success as a person. . . . And I remember him allowing me to have a big imagination. I am not saying he just promoted taking bad shots. But he let you push the envelope a little as far as your freedom on the court. I think that is a reason why we were so successful."

SALUKI RUN: COACHING CHANGES DON'T DETOUR SIU

Southern Illinois University's revolving-door coaching era bred great success in the Missouri Valley Conference. From 2003 through 2005, the Salukis had three different head coaches—Bruce Weber, Matt Painter, and Chris Lowery—win three MVC regular-season championships.

Counting SIU's regular-season co-title in 2001–02 under Weber, the Salukis claimed four straight MVC regular-season titles. That's a feat not accomplished since Cincinnati claimed six straight (five undisputed) MVC titles from 1958 to 1963. During the four-year title run, SIU compiled a 62–10 record in MVC regular-season games, including a 36–0 mark at the SIU Arena in league games.

WEBER'S FIRST TITLE

Southern Illinois' four-year regular-season title run began in 2001–02. SIU guard Kent Williams from nearby Mount Vernon, Ill., was an outside scoring threat as a junior that season, and 6-6, 250-pound senior center Rolan Roberts, a transfer from Virginia Tech, handled the inside defense and rebounding.

During a 28–8 season, Weber's SIU team defeated 2002 NCAA runner-up Indiana, Saint Louis, Iowa State, and nearly upset powerhouse Illinois. "The Illinois game (a 75–72 loss) really gave us confidence," Williams said. "We were on a neutral floor and almost beat Illinois. They were ranked No. 2 in the country. Then the Indiana game was sold out here, and we maybe played our best game of the year (72–60 victory). We went in expecting to win that game."

Williams and Roberts led the Salukis to a first-place tie with Creighton during the MVC regular season and the 2002 NCAA Tournament's Sweet 16 in Weber's fourth season at the school. Connecticut eliminated the Salukis in the region semifinals. "Kent Williams coming into our program was the start of our success," said former SIU player,

Bruce Weber

assistant and current head coach Chris Lowery. "With that team, we had such a dominating presence in Roberts, the league hadn't seen in a while. I think he really helped set the tone the way our defense was played."

WEBER'S SECOND TITLE, THEN EXIT

The following season, 2002–03, SIU won the MVC regular-season title with a 16–2 record, a game ahead of Creighton. Williams starred again and finished as the school's second all-time leading scorer, but Roberts' defensive presence inside was missed, before the Salukis adjusted. "It took some defeats on the road where we were embarrassed," Weber said of losses at Illinois–Chicago, Charlotte, and Saint Louis. "We had to learn we have to guard people." SIU regrouped and lost only at Creighton and at Bradley during the MVC season. After some nervous moments following a 24-point loss to Creighton in the MVC Tournament final, SIU made the 2003 NCAA Tournament.

Weber left for Illinois after a bitter 72–71 first-round NCAA Tournament loss to Missouri when forward Jermaine Dearman was whistled for a controversial blocking foul in the closing seconds. Following Weber's departure, the youthful Painter moved one seat down to become SIU's head coach, and the Salukis played a more free-wheeling style, which relied on defensive pressure to create turnovers and easy baskets. "He was the same guy, a blue-collar guy from when he was an assistant," all-conference guard Stetson Hairston said of Painter when he became SIU's head coach. "He didn't treat people differently."

PAINTER'S TITLE

Under Painter, the Salukis beat Creighton twice during the regular season and finished five games ahead of the Bluejays and two other teams in the 2004 MVC race. SIU was the biggest runaway regular-

Weber issues orders from the sidelines

Matt Painter (right) receives the Coach of the Year award from Rawlings' representative Jeff Rich

Darren Brooks

season winner in the MVC in 18 years since Bradley was 16–0 in league play. "Painter either recruited or had a hand in recruiting all those players," said former SIU player Rick Shipley. "And he understands the game of basketball and can coach it to 20 year olds. He was limited as a player, so he had to understand it better. He only got respect initially when they made the trip to Europe (before the season). They felt like a younger guy could relate to them."

The Salukis won their first 17 conference games before losing at Northern Iowa in the final game. "To be 17–1 and to literally not know where our next basket is going to come from, and when I say that, that is a compliment," Painter said of the balanced scoring led by guard Darren Brooks, the MVC's Most Valuable Player in 2004 and again in 2005. "We just have nine guys who play hard and get after it. (He knew SIU would have a good team) when the guys got after each other in practice."

"They were more athletic across the board (in 2003–04) than in past years," said Lowery, who was an assistant for Weber's Illinois team that season. "I think that is what overwhelmed people. So many people could come in and guard. When you can bring in guys who can really defend the basket and change the tempo of the game, that gives you an obvious advantage because they get transition baskets off steals and put backs."

AND FINALLY LOWERY
Former Assistant Lowery returned as head coach at SIU in 2004–05 after Painter left for Purdue, and Southern Illinois' regular-season title run hit four with the 2005 crown.

The Salukis lost non-conference road games at Hawaii, Arkansas–Little Rock, and Louisiana–Monroe, and they dropped league road games at Wichita State and Missouri State before kicking into high gear with the same swarming pressure defense and a better half-court offensive game.

"When we came in as freshmen, SIU wasn't winning many games," said SIU's Brooks, who was the MVC Player of the Year again in 2005 and played on all four title teams. "Going to the Sweet 16 our first year, that let us know what hard work can do. They (new players) came in big-headed and didn't know what it took. Me and him (Lowery) knew what it took."

Chris Lowery

Lowery was named MVC Coach of the Year, the third straight season an SIU Coach had won it—Weber, Painter, Lowery. "It is a big deal to have three different coaches," Hairston said. "And in the last three years a Southern Illinois coach has won Coach of the Year. For Coach Lowery to get it, that's what we wanted to accomplish."

Despite SIU's regular-season successes over the four-year period, the Salukis failed to win an MVC Tournament crown. SIU fell to Creighton in the title game in 2002 and 2003, and the Salukis lost to Missouri State in the semifinals in 2004 and 2005. Each year, however, the Salukis qualified as an at-large entry to the NCAA Tournament, which is the longest stretch of consecutive NCAA Tournament appearances (four) in SIU history.

KENT WILLIAMS

SIU guard Kent Williams started every game in his career in Carbondale—130 straight contests. He finished as the Salukis' second all-time leading scorer and led SIU to back-to-back Missouri Valley Conference regular-season titles and NCAA Tournament appearances in 2002 and 2003. Williams is the only player in Southern Illinois history to lead the Salukis in scoring four straight seasons (2000–2003).

Lowery receives the 2006 MVC tournament championship trophy

team. I didn't showcase myself like some players have. My teammates were my best friends in high school, and I wanted to play with them and make our team better. I played baseball, too, and didn't want to take a big chunk out of that season. I was a small-town guy from Mount Vernon, and I didn't get recruited like a lot of the big-time guys did."

During Williams' senior season in high school, he finished second in the state of Illinois for Mr. Basketball honors behind Brian Cook, who wound up at Illinois. Williams scored 48 points against Seattle Ranier in the KMOX Shootout at the Savvis Center in St. Louis. His performance broke the prestigious tournament's individual scoring record of 46 points by Teddy Dupay, who later played at Florida.

In the 2002 NCAA Tournament, Williams was the outside scoring threat in SIU's upsets of Texas Tech and Georgia in the first two rounds at the United Center. SIU became the first MVC team to advance to the NCAA's Sweet 16 since Missouri State in 1999. "A guy comes up behind me while I was doing an interview on the telephone (following SIU's victory over Texas Tech) and he slapped me on the back," Williams said. "It was Bob Knight. I dropped the phone in the middle of the interview. He said, 'You played a great game.' He told me I played the kind of style he likes. He told me, 'I like to have guys like you on my team.'" While Knight was at Indiana, he was interested in Williams.

The 6-2, 185-pound Williams was recruited to play baseball at SIU as well. He played shortstop and second base for the nearby Mount Vernon Township High School Rams when not leading the basketball team, but he never went to a baseball practice at SIU.

Williams was a virtual unknown until the summer before his senior year in high school when he went to the Nike All-American Camp in Indianapolis and played on the Eagles AAU team in St. Louis. Utah, Wisconsin, Northwestern, Saint Louis, and Richmond recruited him along with many MVC schools.

"I maybe was a little bit of a late bloomer," Williams said. "I went to summer events with my high school

"I started getting more phone calls after that game," Williams said. "But I already had committed to SIU. . . . I had grown up watching their games. It was close to home and I would have a chance to play in front of my family. . . . I was sold on Coach Weber. He gambled on me. I signed with him before his first game here. I knew he ran the motion offense, like we ran in high school, and I knew I had a good shot at playing and showing what I could do."

CHARLOTTE WEST

Dr. Charlotte West has been a trailblazer for women's sports for more than a half century. She's also perhaps the most important architect of the current Missouri Valley Conference men's and women's sports governance structure.

She sealed the deal. West, a Southern Illinois faculty member, coach, and administrator for 42 years, helped craft an agreement that allowed the merger of men's and women's sports program under the MVC banner in July 1992.

Compromise was definitely needed. Tulsa, an MVC member at the time, didn't sponsor women's basketball and was refusing to budge on its opposition of a proposed rule that would require all schools to sponsor that sport, as well as women's volleyball and softball and men's basketball.

"Charlotte showed significant statesmanship in basically coming back with a compromise that we proceed on faith," said Missouri Valley Conference Commissioner Doug Elgin. West convinced the MVC to not only waive Tulsa's women's basketball sponsorship requirement, but also to relent on mandatory staff and scholarship minimums in women's sports. She truly had faith that schools would do the right thing.

Such was the reputation of West, who was known as an opinionated but tactful administrator who could weave her way through difficult situations. She loved the women's programs being in the Gateway Conference, which had been formed in 1982. "I wasn't real supportive of it (MVC taking in women) at the time because the Gateway was so successful," West said. "We were extremely cost-efficient. We were doing our own thing. And we didn't know if we wanted to affiliate with non-Gateway schools in the Valley. We didn't know if they would enhance our success. . . . The vote was for the Valley to take over women's programs. Once that happened, I worked for that to become as good as it could be. I was on the transition committee and that's when I started working with Doug (Elgin). And we wanted to make the merging of Valley with the women as strong for everybody as we could."By the fall of 2006, the MVC's sports structure is working well and serving as a model for other leagues.

Dr. Charlotte West

West landed at Southern Illinois in 1957 as a physical education instructor and she never left. From 1960 to 1986, she was director of intercollegiate athletics for women at SIU. "At that point (1957) you could go anywhere because there was a huge demand for teachers," West said. "The reason I came here (to SIU) was they had a program of playing other colleges. . . . They called it extra-mural. They didn't call it varsity at the time, but we played against Eastern Illinois, Illinois State, University of Illinois, and Tennessee–Martin. We competed in a comfortable geographic area."

By the time the women's and men's programs merged at SIU in 1986, West had turned a women's program that was funded by bake sales and car washes in the early years into one that had 11 sports and a $1 million budget. Women's sports were taking off. West became involved in men's sports as well, serving as SIU's interim athletic director for the combined programs in 1987–88.

West, who retired as SIU's associate director of athletics in 1998 and has an SIU softball stadium named after her in Carbondale, is proud of the MVC. "The Missouri Valley had the luxury of restructuring how we would govern ourselves when women's sports were added in 1992," said West. "We established a model that other conferences have subsequently copied. It is a tribute to our presidential and conference leadership that we now have a structure where the director of athletics and the senior woman administrator sit around one table, each with an equal voice and vote. Many people from outside the conference have asked me, "Tell me how you accomplished this."

The MVC appreciates her as well. She was inducted into the MVC Hall of Fame in 2005 and has a league award given in her name.

Fifty years after competing in the industrial league in Florida, she is still getting calls to do seminars on women's sports. She truly is an MVC treasure. "Dr. West has been such an important figure for women's athletics, not just at SIU, but all over the country," said Southern Illinois softball Coach Kerri Blaylock. "She's well known and well respected everywhere. When I go to conventions and recruiting, I always run into someone who mentions her name and asks if I know her or worked for her."

Indiana State's Larry Bird

INDIANA STATE

INDIANA STATE

Founded in 1865, Indiana State University is located in Terre Haute. The Sycamores have been a member of the Missouri Valley Conference since 1976. The history of their men's basketball program is dominated by one of the sport's all-time greats, Larry Bird, who led the Sycamores to an MVC championship and an NCAA Tournament final in 1979.

LARRY BIRD MADE IT HAPPEN IN 1979

Carl Nicks still finds himself bombarded by questions about Indiana State's dreamy 1978–79 season. He has worked at Methodist Hospital in Indianapolis directing a program for behavioral kids who weren't even alive when he was starring for the Sycamores. The aura of playing with the state's favorite son, Larry Bird, surrounds Nicks more than 25 years later.

The Sycamores won 33 straight games that season, with a rookie head coach, Bill Hodges. They boasted a 16–0 record in the Missouri Valley Conference regular-season race, the first team to win that many games. And they came within one game, an NCAA title-game loss to

Bill Hodges

Magic Johnson and Michigan State, of completing a storybook finish. Still, the 1979 NCAA final was the highest-rated televised NCAA Tournament basketball game of all time and showcased college basketball's and later the NBA's two greatest stars, Bird and Magic. "Everybody asks about it," Nicks said. "It is just like yesterday. It is still new. When the NCAA Tournament time comes around, it is just unbelievable."

Nicks, a 6-3 guard from Chicago, still can remember Bird's passes and coaching his big men how to catch them. "Larry had eyes in the back of his head," Nicks recalls. "He was such an intelligent player. He could read a play way before it developed. He would make a sharp pass ahead of time. He would catch you off guard while you were making the cut. . . . He could thread a needle and get you a pass in traffic behind his neck or back. You better pay attention . . . I never had problems. That's what I had to do as guard. The big men got clobbered in the face and didn't know what to do. I told them to keep their hands up and be ready. It was hard to catch the ball with your face."

Former New Mexico State Coach Ken Hayes remembers one of those scintillating plays between the 6-9 Bird and Nicks during a 1979 game featuring the Aggies and Sycamores in Las Cruces. "Bird goes up for a rebound inside the free-throw line in our offensive end and he throws a pass like a Don Drysdale pitch, left-handed over his right shoulder," Hayes recalled. "It is a blind pass to the other end, but there's nobody there. Carl Nicks is streaking (to the basket) catches it, lays it in the basket and the ball never touches the floor. Bird had a sense basketball-wise other guys didn't have."

Hodges instructs Carl Nicks

"Bird is by far the best collegiate player I ever saw," Hayes continued. "I said that back then—he was the greatest passer I had ever seen. And I made the statement coaches should not go to coaching clinics. They should go watch Bird."

By the time Bird left Terre Haute, Indiana State was on the collegiate basketball map. Bird scored 2,850 points in three seasons, (30.3 ppg average), was MVC Player of the Year his junior and senior seasons when Indiana State was eligible to play for the MVC title, and in 1978–79 was the consensus National Player of the Year.

He had left his calling card throughout the Midwest in gyms and arenas, some of which have since been put in mothballs, such as Drake's rowdy Veteran's Auditorium. On Jan. 14, 1978, Bird scored 45 points in a 92–80 victory over Drake, breaking the Veterans' Auditorium individual game scoring record. Bird's mark was topped nearly two years later by Drake's Lewis Lloyd (47 points against Wisconsin-Superior).

Indiana State's Larry Bird and Carl Nicks

Former Drake Coach Bob Ortegel remembers how Bird was frustrated at the beginning of that 1978 game, then went on a rampage. "I had a guy name Gregory Johns, a kid out of Crenshaw High School in Los Angeles," Ortegel said. "He was a big kid and had a great basketball body. I started him against Larry Bird. With about six to seven minutes to go in the first half, Bird hadn't scored. Johns had done a pretty good job on him. We take a timeout, true story, he gets in Bird's face walking off the floor. And I just went out and grabbed him (Johns) by the jersey and told him in no uncertain terms what a stupid thing that was to do. All that does is motivate Bird. The tougher the situation, the tougher he was . . . All Bird did was get 45 points . . . leave a sleeping dog lie."

DEVELOPMENT OF A LEGEND
Bird, from tiny French Lick, Ind., originally signed with Bob Knight's Indiana Hoosiers, but he believed the campus was too large and lasted only 24 days in Bloomington. He transferred to Indiana State, sat out a season, and then starred from 1976 to 1979 for the Sycamores.

"We knew he was a very fine player," said Ed McKee, Indiana State's sports information director at the time. "We didn't know he would be a franchise maker. He sat out that season (1975–76) and practiced. We finished 13–12 and won our last game. Larry and the substitutes would scrimmage the varsity starters, and they were beating them on a daily basis. It was somewhat frustrating to play without him."

Larry Bird

Competing as an independent, the Sycamores, in Bird's sophomore season, posted a 25–3 record in 1976–77. Bird served notice of what his future would hold during his first two games as a Sycamore when he registered triple-doubles (31 points, 18 rebounds, 10 assists vs. Chicago State and 22–16–10 vs. St. Ambrose).

Indiana State lost only two games during the 1976–77 regular season—at Purdue and at Illinois State—and accepted a bid to the 1977 National Invitation Tournament. The Sycamores lost to eventual NIT runner-up Houston and guard Otis Birdsong, 83–82, when Bird scored 44 points, but he missed a last-second baseline jumper that would have won the game.

By the beginning of the next season (Indiana State's first as an MVC member), Bird was getting noticed nationally. He appeared on his first of 15 *Sports Illustrated* covers as collegian or pro on Nov. 28, 1977, with two ISU cheerleaders. He also showed up at the MVC Basketball Tip-Off interviews in Omaha after finishing as the nation's third-leading scorer the previous season. Bradley's

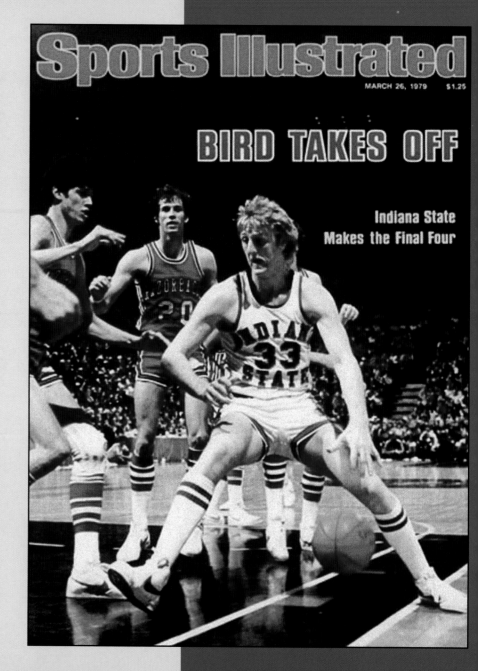

Sports Illustrated

MARCH 26, 1979 $1.25

BIRD TAKES OFF

Indiana State
Makes the Final Four

1977 Indiana State Sycamores

Roger Phegley, however, had been eighth in scoring nationally and was considered every bit the threat Bird was to win MVC Player of the Year honors in 1977–78.

"I thought he (Bird) was a big, fat white guy who was over-hyped," said Hayes, who had yet to coach against Bird in a game. "I thought this guy can't be that good. Besides, I was in love with Phegley. I thought he was the best player. Then the first time we met them, we played a zone and a two-man chase," Hayes continued. "By half time their second leading scorer hadn't scored. But Bird had 20, and we were running a man chase on Bird! We couldn't keep him off the offensive boards. He had a knack of knowing where the ball was. He knew how to use his thighs and belly."

Indiana State zoomed to a 13–0 start in 1977–78, including a 5–0 record in the Missouri Valley Conference. During that stretch the Sycamores demolished Purdue, 91–63, when Bird notched 26 points, 17 rebounds, and eight assists and nearly had his fourth career triple-double. That performance prompted Purdue Coach Fred Schaus to quip: "I thought he should have turned pro last summer. He can play with any team in the country—pro or college."

The Sycamores dropped their first league game, at Southern Illinois in mid-January, starting a five-game losing skid, three in the MVC, when center Richard Johnson was out with a broken foot.

Bill Land, play-by-play man for Wichita State, remembers one of those Indiana State losses, 74–70 in overtime in Wichita, where Bird was playing for the first time. Wichita State Coach Harry Miller called a late timeout to make sure everybody was on the same page, and the Shockers let the Sycamores score on the final play. "They inbounded the ball to Bird, and he got it at the top of the key, took a dribble and wind-milled it," Land said. "He went up, caught it, and dunked it. And, just as the buzzer sounded and the ball came through the basket, he took the ball and pounded it on the floor. Before everybody started cheering, there was almost this quiet which came over the arena, like, 'Did you see that? Did that guy just do that?' To me it was kind of a statement from Bird: 'You better enjoy this because there will be hell to pay when you come to Terre Haute.'"

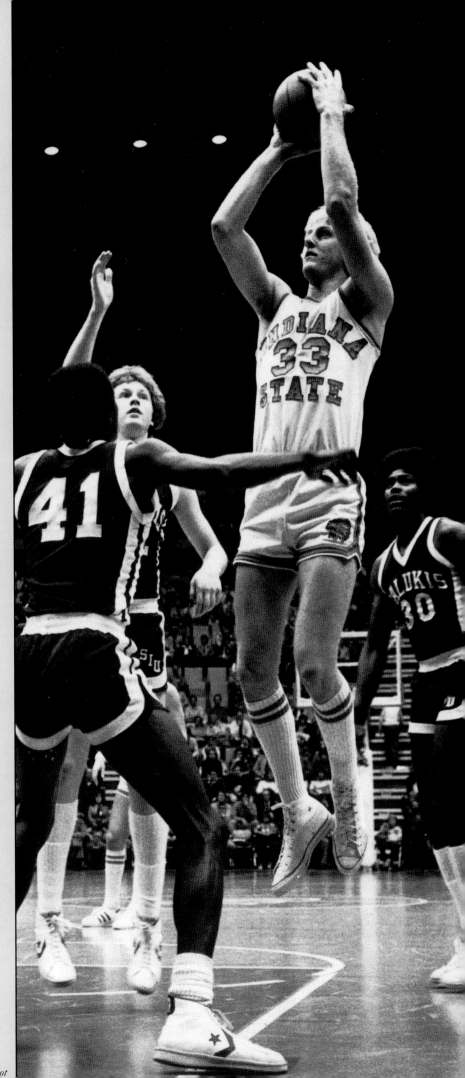

Larry Bird—the definition of a perfect jump shot

A Bird in a cage

1907   2007

100 YEARS OF ATHLETICS EXCELLENCE

Indiana State won the return match with Wichita State, 72–56, but could never fully recover from the midseason losing streak and finished in a tie for second with SIU, a game behind Creighton in the MVC regular-season race. The Sycamores also fell to the Bluejays, 54–52, in the MVC Tournament final.

A rather disappointing loss—57–56 to Rutgers in a second-round NIT game—ended the Indiana State season, but Bird elected to stay for his senior season, principally to finish some business.

THAT INCREDIBLE 33–1 SEASON

Bird was the only returning starter from a 23–9 team of 1977–78. Several new faces dotted the roster. Coupled by the fact that Head Coach Bob King had to resign because of health reasons before the season, there was no reason to believe a rookie coach, the 35-year-old Hodges, would have a banner year.

The buildup for Bird for National Player of the Year would hit a crescendo heading into the season. With Bird coming off an MVC Player of the Year season, the league office's first-year publicist, Jeff Hurd, put a painting of the Indiana State star on the front cover of the league's basketball media guide.

As a junior, Bird had averaged 30 points, 11.5 rebounds, and shot 52.4 percent. He certainly was a National Player of the Year candidate, and the league office wanted to capitalize on his celebrity. "A lot of coaches were irritated," Hurd said of the cover. "I got a call from Bradley Coach Dick Versace, and he said, 'If our university paid one cent for the media guide, we should get it back.' He wanted us to re-do the cover."

It stuck. And Bird would live up to all the hype— and then some as the Sycamores redefined their team. They welcomed back Nicks after a year at Gulf Coast Community College (in Fla.), where he polished his game by learning to play more under control and became academically healthy. "They were all tough, tough guys and loved the game,"

former Indiana State Assistant Coach Earl Diddle said. "I remember that spring (after Bird used up his eligibility). They all stayed and played at 4 o'clock. They were friends. They golfed together and fished together."

Two first-year transfers, 6-5 junior Bob Heaton and 6-4 senior Leroy Staley, played major roles off the bench. Sophomore Steve Reed stepped in to handle the point guard chores with Nicks, who was the team's second-leading scorer. Junior Alex Gilbert, 6-7, was a leaper and rebounder, and 6-8 junior Steve Miley was a defensive specialist.

"We thought we would be pretty good, but not necessarily No. 1 or No. 2, " said Heaton, who transferred from Denver. "In our first exhibition game we played the Soviet National Team. We beat them in a close game, and right then we thought we got something if we can beat those guys."

Nicks said the transition to Hodges, who was King's assistant coach, wasn't difficult. "His philosophy was just like Coach King's," Nicks said. "They had the same defensive techniques. Everybody liked Coach Hodges. He recruited us. Bill Hodges would let you play your game. There were not a lot of restrictions as long as you stayed in the team concept. Larry's status had an impact on our whole team. We followed his quiet leadership."

The stars were aligned right for Indiana State that season, and the team never stopped winning until the very end, although it had several close calls before the Michigan State game. The Sycamores won by one point at Southern Illinois, by two at New Mexico State, and by two in NCAA Tournament games over Arkansas and DePaul.

Heaton became known as the "Miracle Man" because of his heroics at the end of four games that season. He initially received the nickname after he made a 50-foot bank shot that sent a game at New Mexico State into overtime on Feb. 1, where the Sycamores won, 91–89. "New Mexico State was shooting a one-and-one, and the guy missed the front end," Reed said. "Miley rebounded and threw to Heaton and he chucked it from half court. We had two or three starters (fouled out) on the bench in the overtime, but I remember how the momentum shifted to us after that shot. . . . After the game, we looked at each other in the locker room and thought there must be some destiny on our side. It was at that point, I thought it might be a very special year for us. Fate seemed to play a big role."

The victory at New Mexico State raised Indiana State's record to 19–0 and created a buzz nationally. Most teams figured they couldn't beat Indiana State covering Bird the conventional way, which led to opportunities for other players.

Bob Heaton

Later in the season at Bradley, Bird was held to single digits (four points) for the only time during his college career. Versace installed the "Bird Cage" defense, focusing on stopping him, in a 91–72 Indiana State victory. The Sycamores clinched the MVC regular-season title as Nicks tied and Reed posted a career high by making wide-open shots against the Braves. "The idea was that we had very little chance of beating that team unless we cut Bird's points off," said Tony Barone, a former Bradley assistant coach. "We put a man directly in front of him and a big man in back of him, and another on the ball side of where he was. Eventually, what happened in the second half, the first three times we came down the court, he was the defender. He intercepted passes and went down and scored."

Bird's national coming out party came in his last home game in Terre Haute. Before an NBC national television audience (his first), Bird scored a career-high 49 points in a victory over Wichita State to complete a 50–1 home record during his three seasons. There were leaks in the arena's roof from all the snow that had hit the area, but there were none in Bird's game.

BIRD-MAGIC SHOWDOWN
After winning the 1979 MVC Tournament rather comfortably, Indiana State remained the top-ranked team in country and the 16th unbeaten team in history to go into the NCAA Tournament. The Sycamores

Alex Gilbert

LeRoy Staley

Steve Reed

were the first MVC team to finish the regular season ranked No. 1 since Cincinnati in 1963. And Hodges became the second first-year coach of the modern college era (since 1938) to finish the regular season with an unbeaten record. "We won 25 games and then won the MVC Tournament. I thought nobody can beat us, we are going through this undefeated," Nicks said.

Michigan State entered the NCAA Tournament as the No. 2 seed in the Mideast Regional and won games by 31 over Lamar, 16 over LSU, 12 over Notre Dame, and then 34 points over Penn in the other Final Four semifinal. Magic, just a sophomore, had his team peaking at just the right time.

Indiana State registered its first NCAA Tournament victory over Virginia Tech (86–69) and then polished off the Big Eight champion Oklahoma (93–72) in the second game. After the second round, things got a lot tougher for Bird and Co.

Against Arkansas in the Midwest Regional final, with a Final Four berth at stake, Heaton's left-handed heroics entered the picture again. He made a basket in the lane in the final seconds to beat the Razorbacks, 73–71. "With 20 seconds to go in the game, we call a timeout, and we were planning on getting Larry the ball," Heaton said. "But he was guarded quite closely by Sidney Moncrief. Steve Reed had an open shot. He passed me the ball (to me) at the last moment. . . . The reason I went up with my left hand was Scott Hastings, who was 6-9, and he was between me and the basket, and I thought he might block the shot. I went to the left hand to shoot it. The ball went in and that was it."

In the next game, Heaton again made the winning basket, in the final minute of the semifinals against DePaul, to win 76–74, setting up the showdown with Michigan State. The homespun Bird, who scored 35 points on 16 of 19 shooting against the Blue Demons and Mark Aguirre, remarked to reporters after the game: "Sometimes I feel sorry for the guys I'm playing against, and today I was yelling for the ball."

The story of the 1979 NCAA title game was Michigan State Coach Jud Heathcote's match-up zone, which put pressure on Bird. Continuing to play with a hairline fracture on the thumb of his shooting hand, Bird made only seven of 21 shots and finished with 19 points. Several players 6-7 or taller—Magic, Greg Kelser, Jay Vincent, Ron Charles—forced Bird and the rest of the Sycamores into uncomfortable shooting positions. "They ran that as effectively or more effectively than anyone we had played against all year," Reed said. "That was definitely a key to the game. It didn't allow us to do things that we had been doing all year. Michigan State had jelled at the right time and was at the top of its game during tournament time. They came together as a team."

Still, Indiana State clawed back within 52–46 in the second half. But a play that was featured on the cover of *Sports Illustrated* started to deflate the rallying Sycamores, who wound up losing 75–64. The 6-8 Magic, who scored 24 points, went in for a layup and scored. On the same play,

The MVCs Larry Bird Player of the Year trophy

Bird and Miley

Magic Johnson and Larry Bird at the 1979 NCAA championship game in Salt Lake City

Larry Bird

1979 Indiana State Sycamores

an undercut foul (two shots) was called on Heaton. Michigan State wound up with a four-point play and was out of trouble. Hodges said the controversial play broke his heart.

"There was never a doubt in my mind, we still had an opportunity to win," Nicks said. "But I fouled out. Larry was still in a cage. We just ran out of time basically."

At the time, Bird became the fifth-highest (career) scoring player in NCAA history during the game, but it wasn't enough to overcome Michigan State's overall balance. Bird chipped in 13 rebounds and played the entire 40 minutes.

In February 2004, during a 25-year anniversary celebration of the game when Bird's jersey was hung in the rafters of the Hulman Center, he reflected to the attending fans his one regret during his days at Indiana State. "I've always been heartbroken that I couldn't bring the championship back to Terre Haute," Bird told the crowd.

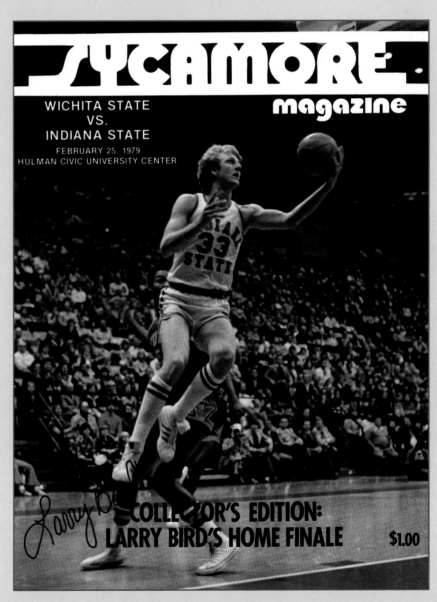

SYCAMORE. magazine

WICHITA STATE
VS.
INDIANA STATE

FEBRUARY 25. 1979
HULMAN CIVIC UNIVERSITY CENTER

COLLECTOR'S EDITION:
LARRY BIRD'S HOME FINALE

$1.00

Kevin Stallings

ILLINOIS STATE

Illinois State University was founded in 1857 in the centrally located town of Normal as the first institution of higher learning in the state of Ilinois. The Redbirds officially joined the MVC in 1980.

Rico Hill

Redbird Arena

Coach Will Robinson and superstar Doug Collins laid the foundation in the early to mid-1970s. Coach Gene Smithson built upon it and made the Redbirds an independent men's basketball power in the Midwest in the mid- to late 1970s. But none of the three was around central Illinois when Illinois State finally played a men's basketball game in the Missouri Valley Conference during the 1981–82 season. By that time, Bob Donewald, a former Bob Knight assistant, was coaching the Redbirds.

By Illinois State's second season in the MVC, the Redbirds already were making their presence felt. They won the MVC Men's Tournament title in 1983 with double-digit victories over Southern Illinois, Bradley, and Tulsa.

The MVC's initial attraction to Illinois State was its central Illinois location to Bradley and the fact that it was a rising basketball power in the late 1970s. As New Mexico State withdrew from the league, Illinois State also geographically began to cement the central core of the MVC.

Doug Collins gets instruction from coach Will Robinson

Bob Bender

In 11 seasons, Donewald posted a 208–121 record at Illinois State, 79–47 against MVC teams in eight of those seasons in the league. He was the first coach to take the Redbirds to the NCAA Tournament.

However, Illinois State's men's basketball success in the MVC has come in spurts during the school's more than two and a half decades in the league. Coach Bob Bender, who played for Knight at Indiana, won Illinois State's next tournament title in 1990 when Rickey Jackson was named the Most Outstanding Player of the Tournament. The Redbirds were a hot ticket in the MVC during those days, leading the league in attendance from 1990 to 1993, corresponding closely with the opening of 10,200-seat Redbird Arena in 1988–89.

Illinois State won the MVC regular-season title in both 1992 (tie, with Southern Illinois) and 1993 but lost in the league's postseason tournament each of those years and failed to make the NCAA Tournament as an at-large entry. Bender was named MVC Coach of the Year in 1992, a year after his team had finished 5–23.

Bender left for the University of Washington following the 1992–93 season, but Coach Kevin Stallings came in and took the Redbirds to a couple of National Invitation Tournament berths before leading them back to the top of the MVC.

Under Stallings, the Redbirds remain the only school (as of 2005–06) in MVC history to claim outright MVC regular-season men's titles in 1997 and 1998 and also win the postseason tournament title (back-to-back) during the same years. Stallings was MVC Coach of the Year in 1998, and the Redbirds' Rico Hill (1997) and Dan Muller (1998) were the Most Outstanding Players of those MVC Tournaments.

Illinois State didn't win its first women's postseason tournament basketball title until 2005.

Although Illinois State has been in the league less than three decades, it trails only Wichita State in MVC All-Sports Trophies, 15–10. The Redbirds won four straight MVC All-Sports titles from 1996 to 1999 and five of six from 1996 to 2001.

Rickey Johnson

Men's basketball has always been the men's staple at Illinois State. The 1982–83 season was the first of three straight NCAA Tournament appearances and 20-victory seasons under Donewald, whose Redbirds tied Tulsa for the 1984 MVC regular-season title. Donewald was named the 1984 MVC Coach of the Year.

Dan Muller

Jackie Stiles

MISSOURI STATE

Founded in 1905 and formerly known as Southwest Missouri State University, the school became Missouri State 100 years after its founding. Missouri State is a recent addition to the Missouri Valley Conference, joining the league in 1990. The women's basketball program has proved to be dominant, winning the MVC championship nine times in 17 member seasons.

Cheryl Burnett

JACKIE STILES:
AN ALL-TIME VALLEY AND NCAA GREAT

At age 12, Jackie Stiles already had been spotted by a Southwest Missouri State assistant coach. A basketball legend was in the formative stages of development about the time Lady Bears basketball took off in the early 1990s. "Actually it was at my first AAU Tournament, and my first game with the team," said Stiles of the chance meeting in the summer of 1991. "(SMS) Assistant Coach Lynnette Robinson was sitting close to dad. She asked him, 'Who is No. 5?' My dad says, 'That is my daughter.' She was killing time watching the younger kids play. She told me if I would keep working, I could get a Division I scholarship. Being from Claflin (Kan.), I didn't know how good I had to be."

The following spring in 1992, the Lady Bears went to the Final Four in their final season in the Gateway Conference before moving into MVC competition. The Final Four appearance made an impression on Stiles, who attended the Southwest Missouri State camp in Springfield, Mo., five straight years before her senior season at Claflin.

Cheryl Burnett was building a national power in Springfield and had recruited Melody Howard, who would become the first women's basketball player to be inducted into the MVC Hall of Fame in 1999. "She struggled her first few years," remembers Southwest Missouri State Athletic Director Bill Rowe of Burnett. "She got these girls from Marshfield (Mo.). She got Melody Howard from there, and Tina Robbins from Joplin. They had a good team, too. The thing about it was Marshfield was just 23 miles out of town, and their fans started to come to our games. And it just mushroomed.

"It started by us recruiting those two young ladies. We got Melody's sister a year or two later. We got some more local players. We went to the Final Four in 1992, and it just kept building and has never gone away."

Southwest Missouri State still nearly lost Stiles because news of her legend spread all the way to the East Coast. Perennial national power Connecticut saw Stiles at a Nike All-America Camp in Indianapolis. She also was invited to try out for the USA Basketball Team in the spring of her junior year in high school. She was well on her way to becoming Kansas' all-time leading high school scorer.

She became a major focal point of the Huskies' recruiting. "Basically I narrowed it to SMS, UConn, and Kansas State," said Stiles. "I felt like all three were good choices. I was going to sign a letter of intent with UConn. I said I would sleep on it. It didn't feel right. My heart was with SMS. I tried to listen to everybody. People couldn't fathom turning down UConn, and they couldn't understand why I would not stay in state. I finally had the guts to stand up and tell them I was going to SMS. I had people disappointed on that day. It was the best decision of my life. My instincts told me to go SMS."

In her high school career, Stiles scored 3,603 points, grabbed 829 rebounds, handed out 523 assists, and made 326 steals. A four-year first-team Kansas All-State selection, Stiles was the leading high school scorer in the state's history through the 2005–06 season. She never dropped off in college.

GETTING STARTED IN THE MVC

Stiles led the MVC in scoring (20.6 ppg) her freshman season and was the top freshman scorer in Division I in 1997–98. She failed to score in double figures only once, with six points against Southern Illinois.

Southwest Missouri State, which finished second in the MVC regular-season race, also lost to Drake in the final of the MVC Tournament and fell to Notre Dame in the first round of the NCAA Tournament. Stiles, however, had served noticed she was going to be a major force in women's basketball. "The Missouri Valley was able to use her in regards to gaining national attention," said long-time Northern Iowa coach Tony DiCecco. "She kind of put a stamp on it being a great, great league. One thing that also helped, she gave the MVC an identity in the country. Everyone knew of

Melody Howard

Stiles and knew of Southwest Missouri State and kne of the conference."

Stiles' shooting skill was obvious from the beginnir because she shot 52.5 percent from the field as a freshma and was an 81.8 percent free throw shooter. That wa partly attributable to the fact that she took 1,000 shots day in practice during her high school career because of broken wrist. "My sophomore year in high school, early i the season, I went up for reverse layup and broke my rigl

As a sophomore, Stiles won the first of three MVC Player of the Year awards, and claimed the MVC regular-season title. Stiles was the first sophomore in the MVC's history to win the league's Player of the Year award.

wrist," Stiles said. "I thought my world was ending. I was out four weeks with a hard cast, and I had to play four weeks with a soft cast and shoot with my left hand. My shot was really inconsistent. . . . I still until this day can remember the semis of the state (Kansas) tournament. If we win the game we will play for the championship. I went 4-for-21 from the field, and we lost by few points. I decided at that point I wanted to be a better shooter. I started shooting 1,000 shots a day until I was a freshman in college."

Of course, it paid off. As a sophomore, Stiles won the first of three MVC Player of the Year awards and Southwest Missouri State claimed the MVC regular-season title. Stiles was the first sophomore in history to win the league's Player of the Year award as she improved her scoring average to 25.7 ppg and both her shooting (52.9 percent) and free-throw shooting (83.8 percent).

Eventually, Southwest Missouri State lost in the MVC Tournament in the semifinals to Evansville, despite Stiles' 32 points, but the Lady Bears won a first-round 1999 NCAA Tournament game. "I wanted to improve in every category, not only on the floor but even in conditioning," Stiles said. "I didn't want to look back with any regrets. I wanted to make the most of this incredible opportunity. I worked hard every summer and played USA Basketball every summer. I played year-round for four years."

"I think her basketball skills speak for themselves," said Bradley Coach Paula Buscher. "She brought a level of intensity to the game, a compassion for the game. She was a class act . . . and went about it in the right manner. . . . She played the game the way it was supposed to be played. She was a respected player on the floor and off the floor."

During her junior season, the 5-8, 144-pound Stiles not only led the MVC in scoring for a second straight season, she led Division I (27.8 ppg). She scored a school record 56 points in an MVC Tournament victory over Evansville. She registered 25 or more points 22 times during that season. Southwest Missouri State, which finished in a three-way tie for second place in the MVC, lost to Auburn in the first round of the NCAA Tournament.

"I wasn't at her practices," said DiCecco. "But I was close friends with Cheryl, and she always talked about her regimen—her routine and work ethic and the amount of

Cheryl Burnett argues a call

time Jackie put in the game and . . . being in a great environment of the Hammons Center, she capitalized on that. And I think she was extremely well coached."

ON TO THE SCORING RECORD, FINAL FOUR

Stiles entered her senior season (2000–01) already a highly decorated player, but her last collegiate season would be the highlight of her career. Stiles became the first NCAA Division I women's player to score 1,000 points in a season when she averaged 30.3 ppg (1,062 points). She became the leading career scorer (3,393 points) in NCAA Division I women's history, and she led Southwest Missouri State to its second Final Four appearance at the Savvis Center in St. Louis.

Stiles gives Burnett, who later became the head coach at Michigan, a big assist in her development. Stiles won the Wade Trophy in 2001, which annually is awarded to the top player each season in women's college basketball. "She was a big influence," Stiles said. "I wanted a coach who would make me the best player I could possibly become. I wanted some intensity, discipline, and someone to push me. She forced me to

Jackie Stiles

Jackie Stiles

During the 2000–01 season, pressure also mounted on Stiles to break the NCAA Division I women's scoring record held by Mississippi Valley State's Patricia Hoskins (1985–89). "I had an emotion of relief," Stiles said of finally breaking the record. "It was so hyped leading up to it. I felt so much pressure. I played at Wichita State (the game before), and I would have had to score 40 points to break it. The Creighton game was the game before Senior Night, and I didn't want to take away from Senior Night. My teammates were sick of talking about it. Our goal was to get to the Final Four. . . . I turned on the radio, and that is all anybody talked about. I got mobbed at Taco Bell, people talking about breaking the record. I couldn't escape it. My first shot went in against Creighton and that loosened me up. It was high pressure. It was a relief to be able to accomplish it."

In the history of the college game, five players still have scored more than Stiles before women's basketball came under NCAA control in 1982. But on March 1, 2001, Stiles became the NCAA leader when she sank a three-pointer early in the second half of a victory over Creighton. "When she was passing the person who had the scoring title, Mr. (John Q.) Hammons flew that woman (Hoskins) from Itta Bena, Miss.," Rowe said. "It was a phenomenal evening. I will never forget it as long as I live."

Breaking the record allowed Stiles to focus on the remaining goal—making the Final Four in St. Louis. Drake and Southwest Missouri State tied for the MVC regular-season title with 16–2 records, but the Lady Bears beat the Bulldogs, 84–69 in the MVC Tournament title game to earn the league's automatic berth into the NCAA Tournament.

In the first round of the NCAAs, Stiles suffered a concussion and scored only 13 points before leaving the game. But the Lady Bears still beat Toledo, 89–71. In the second round, SMS faced another major hurdle—playing Rutgers on its home floor. The previous season Rutgers had advanced to the Final Four. "They hadn't lost a home game all season," Stiles said. "I knew their team was extremely athletic. We were disappointed because we thought we would be getting to host first- and second-round games. Beating Rutgers and beating them on their home court gave us confidence we could beat anybody."

Stiles scored 32 points in Southwest Missouri State's 60–53 victory over Rutgers, propelling the Lady Bears

learn the defensive side . . . and she made me a complete offensive player. She taught me to move away from the ball, set screens, and read screens. You look at the teams we beat to get to the Final Four. We didn't have near the talent. She had teams playing together, and they had great chemistry. She made players understand their roles."

Stiles was still a marked woman in the MVC, especially during her senior season. "We put a box on her on our court. FSN Midwest was doing the game," DiCecco said. "We didn't use it in the first half and we had a lead like 43–40. She might have had 28 at halftime. She was going to go off for somewhere in the 40s or 50s. We surprised her in the second half (with the box). We frustrated her quite a bit and ended up winning the game. . . . We played a fluke thing and won with it."

2001 NCAA® DIVISION I WOMEN'S BASKETBALL CHAMPIONSHIP
Savvis Center • St. Louis, Missouri • March 30 & April 1

into the Sweet 16 against Duke, the region's top seed. "No one wanted their careers to end," said Stiles, who scored 41 points in an 81–71 victory over the Blue Devils in Spokane, Wash. "No one was giving us a shot on ESPN. We believed it, truly believed it, we could win. It helped us that we were a group of seniors. We were just determined. We were down 10–15 points, but we were confident we could come back and win."

A 104–87 victory over Washington in the West Region final—in which Stiles scored 32 points before fouling out for the third time her senior season—sent the Lady Bears to St. Louis. "She had made women's basketball fans out of the St. Louis community," said MVC Senior Associate Commissioner Patty Viverito. "There were a lot of skeptics in this town when we brought the Final Four to St. Louis for the first time in 2001. I think especially among the media. . . . And then, Jackie Stiles had this incredible run through the opening rounds of the tournament, and this community, and especially the media, just fell in love with her."

Stiles remembers the whirlwind of events surrounding the week of the Final Four. The team was swarmed at the Springfield, Mo., airport by adoring fans. "People were trampling others to get an autograph," Stiles said. "*USA Today* was there. It was amazing. We get home

Tuesday night and we are on a bus Wednesday to the Final Four. It was a complete and total whirlwind."

At the open practice, thousands of fans jammed the Savvis Center to catch a glimpse of Stiles, who by now was a Missouri legend. "One of my favorite moments of the open practices was this group of maybe 10–12 year-old boys all through Southwest Missouri State's open practice, chanting, 'Jackie, Jackie, Jackie,'" Viverito remembers. "They were groupies. That was very unusual in women's basketball in a community outside of the institutional community."

Southwest Missouri State fell to Purdue, 81–64, in the NCAA semifinals, but Stiles finished her college career leading Division I scoring for two straight seasons. "If we had played like we had in the earlier rounds. . . ." Stiles said of what might have been in St. Louis. "We had to go from New Jersey to Washington (the state). We were the only team in the Final Four which didn't host games. We were tired. We hit a wall. We were just exhausted. We played Monday and some teams played their last game Sunday. But I have been to Final Fours which are nothing like that. And to be in your home state, it was an amazing atmosphere."

As a token to show its appreciation for Jackie Stiles, during the fall of 2005 the MVC named its Women's Player of the Year award after her. Stiles was in good company. The equivalent men's MVC award was named after Larry Bird, Indiana State's legendary star.

The MVC's Jackie Stiles Player of the Year Trophy

"SPOONBALL" TAKES HOLD IN MISSOURI VALLEY

The marriage of the Missouri Valley Conference and Missouri State men's basketball was an instant hit because of Charlie Spoonhour's infectious personality and his team's tireless defensive play known as "Spoonball."

The Bears entered MVC basketball competition starting with the 1990–91 season, and Spoonhour coached two seasons in the MVC before becoming the head basketball coach at Saint Louis University, a former MVC member.

Charlie Spoonhour

"From my perspective, the Mid-Continent had been very good for us," Spoonhour said of the Bears' previous conference before joining the MVC. "If we could be in the Valley, though, we fit in so many ways geographically. Also it (the MVC) had a great history. It would enhance our program."

In both of Spoonhour's MVC seasons, the Bears advanced to the title game of the league tournament and finished one game behind the league champions during the regular-season race.

In 1991, Missouri State lost to Creighton, 68–52, in the MVC title game, but Spoonhour's Bears won the 1992 MVC Tournament with a 71–68 victory over Tulsa when guard Jackie Crawford was named the tournament's Most Outstanding Player. "I loved him," Spoohour said. "He was one of my favorite players. Arnold Bernard was another. We made a living with little guards. Jackie liked to get after. We wanted our guards to defend. Rodney Perry could really defend. We had good guys. We would have Valley-type kids, who played through their senior year. They would play hard and listen to the coach for the most part."

LOSING TO INDIANA STATE HURTS "THE SPOON"

Southwest Missouri State entered the final game of the 1992 MVC regular season tied with Southern Illinois and Illinois State for the conference lead. Indiana State guard Greg Thomas made a half-court shot to beat the Bears, 55–54, and deny them a piece of the regular-season title.

Southwest Missouri State Athletic Director Bill Rowe had instituted performance bonuses in coaches' contracts for winning league titles, postseason league tournaments, and advancing in NCAA play.

As Southwest Missouri State Coach Charlie Spoonhour went down to shake hands with Indiana State Coach Tates Locke after losing the game, he wasn't too distraught. "I said to myself, 'If I had to lose a game, I feel all right it was to Tates," Spoonhour said. "I said to him, 'Coach, we are going to win the tournament.' I was confident in the kids. Then, Bill Rowe came up to me and said, 'I am really amazed you would be so pleasant. You lost your bonus. You would have gotten a $5,000 bonus.' I said, 'What! I hadn't even thought of that.'"

Spoonhour managed to collect another contract bonus from MSU that season, because the Bears rebounded to win the MVC Tournament.

Spoonhour, who coached at UNLV after his stint at Saint Louis University, was 24–10 in MVC games (70.6 winning percentage) and 5–1 in league tournament games (83.3 winning percentage). "I can't think of a bad memory other than losing a game," Spoonhour said of his MVC days. "I can't think of being treated anywhere in a bad manner. . . . I love doing their games now (on television). I just love doing it."

STEVE ALFORD

Before the 1999 NCAA Tournament, Southwest Missouri State Coach Steve Alford was considered a top candidate for the University of Iowa head coaching job.

Bill Rowe, right, with host John Goodman and Doug Elgin at the 1995 ESPY Awards. Rowe has spent over 45 years at Southwest Missouri Sate building the Bears' athletics program

Bill Rowe, right, with Steve Alford

During the tournament, Alford's name was linked to openings at Georgia and Notre Dame. And shortly after the Bears made the Sweet 16 and were eliminated by the East Region's top seed, Duke, 78–61, Alford completed his stay in Springfield, Mo.

He was named the new Iowa coach at the age of 34 after compiling an overall 78–48 record during four seasons at Southwest Missouri State.

Alford, a former Dallas Maverick and Indiana star, became a hot coach during the 1999 NCAA Tournament when the Bears, a No. 12 seed and an at-large entry, breezed past fifth-seeded Wisconsin (Big Ten) and fourth-seeded Tennessee (SEC) in the first two rounds. Alford was actually not surprised his spunky Bears upset teams from the bigger, more highly publicized conferences. "We have been in the top 38 all season long in the RPI (Rating Percentage Index)," Alford said. "And this team can play a lot of different styles."

In the first round, Southwest Missouri State held Wisconsin to 32 points, a 50-year low for NCAA Tournament games. The Bears then crushed Tennessee by 30 in the second round to advance to the school's first Sweet 16 in the Division I Men's Tournament play.

During the 1999 March run, Alford drew on his NCAA Tournament experience. In his senior year of college, 1987, Indiana won its most recent title under coach Bob Knight. Alford was the shooting star of the Hoosiers, who beat Syracuse, 74–73, in the title game on Keith Smart's shot from the corner in the closing seconds.

Alford's father, Sam, who was an assistant coach on the SMS staff and later at Iowa, said Steve still remembers 1987. "He has the notebooks from his playing days at

Indiana, and he keeps looking at what they did at this stage (of the tournament)," said Sam Alford, who joined his son's Southwest Missouri State staff in 1995 after a 20-year stint as a high school coach in New Castle, Ind.

"He explains to us that he has been there and what it feels like to advance in the tournament," SMS guard Kevin Ault said in 1999. "Just from listening to that, just wanting to experience that for ourselves, it makes us want to play harder and play the best we can."

Alford was stern on the bench and demanding in practice. But he would actually compete against many of his players during the down times. He chest-bumped with them. He set up indoor whiffle ball games and a version of H-O-R-S-E (basketball golf) as diversions to loosen up his players.

Alford had a mission in mind when he first arrived in Springfield from Manchester College (Ind.), a Division III program he built into a national power. And he accomplished it before moving on to Iowa. "We upgraded the schedule and played a very competitive schedule here," Alford said of Southwest Missouri State. "And those major schools were not jumping through hoops to play us at our place. We have been able to play 15 majors in 2 years, and only three have come to the Hammons Center. But we have shown consistency and (the Missouri Valley Conference) has risen to the level of the Atlantic 10 and the WAC."

Southwest Missouri State Athletic Director Bill Rowe had hoped he wouldn't have to refer to that list of potential coaching names filed away in his briefcase. But he did and hired Barry Hinson away from Oral Roberts to replace Alford.

Steve Alford

NORTHERN IOWA

Northern Iowa was admitted to the Missouri Valley Conference in 1991, and 15 years later the Cedar Falls–based school is right at home in the 10-team league that spreads across six states. "They have earned their spurs, overcoming a lot of the preconceived notions, with their facilities and success in the men's basketball tournament," said MVC Commissioner Doug Elgin. "Their women's volleyball is perennially in the Sweet 16, their football is national championship caliber, and their baseball has been a championship contender (winning the 2001 MVC Baseball Tournament)."

UNIVERSITY OF NORTHERN IOWA

University of Northern Iowa made its first MVC Men's Basketball Tournament final in 1994 and lost to Southern Illinois. Cam Johnson of the Panthers was named the Most Outstanding Player of the tournament.

It was a decade before the Panthers returned to the MVC Tournament title game in 2004, although in 1997 UNI's Jason Daisy and Panthers' Coach Eldon Miller were named MVC Player and Coach of the Year, respectively, for the league's regular season. A 16–12 record in 1996-97 was UNI's last winning one in men's basketball team until the 2003–04 season when the Panthers were 21-10.

In 2001, UNI Athletic Director Rick Hartzell hired Coach Greg McDermott, a former UNI basketball star, to pilot the Panthers' men's basketball program. "This program was in horrible shape and he fixed it," Hartzell said of a team that finished 7–24 overall in

Then-Northern Iowa President Dr. Constantine Curris speaking at the press conference in 1991 to announce UNI being admitted into the MVC

2000–01 and was in last place the year before McDermott arrived.

Three years after McDermott took the reins, the Panthers finished tied for second during the MVC regular season and then won their first men's MVC Tournament title in 2004. Sophomore guard Ben Jacobson was the Most Outstanding Player after scoring 26 in the title game, a 79–74 double-overtime victory over Missouri State.

McDermott, the school's field-goal percentage leader during three seasons (1986–88), knew a good shooter when he saw one. "When he (Jacobson) has it going, you let him go and you let him decide what's a good shot and what's a bad shot," McDermott said.

McDermott led the Panthers to three straight NCAA Tournaments (2004–06) and corresponding 20-victory seasons (both school firsts) before Jacobson graduated and McDermott took a job at Iowa State following the 2005–06 season.

McDermott was replaced, oddly enough, by assistant Ben Jacobson (no relation to the player), who will coach UNI in the new 7,000-seat McLeod Center in the fall of 2006. "Once their arena is finished, UNI will have what arguably might be the finest athletics facility in the conference," Elgin said. This is a credit to Rick Hartzell and the entire university."

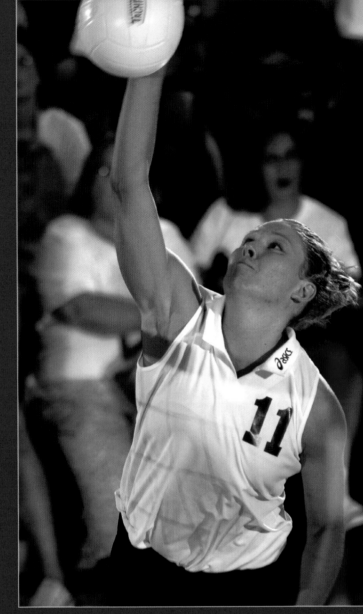

University of Northern Iowa's middle blocker, Molly O'Brien (2000–03) was a three-time MVC Player of the Year.

Joey Woody

Gold Medalist
World Championships 1999

World Recordholder
4 x 800 Relay
2000

NCAA Champion
400-Meter Hurdles 1997

All-American
Indoor 800 Meters
1996
400-Meter Hurdles 1994-95

Kurt Warner

NORTHERN
IOWA

Jim Crews on the sidelines

EVANSVILLE

Founded in 1854 as Moores Hill College, the University of Evansville is the newest member of the Missouri Valley Conference, joining the league in 1993, and beginning play the following year.

UNIVERSITY OF EVANSVILLE

With the addition of Evansville, the Missouri Valley Conference became an 11-school league in 1994–95. The 11-school configuration, which lasted two years before Tulsa departed for the Western Athletic Conference in 1996, was the largest in MVC history. "We didn't know Tulsa was going to leave, but we anticipated they might," said Missouri Valley Conference Commissioner Doug Elgin concerning the necessity for

Jim Crews

McCutchan Stadium

the conference to seek new members. "Evansville was drawing huge crowds (in men's basketball) and they had great tradition."

Evansville, which had been a Midwestern Collegiate Conference power, was the 32nd and last school to join the MVC in the 20th Century. The Aces instantly were a factor in MVC men's basketball when they finished in the middle of the standings their first two seasons and led the league in home attendance with 10,489 per game in 1994–95 and 10,457 in 1995–96. In their inaugural MVC season, senior Andy Elkins became the Aces' first All-MVC basketball player.

Long known as a college division power, the Aces won their first MVC regular-season championship in 1999. Coach Jim Crews' team finished 13–5 in the MVC that year and advanced to the NCAA Tournament as an at-large entry, losing in the first round to Kansas to finish 23–10. Marcus Wilson of the Aces was named All-MVC for the second straight season in 1999, and Crews, who played on the Indiana 1976 NCAA title team, was named the MVC Coach of the Year.

Arad McCutchan

Evansville's membership further helped to geographically solidify St. Louis as the hub and home of the conference office and the men's basketball tournament. An MVC Men's Tournament total attendance record was set in St. Louis in 1995, the first year Evansville was in the league. It has subsequently been broken several times.

By joining the MVC, Evansville continued the long-time basketball series with member schools such as Southern Illinois and Indiana State. "Long-term stability within a conference" was the goal of Evansville officials when they joined the MVC, which they have achieved.

In 2004, Arad McCutchan, the highly successful Evansville basketball coach from 1946 to 1977 (514–314), was given a lifetime achievement award posthumously by the league and was inducted into the MVC Hall of Fame.

Marcus Wilson

Southwest Missouri State's Melody Howard

IRV BROWN (MVC OFFICIAL)

I rv Brown, who was based out of Denver, worked several Missouri Valley Conference basketball games during the 1960s and 1970s. He officiated in six Final Fours, including five NCAA title games ('69, '71, '72, '74, '76) and a third-place NCAA game in 1977.

Brown, who was considered a demonstrative and showy official, worked in multiple leagues but always believed the MVC was the tops during that era. "The Valley at the time was the toughest overall league," said Brown, who worked MVC games with Johnny Overby and later worked for Overby when he was the MVC supervisor of officials.

Brown said early in his officiating career that MVC Commissioner Norvall Neve would require MVC officials to use a red whistle. Brown said it was a sign of pride for the MVC officials and showed unity. "Norvall one time told me, 'I have watched you and you are not the best official out there on the floor, but at the end of the game you have them convinced that you are,'" Brown recalled with a laugh.

PERFECT GAME

Wichita State was ranked No. 1 for one week during the 1964–65 season, then they lost an 87–85 thriller to Michigan on Dec. 14, 1964, at Cobo Hall in Detroit. It was a dazzling encounter between All-Americans Dave Stallworth and Michigan's Cazzie Russell.

Russell's long shot as time expired made the Wolverines a winner. "It was as far as I was concerned the best-played game I have ever been associated with," former Wichita State coach and player Gary Thompson said. "The talent on both teams, both All-Americans, Russell and Stallworth, had excellent games. It was an almost flawless, mistake-free game."

Gary Thompson, Wichita State

MILLER'S TRADEMARK: A STURDY STOOL

Wichita State Coach Ralph Miller sat on a stool in front of the bench during basketball games at Wichita State, and when Wichita State played at Bradley's Robertson Field House, with the court up on a stage, he improvised. "At Bradley, you would come down off (the stage) and then you go sit down, in order to get off the floor there was a step stool there, a second step then up on the floor," said Bob Ortegel, who played for the Braves. "It used to infuriate Ozzie Orsborn (Bradley coach), Ralph Miller would pull out that step stool, which wasn't anchored, and he would sit on the top step and be about floor level with his head. And he would orchestrate his team from

Ralph Miller, Wichita State

there. He wasn't up on the floor, but he wasn't at the bench, either. It was always interesting because something would be written about it."

OFFICIAL FEETE: AN MVC LEGEND

Missouri Valley Conference official Jack Feete was a legendary figure in the league. The late Feete, who also officiated MVC football games, was suspended by the league office for inviting a man into the officials' dressing room during halftime of Wichita State's 88–66 victory over Tulsa on Jan. 11, 1964.

The Tulsa World reported that the fan had been heckling Feete during the first half of the game, taking up what an usher also had been doing. Feete then asked the fan to come into the officials' dressing room where the two fought. One Wichita State source said the fan emerged bleeding. Feete came onto the court with his shirt torn. According to eyewitnesses, Wichita State's Ralph Miller noticed Feete's unruffled nature when he returned to the court.

MVC Commissioner Norvall Neve suspended Feete for the rest of the season because he was in violation of the league rule that prohibits having visitors in the officials' dressing room 30 minutes before the game or during intermission.

Feete was also a major-league baseball umpire and later an NFL official who officiated five Super Bowls. He was known over the years as a no-nonsense yet great official who had rabbit ears.

Johnny Overby, former MVC official and later supervisor of officials, remembers another incident involving Feete in the early 1960s at Wichita. Overby had officiated a freshman game prior to the varsity game and was sitting nearby. "Bob Kirkpatrick, the AD at Wichita, was at the north entrance near the tunnel and he was giving Jack a hard time about his bald head," Overby remembers. "So Feete goes over to Ralph Miller and tells him, 'I am going to throw that guy (Kirkpatrick) out of the field house if he doesn't shut up.'"

Did Feete know who Kirkpatrick was? "Yes," Overby said. "In those days the AD gave the official a check before the game. I learned a lesson from him: take no crap off anybody."

IBA: HE OWED HIS COUNTRY

Coach Henry Iba's nephew, Gene Iba, remembers a conversation he had with his uncle during a fishing trip in the early 1970s. Coach Henry Iba had directed the

United States to gold medals in the 1964 and 1968 Olympics and was asked to be the coach for a third straight Olympics. The 1972 Olympics in Munich was going to be more difficult. The rest of the world was catching up with the Americans. Henry Iba didn't get to pick the American team, either.

"I said, 'Why go?'" Gene Iba recalled. "Pretty soon we will get beat. There is no sense in being part of it."

Henry Iba said, "Because it was my country and they asked me."

"He was very, very patriotic," Gene Iba said, recalling in his uncle's bedroom a 5 x 7 picture of another Missourian, President Harry Truman, autographed: "To Henry Iba, My Favorite Basketball Coach."

CALLING UP A STAR

Oklahoma A&M center Bob Kurland remembers getting ready to play Kentucky in the National Invitation Tournament in 1944 when one of the Aggies' top players, Floyd Burdette, mysteriously had his leave cancelled and was called up for Air Force duty. "I had

Oklahoma A&M center Bob Kurland takes a rebound off the Aggies' basket in their 1945 game against NYU in Madison Square Garden. Also pictured are Aggies' Blake Williams (77) and NYU's Alvin Most (14)

learned most of my post moves from Floyd," Kurland recalled. "But he was asked to return to his base near Stillwater immediately. The senator from Kentucky at the time was Happy Chandler." Kentucky won easily, 45–29. Kurland said he saw Chandler later and asked him if he had intervened to get Burdette called up so the Wildcats would face an undermanned Oklahoma A&M team. "He said, 'Well, Robert, you know I would never do anything like that,'" Kurland said.

ON-THE-FLOOR MEETINGS
Coach Henry Iba had a certain way of getting the attention of his players during timeouts. He had them lay on the floor in a semi-circle, instead of sitting on the bench or on chairs or just standing while he lectured them. "He explained to me they had to look up at him while he was talking," said his son, Moe Iba. "And he could see their faces. I think the main thing he wanted to see their faces and make sure they were listening to him during timeouts. We were the only team I saw do it."

"The reason he stopped it, they started putting ice on the floors (for hockey), and it got too cold for that," said his nephew, Gene Iba.

BILL LAURIE (MEMPHIS)
Bill Laurie was a Memphis State guard who played on the 1973 team that finished second to UCLA in the NCAA Tournament. He later married his high school and college sweetheart Nancy Walton, daughter of the late Bud Walton and niece of the late Sam Walton, brothers of Wal-Mart fame. Despite his connection with Memphis State, Laurie grew up and lived in Missouri and became a major supporter and contributor for the University of Missouri basketball program. He and his wife recently sold the St. Louis Blues NHL team. He was formerly a high school basketball coach and breeds horses.

BOB ORTEGEL (BRADLEY AND DRAKE)
Bob Ortegel is the current Dallas Mavericks broadcaster, but he had the unique perspective of either playing against, coaching against, or covering three members of the MVC's charter Hall of Fame induction class of 1997. Ortegel was on the Bradley basketball roster and actually played against Cincinnati's Oscar Robertson (1957–60). He was head basketball coach at Drake (1974–81) and coached against Indiana State's Larry Bird (1976–79). Finally, he was an MVC broadcaster in the 1980s and covered Bradley's Hersey Hawkins (1984–88).

Drake's Bob Ortegel coaching the 1977–78 team

Ortegel was also a teammate of MVC Hall of Famer Chet Walker at Bradley and coached Drake's Lewis Lloyd, who led the league in scoring in 1980 and 1981 and in rebounding in 1980. "Since my freshman year in 1958, I thought, wow!" Ortegel said. "I played with Chester Walker. I played against Oscar Robertson. Then I coached three years against Larry Bird at Indiana State when I was head coach at Drake. I coached Lewis Lloyd, and I was doing television for the games with Hersey Hawkins. And those are five of the biggest names in the history of that league."

GUY LEWIS (HOUSTON)
Houston's Guy Lewis got his start as a head basketball coach in the Missouri Valley Conference in 1956, but Lewis never finished above fourth place (tie) in the MVC standings from 1956 to 1960. His record in MVC games was 21–35, although he was an assistant coach on the 1955–56 Houston team that won the MVC and advanced to the NCAA Tournament

In 1959–60, Gary Phillips and Ted Luckenbill led Houston to a 13–12 record, Lewis' only winning overall record during his four-year head coaching stint in the MVC, which ended after that season. But the Cougars, who finished in a tie with Wichita State for fourth in

Houston's Coach Guy Lewis

1960, were responsible for Bradley's stinging 63–58 defeat late in the season. That loss to Houston cost the Braves a share of the MVC title with Cincinnati.

Lewis later took Houston to five Final Fours and two NCAA title games, but all those occurred when Houston was either an independent or a member of the old Southwest Conference. In the mid-1960s, he was able to first recruit African American athletes—initially, Elvin Hayes and Don Chaney—and make the Cougars a national power in 1967 and 1968.

MELODY HOWARD (MISSOURI STATE)
Melody Howard was the MVC Women's Player of the Year in 1994 and was the first women's basketball player to be inducted into the league's Hall of Fame in 1999. Howard tied an NCAA women's record by making 11 three-point shots in a game against Drake in 1994 and has had her jersey retired. She scored 1,944 points during her college career, as Missouri State won four straight league regular-season titles and four consecutive league postseason tournament crowns from 1991 to 1994. Howard helped lead Missouri State to the 1992 Final Four when the Lady Bears were members of the Gateway Conference.

A LOT TO HOLD IN SEVEN OTs
Radio play-by-play man Dave Snell can remember Bradley's 75–73 seven-overtime loss to Cincinnati on Dec. 21, 1981, because of the pain he felt by the time it was over. During the long evening, he had drank a lot of water because he had a sore throat. Snell needed to relieve himself during the extra periods. But because the radio booth was located up in a corner of Robertson Field House, Snell never had time to go down and do so, until he made a mad sprint after the game. "I am sure I have permanent kidney damage because of it," Snell said.

The game very well could have gone into an eighth overtime. Cincinnati took a two-point lead with just seconds to go in the seventh overtime. "We throw it in and the guy who catches it is Kerry Cook, who played professional baseball as a pitcher," remembers former Bradley Assistant Coach Tony Barone. "And he catches it two steps outside the foul line. And he is wide open. . . . He has such an open shot, he doesn't know it. He shoots it. It rims out."

One Cincinnati player in that game, Mike Williams, ended up transferring to Bradley and played for the Braves from 1984–86.

ROBERTSON MAGIC
Bradley fans voted the Braves' 91–90 victory over No. 1 Cincinnati in 1960 as the greatest game in school history, but the Braves' 107–106 loss to No. 4 UNLV in 1977 ranks right up there in entertainment value on the raised stage where the lights focused only on the floor.

In 1977, Bradley was going nowhere and finished with a 9–18 record. UNLV, behind Reggie Theus, Eddie Owens, and Glen Gondrezick, was on the way to the Final Four. But on one magic night that season the Braves nearly pulled off the impossible behind Roger Phegley's 46 points. "The Field House gave us a chance to win any game on any given night and the best example of that was on Feb. 1, 1977, when we lost to UNLV," said former Bradley SID Joe Dalfonso.

STOWELL, JACKSON TO THE RESCUE
In the late 1980s, during an MVC road trip, former Bradley Coach Joe Stowell, who was on the Braves' radio team, and Luke Jackson were outside their rooms at the Holiday Inn. They spotted an elderly couple who had just checked into the hotel and was robbed. "There was this guy, and he was trailing this old couple," said Braves' radio play-by-play man Dave Snell. "And he followed them to their room and he grabbed her purse. That's when Stowell and Luke Jackson saw him. She was yelling, 'Stop him! Stop him!' So Luke took off after him and Coach Stowell was right there, too. He was in his shorts. They caught him."

NCAA RECORD WAS IN RANGE FOR BRADLEY'S HAWKINS

The NCAA Division I scoring record was in range for Hersey Hawkins when he set an MVC single-game scoring record with 63 points against Detroit on Dec. 22, 1988.

At the time, LSU's Pete Maravich owned the record of 69 points, later surpassed by Kevin Bradshaw of U.S. International in 1991, when he scored 72 against Loyola Marymount.

"That was one of the games I regret at Bradley," Hawkins said. "If I had known what was at stake. . . . I pretty much shut down the last three or four minutes of the game. I could have had 70 points if I had wanted to. If I had known I was getting close to 70, I would have shot more and looked to get to the free-throw line more."

SOUTHERN ILLINOIS' REBOUNDING KINGS

From 1990 to 1994, Southern Illinois had four different players who led the Missouri Valley Conference in rebounding during a five-year period. "We really focused on rebounding," said Chris Lowery, a point guard for Coach Rich Herrin. "His whole thing was getting and going with it. We always wanted to have the ball."

Through the end of the century, the only other time one school dominated the MVC in rebounding was Wichita State from 1981 to 1985, when Cliff Levingston (1981–82) and Xavier McDaniel (1983–85) combined to win five individual MVC rebounding titles.

Year-School-Player	Games	Rbds.	Aver.
1990 SIU–Jerry Jones	33	341	10.3
1991 SIU–Rick Shipley	32	289	9.0
1992 SIU–Ashraf Amaya	30	308	10.3
1993 SIU–Ashraf Amaya	33	354	10.7
1994 SIU–Marcus Timmons	30	293	9.8

MIKE REIS' TOP SALUKIS TEAM/GAME

Announcer Mike Reis has been a part of radio broadcasts of Southern Illinois basketball games for more than a quarter of a century, and he says the Salukis' 2002 Sweet 16 NCAA Tournament showing was the top achievement by a Salukis basketball team during his tenure and maybe in the history of the school.

No. 11 seed SIU beat sixth-seeded Texas Tech, 76–68, in the 2002 first round, then upset No. 3 seed Georgia, 77–75, in the second round of the NCAA Tournament at

MVC great, SIU's Mike Glenn

the United Center in Chicago before losing to No. 2 seed Connecticut, 71–59, in the region semifinals.

"Long-time fans think the 1967 team is the best," said Reis of the National Invitation Tournament champions led by star guard Walt Frazier. "But I think the 2002 team because it was bigger. The Georgia game at Chicago in the NCAAs, and what they did to get so far down in the first half and for Southern to have 20,000 fans cheering for them. And 15,000 of those fans were Illinois fans."

GLENN: SIU'S FIRST MVC STAR

Southern Illinois joined the Missouri Valley Conference in the mid-1970s and had early success behind guard Mike Glenn, who led the Salukis to a second-place finish in 1976 and a first-place tie in 1977 during the Salukis' second year competing in the MVC. Glenn, who was MVC Player of the Year in 1975–76, finished with an 18.1 ppg career scoring average and went on to a 10-year career in the NBA.

In one of the most thrilling games in MVC history, Glenn scored a career-high 40 points in SIU's 91–90 double overtime loss at Wichita State on Feb. 5, 1977. Glenn also ended his Saluki career with two sensational games in the 1977 NCAA Tournament, when he scored 35 points in an 81–77 victory over Arizona and 30 points (on 15 field goals) in an 86–81 loss to Wake Forest.

Morgan Taylor, Grinnell

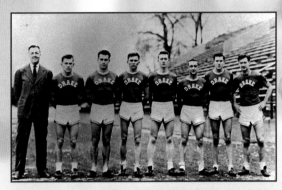

Top: 1944 Drake NCAA Men's Cross Country team
Middle: 1945 Drake NCAA Men's Cross Country team
Bottom: 1946 Drake NCAA Men's Cross Country team

NATIONAL TEAM CHAMPIONSHIPS
(NCAA, unless noted)

1922 – Kansas men's basketball (Helms Foundation)
1923 – Kansas men's basketball (Helms Foundation)
1944 – Drake men's cross country
1945 – Oklahoma A&M men's basketball
1945 – Drake men's cross country
1946 – Oklahoma A&M men's basketball
1946 – Drake men's cross country
1948 – Saint Louis men's basketball (NIT)
1954 – Oklahoma A&M men's cross country
1956 – Houston men's golf
1957 – Bradley men's basketball (NIT)
1957 – Houston men's golf
1958 – Houston men's golf
1959 – Houston men's golf
1960 – Bradley men's basketball (NIT)
1960 – Houston men's golf
1961 – Cincinnati men's basketball
1962 – Cincinnati men's basketball
1964 – Bradley men's basketball (NIT)
1981 – Tulsa men's basketball (NIT)
1982 – Bradley men's basketball (NIT)
1983 – Southern Illinois football (I-AA)
1989 – Wichita State baseball
2004 – Creighton women's basketball (WNIT)
2005 – Missouri State women's basketball (WNIT)

INDIVIDUAL CHAMPIONSHIPS (NCAA only)

DRAKE
Outdoor Track & Field National Champions (M)
1935 – Linn Philson, High Jump (6-4 7/8)
1952 – Jim Ford, 220-Yard Dash (21.0)
1970 – Rick Wanamaker, Decathlon (7,406 points)
Cross Country (M)
1944 – Fred Feiler (21:04.20)
1945 – Fred Feiler (21:14.20)

ILLINOIS STATE
Indoor Track & Field National Champions (M)
2002 - Christian Goy, One-Mile (4:00.06)

Outdoor Track & Field National Champions (M)
1987 – Tom Smith, High Jump (7-5 3/4)
1988 – Tom Smith, High Jump (7-7 3/4)

INDIANA STATE
Indoor Track & Field National Champions (M)
2001 – Aubrey Herring, 60-Meter Hurdles (7.61)
Indoor Track & Field National Champions (W)
1993 – Holli Hyche, 55-Meter Dash (6.76)
1993 – Holli Hyche, 200-Meter Dash (22.98)
1994 – Holli Hyche, 55-Meter Dash (6.70)
1994 – Holli Hyche, 200-Meter Dash (22.90)

Outdoor Track & Field National Champions (M)
1990 – Chris Lancaster, 110-Meter Hurdles
  (13.45)
Outdoor Track & Field National Champions (W)
1993 – Holli Hyche, 100-Meter Dash (11.14)
1993 – Holli Hyche, 200-Meter Dash (22.34)
1994 – Holli Hyche, 100-Meter Dash (11.23)

UNIVERSITY OF NORTHERN IOWA
Indoor Track & Field National Champions (M)
2001 – Jacob Pauli, Pole Vault (18-7 1/2)
Outdoor Track & Field National Champions (M)
1997 – Joey Woody, 400-Meter Hurdles (48.59)

SOUTHERN ILLINOIS
Swimming & Diving (W)
1985 – Wendy Lucero, 1-Meter Diving (468.65)*
Indoor Track & Field National Champions (M)
1985 – Michael Franks, 400-Meter Dash (46.27)
Outdoor Track & Field National Champions (M)
1976 – Phil Robbins, Triple Jump (54-8 1/4)
1978 – Bob Roggy, Javelin (283-9)
1980 – David Lee, 400-Meter Hurdles (48.87)
1991 – Darrin Plab, High Jump (7-6 1/2)
1992 – Darrin Plab, High Jump (7-8)

WICHITA STATE
Indoor Track & Field National Champions (M)
1996 – Einars Tupuritis, 800-Meters (1:45.80)
Outdoor Track & Field National Champions (M)
1996 – Einars Tupuritis, 800-Meters (1:45.08)

GRINNELL (1918-19 – 1938-39)
Outdoor Track & Field National Champions (M)
1921 – Leonard Paulu, 100-Yard Dash (10.0)
1922 – Leonard Paulu, 100-Yard Dash (9.9)
1922 – Leonard Paulu, 220-Yard Dash (21.8)
1925 – Morgan Taylor, 220-Yard Low
  Hurdles (24.0)
1933 – Michael Pilbrow, Two-Mile Run (9.22.80)

HOUSTON (1950-51 – 1959-60)
Cross Country (M)
1959 – Al Lawrence (20:35.7)
Golf (M)
1957 – Rex Baxter, Jr.
1958 – Phil Rodgers
1959 – Dick Crawford
1960 – Dick Crawford

Outdoor Track & Field National Champions (M)
1959 – John Macy, 3,000-Meter Steeplechase
  (9:19.1)
1959 – Jack Smyth, Triple Jump (49-7 1/4)
1960 – Al Lawrence, Three-Mile Run (14:19.8)

IOWA STATE (1907-08 – 1927-28)
Outdoor Track & Field National Champions (M)
1922 – Lloyd Rathbun, Two-Mile Run (9:32.1)
1927 – Ray Conger, One-Mile Run (4:17.6)

KANSAS (1907-08 – 1927-28)
Outdoor Track & Field National Champions (M)
1923 – Tom Poor, High Jump (6-1)

KANSAS STATE (1913-14 – 1927-28)
Outdoor Track & Field National Champions (M)
1921 – Ray Watson, One-Mile Run (4:23.40)
1923 – Ivan Riley, 120-Yard Hurdles (15.20)

MISSOURI (1907-08 – 1927-28)
Outdoor Track & Field National Champions (M)
1925 – Thomas Bransford, High Jump (6-2)
1925 – Kenneth Lancaster, Pole Vault (12-4)

NEBRASKA (1907-08 – 1918-19; 1920-21 – 1927-28)
Outdoor Track & Field National Champions (M)
1926 – Roland Locke, 100-Yard Dash (9.9)
1926 – Roland Locke, 220-Yard Dash (20.9)

OKLAHOMA (1919-20 – 1927-28)
Outdoor Track & Field National Champions (M)
1925 – Frank Potts, Pole Vault (12-4)

OKLAHOMA A&M (1925-26 – 1956-57)
Golf (M)
1953 – Earl Moeller
Outdoor Track & Field National Champions (M)
1955 – J.W. Mashburn, 440-Yard Dash (46.6)
1956 – J.W. Mashburn, 440-Yard Dash (46.4)
1956 – Jim Graham, Pole Vault (14-8)

NBA DRAFT PICKS

THE VALLEY
MISSOURI VALLEY CONFERENCE

FIRST-ROUND NBA DRAFT PICKS OF THE MISSOURI VALLEY CONFERENCE

1951 – Gene Melchiorre, Bradley (by Baltimore) – No. 1 Overall Pick
1958 – Connie Dierking, Cincinnati (by Syracuse) – No. 6 Overall Pick
1959 – Bob Ferry, Saint Louis (by St. Louis) – No. 6 Overall Pick
1960 – Oscar Robertson, Cincinnati (by Cincinnati) – No. 1 Overall Pick
1962 – Paul Hogue, Cincinnati (by New York) – No. 2 Overall Pick
1963 – Tom Thacker, Cincinnati (by Cincinnati) – No. 5 Overall Pick
1964 – George Wilson, Cincinnati (by Cincinnati) – No. 8 Overall Pick
1965 – Dave Stallworth, Wichita State (by New York) – No. 3 Overall Pick
1965 – Nate Bowman, Wichita State (by Cincinnati) – No. 6 Overall Pick
1968 – Wes Unseld, Louisville (by Baltimore) – No. 2 Overall Pick
1969 – Bobby Smith, Tulsa (by San Diego) – No. 6 Overall Pick
1969 – Butch Beard, Louisville (by Atlanta) – No. 10 Overall Pick
1969 – Willie McCarter, Drake (by L.A. Lakers) – No. 12 Overall Pick
1969 – Rick Roberson, Cincinnati (by L.A. Lakers) – No. 15 Overall Pick
1970 – Jim Ard, Cincinnati (by Seattle) – No. 6 Overall Pick
1971 – Dana Lewis, Tulsa (by Philadelphia) – No. 12 Overall Pick
1975 – Junior Bridgeman, Louisville (by L.A. Lakers) – No. 8 Overall Pick
1978 – Larry Bird, Indiana State (by Boston) – No. 6 Overall Pick
1978 – Roger Phegley, Bradley (by Washington) – No. 14 Overall Pick
1980 – Carl Nicks, Indiana State (by Denver) – No. 23 Overall Pick
1982 – Cliff Levingston, Wichita State (by Detroit) – No. 9 Overall Pick
1982 – David Thirdkill, Bradley (by Phoenix) – No. 15 Overall Pick
1982 – Paul Pressey, Tulsa (by Milwaukee) – No. 20 Overall Pick
1983 – Antoine Carr, Wichita State (by Detroit) – No. 8 Overall Pick
1985 – Benoit Benjamin, Creighton (by L.A. Clippers) – No. 3 Overall Pick
1985 – Xavier McDaniel, Wichita State (by Seattle) – No. 4 Overall Pick
1985 – Steve Harris, Tulsa (by Houston) – No. 19 Overall Pick
1988 – Hersey Hawkins, Bradley (by L.A. Clippers) – No. 6 Overall Pick#
1997 – Anthony Parker, Bradley (by New Jersey) – No. 21 Overall Pick^
2006 – Patrick O'Bryant, Bradley (by Golden State) – No. 9 Overall Pick

#Philadelphia traded rights to Charles Smith to L.A. Clippers for rights to Hersey Hawkins and a 1989 first-round draft choice;
^Philadelphia trades Don MacLean, Michael Cage, Lucious Harris, and rights to Keith Van Horn to New Jersey for Jim Jackson, Eric Montross, and rights to Tim Thomas and Anthony Parker.

NATIONAL ACADEMIC PLAYERS OF THE YEAR

1990 – Jan Jensen, Drake (WBB) – USBWA Academic All-American of the Year; WBCA Scholar-Athlete of Year*
1991 – Jan Jensen, Drake (WBB) – GTE/CoSIDA Academic All-American of the Year*
1991 – Cheryl Venorsky, SIU (SB) – GTE/CoSIDA Academic All-American of the Year*
1992 – Charlie Giaudrone, WSU (BB) – GTE/CoSIDA Academic All-American of the Year
1995 – Mike Drumright, WSU (BB) – GTE/CoSIDA Academic All-American of the Year
1996 – Tricia Wakely, Drake (WBB) – GTE/CoSIDA Academic All-American of the Year
1996 – Christine Knotts, SIU (SB) – GTE/CoSIDA Academic All-American of the Year
1998 – Lisa Davies, Missouri State (WBB) – USBWA Scholar-Athlete of the Year, GTE CoSIDA Academic All-American of the Year
2001 – Luchi Gonzalez, SMU (MSOC) – Verizon/CoSIDA Academic All-American of the Year
2003 – Michael Lindeman, Creighton (MBB) – NACDA I-AAA Scholar-Athlete of the Year
2006 – Anthony Tolliver, Creighton (MBB) – NACDA I-AAA Scholar-Athlete of the Year

NATIONAL PLAYERS/COACHES OF THE YEAR – MISSOURI VALLEY CONFERENCE HISTORY

1923 – Paul Endacott, Kansas (Men's Basketball) – Helms Foundation
1924 – Charlie Black, Kansas (Men's Basketball) – Helms Foundation
1945 – Henry Iba, Oklahoma A&M (Men's Basketball Coach)
1946 – Henry Iba, Oklahoma A&M (Men's Basketball Coach)
1946 – Bob Kurland, Oklahoma A&M (Men's Basketball) – Helms Foundation
1948 – Ed Macauley, Saint Louis (Men's Basketball) – Helms Foundation
1949 – Ed Macauley, Saint Louis (Men's Basketball) – AP
1958 – Oscar Robertson, Cincinnati (Men's Basketball) – UPI, The Sporting News
1959 – Oscar Robertson, Cincinnati (Men's Basketball) – UPI, USBWA, The Sporting News
1960 – Oscar Robertson, Cincinnati (Men's Basketball) – UPI, USBWA, The Sporting News
1963 – Ed Jucker, Cincinnati (Men's Basketball Coach) – UPI, USBWA
1969 – Maury John, Drake (Men's Basketball Coach) – USBWA
1973 – Gene Bartow, Memphis (Men's Basketball Coach) – NABC
1979 – Larry Bird, Indiana State (Men's Basketball) – AP, UPI, USBWA, NABC, Wooden Award,
        NABC, Naismith Award
1979 – Bill Hodges, Indiana State (Men's Basketball Coach) – AP, UPI, The Sporting News
1981 – Joe Carter, Wichita State (Baseball) – The Sporting News, All-America Baseball News
1982 – Bryan Oelkers, Wichita State (Baseball) – All-America Baseball News (Pitcher of the Year)
1982 – Phil Stephenson, Wichita State (Baseball) – All-America Baseball News
1982 – Gene Stephenson, Wichita State (Baseball Coach) – All-America Baseball News
1983 – Ray Dempsey, Southern Illinois (Football Coach) – I-AA Coach of the Year
1986 – Dick Versace, Bradley (Men's Basketball Coach) – USBWA
1986 – Jim Les, Bradley (Men's Basketball) – Frances Pomeroy Naismith Award
1986 – Wanda Ford, Drake (Women's Basketball) – Women's Sports Federation*
1988 – Hersey Hawkins, Bradley (Men's Basketball) – AP, UPI, USBWA, Basketball Times
1989 – Gene Stephenson, Wichita State (Baseball Coach) – The Sporting News, ABCA
1991 – Scott Stahoviak, Creighton (Baseball) – ABCA
1991 – Jim Hendry, Creighton (Baseball Coach) – Baseball America
1993 – Gene Stephenson, Wichita State (Baseball Coach) – Baseball America
1993 – Darren Dreifort, Wichita State (Baseball) – Golden Spikes, NCBWA, R.E. Smith Award
1995 – John Coughlan, Illinois State (Women's Indoor Track & Field Coach) – USTFA
1996 – Johnny Torres, Creighton (Men's Soccer) – Soccer America
1997 – Johnny Torres, Creighton (Men's Soccer) – Hermann Trophy, Missouri Athletic Club
1999 – Iradge Ahrabi-Fard, UNI (Volleyball Coach) – AVCA
2001 – Jackie Stiles, Missouri State (Women's Basketball) – Wade Trophy, Honda-Broderick Cup, WBCA
2001 – Luchi Gonzalez, SMU (Men's Soccer) – Hermann Trophy, Missouri Athletic Club, NSCAA,
        Soccer America
2002 – Bobbi Peterson, UNI (Volleyball Coach) – AVCA
2004 – Ryan Pore, Tulsa (Men's Soccer) – Soccer America

Key
UPI – United Press International; USBWA – United States Basketball Writers Association; AP – Associated Press; NABC – National Association of Basketball Coaches; USTFA – United States Track & Field Association; AVCA – American Volleyball Coaches Association; NSCAA – National Soccer Coaches Association of America; NACDA – National Association of Collegiate Directors of Athletics; CoSIDA – College Sports Information Directors of America; ABCA – American Baseball Coaches Association; NCBWA – National Collegiate Baseball Writers of America; WBCA – Women's Basketball Coaches Association; *Drake and Southern Illinois competed under Gateway Collegiate Athletic Conference umbrella until 1992.

CREDITS

The author and the Missouri Valley Conference staff wish to thank member schools, past and present, for their assistance with gathering information and illustrations. The photographs in this book were compiled from the archives and sports information departments of past and present MVC member institutions and from the MVC archives. Photographers Doug DeVoe, and St. Louis based photographers, William Greenblatt and Dave Preston provided photographs for the publication through the files of the MVC. Additional photographs were provided by William Edward Mathis.

The list that follows includes individuals who made our lives easier by leading us toward the perfect photographs. We are eternally indebted for your help.

Bradley University: Ken Kavanagh, Virnette House-Browning, Bobby Parker, and Jim Rea, Athletics Department; and Special Collections Center, Bradley University Library

University of Cincinnati: Brian Teter, Athletics Department

Creighton University: Bruce Rasmussen, Sharon Hanson, Rob Anderson, and Rob Simms, Athletics Department

Drake University: Dave Blank, Jean Berger, Mike Mahon, Paul Morrison, and Jolene Ostbloom, Athletics Department

University of Evansville: Bill McGillis, Sarah Solinsky, Bob Boxell, and Tom Benson, Athletics Department

Grinnell College: Jordan Gizzarelli, Robert Boxwell, Athletics Department; Cheryl Neubert, Library Assistant

Illinois State University: Sheahon Zenger, Leanna Bordner, Todd Kober, Tom Lamonica and Heather Freehill, Athletics Department

Indiana State University: Ron Prettyman, Gail Barksdale, Jason Yaman, and Ace Hunt, Athletics Department; Susan Davis, University Archivist

University of Iowa: Kathy Hodson, University Libraries - Special Collections Department

Iowa State University: Tanya Zanish-Belcher, Iowa State University Library/Special Collections Department

University of Kansas: Becky Schulte, University Archives

Kansas State University: Cindy Harris and Pat Patton, University Archives, and Tony Crawford, Special Collections

University of Louisville: University Archives and Records Center; Tom Jurich and Kenny Klein, Athletics Department

Memphis State University/University of Memphis: Bob Winn and Lamar Chance, Athletics Department; Mississippi Valley Collection, Special Collections Department, University Libraries

University of Missouri: Gary Cox, University Archives

Missouri State University: Bill Rowe, Darlene Bailey, Mark Stillwell and Erin Smith, Athletics Department

University of Nebraska: Carmella Orosco, University Archives

North Texas State University: Richard Himmel, University Archives

University of Northern Iowa: Rick Hartzell, Julie Bright, Josh Lehman, Brandie Glasnapp and Colin McDonough, Athletics Department

University of Oklahoma: John Lovett, Western History Collections

Oklahoma State University: Kay Bost and David Peters, Special Collections and University Archives

Saint Louis University: Doug McIlhagga, Athletics Department

Southern Illinois University: Paul Kowalczyk, Kathy Jones, Tom Weber, Jeff Honza and Shalae Schulte, Athletics Department

University of Tulsa: Don Tomkalski, Athletics Department, and Lori Curtis, McFarlin Library

West Texas State University: Sidnye Johnson, Special Collections, University Archives; Cornette Library, West Texas A&M University

Wichita State University: Jim Schaus, Becky Endicott, Larry Rankin, Tami Cutler, and Mike Ross, Athletics Department; Mary Nelson, Wichita State University Libraries, Department of Special Collections

Stanford University: University Libraries, Department of Special Collections, Patricia E. White, Archives Specialist

Washington University in St. Louis, University Archives, Sonya McDonald and Miranda Rectenwald

Nebraska Football
Early 1900s

MISSOURI VALLEY CONFERENCE SCHOOLS, PAST AND PRESENT:*

95 Drake (1907-08 – 1950-51; 1956-57 – present)
62 Tulsa (1934-35 – 1995-96)
62 Wichita State (1945-46 – present)
55 Bradley (1948-49 – 1950-51; 1955-56 – present)
49 Creighton (1928-29 –1942-43; 1945-46 –1947-48; 1976-77– present)
39 Washington (Mo.) (1907-08 – 1909-10; 1946-47)
36 Saint Louis (1937-38 – 1942-43; 1944-45 – 1973-74)
33 Southern Illinois (1974-75 – present)
32 Oklahoma A&M (1925-26 – 1956-57)
31 Indiana State (1976-77 – present)
27 Illinois State (1980-81 – present)
21 Grinnell (1918-19 – 1938-39)
   Iowa State (1907-08 – 1927-28)
   Kansas (1907-08 – 1927-28)
   Missouri (1907-08 – 1927-28)
20 Nebraska (1907-08 – 1918-19; 1920-21 – 1927-28)
19 North Texas State (1957-58 – 1974-75)

17 Missouri State (1990-91 – present)
16 West Texas State (1970-71 – 1985-86)
   Northern Iowa (1991-92 – present)
15 Kansas State (1913-14 – 1927-28)
13 New Mexico State (1970-71 – 1982-83)
   Cincinnati (1957-58 – 1969-70)
   Evansville (1994-95 – present)
11 Louisville (1964-65 – 1974-75)
10 Houston (1950-51 – 1959-60)
 9 Oklahoma (1919-20 – 1927-28)
   Detroit (1949-50 – 1956-57)
 8 Washburn (1934-35 – 1940-41)
 6 Memphis State (1967-68 – 1972-73)
 4 Iowa (1907-08 – 1910-11)
 2 Butler (1932-33 – 1933-34)

* Eight of 10 current Valley members (all but Creighton and Evansville) were Gateway Conference members for their women's sports from 1983-92. List does not include single-sport affiliate members.

ON THE COVER:

1. Dana Altman	8. Phog Allen	15. Tubby Smith	22. Eddie Hickey
2. Debbie Antonelli	9. Bobbi Becker	16. Kevin Stallings	23. Johnny Torres
3. Mitch Holthus	10. Johnny Bright	17. James Naismith	24. Oscar Robertson
4. Jackie Stiles	11. Marcus Wilson	18. Hersey Hawkins	25. Joe Stowell
5. Larry Bird	12. Cam Johnson	19. Kyle Korver	26. Bruce Weber
6. Henry Iba	13. Dick Versace	20. Bob Kurland	27. Ed Macauley
7. Clark W. Hetherington	14. Xavier McDaniel	21. Glenn Dobbs	28. Ed Jucker
			29. Gene Stephenson

1907

1948

1945

1928

1990

1980

1974

1976

1994

1991